THE METHUEN DRA
CONTEMPORARY SC
THEATRE

In the same series from Bloomsbury Methuen Drama:

THE METHUEN DRAMA GUIDE TO CONTEMPORARY
AMERICAN PLAYWRIGHTS
*Edited by Martin Middeke, Peter Paul Schnierer, Christopher Innes and
Matthew C. Roudané*
ISBN 978-1-4081-3479-5

THE METHUEN DRAMA GUIDE TO CONTEMPORARY
BRITISH PLAYWRIGHTS
Edited by Martin Middeke, Peter Paul Schnierer and Aleks Sierz
ISBN 978-1-4081-2278-5

THE METHUEN DRAMA GUIDE TO CONTEMPORARY
IRISH PLAYWRIGHTS
Edited by Martin Middeke and Peter Paul Schnierer
ISBN 978-1-4081-1346-2

THE METHUEN DRAMA GUIDE TO CONTEMPORARY SOUTH AFRICAN THEATRE

Edited by Martin Middeke, Peter Paul Schnierer and Greg Homann

Bloomsbury Methuen Drama
An imprint of Bloomsbury Publishing Plc

B L O O M S B U R Y
LONDON • NEW DELHI • NEW YORK • SYDNEY

Bloomsbury Methuen Drama

An imprint of Bloomsbury Publishing Plc

Imprint previously known as Methuen Drama

50 Bedford Square	1385 Broadway
London	New York
WC1B 3DP	NY 10018
UK	USA

www.bloomsbury.com

**BLOOMSBURY, METHUEN DRAMA and the Diana logo are
trademarks of Bloomsbury Publishing Plc**

First published 2015

© 2015 Martin Middeke, Peter Paul Schnierer and Greg Homann

Martin Middeke, Peter Paul Schnierer and Greg Homann have asserted
their right under the Copyright, Designs and Patents Act, 1988, to be
identified as editors of this work.

British Library Cataloguing-in-Publication Data
A catalogue record for this book is available from the British Library.

ISBN:	HB:	978-1-4081-7670-2
	PB:	978-1-4081-7669-6
	ePDF:	978-1-4081-7672-6
	ePub:	978-1-4081-7671-9

Library of Congress Cataloging-in-Publication Data
A catalog record for this book is available from the Library of Congress.

Typeset by Fakenham Prepress Solutions, Fakenham, Norfolk NR21 8NN
Printed and bound in India

CONTENTS

ABOUT THE EDITORS

Professor Martin Middeke is Chair of English Literature at the University of Augsburg, Germany, and Visiting Professor at the University of Johannesburg, South Africa.

Professor Peter Paul Schnierer is Chair of English Literature at the University of Heidelberg, Germany.

Greg Homann is an independent academic and multi-award-winning theatre director based in Johannesburg, South Africa.

Acknowledgements

The editors are grateful to all of the above, to the efficient and patient staff at Bloomsbury Methuen Drama, and many others. Once again, we wish to convey our greatest debts of gratitude to Adriana Lopez, Nadja Rehberger, Tim Sommer, and Katja Utz for their diligent work on the manuscript during various stages.

INTRODUCTION
Greg Homann, Martin Middeke and Peter Paul Schnierer

South Africa has a very rich and diverse theatre that has brought together local and international performance traditions, differing theatre practices and varied forms that are seen in the vibrant scope of drama it produces.

This book focuses on the first twenty years of new plays written and produced in democratic South Africa. It surveys indigenous South African drama that is written predominantly in the English language. Through the analysis of more than 100 plays (while many more are mentioned on the way), a detailed history emerges of the struggle against apartheid, including an account of the country's remarkable and unprecedented transition into democracy.

South African drama is internationally most recognized through the widely produced plays written by Athol Fugard, but the country's rich tradition of drama is not predominantly grounded in playwriting, nor is it a theatre that has historically been driven by the interests of playwrights. From around 1970 a tension has existed in South Africa between the practice of writing a play as a solo playwright and the workshop tradition of play making. The latter arguably became the dominant mode of play creation. By the 1980s a well-established collaborative theatre was at its height, coinciding with a State of Emergency in the country.[1]

In order to straddle the full range of plays workshopped, written, developed and produced during the first twenty years of South Africa's democracy, it has been important to allow for chapters that do not focus solely on a particular playwright's work. The introduction is hence followed by six systematic chapters that either focus on successful collaborations, or that allow particular modes of play making or similar types of plays to be discussed together. In the second part of the book we have chosen to include twelve essays that deal exclusively with the most established playwrights working over this twenty-year period. Each of these chapters provides information on biographical aspects of a particular playwright's life and career. Representative plays are then discussed in detail before concluding remarks summarize major topics and aesthetic strategies of the playwright at issue. These chapters are followed by one centring on emerging playwrights and a view into the future of South African theatre and drama. The book closes with an interview with Aubrey Sekhabi, the Artistic Director of the South African State Theatre in Pretoria. Not only does Sekhabi discuss aspects of his own work, but he also gives insight into the situation of South African theatre today including the issues of funding and developing new work.

***

Legislated racial segregation, or apartheid, governed South Africa from 1948 to 1994.[2] Laws of separation and censorship impacted on all sectors of society. Music, art and theatre, however, became a thorn in the side of the apartheid government.

Oppressive laws were designed to limit, amongst other things, 'undesirable' public performances. The apartheid government policed multiracial inter-action and promoted staunch censorship legislation. The Publications and Entertainment Act of 1963, later updated to the Publications Act of 1974, was one example of many. This act prohibited work that was labelled as harmful to the state, offensive or obscene, a threat to peace and order, or a risk to what was defined as moral decency. The Group Areas Acts of 1950, 1957 and 1966 enforced segregation across residential, social and business lines, affecting both the way audiences attended plays and the way makers made them. The State of Emergency clauses that were enacted in the 1980s further obstructed the possibilities of public performances. Over four decades, playwrights, actors, musicians and other artists found themselves banned, imprisoned, tortured and beaten.

International artists and cultural activists offered their support to South African artists through various strategies. A cultural boycott against South Africa began in 1961 when the British Musicians' Union prohibited its members from performing in apartheid South Africa. On 25 June 1963, forty-five, predominantly British, playwrights and theatre makers, including Samuel Beckett, Harold Pinter, Arthur Miller, Spike Milligan, John Barton, Robert Bolt, John Osborne and Iris Murdoch, signed the following declaration:

> While not wishing to exercise any political censorship over their own or other works of art, but feeling colour discrimination transcends the purely political, the following playwrights, after consultation with the Anti-Apartheid Movement and with South African artists and writers, as an expression of their personal repugnance to the

policies of apartheid and their sympathy with those writers and others in the Republic of South Africa now suffering under evil legislation, have instructed their Agents to insert a clause in all future contracts automatically refusing performing rights in any theatre where discrimination is made among audiences on grounds of colour.[3]

This was the beginning of the International Playwrights Boycott. A year later, twenty-eight Irish playwrights added their names to the declaration and a decade later even more international playwrights pledged themselves to withholding rights to their work.

International pressure on the apartheid government grew. This had an unexpected and surprising impact on the theatre landscape. The apartheid laws and the way in which artists responded to them forced a truly South African theatre tradition to emerge. The new home-grown protest, resistance and agit-prop plays that highlighted the oppression by apartheid government came to local and then international prominence. The majority of these brave works were cultivated through illegal multiracial and non-racial collaborations, and as a response to the very rigid limitations that theatre producers and directors were under, including the absence of international English language plays available for production.[4] In short, apartheid legislation, censorship laws and boycotts ironically contributed to the groundswell of new indigenous South African English plays rather than stifling it.

The most cited early example of a multiracial collaborative work is the African Jazz Opera *King Kong* (1959), which saw black musicians and performers working alongside white collaborators to tell the story of a black boxer who was not allowed to compete across the line of racial segregation. *King Kong* was an overnight sensation playing at Wits University, an institution that rejected the apartheid segregation laws that governed who could or could not attend performances. It played to multiracial audiences locally before touring to London where it helped launch the careers of South African icons Miriam Makeba and Hugh Masekela. More politically engaged work followed, like John Kani's, Winston Ntshona's and Athol Fugard's collaboration creating *The Island* (1973) and *Sizwe Bansi is Dead* (1972), which won Tony Awards for Kani and Ntshona. Many other formalized and informal collaborations throughout the 1960s, 1970s and 1980s brought forth locally and internationally produced plays that became the identity of what has often been called South Africa's unique theatre tradition.

At the start of the 1980s, Mbongeni Ngema and Percy Mtwa approached co-founder and artistic director of the world renowned Market Theatre in Johannesburg, Barney Simon. Together the trio created *Woza Albert!*, widely considered South Africa's seminal play to date. By the height of the apartheid uprising in the mid-1980s, there was an abundance of new plays telling the story of an oppressed majority during a time when local newspapers and media were being silenced and censored. As Barney Simon reportedly said, 'Theatre was the newspaper of the day.'

A distinct style of performance had emerged, bold in characterization and incorporating a diverse fusion of song, text, dance and physical story-telling. Although primarily in English, these plays integrated other South African languages in order to enhance a regional texture or as a linguistic coding for certain characters. It was a theatre dominated by politically engaged and issue-driven drama.

By the early 1990s it was clear that apartheid rule was nearly over. On 2 February 1990 President F. W. de Klerk announced the unconditional unbanning of the South African Communist Party (SACP), Pan Africanist Congress (PAC) and African National Congress (ANC), as well as the immediate release of Nelson Mandela from his 27 years in prison. The transition from an oppressive state to a democratic society had formally begun. But what did this mean for theatre and for the makers and playwrights who had almost entirely been creating protest and political theatre for over thirty years?

The transition into the emergence of post-apartheid South African drama was slow. To begin with, many of the key collaborations that had been fuelled by the anti-apartheid cause dissolved. The monologic and often didactic plays that thrived in a heavily censored and oppressed society were now looked on as stale, out of date and irrelevant. A few playwrights persisted.

Playwright, poet and novelist Zakes Mda quickly turned to criticizing the new democracy and to warning an audience against complacency. His plays of ideas – *The Mother of All Eating* (1992) and *You Fool, How Can the Sky Fall?* (1995) – fell on deaf ears as South Africa was still drunk on the euphoria of its success. The country had avoided a civil war and had come through an unprecedented transition; it was far too soon to offer a pessimistic account of the challenges that lay ahead.

The politics of exile and return surfaced as a theme, as did re-urbanization of the larger cities. Paul Slabolepszy's *Mooi Street Moves* (1992) was set in the quickly changing inner-city suburb of Hillbrow in Johannesburg.

In Sue Pam-Grant's *Curl up and Dye* (1989) the setting is again Hillbrow, but this time a rapidly deteriorating hair salon. Through the eyes of a few struggling women trying to get by, Grant explored the loss and loneliness of a hard life on the edge of the city.

Fatigue set in with audiences not wanting to see political drama. Plays shifted in tone and subject matter. Drama suffered, although a few comedy writers like Paul Slabolepszy and the odd satirist, like Pieter-Dirk Uys, managed to capitalize on the audiences' almost palpable plea to avoid strong political messages. From 1990 to 1996 there was plenty of patting on the back, casino-style dance curio shows and celebratory theatre, and that did not make for great drama. Where was the conflict?

South Africa's Truth and Reconciliation Commission (TRC) ran from April 1996 to October 1998 during which 1,674 public hearings of violations committed under apartheid were heard. Amnesty was offered to perpetrators who committed politically motivated violence between March 1960 and May 1994. Rory Bester explains that, 'running on the slogan "Truth, the Road to Reconciliation", the commission tried to paint a "true" picture of the history of political trauma in South Africa, and thereby to contribute to the reconciliation of a society polarized by racial prejudice' (2002: 163). The TRC became a major influence on post-apartheid drama.

Unique to South Africa's truth commission was that hearings were not held in camera but rather in public, where the audience witnessed the testimonies in situ – this was theatre of a special kind. The conversations and debates that the TRC produced became a foundation vocabulary clearly evident in contemporary South African plays. People for the first time had a chance to tell their personal story in a way that validated themselves, their culture, their community and their identity, and that recognized in some small way the deep trauma that they had suffered. This helped shift playwriting and play making from a monological argument, where all the characters within a play spoke to or at an issue – almost always the anti-apartheid diatribe – to a dialogic debate where characters argue their differing positions and perspectives.

The TRC essentially developed and nurtured a desire to explore personal truth, truth telling and memory. Concerns that were fuelled by 'theatre' were witnessed by ordinary South Africans on their televisions, the radio and in local community halls almost every day for 18 months. The TRC was the dominant theatre of this brief period, but the themes that stem from this period are vividly evident throughout the first twenty years of post-apartheid drama.

***

A survey of the chapters in this book illustrates major thematic and aesthetic trends in contemporary South African drama. Pioneers such as Barney Simon, Mannie Manim, Mbongeni Ngema, Maishe Maponya, Gcina Mhlope, Phyllis Klotz or Smal Ndaba formed a multifaceted and by no means uniform bridge between the apartheid past and the post-apartheid present. Obviously, their work is built on the legacy of plays like *The Island*, *Sizwe Banzi is Dead* or *Woza Albert!* They take the cue from the formal characteristics of these latter plays: their multilingualism, their emphasis on physicality and the co-presence of music, song and storytelling inherent to them. As these plays highlighted plurality in that they juxtaposed literacy and orality or engaged in history and politics, they epitomized protest and, thus, worked towards a democratic present. However, while Simon and Manim accordingly made the theatre a challenge to discrimination and segregation by going beyond the protest advocating and encouraging experiment and condoning failure, Ngema's activist and often thoroughly satirical drama focuses on the hard facts of social reality (i.e. AIDS, HIV) in the service of consciousness raising. In still another aesthetic vein, Mhlope's hybrid approach is more literary as it combines aspects of folklore and oral tradition with modern life and technology. As Sarah Roberts points out in her chapter on these pioneers, the common denominator of their work is the ethical endeavour to awaken or retain a sense of responsibility in the spectator. In a post-apartheid context, this is of particular importance because the way to democracy entails the convergence of communal as well as individual concerns.

This impression is borne out by contemporary collaborators such as William Kentridge, Jane Taylor and the Handspring Puppet Company or Mark Fleishman's and Jenny Reznek's Magnet Theatre. Kentridge/Handspring/Taylor explore the theatricality of the events they are staging, experimenting with different expertises, materialities and genre boundaries. Magnet Theatre's concept comprises physical aspects of collaboration with different communities and companies, stylistic aspects juxtaposing various approaches to physical theatre, as well as paradigmatic approximations of African and European styles and traditions, plus concepts of history, memory and the body. As Yvette Hutchison demonstrates, works such as *Medea* include multiracial casts and multilingual scripts to make a plethora of South African experiences and cultures interact. Moreover, a clear-cut boundary between professional and community theatre is definitely deconstructed by Magnet Theatre's collaboration with UCT Drama School. Verbal and non-verbal forms of expression go hand in hand with each other, challenging traditional ways of reception and spectatorship. Physical theatre, as Robyn Sassen makes clear, includes storytelling and the convergence of clear-cut boundaries between 'straight' theatre, performance art and contemporary dance, highlighting the joint effort of writing, narrating and sequencing movement. Much of this, in fact, is also shared by South African solo artists and their one-person performances where a single actor inhabits many characters. These formats negotiate and, thereby, accentuate the perviousness and fluidity of cultural identity. Veronica Baxter demonstrates how memorable work by such key representatives as Pieter-Dirk Uys, Andrew Buckland, Greig Coetzee, Rajesh Gopie, Bheki Mhkwane, Omphile Molusi and Philip M. Dikotla turns to multiple social, political, cultural and psychological clashes in multiple formal ways which range from the tragi-comical and farcical to the satirical including storytelling, jokes, puns or parody. The underlying appeal of these productions is to emphasize the necessity for a rethinking and reconstitution of the community, which would take heed of aspects of communal experience and, at the same time, acknowledge multiple forms of individual experience and, thus, ultimately enlarge the spectator's scope of collaborative being. The pluralistic democracy gained from such collaboration is also manifested by the testimonial plays of Yaël Farber. These plays are not verbatim drama, but rather employ interviews to construct dialogue, gestures and songs in a workshop atmosphere. Oppression, poverty and violence are made tangible, and audience members are thereby given the experience to participate and bear witness to grief and suffering.

The seminal plays of the last twenty years detailed in this book reflect a nascent democracy that is striving to define and redefine a country against the backdrop of a very difficult history. The plays deal with issues of identity, notions of land, reconciliation, negotiation, xenophobia, generational conflict, corruption, violence, abuse and prejudice. Drama and theatre have been functioning as influential and powerful counter-discourses against a society dominated by segregation, exploitation and oppression. During apartheid, theatre became an act of resistance and defiance. The theatre of the post-apartheid South Africa is still a place of socio-political idealism reacting to the experience of transformation and redress.

As far as its topics are concerned, race/racism and related issues such as obedience, civil disobedience, brotherhood, politics and justice, freedom – both in the sense of bodily freedom and freedom of the mind – as well as (traumatic) memory and the painful and difficult way to post-traumatic existence have invariably been prevalent in contemporary South African drama. While Mike van Graan's *Green Man Flashing* and *Some Mother's Sons* raise questions of integrity and legitimacy, Craig Higginson's shocking *Dream of the Dog* emphasizes the contingency and inevitable subjectivity inherent in human memory, which, of course, gains true historical and psychological momentum against the backdrop of the Truth and Reconciliation Commission and its teleology of confession. In the same vein, Lara Foot's plays juxtapose memory, imagination and the transformative power of performance.

Many plays deal with Afrikaner history. Peter-Dirk Uys's controversial look at the Afrikaner family in *God's Forgotten* is endorsed in Reza de Wet's *African Gothic*, a biting critique and de-mythologizing of Afrikaner identity. Higginson's aforementioned *Dream of the Dog* negotiates the question of dispossession: the 'farm' – one of the central metaphors of the South African imaginary – becomes the cipher of colonization on the one hand and cultural change on the other. One individual mythology, so it seems, is followed by another one, and a 'natural' association of history, land ownership and existential belonging is, thus, deconstructed. Mike van Graan's *Die Generaal* evaluates land claims and language issues of the Afrikaner. In this context, violence is an omnipresent topic on stage, most recently and most controversially confirmed by Brett Bailey's *Exhibit A: Deutsch Sudwestafrika*, *Exhibit B* and *Exhibit C* (2010, 2014, 2015).

All such despondency notwithstanding, South African drama has always been characterized by the presence of hope and, if only in a utopian way, faith in potential transformation. Lena's dance in Fugard's *Boesman and Lena* immediately springs to mind, or the conclusion of *The Island*, which sees a potential of reconciliation in the solidarity of suffering. Fugard's *Playland* shares this view and aims at an appeal to mutual forgiveness. Zakes Mda's *Mother of All Eating* looks upon social development as the means to overcome inequality and injustice. In a less didactic, but more experimental way, even Higginson's *The Girl in the Yellow Dress* argues in favour of a common humanity, albeit acknowledging its provisionality and contingency.

South Africa is a country with eleven official languages. Again and again, perspicuously, South African drama presents the construction of what we are or of how we construct ourselves as a matter of language. During the apartheid era, language was implicated hegemonically and aligned with policies of segregation and racism. Nevertheless, landmark plays such as

The Island, *Sizwe Banzi is Dead*, *Woza Albert!* or *Asinamali!* have decidedly expressed a multilingual emphasis rather than remaining constrained to the official languages under apartheid, Afrikaans and English. In the post-apartheid context, these issues have become more complex. Many South Africans feel a need to reclaim what has been lost culturally, and at the same time English is perceived as the language of progress and an avenue to opportunity on a national as well as international basis, while simultaneously standing as a symbol of colonial oppression. Reza de Wet's plays spring to mind, with their parody of Afrikaner society. Two of her plays, *Worm in the Bud* and *Concealment*, were commissioned in English, but attack English colonialism in South Africa and ensuing patronizing attitudes. Gcina Mhlope's work, by contrast, uses English as a means of overcoming differences in the cultural diversity of twenty-first-century South Africa. Physical theatre, generally, is characterized by the inclusion of multiple languages. Productions such as Khaylihle Dominique Gumede's *Milk and Honey* integrate a number of indigenous languages, and in the face of their relative fluidity and instability, the element of the body in physical theatre functions as a constant that is able to cross language and literacy barriers. Paul Grootboom's and Aubrey Sekhabi's work is characterized by a mix of languages, slang, oral narrations and multilingual expressions during performances – a characteristic feature that often is lost in the printed versions of the plays. In a totally different aesthetic fashion, yet still very much centred on language, Paul Slabolepszy's work is a unison of well-observed South African English dialects, body language and masterly crafted rhythms of everyday speech. And, quite unforgettably of course, it is Pieter-Dirk Uys's or his alter-ego Evita Bezuidenhout's language that fathoms the rights of the Afrikaans woman.

In this connection, post-apartheid South African drama and theatre have witnessed the growing interest in feminist politics and gender issues. Taking the cue from early plays such as Athol Fugard's *The Road to Mecca* or Zakes Mda's *And the Girls in Their Sunday Dresses,* which refuses a status quo for women, Fatima Dike's work, for instance, examines feminist and gendered perspectives on South African life and female identity. Lara Foot's characters likewise inhabit a world of suffering where women and girls are raped, mutilated and killed, but to which they still offer resistance. Rape, violent assault and death are also key concerns of Yaël Farber's *Nirbhaya*. The fact that the play at first sight draws on conditions in India can hardly detract from the high number of rapes and incidents of sexual violence in South Africa. Farber's *Mies Julie: Restitutions of Body and Soil Since the*

Bantu Land Act No 27 of 1913 & Immorality Act No 5 of 1927 unmistakably makes clear that there are no easy solutions to these questions of race, class, gender and power – a diagnosis that is met by Lara Foot's *Tshepang*, which deals with the real-life event of the rape of a nine-month-old baby, but also seeks to establish and restore a flicker of dignity amidst all the bleakness. Sexuality and eroticism are omnipresent on the contemporary South African stage: the strong erotic undercurrents of Reza de Wet cross one's mind, as does Mpumelelo Paul Grootboom's provocative, Arthur Schnitzler-based, depiction of sexual morals in *Foreplay*. Paul Slabolepszy's work very much centres on masculinities, homo-erotic roots of male friendship and the nature of male bonding.

There is a wide range of aesthetic, formal and structural consequences which these topics entail. On the one hand, and understandably so, South African drama has for a long time been grounded in a recognizably realist tradition covering social realist depictions of the milieu as well as subjectively heightened forms. Quite cogently, the didactic impact of such aesthetics is relatively high. Zakes Mda's plays, for instance, interrogate how the poor masses continue to be discriminated against by the political and economic elites, who use their positions of power to perpetuate some of the socio-economic inequalities and injustices of the past. The socio-political 'message' about a post-apartheid South Africa in Mda's theatre is, thus, ostensibly clear. Moreover, even if plays such as *Saturday Night at the Palace* are of a more heightened realism, Paul Slabolepszy's tragi-comedy straight-forwardly appeals to moral conscience and is recognizably engaged in the raising of socio-political consciousness. Pieter-Dirk Uys's mask of Evita is a means of satire and hence is able to attack and debunk sexual and moral behaviour as well as challenge publicly accepted sexual norms.

On the other hand, more experimental forms are still developing in post-apartheid times. Already Athol Fugard's circular plot structures, their compressed dialogues and minimalist props recall the sparse reductions and absurdity at work in Samuel Beckett's plays. Reza de Wet and Lara Foot employ techniques from magic realism which have strong evocative qualities and thus present formerly fixed boundaries of the real and the imaginary as increasingly blurred. De Wet, in fact, emphasized that theatre was not to have a didactic function, but was rather to construct an alternative, imaginary world.

Many contemporary South African plays are characterized by a very high degree of intertextuality. These plays highlight their own self-reflexivity as they lay bare their own fictional status reflecting upon unstable identity formations in the social reality they relate to or, in a more playful fashion, assert their status as artefacts in the face of otherwise oppressive social surroundings. Reza de Wet has written highly intertextual pieces drawing, for instance, on Chekhov's *Three Sisters*. Chekhov has also been an important pre-text for Pieter-Dirk Uys's *God's Forgotten* and John Kani's *Nothing But the Truth*. As mentioned above, Paul Grootboom's *Foreplay* draws on Schnitzler's *Reigen*, and in as much as *Foreplay* is an important and energetic portrayal of sexual mores in contemporary South African urban life, it is also a metadramatic play about playacting and theatre which skilfully connects elements from the traditions of both African theatre and postmodernism. In fact, the traditional forms and, inherently, the direct responses from the audience during the performance have widely been combined with European aesthetic strategies. Lara Foot's *Karoo Moose*, for example, is influenced by Jacques Lecoq's principles and Jerzy Grotowski's Poor Theatre as well as by the alienation effects of Bertolt Brecht's Epic Theatre. Much of the work of the Pioneers is following Brecht's aesthetics, turning drama into an exercise in responsible citizenship. Moreover, story-telling as a dramaturgical strategy is omnipresent on the South African stage. Yaël Farber's work integrates elements from Greek tragedy, Shakespeare and modern international drama of the twentieth century. In an apparently revisionist way, Farber resituates these intertexts in contemporary South Africa. By turning to myth, Farber makes formerly hardly mentionable questions of race, class, politics or individual trauma representable. In a similar vein, Brett Bailey's *Orfeus* retells the Greek myth only to transform it to a passageway into an African underworld where the sins of the nation find their just punishment. Bailey's work challenges the boundaries of theatre and performance (art), and clearly accentuates aspects of performa-tivity (of gender, class, race, etc.). Bailey's work is deliberately ambiguous, provocative and – as the London scandal about *Exhibit B* amply illustrates – as such explosive political matter. The literary aspects of Bailey's drama can never be separated from their non-verbal aspects of performance: music, folklore, ritual, rhythm, dreamlike states, historical and symbolic charging of images and action, and visual elements enter into an atmos-pheric connection which is evocative throughout. Plays like *iMumbo Jumbo*, *ipi zombi?* and *Heartstopping* draw their audience into their performa-tivity and make them experience a reality that is not rigid and stable but ever-changing and fluid. In much the same way, though very different in their concrete aesthetic design, Craig Higginson's plays also give aesthetic answers to ethical problems. They integrate classical and contemporary elements freely and, in this, no longer work as political or even national allegories. They rest themselves on the idea of a fundamental plurality that affects both individuals as well as communities and society in general. They neither deny nor ignore the psychological/individual as well as the political/historical past, yet they root in the vital belief in an imaginative, fluid coexistence of subjectivity and communal concerns which allows for further change and development.

***

No matter whether of a more realistic and didactic or experimental and pluralistic bent, at the heart of South African drama remains the evaluation and delineation of identity. Race and gender are important fields which have witnessed a constant redefinition in post-apartheid drama. Likewise, issues of history and memory are still looming large on the contemporary South African stage. And while apartheid history is more and more left behind in a society that unanimously rejects apartheid, social as well as ethical issues and interpersonal relationships in a globalized, (post)modern world are increasingly foregrounded. Many plays and many writers for the stage integrate European aesthetics into their formal designs. Moreover, plays and writers seek for European – or worldwide at that – productions and, thus, acknowledgement. Whether or not this positively or negatively impinges on 'South African-ness', or whether or not that very South African-ness does or should exist at all in a normative way, is left for further debate.

South African drama is concerned with its home ground in much the same way that Irish theatre even today remains focused on the island's own history and present tribulations. This makes for strong stories and characters that require little or no mediation to be appreciated by local audiences. Yet paradoxically, and again like the Irish, South African playwrights and performers enjoy international visibility far in excess of, say, Australian or New Zealand companies. The following chapters assemble many instances of productions taken on tour abroad or even reaching 'home' only after prolonged exposure to foreign audiences, sometimes years after their first nights. This is to some extent due to the continued hospitality of old, apartheid-era contacts, but without the readiness of sizeable audiences in Vienna or London to go and see new South African work there would not be such a lively presence today. Evidently these pieces speak to needs beyond their own African communities: the local becomes, if not quite the global, then at least the recognizable, the representative and the metonymic.

As far as aesthetics is concerned, the rich scene of South African drama in the first decade of the twenty-first century suggests that a growing number of theatre makers, playwrights and audiences alike are more keen on open and more fluid issues and forms, more truly dialogical drama which just like all those many multifaceted collaborative efforts on the South African theatre scene seems more appropriate to democracy and, ultimately, to post-liminal existence, where the value of each individual subject goes hand in hand with the ethical obligation to preserve a sense of responsibility.

Notes

1. Significant workshopped plays from the 1980s include *Woza Albert!* (1982), *Marabi* (1982), *This is For Keeps* (1983), *Black Dog/Injèmnyama* (1984), *Born in the RSA* (1985), *Sophiatown* (1986) and *You Strike the Woman, You Strike the Rock* (1986).

2. South Africa's first democratic elections were held on 27 April 1994 although it is worth noting that on 2 February 1990 President F. W. de Klerk began the process of demolishing apartheid legislation and rule. This was followed by a whites-only referendum in 1992 that approved the reform process towards democracy.

3. The digital copy of the original signed declaration can be viewed at http://aamarchives.org/file-view/file/4003-60s17-playwrights-against-apartheid.html?tmpl=component&start=20 (accessed 17 March 2015).

4. A distinction must be made between multiracial collaboration and non-racial collaboration. Where multiracial collaboration simply means a working together of people from different racial groupings, non-racial collaboration is a more nuanced and politicized term that was popularized in South Africa by the United Democratic Front (UDF) when that organization launched itself as a non-racial coalition in 1983. Where the term multiracial acknowledges the different races involved, non-racial is a term that rejects racial groupings altogether and strives for a society without racial categorizing.

Bibliography

Anders, Peter and Matthew Krouse (eds), *Positions: Contemporary Artists in South Africa* (Johannesburg: Jacana Media Ltd, 2010).

Bester, Rory, 'Trauma and Truth', in Okwui Enwezor et al. (eds), *Experiments with Truth: Transitional Justice and the Process of Truth and Reconciliation* (Ostfildern-Ruit: Hatje Cantz Publishers, 2002), 155–73.

Boyden, Matthew, with contributions from Nick Kimberley, *Opera: The Rough Guide* (London: Rough Guides, 1999).

Coplan, David B. *In Township Tonight! Three Centuries of South African Black City Music and Theatre* (London and New York: Longman, and Johannesburg: Raven Press, 1985).

Franklin, Benjamin. *The Autobiography and Other Writings.* (Harmondsworth: Penguin, 1986).

Fuchs, Anne, *Playing the Market. The Market Theatre Johannesburg 1976–1986* (London: Routledge, 1990).

Gunner, Liz (ed.), *Politics and Performance: Theatre, Poetry and Song in Southern Africa* (Johannesburg: Wits University Press, 1994).

Hauptfleisch, Temple, *Theatre and Society in South Africa: Reflections in a Fractured Mirror* (Pretoria: J. L. Van Schaik Publishers, 1997).

Homann, Greg (ed.), *At This Stage. Plays from Post-apartheid South Africa* (Johannesburg: Wits University Press, 2009).

Homann, Greg (ed.), 'Landscape and Body', *South African Theatre Journal* 23:1 (2009): 149–76.

Jamal, Ashraf, *Predicaments of Culture in South Africa* (Pretoria: University of South Africa Press, 2005).

Krueger, Anton, *Experiments in Freedom: Explorations of Identity in New South African Drama* (Newcastle upon Tyne: Cambridge Scholars Publishing, 2010).

Kruger, Loren, *The Drama of South Africa: Plays, Pageants and Publics since 1910* (London: Routledge, 1999).

Ndebele, Njabulo S., *Rediscovery of the Ordinary: Essays on South African Literature and Culture* (Johannesburg: COSAW, 1991).

Perkins, Kathy A. (ed.), *Black South African Woman: An Anthology of Plays* (New York: Routledge, 1998).

Stephanou, Irene and Leila Henriques, *The World in an Orange: Creating Theatre with Barney Simon*, ed. Lionel Abrahams and Jane Fox (Johannesburg: Jacana Media Ltd, 2005).

Strunk, Oliver, *Source Readings in Music History: The Romantic Era* (New York: Norton, 1950).

Taylor, Jane, 'Taking Stock: The Making of a Bourgeois Life. The Confessions of Zeno', *South African Theatre Journal* 17 (2003): 234–44.

Taylor, Jane (ed.), *Handspring Puppet Company* (Johannesburg: David Krut Publishing, 2009).

Truth and Reconciliation Commission of South Africa, *Report: Volume 1* (Cape Town: CTP Book Printers (Pty) Ltd, 1998).

Twijnstra, Roel and Emma Durden, *Theatre Directing in South Africa: Skills and Inspirations* (Johannesburg: Jacana Media Ltd, 2014).

Walder, Dennis, *Athol Fugard*, Writers and Their Work (Plymouth: Northcote House Publishers Ltd, 2007).

Winnicott, Donald. W., 'The Theory of the Parent–Child Relationship', *International Journal of Psycho-Analysis* 41 (1960): 586–95.

PART I
OVERVIEW ESSAYS

CHAPTER 1
THE 'PIONEERS'
Sarah Roberts

Defining the 'pioneers' and the context of their early work

> 'Politics' is a word that describes life. You don't decide to be in a
> politically explosive part of the world. You are born there and you
> are governed by what happens – whether the sun shines or it rains
> for months. These things affect people in different ways. Some people
> would find cause to celebrate, others to mourn.
>
> Gcina Mhlophe[1]

Forming a kind of living bridge, the 'pioneers' straddle apartheid past and
democratic present. The 'pioneers', although not the first generation of
dramatic voices, are defined as those making theatre in the last decades of
apartheid rule and who continue to do so today. Their practice was informed
and guided by the imperatives of addressing accelerating socio-political
tensions from 1976 onwards and their early works synthesize life as it was
lived and experienced in South Africa with mobilizing theatre according
to the liberation principle that 'culture is weapon'. The public and instrumental act of play making in these circumstances was constantly informed
by the understanding that presenting narratives that emerged directly
from a society dominated by segregation, exploitation and oppression was
an act of resistance in defiance of state imperatives. Their current work
continues to be undergirded by generative tensions between socio-political
idealism and the experience of complex pressures of transformation and
redress characterizing the two decades of a post-apartheid society. Beyond
the somewhat instrumentalist definition attributed to 'ground-breaking
activity', two related questions emerge from reconsidering their work from
a contemporary perspective: first, what common features, if any, can be
ascribed to this corpus; and second, have these qualities survived into the
present or are the principles, to some extent at least, under threat?[2]

Works produced by key director-dramatists in 'mainstream' theatre
during the period 1976–94 are seminal to the emergent South African

dramatic tradition and have been revived in the Market Theatre programme in what Malcolm Purkey calls a 'second look'. Plays like *The Island, Sizwe Banzi is Dead, Woza Albert!* and *Asinamali!* share a distinctive immediacy of local subject and theme, augmented by notable formal attributes, namely, a multilingual actor-centred emphasis (rather than remaining constrained by the two official languages, English and Afrikaans), heightened physicality, the integration of song and storytelling episodes and an actor-centred *mise-en-scène*. It is this body of work that constitutes a legacy through which contemporary dramatic writing may be contextualized and its achievements set in perspective.

The current output of the 'pioneers', despite an ostensible decline, continues to be significant, and their practice testifies to the extent that the socio-cultural landscape has shifted from the intense and generative period immediately prior to transition to a new dispensation and social order.[3] The ethos of egalitarian teamwork was a hallmark of works produced in contrast to a discernible current tendency towards valorizing singularity through asserting the auteur status of the director or dramatist along with asserting a hierarchical authoritative order in theatre making. As Klotz puts it:

> They want us to emulate European playwrights, but that's not what our theatre is about; it's about the collective and that has another life. I'm not saying there's not a place for playwrights or that we should eradicate them, but trying to develop the cult of the writer … we're in Africa and we don't have that history.[4]

Key features of the 'plays' and the method through which they were derived include: prioritizing a plurality of voices; grappling with tensions between literacy and orality in interpersonal encounters as a means of negotiating disparate cultural traditions; engaging with history and politics (not only in terms of published records, but as defined by the experiences of ordinary people); and, finally, to the extent that they epitomize the 'genre' of 'protest theatre',[5] the plays (along with their mode of production) are anticipating an egalitarian democracy. Audiences were invited to address the rights and obligations of active citizenship as advanced in a critique of contemporary politics by activist and public intellectual Dr Mamphela Ramphele:

> The myth that South Africans were passive recipients of freedom from a liberation movement has disempowered many into believing that they owe their freedom and future prosperity to the ANC as a

1276

ORBURY FOOD & WINE
398 LONDON ROAD
540436505096727
ID36560995
ID : A0000000041010
ebit MasterCard

ASTERCARD DEBIT

*** **** **** 8443
XP 09/20   START 09/17
ONTACTLESS   PAN. SEQ 01
ALE

ERCHANT COPY

ALE   21.75
0:27 15/10/19
UTH CODE: 597300
ECEIPT 0521

liberation party[6] ... The citizenship rights and responsibilities are undermined by this myth which perpetuates the subject status of citizens ... the antithesis of freedom.[7]

Reassessing the significance of plays of the so-called South African canon through evaluating their mode of authorship (rather than in purely formal terms) thus opens up the scope to consider these plays as something more than expressions of dissent demanding social justice. Their value is recast by acknowledging the process of their construction as models through which an ideal nation state may be forged. In accordance with the Brechtian template, the plays, on this reading, served as experiments in citizenship of the future and the notion of 'ensemble' has some parallels with Ramphele's notion of an 'engaged (rather than self-serving or passive) citizen'.[8]

During the 1980s, the impetus to forge productive allegiances, hybrid collaborations and oppositional platforms operating in direct antithesis to the state and its apparatuses united a small fraternity of individuals from different backgrounds and geographically disparate parts of the country. It also provided a potent well-spring of diverse experiences on which to draw in terms of developing new material and its presentation style. These features, entrenched by habit, not only underpin a contemporary work ethic but also begin to account for the resilience and reach of these theatre-practitioners today. The survival of the veterans of the struggle years depended on a firm foundation in tenacity of purpose, resourcefulness and initiative: access to resources was neither a right nor prerogative; rather, new plays emerged directly from pressing crises in a harsh and testing environment. In Barney Simon's words,

> In the beginning there was work. Work of a specific passion, relevance and commitment. Work intended for all the people of South Africa, work that attempted to address our place and time ... When we began in 1976, we lived in a terrible but deceptively simple time. Today complexity is our given. The world we live in changes every day – marked by States of Emergency, news clampdowns, strikes, stayaways, sanctions and cruel factionalism ... [T]o penetrate any kind of truth that speaks for all of us is virtually impossible.[9]

The inadvertent outcome of the playwrights' boycott of 1963 was to prove unexpectedly productive in creating a void through denying performance rights for much contemporary world drama. Local theatre makers responded with some alacrity: collectives 'redefined' the 'lack' by actively committing to developing original South African material. While the political climate enforced fertile productivity, the introduction of television on 5 January 1976[10] was also to have a profound impact on theatre attendance as much as on the evolving dramatic style. From the outset the novelty of broadcasts not only showed signs of a capacity to erode the extant audience bases, but the electronic medium constituted a challenge urging a redefinition of what is unique to the live encounter between actor and audience. Experiments with narrative form and heightened presentation modes became a means of asserting a distinctive theatrical idiom.

The role played by the Market Theatre, founded by Barney Simon and Mannie Manim, as a structure and institution is reasonably comprehensively archived. Dedicated to opposing state authority and the pervasive implementation of nationalist apartheid policy, the Market Theatre was a platform for resisting all aspects of racism and actively committed to challenging discrimination, separatism, segregation and oppression. The principle of bold independence was instrumental in forging an ideologically based work ethic and inculcated resistance to forms of hierarchy and privilege. The Market's achievements were produced through the efforts and persistence of the two individuals who strove for its foundation on an ethical basis in what Ronge calls a 'great epic struggle' documented by Schwartz and succinctly summed up in the obituary to Simon as:

> an event which was a catalyst in SA theatre history. It unleashed talents and theatre events that changed the face of theatre in this country.[11]

And as Michael Gardiner puts it (in an article on the life and work of Lionel Abrahams, Bill Ainslie and Barney Simon), 'despite being male, white and middle-class, the three asserted, for those who wished to participate in the arts, alternatives to the dominant bourgeois and nationalistic cultural values that characterized the formal activities in the city of Johannesburg'.[12] Malcolm Purkey explains the continued value of the Market as an institution:

> The magic of the Market was that it is a beautiful space supported by imaginative leadership and a model of production that centred on partnerships with satellite companies. And that model of partnership was that the satellite companies created the work, the entire package, so to speak ... and that was their contribution to a 50% partnership in

presenting new works. That model is no longer possible today in the same way in relation to income and expenditure. The other big point is that actors and artists subsidized the venue and are less prepared to do so today.[13]

The objective of the Market Theatre was to foster the development of new writers, and Barney Simon as artistic director and dramaturge routinely interrogated the narrative clarity and expression of a new production in the final phases of rehearsal. Any challenge that he made was guided by an instinct for the reception of the play by its local audience. His sudden death 'left a gap in South African theatre that is incalculable'.[14] His stature and the trust that he enjoyed was attributable to his genuine pleasure and enjoyment in the company of those he encountered and worked with, his mischievous sense of humour, his humility and gentleness. His strength lay in constancy to a vision that inspired and sustained the development of others. Ronge succinctly describes how this vision was manifest in the work and plays produced: 'He never divided his theatrical imagination from his social awareness or his own moral consciousness. His declared intention was "to serve the life rather than the literature of the piece".[15]

Simon often repeated the maxims which guided his life on the first day of developing a new play, among them, after Camus, 'A man's work is little more than his journey through his life (through the byways and detours of art) in order to discover the one or two great and simple images that first found access to his soul', or (another favourite), 'In this whole world there is only one really tragic thing: each of us has his/her own reasons.' He also resorted to an understanding of the value of art expounded by Braque, recorded by Mary Benson as having considerable impact on his thinking:

[D]uring the First World War, [Braque] had begun to understand art when he saw a batman take a bucket which had contained water and punch holes in it until it became a brasier [sic] to carry fire. This potential metaphor in all things, said Braque, is what we search to express in art. The stone on the beach, in my hand can become part of a wall, a piece of sculpture, a weapon: there are possibilities for transformation in all things.[16]

Simon was a feisty advocate of the need for artists to risk experiment, secure in the knowledge of the 'right to fail'. Such was his standing and influence that this principle of tolerance accommodated and affirmed the rights of aspiring writers/directors. He construed failure not so much as a disgrace, but as an integral component of the learning experience and crucial to the process of development. It is difficult, from a contemporary perspective, to assess just how significant this attitude proved to be: the importance of achievement and reward resonates loudly in current discourses and it may be that the imperative towards success and the reluctance to confront or interrogate the prospect of mediocrity prohibits rigorous critique of new work along with foreclosing on more adventurous innovation or radical experiment.

Michael Gardiner ascribes the integrity of Simon's method of 'devising' new work to underpinnings in Joseph Beuys' view that 'workshops are "social sculpture"'.[17] Furthermore, Gardiner makes a discerning comment about the ways in which Simon's mode of workshop was predicated on contesting traditional and patriarchal modes of transmitting ideas and knowledge systems:

> The real and genuine workshop is a radical alternative form of learning and interacting, which is rarely provided or experienced except in the notorious form of 'group work', a static and most commonly unproductive process employed by bewildered teachers.[18]

Simon's method avoided these pitfalls, as explained by Gardiner:

> One of Simon's approaches to the preparation of characters for a stage production was to send out the actors to become as close as possible to that which they were seeking to portray. Then they would return to the theatre and discuss what it was that they had observed and felt and discovered. Simon had the disconcerting knack of deciding which insights were truthful, those which were true to the character, and those which were bogus, especially the ideas that came from the assumptions and presuppositions of the actors themselves. Once he was satisfied that the actor had penetrated to the genuine heart of the character, the actor was sent off to write up all that had been discovered. This written account was then 'fictionalized' by Simon and the actor, together. So the brute truth was transformed eventually into something that had its own verisimilitude and which was capable of being incorporated into the bigger scheme of the play as a whole.[19]

Simon was at the hub of a network of personal associations and the driving force behind supporting independent ventures of actors that he had worked with. Mbongeni Ngema, Percy Mtwa, Gcina Mhlophe, Neil McCarthy and Mark Fleishman worked with him as actors prior to establishing themselves as 'writers', while Lara Foot sat alongside him as an intern director, and Craig Higginson as his assistant. This is not to suggest that the work of these play makers bears Simon's signature, but rather how he enabled a range of diverse personalities to hone their own emergent voices. His emphasis lay, always, on respecting the dignity of each individual while appreciating their role within a collective. Seldom didactic or literal and never dictatorial in his directives, his writing or editing, Barney took recourse to parables, metaphors or analogies in order to trigger the creative agency of whoever it was that he was addressing. In Grahamstown in 1989, we went to look at the Standard Bank collection and lingered over the display of Tsonga shawls. These were anonymously produced 'craft objects' in which plain cotton cloth had been comprehensively ornamented with beads and hundreds of small gold safety pins. Barney's observation memorably reflected his insistence on probing and reworking everyday objects, respecting what is ordinary: '[T]hat's how we must work: use the simple everyday things and re-arrange them so that they create patterns – patterns that can transform ways of seeing the commonplace. The way of art lies in selecting and arranging these things with care.' Braques' idea is concretely manifest, trans-posed and autonomously expressed in African terms.

Born in the RSA, described by some as a docu-drama and by others as a 'living newspaper', explicitly crystallized the notion of theatre as testimony – a tapestry of interwoven individual voices. This emphasis on personal narrative later became a key concept and mechanism of the Truth and Reconciliation Commission hearings. In both instances the core value of the personal narrative lay in its juxtaposition and integration with other narratives, creating a complex of multiple perspectives, the montage consti-tuting a 'social or dialogic truth': no single individual account could lay greater claim or insight to the South African experience than any other.

Simon's output in terms of new texts is comparatively slight; his corpus included directing classics (*The Dybbuk*, *Hedda Gabler* and *East*), directing new plays by other authors (*Death and The Maiden* (by Dorfman), *Flight* and *So What's New?* (by Dike)) and staging adaptations of literary works as in *The Suit* (1986), Can Themba's short story. Ultimately, his project as artistic director was to nurture the work of others and it was to this that he devoted considerable energy. His unequivocal sense of purpose in mentoring and celebrating the emergence of a generation of play makers is hinted at in words taken from his acceptance of the Jujamcyn Award: 'We are very far from the completion of our journey which is as various and difficult, as extraordinary as any that strive for dignity and clarity in our time.'[20]

The quest for a dramatic idiom that clearly articulated a sense of shared humanity and dignity was Simon's life project, and during the production week of *So What's New?*, he speculated on the direction that new modes of dramatic writing might take. He foresaw that plays exploring affinities across cultural and racially defined categories would appeal to the popular imagination. He delighted in his sense that the soap opera *The Bold and the Beautiful* (around which, in his view, Dike's play was structured) served as a binding mechanism between residents of working- and middle-class suburbs of Johannesburg and Soweto. He imagined that a shared engagement with popular culture may, in the future, prove to be an instrument of transformation capable of negating ingrained prejudice and preconceptions of difference.[21]

Understanding Simon's ideas profits from drawing on the theoretical perspective of Njabulo Ndebele outlined in his anthology of critical essays. In *The Rediscovery of the Ordinary: Some New Writings in South Africa*, he assesses the emergent tradition in black South African literature and submits that what is lacking is any 'attempt to delve into intricacies of motive or social process',[22] resulting in forms that he ultimately condemns:

> We can now summarize the characteristics of the spectacular in this context. The spectacular documents; it indicts implicitly; it is demonstrative, preferring exteriority to interiority; it keeps the larger issues of society in our minds, obliterating the details; it provokes identification through recognition and feeling rather than through observation and analytical thought;[23] it calls for emotion rather than conviction; it establishes a vast sense of presence without offering intimate knowledge; it confirms without necessarily offering a challenge. It is the literature of the powerless identifying the key factor responsible for their powerlessness.[24]

His analysis is underpinned by Barthes' essay on wrestling from which he extrapolates the concept of 'the spectacle of excess' which is particularly apposite to the South African social formation. He writes:

> Everything in South Africa has been mind-bogglingly spectacular: the monstrous war machine developed over the years; the random

massive pass raids; mass shootings and killings; mass economic exploitation the ultimate symbol of which was the mining industry; the mass removals of people; the spate of draconian laws passed with the spectacle of parliamentary promulgations; the luxurious life style of whites: servants, all-encompassing privilege, swimming pools, and high commodity consumption; the sprawling monotony of architecture in African locations, which are the very picture of poverty and oppression ... the most outstanding feature of South African oppression is its brazen, exhibitionist openness.[25]

The plays of the 1980s consistently problematized this very 'spectacle of excess' and through juxtaposing the multiplicity of divergent personal testimonies, perhaps these dramatic works resisted the tendency towards stereotyping, unless in accordance with established convention when stereotypes were expressly invited to be recognized as such.

New works: Then and now

Mbongeni Ngema drew on his formative experiences as an actor with Gibson Kente in forming his company, Committed Artists, and in creating two seminal dramatic works: *Woza Albert!* and *Asinamali!*. The musical *Sarafina!* (1987) became a template for most of his subsequent output and consolidated his reputation as an iconic figure locally. While the international appeal of the heady mix of music and a reworking of traditional dance styles proved potently popular, perhaps more than any other it was his elevation of the ensemble as the focal element and defining feature of his various works that invited acclaim.

At the level of content, *Sarafina!* fuses cultural form with the call to collective action. The 'plot' is developed around the defiant and indomitable spirit of township schoolchildren subject to the curbs and constraints of State of Emergency regulations. A fictional class at Morris Isaacson High School is constructed around the figure of Sarafina who, herself, represents the spirit of resistance leadership. The character is a synthesis of the idealization, glamour and romance attached to the role of leadership within the 'struggle' with the more egalitarian capacity for self-effacement. The work explicitly pays tribute to Tsietsi Mashinini in lyrical and dialogic references.[26] Sarafina not only refigures what he represents through gender transpositon, but also transforms his narrative through the process of (fictional) representation and commemoration. It is, however, Victoria Mxenge the activist lawyer (shot and hacked to death in 1985) who is the iconic role model adopted by the adolescent schoolgirl. Mxenge's role in the struggle and her violent death is the subject of Sarafina's first-act monologue, underscored by the entire company in 'Wawungalelani' and leading into the lament 'Mama'. The intertwining of Victoria Mxenge's story with the emotive *response* to that narrative on the part of the ensemble is an important formal feature of the drama and culminates in the first-act finale.

The sequence begins with the classroom routine being disrupted by the arrival of a security policeman who challenges the teacher's lesson on 'the oil producing countries', prompting immediate resistance and retaliation on the part of the students,[27] and ends with the funeral of those who 'die' in this confrontation. The Mxenge monologue recites the events that occur within the life of a specific community and is a concrete instance of what Berger and Calvino claim for the role of oral history and the storytelling tradition. The oral testimony acknowledges the responses of the onstage audience as integral to its shape. The narrative form thus functions as a node around which notions of identity, affiliation, values and ideals can be consolidated. In contrast, colonial texts and their circulation is a motif that recurs throughout the text: the routine of the school day begins with a musical rendition of the Lord's Prayer, followed by a recitation of 'On Westminster Bridge'. The appropriateness of the latter to the curriculum is challenged by Sarafina, who challenges the merits of learning about beautiful cities in England and is quick to recognize that 'Mistress' should teach them 'the history that is not in books', about *Umzabalazi* – the wars of resistance – and the Defiance campaign, in which the role of the collective figures prominently.

The role of the collective in 'recycling' unwritten or repressed narratives was also central to the 'mode of production' which characterizes Ngema's subsequent musicals. In a complete break with conventional norms and theatre protocols, *Sarafina!* was rehearsed and performed without the script being reduced to writing. The explanation for this phenomenon lies as much in the identity of the ensemble as the so called 'workshop mode' and writing 'dialogue' directly into space and time through the voice and body of the rehearsing performer. In addition to effecting an organic synthesis between 'dialogue' and physical action from the outset, the evolution of the playing script through interaction (with the entire company as witnesses and auditors) also meant that any member of the ensemble was capable of stepping into any role as an understudy and was equally capable of delivering the entire text more or less single-handedly. More crucially, the focus of every performer was not only directed on their particular role within a specific scene but was intensely engaged with the unfolding narrative as a whole, imbuing the production with an uncommon level of theatrical intensity. Solo vocalists and dance leaders emerge from within the group without any particular significance being attached to their role or identity, just as the named characters effortlessly 'disappear' within that same collective. What appears to be a homogenous group is consistently revealed as heterogeneous with the personalities, features and expressive range of each individual as a potent intervention regarding both the construction and reception of 'stereotypes'.

Ngema subsequently produced a series of musicals, including *Township Fever!* (1990), *Magic at 4am!* (1993), *Maria! Maria!* (1995) and *Mama!* (1997), all of which toured Europe. As international appetite waned, he turned his attention towards local opportunities developing musicals celebrating Zulu history – *The Zulu* (1999), *House of Shaka* (2005) and *Bhambada 1906* (2006) – or resistance figures such as Gert Sibande (Mpumalanga-based leader of the 'potato boycotts' of the mid-1950s) in *The Lion of the East* (2009), while showcasing the evolving popular musical idiom rooted in indigenous forms intensified, as in *Nikiziwe* (2005). Having founded the KwaZulu Music House (launched at the KwaZulu-Natal Playhouse, 2009), a recording studio serving local musicians, he returned to the stage as a writer-actor in *The Zulu* (2013), which integrated an oral rendering of history with a solo acoustic guitarist as accompanist. The explicit return to the Zulu storytelling idiom draws strongly on oral tradition and cultural forms. His great-grandmother is invoked as a figure whose legacy must be preserved. As he recalls, she was blind, of unknown age (having married his great-grandfather before the Zulu War of 1879) and a repository of pre-colonial experience. Mkhulutshana Manqele did much to inspire his own values and style; he remembers 'as a small child, listening to the wonderful stories of heroic deeds that [she] shared with me … kept a wealth of our history alive, both about our family background and our proud roots as members of the Zulu nation' (http://www.artslink.co.za/news). She emerges as a key figure linking him with his forebears' participation in the Battle of Isandhlwana as a member of the vaunted *Umkhulutshana* regiment. Personal and historical motifs intertwine in a representation that reclaims and asserts his pride in Zulu heritage and nationhood.

***

Ngema's flamboyance and public prominence has a clear antithesis in the quiet presence of Maishe Maponya, playwright and theatre maker, poet and activist. Maponya's early plays are *The Hungry Earth* (1978), *Dirty Work* and *Gangsters* (presented as a double bill in 1983) and *Umongikazi* (1984). He describes how *The Hungry Earth* was first performed at the D.O.C.C. Hall in Soweto, and on the legal advice of Adv. Raymond Tucker was presented at the Wits Box Theatre (a 'private' campus venue),[28] while *Gangsters* was first performed at the Market Laager Theatre. *Gangsters* was, however, obliged to comply with constraints imposed by the Censorship Board, specifically:

2a. [I]t may only be performed in small intimate four-wall theatres, of experimental or avant-garde type.

b. [A] request for approval of any future venue for the performance of the play must be directed via the Directorate of Publications

c. The Laager Theatre in the Market Theatre complex in Johannesburg is an approved venue.

d. If 'Gangsters' is performed as part of a double bill (as with 'Dirty Work' in this case) or together with any other productions in the same venue, the conditions in regard to para. 2 shall apply.[29]

Maponya describes the kind of work that he is committed to making as focusing on 'facts, knowledge and the raising of consciousness' and challenges the current political dispensation, insisting that his work will remain 'socially and politically informed without fear or favour'. He distances himself from what he terms a position of artistic and 'political bankruptcy' and acknowledges that 'it is harder ... to do new plays than before'. He prioritizes developing a new work rather than reproducing existing texts in response to 'new issues'. His recent works *Bombarded* (2010) and *Place of Rock* (2005) testify to this sense of needing to deal with current crises, but neither has received much acclaim. Neither publicity nor marketing departments, nor the CEO of the State Theatre, supported the showcasing of *Bombarded*, with a lack of engagements that Maponya deplores. He attributes this to the way in which the play dealt with HIV, AIDS and charlatan health cures that have proliferated and are publicly advertised on street corners. Working as an HIV- and AIDS-awareness activist, Maponya had trained a group of young actors and researched some of the practices and cures being promoted by unscrupulous, bogus 'healers' in a text that strains the boundaries of magical realism and satire. Exhilarating levels of the fantastical and the bizarre escalate to extremes that comment on the naivety of a stubborn insistence on relying on 'faith-healing' rather than informed and life-saving medical protocols. His most profound indictment is reserved for those who exploit a credulous and desperate client base.

Based on the stories of Tshekiso Solomon Plaatije, *Place of Rock* deals with 'the land question' which is encapsulated in terms associated with colonialism: 'dispossession', 'disenfranchisement' and 'exploitation'. The play deals with the consequences of the Land Act of 1913 and had obvious pertinence at the time of the centenary of this law being passed. Despite the momentous historic impact of this single act, the play, commissioned by Walter Chakela at Windybrow Theatre in Plaatje's honour and hosted for a short season at the Market Theatre in 2007, seems unlikely to be revived. Ever the 'struggle-poet', Maponya asks: '[D]o you think that the ruling party will ever think of allowing us a space to reflect on the impact of that historic declaration? No Ways!'

***

Gcina Mhlophe's work is distinctive because of how her theatrical and dramatic sensibility is informed by a passionate commitment to literature and literacy.[30] Her autobiographically based play *Have You Seen Zandile?* (1986) marked her debut, and increasingly her career and stature has been founded on her commitment to oral storytelling as a crucial means of cultural and personal affirmation.[31] Now celebrated as an ambassadress of literacy and heritage for promoting the value of storytelling,[32] Mhlophe's plays (*Have You seen Zandile?* and *Somdaka* (1989)) are seminal indicators of the style she was to evolve. Both plays are delicately textured studies of life on the cusp of rural and urban living, of the threat to innocence as characters negotiate thresholds of transition between worlds. Both are intimate works, intertwining duologues and solo narratives in which Mhlophe's pithy dialogue and rhythmic command suggest her love of the spoken word. Thematically, storytelling serves as a means of intergenerational communication and as a nurturing force. She posits:

There was time in African culture when the setting of the sun announced that it was time for story telling ... That time is gone now. Now everybody in the family works ... So there's all kinds of breakdown in normal African culture because of the lifestyle we lead, in the cities especially. The television and the radio and the disco are taking over. And that's something that should not be allowed to happen. There's wisdom in folk tales. Folk tales are educational.[33]

Mhlophe's preference for using English as a medium of expression is probed by Tyrone August (1989) and since her project is to celebrate the cultural richness through reviving traditional stories in addition to creating new ones, her choice of linguistic medium is significant. She says: 'I wrote for the very first time in Xhosa ... I think it was only in 1979 that I started writing in English. I don't think it was a conscious decision. I just found myself writing in English. Now I write in both languages. It depends on what is needed at the time'.[34] She submits that an organic connection between theme, expressive purpose and subject governs her linguistic preference and perspicaciously comments on multilingual texts. In her view, the polyglot 'formula' tends, unfortunately and problematically, towards vernacular interpolations for swearing or in moments of comic relief, while English is reserved for 'speak[ing] about serious things'. For her, the audience remains the vital determining factor governing language choice: the cultural diversity of Johannesburg necessitated relying on English as a means of overcoming differences. Her facility to present the same material to a Xhosa or Zulu audience is informed by their preference as she explained in a 1993 interview:

I ask my audience if I am not sure what language they want. I speak three African languages and English. It is a big advantage, because language is a tool for a story-teller ... certain languages are more expressive for what I want to say. For example there are certain emotions and exclamations that you can drive home more easier [sic] in Zulu than you can in English.[35]

Her account of *Lovechild* (1991) conveys her views on the synthesis of the personal and the political:[36]

It was about a person who is born between two language groups. A person who believes that art can be a healing force. I used a traditional folk tale to start with, that talks about two villages that were fighting, but the chiefs were cousins. A young girl called Nomlambo came into one of the villages and fell in love with Mtujnzi, the young man who was looking after the chief because he was not well. She took him to a deep pool in a river. They found a drum with magic powers, took it to the battlefield and, because of its music, the warriors forgot their spears and shields and held hands, dancing to the rhythm of the drum. It carried on to talk about the violence on the Reef, and how the press had labelled it as a Zulu–Xhosa war. Me, being Zulu-Xhosa, I know it was not the case.[37]

Zanendaba (1992) stages much of what Mhlophe is striving towards when she states that 'Story-telling should not conform to theatre rules.'[38] Mhlophe, as performer, takes on the multiple characters in addition to that of narrator. Moreover, as in the *ntsomi* tradition, the presence of the audience is a vital element of the form of theatre that she proposes. Incorporating the formal convention of the opening and closing call-and-response motif is a manifestation of her revival of custom and its role in facilitating a sense of *communitas*. The one-woman presentation signalled the direction that Mhlophe's work would take. As early as 1993 she described her 'shift' from theatre to storytelling as a natural response to public interest, the extent of which she had not initially anticipated. The scope of her venture embraces extensive publication of the stories in addition to solo storytelling performances:

> I had to put a hold on theatre because it was not possible to put as much into theatre at the same time as doing story-telling. There are now fifteen of us involved in the story-telling group *Zanendaba* (Bring me a story). We perform in different places, new stories that are contemporary and very recognizable for children that are growing up now, and relevant to certain situations that they have experienced. We are collecting stories from all over the African continent and abroad.[39]

Despite international success and opportunity, Mhlophe's focus remains local, founded on a profound sense of community. She puts it in these terms:

> I choose to give priority to the people of my country. Black artists don't go to university to learn skills, they learn from the people around them. They should plant back. We owe our community the right to share what we have achieved.[40] [41]

Since the formation of the *Zanendaba Initiative* in 2002 (in collaboration with the Market Theatre and READ),[42] her aim is to ensure the dissemination of this archive within local communities just as her theatrical voice is a hybrid of a proudly revivalist strain with contemporary idiom and technologies.

***

The dramatic output of Phyllis Klotz and Smal Ndaba extends to an ambitious play proposed for 2014 which is currently in the initial phases of fund-raising and research.[43] Since the foundation of the Sibikwa Community Project in 1988 (a visionary venture, formally constituted as a Non-Governmental Organization), located in the industrial section of Benoni,[44] their joint output has been prolific and anchored in organic relations with the community that they serve. A community arts centre, the Sibikwa project is multifaceted and boasts its own theatre at Sibikwa (opened in 1997). Here, their plays have been launched to local audiences, students, parents and local residents. Klotz stresses her view that, while craft and style are crucial to their work, 'the meaning and value of the work is all audience related'[45] (June 2013).

Asked to define what is denoted by the epithet 'community', Klotz observes that such work invariably centres on 'education and training' – hence productions like *Maru* and *Animal Farm* catering to school audiences. Equally the term inculcates distinctions similar to the divide between amateur and professional practice. As she puts it:

> Community … is a concept we've been struggling with. There's a kind of opposition between community and professional. We work with people who haven't had training or experience and are drawn from the metro, which is not to say they haven't talent and ability. We have changed our trading name to Sibikwa Arts Centre.[46]

Pronouncing the pejorative connotations attached to the tradition from which they have come, she says 'the stigma (of being defined as a community theatre maker rather than receiving unqualified acknowledgement) is there …' Ndaba adds quietly, 'I want to come out of *that* before I die'.[47]

Personal and professional lives blend seamlessly in the ventures of this partnership, and boundaries between the domestic and work spheres are porous – their voices are at times interchangeable or one speaks on behalf of another. Their compatibility and reciprocal accommodation of each other's views has its origins in their long-term close allegiance and collaboration.

The duo offer complementary views on relations between literacy and orality from their respective cultural positions. Ndaba stresses the value and authority of personal oral testimony:

> If you hear the story from someone, then you can work with it – if it is your grandmother, then you can ask questions – you can believe it. But if the information is from a book, then it is harder to believe it. The stories from our grandmothers are not just stories – these were things we could learn from.[48]

His view is complemented with considerable equanimity on Klotz's part: 'You've got a completely different approach to trusting the source of material – the perspectives are just so different. A Western view honours that which is written.'[49]

Their relatively autonomous and stable base at Sibikwa, although always subject to the pressures of irregularities in funding and located on the margins of mainstream theatre at some distance from a more diverse theatre-going constituency, appears to have been productive, enabling and a source of profound personal fulfilment, despite constant confrontations with bureaucratic systems. Disregarding her capacity as Board member of the NAC and the State Theatre, Klotz asserts, 'We haven't gone into government – everybody else did, by choice – that's the problem … we're just maverick sprits.'[50] The duo clearly relishes their freedom from constrictions along with their independence. They are relatively unaffected by the constraints congruent with being accountable to associate producers or being commissioned to work for an institution other than their own. Ndaba is diplomatic but firm in indicating the need for autonomy:

> It's very difficult to make [work] to be acceptable. We are not used to that. We don't want to bow down. But we don't want to embarrass people.[51]

Klotz is more forthright in her declaration:

> In a way there's more censorship now – people have to toe the line – they're concerned money will be withdrawn. We've got nothing to lose. Nobody is particularly interested in us. Nobody cares, really, what work we produce.[52]

Discussing ways in which their work profited from being showcased at the Market and subject to Barney Simon's scrutiny in the final phases, Ndaba begins, 'Remember with Barney, he'd get into the thing and ask you "Why did you do that? Do you think it works?"' Their preoccupation lies as much with methodology and formal considerations of medium as with the content. Klotz expands: '[W]e never really had [dramaturgical] input. The only guidance was from Barney on *Strike*.' The process of how the plays were devised and written, in the case of the Sibikwa projects of the late 1980s and early 1990s, is distinctive as Klotz recounts:

> We made our best work when we lived with actors. Like with DET when we rehearsed under the trees somewhere in KwaNdebele ... With monkeys overhead as the audience! We rehearsed *Ghamka* in Cape Town for several weeks and *Ubuntu* for those few weeks at that retreat in Wilgespruit. It was the best way of working – taking people away. We were dealing with raw, township talent in the early 90s – and there was a lot of civil disturbance which made it hard for people to focus.[53]

Returning to the subject of audiences, Klotz makes a penetrating observation regarding the perennial appeal of seminal South African texts which is likewise indicative of the qualities she strives for in her own work. She identifies an 'abiding interest' on the part of audiences, in what she herself relishes as:

> The quirkiness of humanity ... That's what shines through in *Sizwe* and *Woza* ... those plays had humanity about them – nobody in those plays is a victim – everyone is doing their stuff. They deal with circumstances, adapt to it with a kind of resilience and self-sufficiency.[54]

It is just this 'resilience and self-sufficiency' that she and Ndaba epitomize. Klotz describes the approach to the Shaka project as striving towards reflecting a set of personal statements from multiple perspectives and then departs from this theme in a quirky declaration:

> I don't have the distance, but I'd like to a do a play about Smal and myself, our lives together, but I don't have the distance and can't conceive of how to do it.[55]

For them, celebrating past achievements is subsidiary to fresh compulsions:

We've done too many revivals and need to make new work. But it would be wonderful to do a retrospective season before we bow out. Go back over the early lehrstücke like *So Where To?* with D.E.T.[56] and Uhambo.[57]

Reproducing these works is driven by the need to re-examine issues of teenage pregnancy, the fraught condition of secondary school experience and the place of memory in the perpetual role of the struggle for dignity in a society that has not transformed as radically as one might have anticipated from the time in which these plays were first made. Smal Ndaba offers a final statement about making plays and theatre in South Africa today by simply, but nevertheless eloquently, restating what Barney Simon articulated in 1988:

I always feel that there is something good that one can do. There's nothing like 'I'm giving up'. I see more opportunities. We haven't done enough.[58]

Conclusion

It seems a fundamental and deep irony that the post-colonial project of building a unified nation and consolidating a sense of national identity butts up against the postmodern valorization of the individual subject, while respecting the rights of plural minority groups effects a splintering and schismatic separation that seemingly insists on endorsing contained, psychologically-driven narratives. This necessarily brief survey testifies to deploying a montage as an expressive device that accommodates not only cultural and personal difference but positively eulogizes the egalitarian imperatives of the collective play-making process and presents the audience with a textured tapestry of multiple views.

A quotation transcribed by director Lucille Gillwald into her diary from the novel *The Artist* seems an appropriate conclusion.[59] Its articulation, as much as the range of the personal tributes to her memory from widely varied constituencies celebrating the role that she had played in their lives, testifies to what made the theatre-making project so valuable in the 1980s. She records a sentiment that might well undergird the work of the 'pioneers':

Perhaps the most important of all is a sense of responsibility. In the final analysis it may be the only thing that prevents total violence and nihilism in the world – it's the connective tissue between the individual and the tribe. It's the way people stay sane when they do stay sane. Responsibility to others keeps us from spinning off into insanity which is, after all, total loneliness, total disconnection from others.

In this present milieu, the commitment to fabricating 'the connective tissue between the individual and the tribe' seems all the more crucial as the endemic poverty and crime, civil disruption, xenophobic unrest, strike action and violence (epitomized by the events at Marikana) eerily echo what was experienced during the 1980s. Barney Simon's perception of the socio-political complexities of South Africa in 1986 seems frighteningly apt today,[60] although the extent to which theatre continues as a potent form of cultural expression operating within the social domain and grappling with the multifaceted dimensions of South African experience, particularly tensions between autonomy and alterity, is less demonstrable.

Notes

1. Quoted in Elizabeth Gunner, *Politics and Performance: Theatre, Poetry and Song in Southern Africa* (Johannesburg: Witwatersrand University Press, 1994), 277.

2. I acknowledge a method that fuses scholarly research and interviews with personal memories and reflections as an unavoidable consequence of my own engagement with the material being presented. The dual focus of my position as scholar and professional theatre-practitioner suggests a privileged perspective that synthesizes personal experience with the obligations of the dispassionate scholarly method, but subjective bias inevitably renders this account both partial and provisional. The process of constructing any narrative account does, however, depend as much on personal memories as on archival documentation, as Pat Schwartz, in her author's note to *The Best of Company*, acknowledges: 'The Market is the people who created it and its story lives on in their heads rather than on paper in dusty archives' (Johannesburg: AD Donker, 1988), 207.

3. In South Africa in the mid-1980s there were no reasonable grounds to anticipate a negotiated settlement as a conclusion to struggle politics, nor was it possible to imagine the inauguration of Nelson Mandela as the first democratically elected President of South Africa.

4. Phyllis Klotz and Smal Ndaba, interview, 22 June 2013, Johannesburg.

5. Revisiting key texts affirms the extent to which the so-called 'protest plays' viscerally enact the consequences of disenfranchisement and exclusion: the works resonate with the effects of lacking a sense of place or being securely

anchored in a sense of 'belonging' (a consequence of the migrant labour system and land removals) as much as being denied the basic right of the freedom of speech.

6. Ramphele defines freedom as entailing 'the right and the ability to make choices in life' (Mamphela Ramphele, *Conversations with My Sons and Daughters* (Johannesburg: Penguin, 2012)), 67.

7. Ibid., 159.

8. Ramphele writes: 'The critical question is to what extent people are genuinely and meaningfully participating in their own governance. How do you feel about the level of your own participation in shaping the future of your country? Is it meaningful and engaged? ... Some of you confess to not being engaged citizens' (ibid., 17).

9. Schwartz, *The Best of Company*, 205.

10. John Matisonn writes, 'Thanks to the nationalist Government, South African Broadcasting and telecommunications were backward in ways almost incomprehensible to developed economies ... South Africans first saw television broadcast tests in 1929 ... but it would be 1976 before Pretoria would risk its polluting effects here' (John Matisonn, 'Reflections of a Broadcast Regulator in Democratic South Africa', *Focus* 66 (Johannesburg: Helen Suzman Foundation, 2012)), 5.

11. Barry Ronge, *The Saturday Star*, 1 July 1995.

12. Michael Gardiner, 'A Renoster, a Foundation and a Market: The Cultural Import of Three Johannesburg Figures Between 1960 and 1990', *Focus* 61 (Johannesburg: Helen Suzman Foundation, 2011), 21.

13. Malcolm Purkey, interview, 21 June 2013, Johannesburg.

14. Ronge, *The Saturday Star*.

15. Ibid.

16. Mary Benson, *Athol Fugard and Barney Simon: Bare Stage, a Few Props, Great Theatre* (Randburg: Ravan, 1997), 45.

17. Gardiner, 'A Renoster, a Foundation and a Market', 26.

18. Ibid., 27.

19. Ibid.

20. Ronge, *The Saturday Star*.

21. Transformation is a term, concept and trope dominating contemporary discourses most frequently associated with issues of redressing residual imbalances in agency, along with the associated preoccupation with identity and the implications of 'stereotyping' which counters the imperatives of restorative dignity.

22. Njabulo Ndebele, *The Rediscovery of the Ordinary: Essays on South African Literature and Culture* (Pietermaritzburg: University of KwaZulu-Natal Press, 2006), 33.

23. 'Uncritical rhetoric of protest can easily impair the capacity of the oppressed to think strategically' (ibid., 60).

24. Ibid., 41.

25. Ibid., 31.

26. Mashinini organized and led the Soweto uprisings of 1976.

27. The presentation of violence and confrontation is highly stylized and symbolically represented through relatively simple theatrical devices: the pupils mime throwing stones; gun shots and tear gas are signified through the use of staccato drum and percussion instrumentation.

28. Then S.A.C.C. secretary Bishop Tutu referred Maponya to Tucker, who had this to say: 'I am of the opinion that the play would constitute a contravention of the laws relating to racial incitement and the Publications Act and, in addition the presentation would result in severe harassment of both the author and the performers.'

29. Maishe Maponya, interviews, conversations and unpublished correspondence, 9/8/1984.

30. Mhlophe acted in two works generated by Simon with an ensemble, *Injanyma/ Black Dog* and *Born in the RSA,* winning an OBIE award (New York) for her performance in the latter. *The Snake with Seven Heads* (Skotaville: 1989) was subsequently translated into multiple languages, including five African languages. Her career as author has been prolific and much of her work translated into European languages (French, German and Italian) in addition to Japanese. Publications include: *Queen of the Tortoises* (1990), *The Singing Dog* (1992), *Nalohima, the Deaf Tortoise* (1999), *Fudukazi's Magic* (1999), *Nozincwadi, Mother of Books* (2001), *African Mother of Christmas* (2002), *Lovechild* (2002) and *Stories of Africa* (2003).

31. 'I like things that last. How many people saw *Black Dog*? I don't know if it will ever be performed again. But if it's something that's scripted, on paper, I could be dead and the script will still be there' (Gunner, *Politics and Performance*), 277.

32. Her role in promoting literacy is acknowledged in the several doctoral degrees conferred on her, including those from the London Open University and the University of Natal.

33. Gunner, *Politics and Performance*, 274.

34. Ibid., 273.

35. Ibid., 281.

36. '... me giving priority to myself sometimes; it's just that I think of myself as important, as well as national issues. Also, I have a belief that I'm not a unique person. There's got to be somebody who's gone through it before and that gives it another point of view altogether. And because people go through the same kinds of things for different reasons, I think that they have got something to share in my life. I think we need to think of it – the personal and the political

– as equal all the way. Politics changes every day, but the fundamental things that are important to human beings last a long, long time' (ibid., 277).

37. Ibid., 282.

38. Ibid., 275.

39. Ibid., 281.

40. In line with these sentiments, she admires the work of Gibson Kente as being driven by community needs and acting as a 'university' through providing education and skills development through training.

41. Gunner, *Politics and Performance*, 278.

42. A national literacy organization.

43. Currently untitled, the work proposes a multi-perspectival presentation of the life of Shaka drawing on the oral tradition and the written archive. The intention is to perform in Zulu with English surtitles. They have been engaged in research at the Killie Campbell Museum, amassing material from the diaries of Henry Francis Fynn, rewritten largely from memory when the originals were lost, describing his encounters with Shaka, as trader and gun-runner. As Ndaba explains, Fynn became virtually one of Shaka's *Ndunas* (subsidiary chiefs) with his own *izibongo* (praise poet), five wives and many children. But Ndaba is adamant that the written record requires interweaving with what material can be unearthed from the oral tradition: 'We need to find old people in the community. We want *their* interpretation of the history … and all these characters from the past they will come back, these ancestors the *dlozi*. We want to stage, somehow, these multiple spirits of the past.' The objective is for a presentation which is not so much a re-enactment of history as an invocation of identities who remain defined as spiritual presences. 'Mbopha is not a present day person – he can *only* appear today as a spirit of the past in our present', Ndaba reiterates (interview, 2013).

44. Benoni is an Eastern satellite town on the periphery of the industrial complex that makes up the Witwatersrand, with Johannesburg at its centre.

45. Klotz acknowledges that their 'audience base has changed: now our audience is mostly white and they seem to love it. Originally white audiences didn't seem to want to watch our work with its raw edges they seemed to prefer the slick professionalism of Westernized stuff' (interview, 2013).

46. Ibid.

47. Ibid.

48. Ibid.

49. Ibid.

50. Ibid.

51. Ibid.

52. Ibid.

53. The East Rand was a hotbed of violent unrest with continual clashes between Inkatha and ANC factions in the period immediately prior to the 1994

elections and their aftermath, as documented and interrogated by political scientist Ivor Chipkin. Ndaba puts it in personal terms: 'we put the facts together ... like the violence – when we did Ubuntu – it was about their experience – they understood that' (interview, 2013).

54. Klotz, interview, 2013.

55. Ibid.

56. In a remark that suggests that (at grass roots level) life in South Africa has not changed much nearly twenty years into democratic governance, Klotz observes, 'Apart from the one word "Bantustans", which today's generation doesn't understand, when we revived *D.E.T.* everything was still relevant – pathetic really' (ibid.).

57. Ibid.

58. Ibid.

59. The statement was reproduced beneath her photograph on the sheet outlining the order of events at her memorial service which took place in the school hall of St Barnabas College on the western outskirts of Johannesburg.

60. Simon frequently spoke simply and eloquently of the 'insane abnormality' of the asymmetries and imbalances in living conditions generated and governed by apartheid politics. The legacy of that past continues to simmer.

Bibliography

Primary sources

Gray, Stephen (ed.), *Theatre One: New South African Drama* (Johannesburg: AD Donker, 1978).

Gray, Stephen (ed.), *Market Plays* (Johannesburg: AD Donker, 1986).

Ndlovu, Duma, *Woza Africa! An Anthology of South African Plays* (New York: George Braziller, 1986).

Ngema, M., *Sarafina! The Music of Liberation* (New York: Lincoln Center Broadway cast recording, MNMCD002(134)).

Secondary sources

http://www.artslink.co.za/news (accessed 30 June 2013).

Benson, Mary, *Athol Fugard and Barney Simon: Bare Stage, a Few Props, Great Theatre* (Randburg: Ravan, 1997).

Chipkin, I., *Do South Africans Exist?* (Johannesburg: Wits University Press, 2007).

Gardiner, Michael, 'A Renoster, a Foundation and a Market: The Cultural Import of Three Johannesburg Figures Between 1960 and 1990', *Focus* 61 (Johannesburg: Helen Suzman Foundation, 2011): 21–8.

Gunner, Elizabeth, *Politics and Performance: Theatre, Poetry and Song in Southern Africa* (Johannesburg: Witwatersrand University Press, 1994).

Hauptfleisch, Temple, *Theatre and Society: Reflections in a Fractured Mirror* (Pretoria: J. L. Van Schaik, 1997).

Klotz, Phyllis and Smal Ndaba, interview, 22 June 2013, Johannesburg.

Maponya, Maishe, interviews, conversations and unpublished correspondence.

Matisonn, John, 'Reflections of a Broadcast Regulator in Democratic South Africa', *Focus* 66 (Johannesburg: Helen Suzman Foundation, 2012): 4–12.

Ndebele, Njabulo, *The Rediscovery of the Ordinary: Essays on South African Literature and Culture* (Pietermaritzburg: University of KwaZulu-Natal Press, 2006).

Purkey, Malcolm, interview, 21 June 2013, Johannesburg.

Ramphele, Mamphela, *Conversations with My Sons and Daughters* (Johannesburg: Penguin, 2012).

Ronge, Barry, *The Saturday Star*, 1 July 1995.

Sarafina! theatre programme. Lincoln Center Theater. 1988.

Schwartz, Pat, *The Best of Company* (Johannesburg: AD Donker, 1988).

Terreblanche, S., *The Sunday Times*, 28 October 2012.

http://en.wikipedia.orgwiki/Gcina_Mhlophe (accessed 30 June 2013).

CHAPTER 2
CONTEMPORARY COLLABORATORS I: KENTRIDGE/HANDSPRING/TAYLOR
Jane Taylor

Ubu and the Truth Commission; Zeno at 4 am; 2½ or 3: Confessions of Zeno

Introduction

Modern aesthetic conceptions of collaboration seem to derive from the composer Carl Maria von Weber, who celebrated the opera *Undine*[1] as demonstrating how 'partial contributions of the related and collaborating arts blend together, disappear, and in disappearing, somehow form a new world'.[2] This conception of a 'new world' that might arise beyond the capacities of any of the contributing artists is part of the wondrous interest provoked by collaboration. Weber was, in this review, inaugurating an idea that would preoccupy the creative arts in nineteenth-century Germany. It was actually the German writer and philosopher K. F. E. Trahndorff who, in 1827, coined the term *Gesamtkunstwerk*, a conception of the fully integrated multi-modal work of art that was later to become associated with Richard Wagner.

Weber's argument above is engaged with thinking about the question of the collaboration of the elements of the actual work of art; he is looking at an aesthetic end, that 'new world' which the endeavour precipitates. My purpose is to consider the processes and practices of collaboration, that coming together of sensibilities, persons, gifts, predispositions that occurs when several beings apply their differences to the exploration of a joint undertaking.

Rather like the two-faced figure of Janus, the term 'collaboration' looks in both directions at once. On the one hand it carries all of the positive and affirming values associated with a shared endeavour, a joint project arising from a team of individuals who merge their interests, subordinating each distinct objective to a unified end. Collaboration in such terms is often identified with creative or artistic engagement, or projects aimed at supporting a collective good.

Since the Second World War, though, the term has been inflected with the negative, as it became associated with groups or individuals within communities who, when occupied by totalitarian forces, capitulated to their captors and worked for Nazi interests. In such historical instances, the word 'collaboration' usually implies that there has been some kind of substantial regime change, because the one labelled a 'collaborator' would for futurity be associated with a political faction associated with an ousted regime. French citizens who aligned themselves with Vichy France were named 'collaborators'.

In South Africa, 'collaborators' were citizens (usually black or legally of 'non-white' status) who had covertly worked for the apartheid state; in particular, it was used as a shorthand for the schizoid identities of those who held a citizenship (of a kind) in two states: on the one hand living as a community member subjected to apartheid law that oppressed them, while simultaneously engaging in pro-apartheid pursuits against the interests of their perceived community, through spying or engaging in secret acts of right-wing terror.

It struck me as worth sketching that double legacy of the idea, because the first collaboration which I worked on with Handspring and Kentridge engaged very expressly with the question of political collaboration. It was, after all, in South Africa in the first years of the post-apartheid state.

***

The Kentridge/Handspring/Taylor theatre collaborations are to date two (or three) in number, although we have worked together (in varieties of twos and threes) in several other ways, on intellectual projects, exhibitions, arts activism, books and essays, and anticipate further initiatives. At present we all collaborate on the Handspring Trust, an arts initiative in rural communities, working in contexts of scarcity or political crisis.

The two plays are of distinctly different kinds: the one, *Ubu and the Truth Commission*, is in part what might now be termed a piece of 'verbatim theatre' although the words gathered were not gathered by us, as is generally the case in that theatre practice; rather, we have worked with the testimony generated by the public hearings into human rights abuses during the apartheid era. The play is not, however, in the style of 'verbatim' or documentary theatre. Rather, it is absurd in style. Our purpose was to bring the strong, fragile truths narrated at the commission into a direct confrontation with the grotesque and farcical delinquency of the thugs who were deployed as the blunt instruments of apartheid's terror. The juxtaposition of these asymmetries drives the meaning of the play. That was the first theatre piece we undertook together.

The second collaboration was itself a curious double bill, because the work was initially launched as a short one-act experiment in making an avant-garde puppet opera; and so an additional collaborator, the composer Kevin Volans, was added to the core creative team. That first test piece is *Zeno at 4 am,* a performance piece for voice, puppet and quartet; this was succeeded by a reworking of the material into a three-act operetta, *Confessions of Zeno.*

Ubu and *Zeno* as enquiries were each impelled by their own purposes: political, philosophical, aesthetic, dramatic. Let it be noted from the outset that these plays were from the start already collaborations, because of the lively presence of the ghosts of the writers whose works engaged us: Alfred Jarry, whose wild exuberant *Ubu Roi* (1896) is in our mind's eye; so too is Italo Svevo, with his poignantly wry *Coscienza di Zeno* (1925).

The modes of engaging with the source texts differ substantially between the two cases. Jarry's *Ubu* texts are alluded to only obliquely in our play; Svevo's novel is by contrast on occasion invoked fairly closely in the weaving of the textures of the libretto in collaboration with the composer Kevin Volans. I suspect the character of that collaboration may have had something to do with it. Volans was in Ireland and I in Johannesburg when I was drafting chunks of the libretto. We trafficked passages of text, fragments of music back and forth, a task not quite so easy in the mid-1990s. I suspect that the novel itself provided something of a *lingua franca* as we navigated the meanings of the text/sound environments with one another.

The plays

Ubu and the Truth Commission

Ubu and the Truth Commission was the first creative collaboration by Kentridge/Handspring/Taylor, and it is a multi-modal piece of puppet theatre dealing substantially with the question of political 'collaboration' as outlined in the second definition, above.[3] In 1996 the South African state set in process its Truth and Reconciliation Commission (TRC), the public hearings into abuses by apartheid operatives who had engaged in human rights violations during the last decades of apartheid. Our play sought to engage with the testimonies being generated, in order to explore the theatricality of the events, and to archive the stories being generated through performance. There were the disturbing voices of amnesty applicants, thugs who had engaged in racist violence against powerless individuals with few legal rights and little if any legal recourse. More destabilizing were the applications from the collaborators who for various reasons had been drawn into the assault against their own communities, against their own political interest.

Initially, the idea for such a theatre work arose out of *Fault Lines*, a broad interdisciplinary enquiry I had established in order to draw the arts into the process of considering what the commission might mean: what its key terms 'Truth' and 'Reconciliation' might portend. *Fault Lines* was a series of cultural and arts events aimed at provoking thought about the commission and the materials that it was unearthing. My thinking was, 'Let's use the arts to provoke the public into debating what the legal and political processes of the commission might mean.'

I approached Kentridge with a proposal about making such a play; he had come through the immense projects of directing *Woyzeck on the Highveld* and *Faustus in Africa* with Handspring, and through the partnership they were just beginning to grasp together a new visual language. Kentridge effectively was working with the Handspring puppets as if they were animation figures who could move and react within real time. This was the great gain for him. He could imagine an event, then draw a context – a landscape of some kind – and populate that affectively charged visual field with a walking, talking, breathing being that was not captive to the naturalism of the live actor.

Conventional animation is notoriously time-intensive, with even a simple change of expression requiring any number of distinct drawing events. Kentridge had himself evolved his trademark visual language, using the filming of drawing and erasure, with which he captured 'change' in his films, as a way of speeding up the traditional animation process; however, even then the temporal economy of Kentridge's 'Films for Projection' meant that the making of a three-minute film could take anything up to three months in the studio (excluding the intangible time spent in reflection, research and cogitation). Now, working with puppets, he could draw a minimally altering background, into which a puppet figure could be inserted. The theatrical encounter stitched together the live and the filmed events as integral to one another, and an animation figure could move through the landscape as an agent in the world. With limited preparation, a half-hour scene could now be performed in half an hour. Kentridge was tempted by the idea of testing formal questions, taking the pragmatics of the puppet theatre further. Of course, theoretically and politically he was also immensely provoked by the idea of working in relation to the great event of his time – the TRC was, with the Constitutional court, one of the first great tests of the post-apartheid juridical imagination.

Handspring similarly had much to gain from the sustained encounter with Kentridge. His roughly-drawn expressionistic visual style freed Adrian Kohler (master puppet-maker) into a liberated visual idiom. Having worked for years on the nuance and finesse of the machineries of the puppet, and engaged in solving aesthetic questions about ratios, time and affect in the performance of the puppet, Handspring was prompted, through the dialogue with Kentridge, into considering afresh the expressive capacities of the carved head, and gave fresh attention to how the puppet might capture dynamic emotion inside static form. Both Kohler and Jones had begun their careers within a fine art practice as sculptors, though they had had to forego elements of this practice when they launched a puppet company. The collaboration was prompting them to draw the visual and the performance arts into a more integrated field of meaning. Both Kohler and Jones had been active anti-apartheid activists, and as 'out' gay men had a particular interest in exploring the staging of violent masculinities such as had dominated South African military culture. Testimony from the commission made evident, over and over, that a denied and repressed homoerotics often was deployed in scenes of torture and interrogation.

Initially my approach to Kentridge and Handspring had been made from my purposes as curator of *Fault Lines*, but quite quickly I was drawn into the writing process; I brought to it the questions that as curator I was asking about the commission. What were these testimonies telling us about narrative, about sadism and masochism, about memory and evidence? My interests were in the first instance concerned with language and ideas, and so I was (and remain) particularly interested in verbal forms and structures. How are they used in order to communicate inner states? Do words project meanings into the social through speech acts? What is the relationship between poetic expression, or the well-turned phrase, and authentic feeling? Can metaphor arise during times of urgent honesty? In selecting which testimonial moments to draw on for the making of the play, I was always interested in this set of questions.

This linguistic ordering of priority masks immense ethical questions about the status of testimony and the freedoms of the writer. It was inevitable that we would confront what rights we as artists and intellectuals might have in relation to these first-hand stories. Was this yet another appropriation? My response at the time was that the materials were in the public domain; further, my sense is that if an artist or a scholar attends to a question with real seriousness, there is some legitimacy in that itself. It seems to me foolhardy to proscribe writers and artists from dealing with significant questions – this would be to condemn our artists to trivial enquiry.

So then the resources we brought together into the creative team were several. Through Handspring, there was always going to be a wrestling with materialities, as well as with species and category boundaries. They have over subsequent years demonstrated an increasing commitment to testing the limits of the subject–object–animal continuum. Both of the previous Kentridge/Handspring productions had had an animal central to the artistic language of the work – a rhinoceros in *Woyzeck* and a hyaena in *Faustus*. This is in part a way of disrupting the humanism of modernist thinking: in part a way of celebrating the art of puppetry. It was precisely because of this particular mode of regard that, when the National Theatre in the United Kingdom was considering making *War Horse*, they invited Handspring to work on the horse puppets for that show. Part of the task as they understood it was to find an idiom for capturing the mentality of the animal through its mechanical manipulation. In *Ubu and the Truth Commission* there are several beasts – a crocodile, a vulture, a three-headed dog. Each of the Handspring animals is found in a slightly different position on the spectrum of possible identities ranging from the fully autonomous and 'other' animal, to the fully anthropomorphic, the animal as avatar of the human.

The creatures from *Ubu* put me in mind of the four evangelists (man, lion, ox, eagle). For our production there are the debased human, the vulture, crocodile and dog. The dog and the crocodile have human speech. The dogs are servile, domesticated beasts of various types; the crocodile is interrogative, supercilious; the vulture squawks and is a grotesque version of the parrot of philosophy (the non-human that speaks, beloved of Locke, Defoe and Rousseau). The bird's meanings, as projected text, are thrown onto the upstage screen that carries Kentridge's animations, and these 'utterances' are somewhere between Aesopian phrases and silent movie captions ('It is enough for the zebra to know about grass' and 'The gamewarder's wife wears a fur collar'). I was interested in the vulture as a thinking thing, yet it thinks in idioms that would strike the viewer as somehow sage, resonant, while remaining curiously foreign.

My own thinking about the three-headed dog (based on Cerberus from classical legend) arises from the testimony that is presented at the amnesty hearings, where the structures of dissembling and the performances of self are at once ambiguously narcissistic as well as communitarian. The acts that might be named errors or shameful deeds arise from shared vision, while the capacity for mourning and melancholia remains individual. In other words, sins and errors get attributed to a collective loyalty to the group imperative, while remorse is personal and evidence of a true self.

The many-headed dog provides a strategy for thinking about the varieties of different apartheid agents. The general, the foot soldier and the policeman each had testified in distinct ways at the commission, each locating blame elsewhere. The strategy of the generals is clear: take no blame for the chain of command. As Pa Ubu testifies, 'These vile stories, they sicken me. When I am told what happened here, I cannot believe it. These things, they were done by those above me; those below me; those beside me. I too have been betrayed! I knew nothing.' Dogs have become notorious figures of domestic paranoia in South Africa, and households are ubiquitously patrolled by canines that have been bred for attack. They also, of course, are a mainstay of the military and police units. Bred now largely as weapons, they are, in the Heideggerean phrase, 'ready-to-hand', considered primarily as utilities.

William Kentridge initially thinks about the visual field of the dog. 'Where will it go, with Pa?' His imagination is instantly engaged with landscapes. Handspring imagines how to *realize* the animal: how to make it work. What material are the necks, with elastic, girth and contraction so that the dogs' heads can dart about and then draw back to consolidate close to the body. The solution Adrian Kohler resolves on is a kind of vacuum-cleaner concertina tube that has stretch, mobility and tension. The three dogs are clearly different breeds, each of which is attributed a kind of generic character. The torso of the dog is initially a puzzle – and a problem for simple naturalism. There is, in the end, a kind of existential trade-off between Basil Jones and William Kentridge. Basil will allow his father's Second World War kitbag to become the body of the crocodile if William will allow us to use an item of tremendous sentimental value to himself and to his father (human rights lawyer, Sir Sydney Kentridge). It is the legal briefcase used by Bram Fischer, the human rights hero who had defended Nelson Mandela at the Rivonia Trial. (Fischer himself was put on trial following that case, and was sentenced to life imprisonment.)

Once the dog begins to emerge in its physicality, we begin to generate plot. William imagines an evening perambulation, and I think of a song, a quartet, with Ubu and his three dogs. It is grim and macabre, full of dark humour; Brecht and Kurt Weill are influences in the background.

Several of the Handspring puppeteers here also realize themselves as actors and the collaboration relies on them, too. I would like particularly to mention the outrageous gift for seductive playfulness of Busi Zokufa as Ma Ubu. In a small company such as Handspring's, the demands of the script are always captive to the performance capacities of the individuals. Zokufa has to balance the enormous comic role of Ma Ubu with the great seriousness and subtle philosophy required to perform also at times as a translator in the glass booth, and at times as an occasional puppeteer, manipulating a witness telling her own harrowing story. No greater demand is made of any performer in the play than that required of Busi Zokufa, who has in this past year (2014) performed in the role on tour again.

Dawid Minnaar, as Pa Ubu, holds the arc of the work's meaning. He performs in this play only as a live actor, never as a puppeteer – although he has worked with Handspring before, and has manipulated puppets in *Faustus in Africa*. At some level we are aware, through Minnaar's performance, of Pa Ubu taking his own body as puppet as he prepares himself and rehearses the testimony he will perform before the commission. He has to perform the scene with as much credible seriousness as he can muster. Our question is how to undercut that scene while playing it for its life and death seriousness. In the end we resolve on using Jarry's own instrument – the absurd. While Pa Ubu is testifying, his microphones become animated and turn on him. In rewriting this now, I recollect similar animated microphones from an early Kentridge film – is it *Monument*? – and I recall what I have noted to myself before, that *Monument* (a tribute to Beckett's *Catastrophe*, as Kentridge has noted) is also a treatment of Charlie Chaplin's opening scenes from *City Lights*, in which a microphone produces garbled noises instead of speech. So the final speech, with Pa Ubu at the lectern, is a piece of wild puppetry pyrotechnics. The speech is constructed from fragments that I have inter-spliced from pieces of testimony from amnesty applicants (I am less punctilious with them than with the statements testifying as victims of abuse).

Louis Seboko no longer performs in the piece,[4] but his contribution to the play is also immense, because he brought to his interpretation of the witnesses a kind of radiant integrity, an almost heraldic sense of service to the testimony and to the puppet figures. I remember with great admiration watching the expressive integrity of Louis telling some grim story of a violation. The audience watch for a moment alternately the impassive carved wooden face of the puppet, but now, imperceptibly, the individual viewer in the audience, in their own time, turns to gaze at the radiant face of the puppeteer, just barely visible, that is carrying the truth of the puppet. This is the alchemy, the transcendent projective mesmerism of puppetry through which we grasp the great fable of the human. We are, none of us, individuals; we all partake of a dispersed body; mutuality and reciprocity are foundation to us. As Winnicott so brilliantly asserted, 'There is no such thing as an infant', meaning, of course, that whenever one finds an infant one finds maternal care, and without maternal care there would be no infant.[5] In such terms, then, we might say that the art of puppetry is the fundamental human art: it is the art of holding, of imaginative identification, and in this it is the art that is fundamental to our species' reproduction of itself. In other words, the human being is necessarily a collaboration. All of these allegories are somehow at play when we watch the best of puppetry in performance.

The set design arises from a combination of the double field of the TRC spaces and Ubu's home. Hannah Arendt's observation about the banality of evil (from her keen-eyed account of *Eichmann in Jerusalem*) informs my sense that the world of Pa Ubu's home and the world of the Truth Commission need to intersect. Testimony should pour out of the household tap is how I originally think of it. I am keen to have testimony infiltrate the household of Ubu. This is a plot device, but also a way of thinking about scale – my sense is of the grotesque asymmetries between the obtuse blindness of Pa Ubu, who (true to Jarry's original) rapes, plunders and murders with impunity, and his victims as individuals who have had their lives and households destroyed by Pa's every careless gesture. The play opens with Pa stumbling home, drunkenly kicking over a puppet figure making soup in her home. Her household is demolished while he cannot grasp what has stubbed his toe. It is a farcical reconsideration of the use of scale of Goya's *Colossus*.

At the time of writing the play, I was also curating the exhibition *Fault Lines*. While working with artists who had their own kinds of meaning, I gained access to a range of keen aesthetic intelligences. One of these was Lien Botha, a photographer whose father, Pik Botha, as Minister of Foreign Affairs for the South African state, had authorized raids on bordering countries, engaging in a reckless undertaking of murderous attacks in the attempt to bring a halt to the cross-border raids and insurgency activities being undertaken by the ANC and other anti-apartheid groups in exile. At home, Pik Botha was a notoriously buffoonish figure – rather drunken and dishevelled – yet there he was, wreaking havoc and destruction in the lives of ordinary villagers in Botswana, Lesotho, Mozambique, Angola, countries where communities had been devastated by the laying of land mines and where land and air raids were commonplace.

I had arranged that each of the artists in the exhibition would have a period of residency in the Mayibuye Archive (at the University of the Western Cape, where I was teaching at the time). The archive holds thousands of images and documents from the anti-apartheid struggle. Lien worked in a lonely pursuit in the archive, tracking her father's steps. She ultimately made a remarkable photographic installation of images of villagers whose lives, whose bodies, had been blown apart in raids authorized by her father as minister. She made a washing-line strung with rags, onto which she printed these images. Her mother died during the final days of making the installation; and funerary photographs of her mother were printed on the torn bedsheets, and hung alongside the more public archive of catastrophe. Here was the domestic tragedy inserting itself into the national narrative. All human losses are simultaneously both private and public events.

At the same time there was a significant shift in the visual languages being used by William. Historically he had drawn extensively in charcoal, where the soft line could be rubbed, erased, transformed, blended. While working on drawings for *Ubu*, he shifted from charcoal to white chalk, a much less nuanced medium. Chalk does not blend; it is not a kind medium readily available for blending and tones of grey. Working on black construction paper, the new imagistic language that got added to his repertoire was sharp-edged, unambiguous, Manichean. They returned, in tone though not in style, to Kentridge's early drawings of Soho Eckstein as the brute capitalist.

One final note on how the production foregrounds meanings around the collaborative. My research on the commission has made me particularly attentive to the experience of the interpreters at the hearings. They enable the speech acts that will be at the heart of the new South African state. (South Africa, with transition, identifies 11 official languages, and the TRC is tasked with making all testimony available in all languages. Language has always been contentious in the country: under the Nationalist regime only the two languages associated with colonization, English and Afrikaans, had been official.) In effect the decision for multilingual hearings means that all aural events are piped through headsets, so that the public will be able to identify which language they want to hear in translation. A substantial team of interpreters travels with the commission to every village where hearings are to be held. In all radio transmissions and discussions the textures of multilingualism are apparent. This sound environment provides a visual field in the play, a performance space and an aural texture on stage.

A puppet figure steps into a neutral space that is Pa Ubu's home. Speaking as if at the commission, the figure tells of a personal violation, or the attack on a community, or the loss of a child. A member of the cast steps into Pa Ubu's shower, and the shower head becomes a microphone. Sitting in the audience we hear the voices from various contexts. The puppet, of course, does not speak for itself, so the primary texture of the speech act is already displaced, arising from the puppeteer who stands just behind and to the side of the puppet; half a beat later, the interpreter speaks in another language, holding the utterances in the air, slightly tentative, listening in the act of speaking. In the staging of these scenes my interest is in the aural and linguistic textures of the event, so I spend days listening over and over again to the textures of witness testimony, the sound of evacuated hope in a witness, the tone of 'listening while speaking' in the interpreter. One noteworthy texture of the sound is that the interpreter, not knowing if a witness's sentence or idea is complete as they speak it, is caught suspended, waiting, as it were, for the shoe to drop. As a result, the interpreter's utterances are marked by upward inflections, with every statement suspended, wavering in incompleteness.

William devises a strategy which will use illusion to make that shower-microphone work *as shower*, with projected drawings of jets of water streaming from the shower head. (After a night of killing, Pa Ubu will use the shower to wash the rank smells of his activities from his skin.) Meanwhile the Handspring performers labour with artful care at capturing the affective transfer from manipulator to puppet to manipulator; muscle memory learns how to angle the puppet's head to catch a particular line of the chiselled face that signifies defeat, or another mark that suggests a raised eyebrow. Did I see hope? Was it bitterness that passed across the face like a shadow?

There were other collaborators that brought the show together: the choreography of Robyn Orlin helped to locate Ma Ubu as both voluptuary and as narcissistic child; the music environment created by Warwick Sony and Brendan Jury gives a psychotic depth to the work that also defines the piece in its period. Punctuated sound elements are mastered by Wilbert Schübel. Here, too, Kentridge is learning about his art and his craft. Over the past decades he has become ever-more alert to the sensory information of sound, that a scene is read not so much for its visual information as by what we as audience are informed of through aural cues. Here David Lynch has been something of a trail-blazer, working as he does at the manipulation of proximity and scale through the engineering of sound levels.

Zeno at 4 am

Zeno at 4 am was an experiment that derived largely from a chain of formal and technical possibilities that had thrown themselves up for William. This, to be brief, was again a question of animation as both practice and theory. I will return to the formal questions shortly, but let me begin with a consideration of the inter-text, that Svevo novel.

Kentridge had read the Svevo as a youth and was captivated by its understated confessional mode. He was 'intrigued then about how a novel from the Italy of the 1920s could resonate with his feelings about personal ethics in South Africa.'[6] I myself was at the time working on a research project on the history of sincerity, and the confessional autobiographical text interested me. I was reading everything from Augustine to Rousseau. Benjamin Franklin's *Autobiography* captured my imagination because of the practices of moral accountancy described in the text:

> I transferr'd my Tables and Precepts to the Ivory leaves of a Memorandum Book, on which the lines were drawn with red ink that made a durable Stain, and on those Lines I marked my Faults with a black Lead Pencil, which Marks I could easily wipe out with a wet sponge. (98)

I was fascinated by the double-entry accounting self used to assay the soul here, with its proclivity to mark down commissions of error, but which also had the gift of forgiveness, more remarkably the capacity to forgive the self.

The Zeno character at the centre of the piece is performed by Dawid Minnaar, who had performed Pa Ubu. It is key, when thinking of collaborative theatre, to imagine the significance of performers in that collaboration. If there is a writer, she can imagine the expressive capacities, the embodied gestural nuance of the performer, inside the writing. Pa Ubu's crimes were multiple and grandiloquent: multiple murders and acts of mayhem; while the follies of Zeno are small, bourgeois, insignificant: he has a series of romantic liaisons; he is distressed that his alienated relation to his aging father is not resolved before his father dies; and he cannot give up smoking. It is thrilling to watch Minnaar, as performer, come to terms with two such different embodiments of the contrite male seeking absolution. The small work, an oratorio, unfolds as the 'Dreamwork' of Zeno, who lies on his bed, fixated by his longing for a cigarette. The figure of his father arrives as a visitation. Played by the bass Otto Maidi, Zeno's father is a massive African patriarchal presence whose physical being and rich voice make Zeno's febrile neurotic self all the more feeble. We observe in the father a kind of cerebral event, as the old man attempts to sing a series of interrogations to his son, but he keeps on having lapses of memory, little breakdowns between word and sound. The visit from the father is obviously an oft-repeated dream in which he attempts to console his son, but catastrophically he dies in the middle of that reconciliation. Much of what the father intends to say, he does not; the words are at times stalled, unarticulated, and are projected as thought on the screen upstage. A year before, Kentridge and I had experimented with the composer Philip Miller for a small workshop event in which we projected text above characters on stage. It had quickly become apparent that the audience would readily interpret the text as originating inside the mind of the character onstage. There was a desolate poignancy in seeing the ideas pre-formed inside the father, only to be strangled before they could be articulated to the needy son.

It was initially intended that the dream sequences with the shadow puppet figures would be performed by the Handspring Puppet Company and that this would be filmed and then projected as a video feed above the head of the sleeping Zeno. However, in the first workshop we staged the scene with the puppets live, in order to work out timings. The puppeteers marshalled themselves as a small militia at the side of the stage. Like a series of manoeuvres by toy soldiers, the puppet figures were marched back and forth, a live video feed populating the screen with projected images of bizarre nightmarish figures, or characters from a Max Ernst dream. The bizarre *danse macabre* of the puppeteers is mesmerizing, and I turn to William. 'We have to have the puppeteers on the stage.' In the same instant we both recognize the power of that event onstage; and so ultimately the work would stage the quartet and the puppets as a kind of cerebral activity inside of which is Dawid Minnaar lying on his bed, fantasizing about cigarettes, sisters and his dead father.

It is absolutely significant that when making this piece it was imagined as a short stand-alone experiment. It did not have to sustain the full weight of a bourgeois novel. Several disjointed elements are brought together: a bass singer (Otto Maidi) to play the father; a quartet who will perform on stage, giving the texture of a concert performance; Dawid Minnaar as confessional figure; and a filmed projection of the dream figures that populate Zeno's dreams. At least, that was what was initially intended. William and Adrian went into a feverish process of making black paper puppets. These are figures that when filmed look as if they are shadows and can cast shadows that look as if they are shadows. Herein lies a trick. The puppets are trans-formers, paper puppet figures which, when revolved 90 degrees, will change their form from, say, a man on crutches into a tree; or a hat stand into a damsel.

2½ or 3: Confessions of Zeno

This is the fully-fledged three-act opera that evolves out of *Zeno at 4 am*. The centre of gravity of the work shifts away from the figure of the patriarch and the obsession with smoking, to the more knowable narrative dimension of the novel: the husband, his wife and his mistress. Much of the invention of the piece arises from a certain internal resistance to that impulse toward the familiar operatic plotline. William draws a bourgeois *fin de siècle* household, the context for the sisters who are at the centre of the youthful Zeno's amorous interests in the novel. Our interest is in imagining the sisters as integral to that home, as fundamental to it; yet somehow we want them to be something more than that familiar idea. The great solution arises from the 'transformer puppets' devised for the dream sequences in *Zeno at 4 am*, because it becomes evident that the four sisters could be themselves as well as something else besides – they are to be dining room chairs. All of a similar period, each one is slightly distinctive, an ensemble of household furniture.

Summary

My interest in this brief sketch has been to give some detail of the forms and meanings that result from the distinctive exchanges which are marked by a high degree of playful interrogation as well as mutual fascination. Yes, fascination. We are all fascinated by the processes of one other.

Notes

1. *Undine* (1814). Composer E. T. A. Hoffmann; libretto Friedrich de la Motte Fouqué.

2. Oliver Strunk, *Source Readings in Music History: The Romantic Era* (New York: Norton, 1950), 63.

3. I will give much of my thought in this chapter to considering *Ubu and the Truth Commission*, because it provides an instrument for thinking about the commission; in these terms the question of collaboration here is internal to a set of political imperatives that dominated the creative act in 1996–7.

4. His place has been taken by the fine actor, Mongi Mnthombeni, who is also an exceptionally gifted puppeteer.

5. D. W. Winnicott, 'The Theory of the Parent–Child Relationship', *International Journal of Psycho-Analysis* 41 (1960): 587, n. 4.

6. Jane Taylor, 'Taking Stock: The Making of a Bourgeois Life: The Confessions of Zeno', *South African Theatre Journal* 17 (2003): 234.

Bibliography

Boyden, M. and N. Kimbereley, *The Rough Guide to the Opera* (London: Penguin, 2002).

Franklin, Benjamin, *The Autobiography and Other Writings* (Harmondsworth: Penguin, 1986).

Strunk, Oliver, *Source Readings in Music History: The Romantic Era* (New York: Norton, 1950).

Taylor, Jane. 'Taking Stock: The Making of a Bourgeois Life: The Confessions of Zeno', *South African Theatre Journal* 17 (2003): 234–44.

Winnicott, D. W. 'The Theory of the Parent–Child Relationship', *International Journal of Psycho-Analysis* 41 (1960): 586–95.

CHAPTER 3
CONTEMPORARY COLLABORATORS II: MAGNET THEATRE
Yvette Hutchison

Introduction

In 2012, South Africa's Magnet Theatre Company celebrated its 25th year of creating an original repertoire of performance events that emphasize the primacy of the body. A distinctive aspect of this company has been the ways in which it has collaborated: physically, with various companies and communities; stylistically, as it has explored diverse approaches to physical theatre; and paradigmatically, as it has brought together African and European engagements with history, memory, theatre and the body. However, most of their work has not been published, as co-founder Mark Fleishman (Fleishman and Davids 2007) has wanted to strongly challenge western traditions of prioritizing text over embodied images and privilege somatic engagement with theatre. I will thus explore how he has developed these ideas in and through productions and in particular collaborations with various artists and communities.

Magnet Theatre began in 1987 when Mark Fleishman, a University of Cape Town (UCT)-trained actor, and physical performer Jenny Reznek, who studied for two years at École Jacques Lecoq in Paris from 1984 to 1986, produced Reznek's first one-person performance, *Cheap Flights*. This play explores one woman's fear of the escalating violence which she can only escape in flights of fantasy. From the outset this signalled Fleishman's and Reznek's commitment to engage with pertinent socio-political issues through personal experience and embodied modes of expression.

Magnet Theatre's development has been informed by Reznek's Lecoq training and Fleishman's work with various people in his role as the Market Theatre Laboratory's first administrator,[1] not the least of whom was Barney Simon. In 1991 they produced *The Show's Not Over 'Til the Fat Lady Sings* in Cape Town; and for the next two and a half years the company toured in South Africa, the UK, Hong Kong and Stockholm. They returned to South Africa in 1994 with the intention to collaborate 'with other practitioners on larger scale productions which would encompass a broader socio-political vision', alongside their ongoing commitment to developing Reznek's physical performance style, in part as a strategy to overcome vast language diversities (http://www.magnettheatre.co.za).

Since then they have adapted and staged Herman Melville's epic novel *Moby Dick* (1994); created two new Reznek-inspired performance pieces – *I Do X 22* (1997) and *53 Degrees* (2002); adapted the stories of the acclaimed Mozambican author Mia Couto for the stage in *Voices Made Night* (2000–1 and 2007); created three outdoor theatre productions – *Pump* (1998–9), *Onnest'bo* (*Upside-Down* 2002–6) and *Die Vreemdeling* (*The Stranger* 2010); as well as the large-scale outdoor performance event *Vlam 1* (*Flame* 1999), which celebrated the dawn of the new millennium in collaboration with Jazzart and Southern Edge Arts of Western Australia.

Many of these productions have involved collaborations with various writers and artists, colleagues and students from UCT's Drama Department, where Reznek and Fleishman are members of staff. They have also collaborated with NGOs, like the District Six Museum, with whom they created the outdoor event *Vlam 1* and the physical theatre piece *Onnest'bo*, as embodied ways of negotiating memories of forced removals in the District Six area of Cape Town in the context of post-apartheid South Africa. Their international collaborations include working with Theatre Spirale (Geneva) on a South African version of the Swiss play *The Fire Raisers* by Max Frisch (2004), where seven South African actors worked alongside actors from Mali, Indonesia and Switzerland.

Jazzart Dance Theatre Company has influenced the ways in which Magnet Theatre has developed its physical performance style. Jazzart is the oldest contemporary dance company in South Africa, if not Africa. It has led many innovations in contemporary dance in South Africa, while providing a model for arts engagement in democratic practices and work with marginalized communities since 1973 when Sonje Mayo opened her jazz studio to all, right across South Africa's racial spectrum. In 1978, Sue Parker established the Sue Parker Jazzart Contemporary Dance Company alongside the jazz school. However, the company only performed sporadically due to irregular funding. In 1986, Alfred Hinkel bought the company, changed its name to Jazzart Dance Theatre and took over its artistic directorship. Dawn Langdown, John Linden and Jay Pather provided the dancing, teaching and choreographic backbone. Under Hinkel's direction, a philosophy of professional dance training and performance emerged that recognized the socio-political and economic contexts of Jazzart's students and audiences.

They continued the tradition of non-discrimination in terms of race and gender, and the company both recognized and encouraged the incorporation of the various repertoires and dynamics of diverse South African dance styles which the students brought with them into their creative work. It also consciously engaged with the socio-political struggles of the time.[2] The company has not limited itself to training professional dancers and staging professional performances, but it is also involved in a number of community cultural initiatives including dance groups in Durban and the Free State; and it has an ongoing involvement in community-based programmes in Clanwilliam, Prince Albert and George (largely through focus schools).

Through its collaborations with Jazzart between 1994 and 2007, Magnet has come to occupy an important place in South African contemporary dance history. As a director, Mark Fleishman has co-created ritualistic dance theatre, which has not only grappled with the complexities of South African racial identity and intra-culturalism, but has also created a frame for Jazzart's eclecticism and dance innovations. During this period the Magnet Theatre and Jazzart Dance companies collaborated to create seven new works: *Medea* (1994), *The Sun, the Moon and the Knife* (1995), *Soe Loep Ons ... Nou Nog!* (So we walk ... still!, 1996), *Vlam 1* (*Flame* 1999), *Cold Waters/Thirsty Souls* (2002), *Rain in a Dead Man's Footprints* (2004–5) and *Cargo* (2007).

Medea was a provocative yet pertinent choice of text to frame an analysis of South African society as it approached its first democratic elections insofar as the play explores the birth of a new dispensation from the ashes of an old system marked by conflict and betrayal. This production dealt both with the history of colonization and the complex moral decisions of the liberation struggle, where certain forms of resistance chosen by activists could be compared to Medea killing her children, an act which can be interpreted as revenge and/or as a means of protecting herself and her children.[3]

The multiracial cast and multilingual script, including English, Afrikaans, isiXhosa, isiZulu, tsotsitaal (gangster slang) and Tamil, demonstrated Magnet's commitment to engaging the range of South African experience and cultures. Fleischman and Reznek worked with performers' own stories and incorporated these into South African oral and dance traditions so that this classic play became a fictional frame to explore diverse and contested contemporary South African experiences and memories.[4] Magnet's inclusion of multiple languages, voices and performance styles highlighted the complexities of constituting the 'rainbow nation', as well as the advantages of working with embodied performance through physical theatre, particularly with the skills of the Jazzart performers.

Fleischman's focus on 'core images' meant that this production of *Medea* no longer followed a strongly text-based Aristotelian linear structure.[5] This shift required audiences to draw on different competences to make sense of the play both visually and linguistically, which in turn highlighted the complexities of negotiating narrative and history given South Africans' multiple perspectives on the past. The use of the classic Greek tragedy provided distance from the immediate context, and a reference point for analysing causes of extreme acts of violence.[6] This was particularly important given that in the same year the Truth and Reconciliation Commission (TRC) began its hearings in South Africa. It was also the start of Magnet's engagement with what Fleishman terms 'remembering in the postcolony', which would become Magnet's overt research and creative focus from 2002.[7]

The Sun, the Moon and the Knife was Magnet's first engagement with San narratives, and drew on Stephen Watson's adaptations of the recently rediscovered primary research on San/Bushman[8] language, culture and folklore that German linguist Wilhelm Bleek and his sister-in-law Lucy Lloyd recorded from fewer than twenty /Xam and /Kung adults and children who lived with them at Mowbray in Cape Town for varying periods between 1870 and 1884.[9] Hewitt explains that much material partially published by Lucy Lloyd and Dorothea Bleek 'more or less disappeared from view'[10] between 1936 and 1973, and that scholarly interest in the collection was rekindled from the 1980s onwards through the work of Janette Deacon. Pippa Skotnes published *Claim to the Country* in 2007, and was to influence Fleishman as he re-engaged with the /Xam stories in his collaboration with Jazzart in creating *Rain in a Dead Man's Footprints*. In the article 'Stories like the wind: recontextualising /Xam narratives for contemporary audiences' (2005), Fleishman traces his work with Skotnes and the processes involved in his negotiating and translating a transcribed oral narrative of a culture that has all but disappeared under the brutalities of colonialism and apartheid for performance, particularly as regards accurately representing particular /Xam approaches to time, space, landscape, narrative and cosmology. This physical theatre production, with all the conceptual and physical collaborations involved, reflects on issues related to archaeology, translation and the relationship between oral and literary texts and embodied dramaturgy, and it traces some of the problems involved in intra- and intercultural theatre processes.

Similarly, *Soe Loep Ons ... Nou Nog!*, *Onnest'bo* and *Cargo* have engaged critically in embodied ways with complex, contested and often disavowed memories of coloured people living in the Western Cape, particularly with reference to the histories of slavery and forced removals.[11] Fleishman's critical reflections[12] on these issues in and through collaborative processes trace various aspects of his developing dramaturgy, while inflecting back into research debates on the relationship between archives and performance, and analysing processes of researching in and through performance.

Collaborations with/in community projects

Alongside collaborations with companies to produce theatrical works, Magnet Theatre has worked closely with UCT Drama School and local community groups, running skills workshops and outreach projects alongside their productions from the outset. In 1998 it formalized this aspect of its work by establishing the Magnet Theatre Educational Trust. Through this Trust it has established the Community Groups Intervention, which has mentored eight youth drama groups from Khayelitsha (2002–7). It has established a full-time training programme with young actors from townships in and around Cape Town (2008–10), and worked with students in Western Cape Schools using history, arts and culture and life skills curricula to explore creativity, imagination and theatrical skills, while promoting tolerance and understanding through embodied engagement with ideas and other peoples.

One of Magnet's most significant community involvements has been in the Clanwilliam Arts Project. In 2001, Pippa Skotnes of UCT's School of Fine Art and John Parkington of the Department of Archaeology approached Mark Fleishman as the Artistic Director of Magnet with the request that Magnet Theatre add a performance element to the Clanwilliam Arts Project (CAP), which involved a rural community in the Western Cape about 200 km (120 miles) north of Cape Town. Since 2001, a group of thirty-five researchers and practitioners have worked with local communities in the rediscovery and preservation of cultural material related to the San peoples who lived in the area for thousands of years. It also aims to convey a sense of the relevance of this research and cultural material to the local inhabitants of the area. As Duncan Brown has argued, for many First World nations any claim to belonging in a land is profoundly linked with narrative and storytelling, encapsulated in the question, 'If this is your land, where are your stories?'[13] In the post-apartheid context, many people, including South African poet Antjie Krog, have suggested that while '[w]e have had many years of telling stories', only 'some were heard; others went underground; some were written; some were oral; some were trapped in neglected mother tongues'.[14]

To compound this skewed engagement with diverse Southern African cultures and histories, one of the most dogged issues facing post-apartheid South Africa is that of racial classifications, a complex subject – and the process of dismantling them fraught with conflict. Identity is in flux, and terms of belonging are contested. The Black Consciousness Struggle narrative tends to dominate the political scene, and so many people like those living in the Clanwilliam area who come from mixed racial heritage, including Khoe, San, African and European backgrounds, may well ask: What are our stories? Who are we?

This project is one attempt to address these questions and to reclaim the heritage of the /Xam with the local people by reconnecting story and landscape. Thus the ongoing Living Landscape Project in Clanwilliam has incorporated archaeological materials and exercises into local school curricula, and trains local people as guides, craftspeople and heritage managers.[15] Each year, CAP runs an eight-day-long workshop with 500–700 students, aged between 5 and 18, from diverse communities in Clanwilliam and Okiep, Namaqualand. The project culminates in storytelling events and the annual spring lantern parade which involves the whole community. This is important because, as Fleishman notes:

> It is a small town of a few thousand inhabitants and like all rural South African towns it is split down the middle; on one side an affluent area mostly occupied by the minority white population known as the town and on the other side, a sprawling, run-down area of newish matchbox houses, crumbling cottages and shacks occupied by the majority black population, known as the township.[16]

This event is focused on a different narrative chosen each year from one of the 2,000 notebooks containing 13,000 pages of oral stories told to Bleeck and Lloyd by San informants like //Kabbo, /Han#kass'o and !Kweiten ta // ken who temporarily lived with them in Cape Town. Magnet Theatre in collaboration with Jazzart, Namjive, the Michaelis School of Art, UCT archaeologists and local practitioners combine archaeology, visual art, drama, music and dance to create compelling interpretations of the stories of the San people in the present for the area's contemporary inhabitants. Fleishman argues that this engagement with 'heritage' is not a 'fetishization of "authentic ... physical relics and remains"', but rather,

1. It is something we *do* in the present with the past for our present purposes. It is an active, participatory and performative process or perhaps a set of such processes and involves an embodied engagement with what remains from the past in order to make meaning in the present (Harvey 2001; Smith 2006). It is, therefore, never inert, always contestable, open to engagement and constant re-working.

2. It is, in Alain Badiou's terms, something that has the capacity to change the situation; to bring something new into being, a new way of seeing the world (Badiou 2001: 41). In this sense heritage as an event is aligned to the development of subaltern communities particularly in the context of the postcolony.[17]

The processes involved in the ongoing Clanwilliam project evidence ways in which Magnet Theatre are reimagining approaches to African embodied performances that represent various linguistic and cultural groups and histories in South Africa. At the same time, Fleishman's critical reflections on Magnet's processes and his own developing dramaturgy also suggest how his role as Artistic Director is informed by a broad range of Western and African academic theoretical and critical thinking, including the ideas of Pierre Nora, James Young and Achille Mbembe. It also demonstrates how Magnet's experimentation with 'sensitive sites', archives and contested memories in and through experimental forms of improvisational physical theatre feeds back into these debates.

Magnet's arts interventions have had profound effects in communities because they have been sustained over long periods of time; they have also helped to establish local arts groups like the community-based ensemble Community Networking Creative Arts Group (ComNet), primarily made up of teenagers, that has emerged out of the CAP project. Under the direction of community-based theatre practitioner Lavona de Bruyn, the ensemble has been devising original performances since 2007. One of ComNet's aims is to nurture cross-cultural relationships in Clanwilliam. Magnet has also developed relationships with other organizations like BOSASA (2007–10), which is engaged in rehabilitating young offenders in the area.

A more recent development has been Magnet's shift in focus to its Migration Project, involving UCT and communities just outside of Cape Town. Fleishman details 'three separate interventions that used performance to explore the theme of migration and the experience of being between and on the move that characterises life for many people in Cape Town today'.[18] These three interventions were shaped via three routes: the mythical Cape to Cairo North–South route that traverses the African continent, and today often signifies the route of immigrants or refugees seeking entry into South Africa; the N2 highway that links the Western Cape with the Eastern Cape, which is the traditional home of the amaXhosa; and the N7 highway that links Cape Town with the Northern Cape and Namibian border via the west coast of South Africa. Each of these routes is used to highlight issues related to a specific group's sense of belonging, dislocation and/or xenophobia.

I turn to briefly analyse some of the collaborations and outcomes of this project, beginning with Mandla Mbothwe's collaborations. In his roles as lecturer at UCT's Drama School and Magnet Theatre company member, Mbothwe worked with various communities in Khayelitsha, a partially informal township on the Cape Flats, just outside Cape Town. This collaboration resulted in the intervention *Isivuno Sama Phupha* (Harvest of Dreams, unpublished), which was performed at UCT's Arena Theatre and at the Spier Infecting the City Summer Arts Festival in 2007. This production explored what Mbothwe terms 'the aftermath of decolonisation and a search for an aesthetic that speaks directly to the traditional/postmodern tension experienced by township youth'.[19] It is important to understand that many South African townships are areas with high levels of poverty and unemployment, with associated levels of violence.[20] People living in these townships often feel dislocated, without a clear sense of belonging in terms of their own cultural referents, largely due to the forced removals and migrant labour policies of apartheid.[21]

Mbothwe's 'intention for *Isivuno Sama Phupha* was to develop an African Dream Play for the twenty-first century, one that in substance, aesthetic and in modes of presentation and reception would function as a means of social "redress"'.[22] Inspired by Brett Bailey's uses of ritual, Mbothwe explored how Victor Turner's ideas on social drama could be mobilized to address crisis and reintegrate communities that had become fragmented for multiple reasons. Mbothwe hoped that

through a return to ritual and an incorporation of practices already prevalent in our communities, and through an experience of 'liminality' and 'communitas' in which indeterminacy and determination, anti-structure and structure work in a dialectical relationship with each other, theatre might indeed generate the change of consciousness required in the face of crisis.[23]

By means of poetic language and body images, voice orchestration and symbols, this production wove between places and spaces, between waking-time and dream-time, as it invited its audiences to journey with the performers through their dreams. Through dancing, clapping, singing, poetry and drumming, it drew audiences in and thereby created a sense of possibility, insofar as it helped participants and audience members to recognize their hopes and fears, and so generate a new sense of possibility and optimism for wider inclusion of peoples in South Africa in the post-apartheid context.

Mbothwe extended his experimentation with ritual and the evocation of 'communitas' in his next isiXhosa production, *Ingcwaba Lendoda Lise Cankwe Ndlela* (2009),[24] which was also part of the Magnet Theatre Educational Trust training programme. Mbothwe began a five-day workshop with a group of 11 participants from Khayelitsha community groups, which he later integrated with the group of four second-year UCT drama students with whom he had worked during formal UCT classes. The play explores how on the long road of life we are all searching for somewhere to belong. This play interrogates both the concept and location of 'home' and belonging in the context of African cultures and increasing migration. Drawing inspiration from African traditions related to the umbilical cord, the grave, clans and ancestors and urban rituals, *Ingcwaba Lendoda* explores the physical, emotional, spiritual and intellectual dislocation of young black South Africans whose origins, they are told, lie along the N2 in the Eastern Cape. Like all Magnet Theatre productions, this play uses sound, image and dance to communicate 'the fragmentation and dispersion of families forced to separate in search of work, daughters, seeking lost fathers, wives left husbandless, desperate, workers lured into crime'.[25] It also suggests that without a sense of 'home', one is not rooted or protected, but rather one is blown about, like the wind. This play demonstrates how the legacies of apartheid continue, while analysing the cultural cost of displacement. It was performed in 2009 at the Spier Infecting the City Festival, which was themed 'Home Affair'; for the National Arts Festival Fringe, toured in the Eastern Cape; was part of the Arts Alive 969 Festival in Johannesburg; and again performed at the Artscape Arena in 2010.

The plays *Isivuno Sama Phupha* and *Ingcwaba Lendoda* and the 2010 productions *Inxeba Lomphilisi*[26] and *Die Vreemdeling*[27] challenge the perception of English as a marker of sophistication and upward mobility in relation to black urban identity and South African history. During apartheid the way in which language was implicated hegemonically was clear, particularly insofar as it was aligned with policies of separate cultural and racial development.[28] However, in the post-apartheid context these issues have become more complex. Many South Africans are torn between an internal need to reclaim what has been lost culturally, while continuing to perceive English as the language of progress that will open doors to opportunity both in South Africa and abroad. The decision to produce a number of plays for mainstream venues in isiXhosa in Cape Town and at international festivals questions these perceptions. The isiXhosa text challenged non-speakers, who had to read bodies instead of focusing on narrative; and it challenged mother-tongue speakers, who were asked to engage with different registers of their own language, particularly in and through oral poetic modes. This particularly called for urban youth to critically reconsider their linguistic evaluation of their mother tongue. Citing Afrikaans in the context of estrangement and xenophobia also questions the perception of Afrikaans as the language of those at the centre, and it asks all to imagine what would happen if we open our hearts beyond the fences we build to define insider/outsiderness.

The first play in the Migration collection, *Every Year, Every Day, I am Walking*,[29] brings together issues of belonging in both local and global contexts as it explores issues and experiences of immigration, refugees and xenophobia in the contexts of Cape Town and beyond. It also exemplifies the reach of Magnet Theatre's work. This play was initially created for the African Festival of Youth and Children's Theatre in Yaounde, Cameroon, in 2006. However, its significance is evidenced in its further performances in South Africa at the National Festival of the Arts in Grahamstown (2007 and 2009), in Cape Town (2007 and 2010), in Johannesburg (2008), at the Hilton Festival (2008), at KKNK (2009), in Aardklop (2009) and in nine SADC countries (2008–9); as well as at the London International Festival of Theatre (2006–7), Proyecto Festival, Argentina (2009), Juice Festival, Newcastle-Gateshead (2009), the International Theatre Festival of Kerala, India (2009), Oval House, London (2010), the IDEA Congress, Brazil (2010), Stuttgart, Germany (2012), Brasilia, Brazil (2012), Okinawa, Japan (2012) and the University of Massachusetts, Amherst, USA (2013).

This play traces the story of a young girl and her mother from an unspecified Francophone African country, who lose their family and home brutally and irrevocably and are forced to journey to a new place through many dangers and uncertainties. This play again exemplifies the power of using music, movement and core images to tell a story. It opens with young Aggie (played by Faniswa Yisa) walking and running around the perimeter of a circular floor cloth, changing direction and losing her way, which signals the titular experience of walking 'every day, every year' without a sense of belonging or destination. The play goes on to suggest many reasons for this displacement: violence and civil conflict are the main reasons for Aggie and her mother's displacement, but it also explores economic and social responses to displaced people.[30]

One of the most profound aspects of the play is its use of images, particularly through the performers' use of their shoes as hand-held puppets to reflect the characters' physical and emotional experiences. For example, when journeying, Aggie's and Mama's shoes are made to walk endlessly, crunching across the sand they have spread on the table (33) to somatically communicate something of the experience of displacement. Later, when riding in a train, the shoes are made to walk down their bodies and are scooped up and beat like a heart against their breasts (36) to suggest their fear. Mama's abuse in the refugee camp is suggested by her miming a pair of heavy men's shoes walking over her prostrate body, while she tries to shift herself from under their weight; she is 'crying and her shoes are shaking with sobs' (35). The shoes also invoke joyous memories: for example, Aggie's happy memories of her sister are often linked to a magical blue (origami) bird that emerges from her pink shoe, which her sister would fly in the sky (18, 19), but which disappears when she loses her home and sister (37). The shoes communicate experiences and emotions that are often unspeakable, because they are emotive and often associated with trauma, while avoiding the pitfalls of trauma narration.[31]

Another powerful image in the play occurs after Mama has once again been finger-printed and questioned in English, Afrikaans and Xhosa. Using two plastic bags to create the rhythm of the ocean, 'tossing and lifting them like flotsam and jetsam' (41),

Mama climbs slowly and ceremoniously into the black bag and sweeps the second bag over her head as if she is making a blessing. She covers her head with the second bag so that she has completely disappeared. She sweeps up her shoes into the bag and collapses on to the floor. She rolls slowly on the floor as if she is a bag of human rubbish being blown around by the wind. She climbs out holding her shoes to her chest and looks at the audience. (42)

This image invites an audience member to empathize somatically and thus avoid judging the authenticity of the narrative, or assume a moral or political position relative to migrancy or refugees. This, I would argue, is an example of Fleishman's 'dramaturgy of displacement' (2011), where the company communicate a strong emotion related to a specific experience without speaking for the subject. The style of physical theatre, with its combination of narrative alongside vivid and poignant images, movement and music, invites audience members to engage imaginatively with what they see in the space, while acknowledging the fact that these are affective indicative gestures that work on an embodied somatic level to hint at experiences ubiquitous to migrancy and being a refugee.[32] The audience is then left with the choice as to what to make or do with the residue of this affective experience.

Currently Magnet is collaborating with Cape Town Opera to develop a new musico-dramatic work; and they are working with ASSITEJ SA (International Association of Theatre for Children and Young People) to develop performance pieces for some of the hundreds of crèches and nursery schools in Cape Town and the surrounding townships.

It is clear that collaboration feeds most aspects of Magnet Theatre's work: it reflects their commitment to engage with current socio-political and linguistic issues that affect the widest range of people in southern Africa and beyond. Its membership means that while Fleishman is engaged with conceptual issues like what it means to 'remember in postcolony', or how to develop a 'dramaturgy of displacement', whereby he does not speak for others, Reznek is pushing the limits of physical theatre. Other company members like Faniswa Yisa and Mandla Mbothwe are developing new performance repertoires alongside musicians like Neo Muyanga and sound designer Tony Madikane, who create soundscapes that evolve with the physical theatre repertoires. This developing repertoire that is focused on images and embodied performance challenges audiences in a number of ways. It deconstructs assumptions about what is understood as the relationship and distinction between professional and community theatre, particularly as regards aesthetics. It challenges the relationship between physical and linguistic texts, by foregrounding embodied and non-verbal forms of knowing and communicating. These experiments, in turn, demand that audience members use or develop new competences to make meaning from the performances. Magnet's specifically embodied practice serves to disturb fixed narratives of identity, history and memory and thus encourages all in South Africa to negotiate multiple and often disavowed memories or feelings, and so makes room for more collaborative, inclusive ways of being.

Notes

1. See Mark Fleishman's speech at the 10th anniversary of the Market Laboratory in Irene Stephanou and Leila Henriques (eds), *The World is an Orange: Creating Theatre with Barney Simon* (Johannesburg: Jacana Media, 2005), 364–66.

2. For details on the company's history, see http://www.jazzart.co.za/index.php/about-us/history (accessed 15 April 2015).

3. See Alex Halligey, 'Re-Inventing Mythologies: Arguments towards Cultural Identity in *Medea* and *Rain in a Dead Man's Footprints*', *South African Theatre Journal* 19 (2005): 208–22, on how Fleishman uses mythology to explore cultural identity in this play.

4. See Mark Fleischman, 'Workshop Theatre's Oppositional Form', *South African Theatre Journal* 4:1 (1990): 88–118, on his developing conception of workshop theatre.

5. Kali Francis, 'Theatre of Struggle and Transformation: A Critical Investigation into the Power of Oral Traditions as Used by Director Mark Fleischman', *South African Theatre Journal* 20 (2006): 109.

6. See Betine Van Zyl Smit, 'Multicultural Reception: Greek Drama in South Africa in the Late Twentieth and Early Twenty-first Centuries', in L. Hardwick and C. Stray (eds), *A Companion to Classical Receptions* (Oxford: Blackwell Publishing, 2008), 373–85, and 'Orestes and the Truth and Reconciliation Commission', *Classical Receptions Journal* 2:1 (2010): 114–35, on the use of Greek tragedies in the context of conflict in South African theatre. For further analysis of this play, see Francis, 'Theatre of Struggle and Transformation', and Judith Rudakoff, 'Somewhere, Over the Rainbow: White-Female-Canadian Dramaturge in Cape Town', *TDR* 48:1 (Spring 2004): 133–4. On the significance of the TRC and performing memory, see Yvette Hutchison, *South African Performance and Archives of Memory* (Manchester and New York: Manchester University Press, 2013).

7. Mark Fleishman, '*Cargo*: Staging Slavery at the Cape', *Contemporary Theatre Review* 21:1 (2011): 8–19, and 'For a Little Road it is not. For it is a Great Road; it is Long', in Anthony Jackson and Jenny Kidd (eds), *Performing Heritage – Research, Practice and Innovation in Museum Theatre and Live Interpretation* (Manchester and New York: Manchester University Press, 2011), 234–48.

8. I am aware of the extensive debate about, and problems related to, these terms. Both have been used to refer to the hunter-gatherer first peoples of

Southern Africa who speak related languages. The few who remain today live in South Africa, Botswana, Namibia and Angola. The /Xam represent one particular San group living in the most southern area of southern Africa.

9. When Wilhelm Bleek died in 1875, his work on Bushman folklore and language was not complete; it would take Lloyd another 36 years to finish and publish the results of their joint research, *Specimens of Bushman Folklore* (1911) (see Jackie Loos, 'Portraits in Specimens of Bushman Folklore by Bleek and Lloyd', *Quarterly Bulletin of the South African Library* 52:1 (September 1997): 13).

10. Roger Hewitt, *Structure, Meaning and Ritual in the Narratives of the Southern San* (Johannesburg: Wits University Press, 2008), 3.

11. The term 'coloured' refers to South Africans of mixed racial background, usually from South-east Asian, European or African-European backgrounds. There is much debate about this definition of racial identity: Zimitri Erasmus and Edgar Pieterse ('Conceptualising Coloured Identities in the Western Cape Province', in M. Palmberg (ed.), *National Identity and Democracy in Africa* (Pretoria: Human Sciences Research Council, 1999), 167–87) and Erasmus (*Coloured by History, Shaped by Place: New Perspectives on Coloured Identity in Cape Town* (Cape Town: Kwela and South African History Online, 2001)) have traced the evolution of the term and argue that it may signal political conservativism in the apartheid sense of defining racial difference, and also political radicalism when used as a self-descriptor. See Zoë Wicomb ('Shame and Identity: The Case of the Coloured in South Africa', in Derek Attridge and Rosemary Jolly (eds), *Writing South Africa: Literature, Apartheid and Democracy, 1970–1995* (Cambridge: Cambridge University Press, 1998), 91–107) on colonial historical constructions of degeneracy and shame, and Pumla Dineo Gqola (*What is Slavery to Me? Postcolonial/Slave Memory in Post-Apartheid South Africa* (Johannesburg: Wits University Press, 2010)) on slave memory in post-apartheid South Africa.

12. Cf. Mark Fleishman and Nadia Davids, 'Moving Theatre: An Exploration of the Place of Theatre in the Process of Memorialising District Six through an Examination of Magnet Theatre's Production *Onnest'bo*', *South African Theatre Journal* 21:1 (2007): 149–65, and Fleishman, '*Cargo*: Staging Slavery at the Cape'.

13. Duncan Brown, *To Speak of This Land: Identity and Belonging in South Africa and Beyond* (Scottsville: University of KwaZulu-Natal Press. 2006), 1.

14. Ibid., xix.

15. See http://www.cllp.uct.ac.za (accessed 15 April 2015).

16. Fleishman, 'For a Little Road it is not', 235.

17. Ibid., 237.

18. 'Introduction', Jennie Reznek, Mark Fleishman, Faniswa Yisa and Frances Marek, *The Magnet Theatre 'Migration' Plays* (Mowbray: Junkets Publisher, 2012), 6.

19. Mandla Mbothwe, 'Dissecting the Aesthetics of Identity in *Isivuno Sama Phupha*', *South African Theatre Journal* 24:1 (2010): 241.

20. Katharine Wood and Rachel Jewkes, 'Dangerous Love – Reflections on Violence among Xhosa Township Youth', in Robert Morrell (ed.), *Changing Men in Southern Africa* (Pietermaritzburg: University of Natal Press, 2001), 317–36.

21. Gay Morris, 'Townships, Identity and Collective Theatre Making by Young South Africans', *South African Theatre Journal* 21:1 (2007): 166–79.

22. Mbothwe, 'Dissecting the Aesthetics of Identity', 250.

23. Ibid., p. 241.

24. 'The Grave of the Man is Next to the Road', published in Reznek et al., *The Magnet Theatre 'Migration' Plays*, 55–90.

25. Megan Lewis, 'South Africa's National Arts Festival', *Theatre Journal* 62:2 (May 2010): 275–80.

26. 'The Wound of the Healer', published in Reznek et al., *The Magnet Theatre 'Migration' Plays*, 151–84.

27. 'The Stranger', ibid., 91–149.

28. The issue of language has remained a key concern for deconstructing colonial conceptions of thought and identity in Africa, and South Africa is no exception (Ngũgĩ wa Thiong'o, *Decolonising the Mind: The Politics of Language in African Literature* (London: James Currey; Nairobi: EAEP; Portsmouth: Heinemann, 1994)). As apartheid policy promoted separate cultural development, many South African artists resisted writing in their mother tongues, in order not to reinforce these policies of separate development, and to speak to the widest audiences possible.

29. In Reznek et al., *The Magnet Theatre 'Migration' Plays*, 9–53.

30. The relevance of this play has increased since the shocking wave of violent xenophobic attacks in 2008, which saw tens of thousands of the several million refugees in South Africa displaced and some sixty murdered.

31. See Emma Cox's comparative analysis of this play in the context of verbatim and refugee theatre ('Victimhood, Hope and the Refugee Narrative: Affective Dialectics in Magnet Theatre's Every Year, Every Day, I Am Walking', *Theatre Research International* 37:2 (2012): 118–33), and C. Wake comparing witnessing and spectatorship ('The Accident and the Account: Towards a Theory of Spectatorial Witness in Theatre and Performance Studies', *Performance Paradigm* 5:1 (2009): 1–21).

32. See Magnet Theatre ('Every Year, Every Day, I am Walking', Interviews and Clips from Performances at The Oval House Theatre, London (2011). Filmed by ejcmedia, Caracois Voadores for Vox Africa, TV, https://vimeo.com/19299079 (accessed 22 March 2013)) for interviews with director and actors on the processes and issues they encountered in this play's creation.

Bibliography

Brown, Duncan, *To Speak of This Land: Identity and Belonging in South Africa and Beyond* (Scottsville: University of KwaZulu-Natal Press, 2006).

Cox, Emma, 'Victimhood, Hope and the Refugee Narrative: Affective Dialectics in Magnet Theatre's Every Year, Every Day, I Am Walking', *Theatre Research International* 37:2 (2012): 118–33.

Erasmus, Zimitri (ed.), *Coloured by History, Shaped by Place: New Perspectives on Coloured Identity in Cape Town* (Cape Town: Kwela and South African History Online, 2001).

Erasmus, Zimitri and Edgar Pieterse, 'Conceptualising Coloured Identities in the Western Cape Province', in M. Palmberg (ed.), *National Identity and Democracy in Africa* (Pretoria: Human Sciences Research Council, 1999), 167–87.

Fleischman, Mark, 'Workshop Theatre's Oppositional Form', *South African Theatre Journal* 4:1 (1990): 88–118.

Fleischman, Mark, 'Physical Images in the South African Theatre', *South African Theatre Journal* 11:1–2 (May/September 1997): 199–214.

Fleischman, Mark, 'Stories like the Wind: Recontextualising /Xam Narratives for Contemporary Audiences', *South African Theatre Journal* 19:1 (2005): 43–57.

Fleischman, Mark, '*Cargo*: Staging Slavery at the Cape', *Contemporary Theatre Review* 21:1 (2011): 8–19.

Fleischman, Mark, 'For a Little Road it is not. For it is a Great Road; it is Long', in Anthony Jackson and Jenny Kidd (eds), *Performing Heritage – Research, Practice and Innovation in Museum Theatre and Live Interpretation* (Manchester and New York: Manchester University Press, 2011), 234–48.

Fleishman, Mark and Nadia Davids, 'Moving Theatre: An Exploration of the Place of Theatre in the Process of Memorialising District Six through an Examination of Magnet Theatre's Production *Onnest'bo*', *South African Theatre Journal* 21:1 (2007): 149–65.

Francis, Kali, 'Theatre of Struggle and Transformation: A Critical Investigation into the Power of Oral Traditions as Used by Director Mark Fleischman', *South African Theatre Journal* 20 (2006): 102–27.

Gqola, Pumla Dineo, *What is Slavery to Me? Postcolonial/Slave Memory in Post-Apartheid South Africa* (Johannesburg: Wits University Press, 2010).

Halligey, Alex, 'Re-Inventing Mythologies: Arguments towards Cultural Identity in *Medea* and *Rain in a Dead Man's Footprints*', *South African Theatre Journal* 19 (2005): 208–22.

Hewitt, Roger, *Structure, Meaning and Ritual in the Narratives of the Southern San* (Johannesburg: Wits University Press, 2008).

Hutchison, Yvette, *South African Performance and Archives of Memory* (Manchester and New York: Manchester University Press, 2013).

Lewis, Megan, 'South Africa's National Arts Festival', *Theatre Journal* 62:2 (May 2010): 275–80.

Loos, Jackie, 'Portraits in Specimens of Bushman Folklore by Bleek and Lloyd', *Quarterly Bulletin of the South African Library* 52:1 (September 1997): 13.

Magnet Theatre, 'Every Year, Every Day, I Am Walking', Interviews and Clips from

Performances at The Oval House Theatre, London (2011). Filmed by ejcmedia, Caracois Voadores for Vox Africa, TV, https://vimeo.com/19299079 (accessed 22 March 2013).

Magnet Theatre, http://www.magnettheatre.co.za/ (accessed 17 March 2015).

Magnet Theatre, http://www,magnettheatre.co.za/ (accessed 15 April 2015).

Mbothwe, Mandla, 'Dissecting the Aesthetics of Identity in *Isivuno Sama Phupha*', *South African Theatre Journal* 24:1 (2010): 241–58.

Morris, Gay, 'Townships, Identity and Collective Theatre Making by Young South Africans', *South African Theatre Journal* 21:1 (2007): 166–79.

Reznek, Jennie, Mark Fleishman, Faniswa Yisa and Frances Marek, *The Magnet Theatre 'Migration' Plays* (Mowbray: Junkets Publisher, 2012), 9–53.

Rudakoff, Judith, 'Somewhere, Over the Rainbow: White-Female-Canadian Dramaturge in Cape Town', *TDR* 48:1 (Spring 2004): 126–63.

Stephanou, Irene and Leila Henriques (eds), *The World is an Orange: Creating Theatre with Barney Simon* (Johannesburg: Jacana Media, 2005).

Van Zyl Smit, Betine, 'Multicultural Reception: Greek Drama in South Africa in the Late Twentieth and Early Twenty-first Centuries', in L. Hardwick and C. Stray (eds), *A Companion to Classical Receptions* (Oxford: Blackwell Publishing, 2008), 373–85.

Van Zyl Smit, Betine, 'Orestes and the Truth and Reconciliation Commission', *Classical Receptions Journal* 2:1 (2010): 114–35.

Wake, C., 'The Accident and the Account: Towards a Theory of Spectatorial Witness in Theatre and Performance Studies', *Performance Paradigm* 5:1 (2009): 1–21.

wa Thiong'o, Ngũgĩ, *Decolonising the Mind: The Politics of Language in African Literature* (London: James Currey; Nairobi: EAEP; Portsmouth: Heinemann, 1994).

Wicomb, Zoë, 'Shame and Identity: The Case of the Coloured in South Africa', in Derek Attridge and Rosemary Jolly (eds), *Writing South Africa: Literature, Apartheid and Democracy, 1970–1995* (Cambridge: Cambridge University Press, 1998), 91–107.

Wood, Katharine and Rachel Jewkes, 'Dangerous Love – Reflections on Violence among Xhosa Township Youth', in Robert Morrell (ed.), *Changing Men in Southern Africa* (Pietermaritzburg: University of Natal Press, 2001), 317–36.

CHAPTER 4
PHYSICAL THEATRE
Robyn Sassen

The Well Being; The Ugly Noo Noo; The Anatomical Journey of a Settler Man; Black and Blue; The Miser; The Unspeakable Story; Daddy I've Seen This Piece Six Times and I Still Can't Understand Why They Are Hurting Each Other; High Diving; Milk and Honey; Africartography; Attachments 1–7; Bopha; Asinamali; Thina Bantu; Agreed; Elev(i)ate; Standing By; Rough Musick; The Best of Company; We Must Eat Our Suckers With the Wrappers On; Bunju; Itsoseng; Cadre; Skierlik; Woza Albert!

Introduction

When two men evoke a natural birth onstage armed only with a watermelon, in such a way that all the blood, drama and trauma of this biological event become indelibly seared into an audience's collective memory, that is physical theatre. The birth in question was a moment pivotal to the play *The Well Being*,[1] co-written and directed by Lara Foot and performed and workshopped by Andrew Buckland and Lionel Newton in the 1980s.

'In 1973 I went to Rhodes University in Grahamstown, to do accountancy', said Buckland, today considered one of the progenitors of physical theatre in South Africa. 'It was mainly to get out of forced conscription, but it was also a logical choice. My father was an accountant. But that did not work out for me and I switched to Physical Education.'

Movement was taught by a newly employed Gary Gordon in Rhodes' Physical Education department. 'Thanks to Gary's teaching, my enjoyment of movement became primary. It was not about intellectually understanding the body, it was all physical.'

Buckland diversified in his approach to learn classical, contemporary and jazz dancing. 'It was an amazing combination of physical input. The more I understood technique as a means of liberating myself, the more I was developing my own language. For me this was like a match struck in an environment ripe to be set alight.'

In 1982 he moved to Johannesburg; in 1993 he moved back to Grahamstown, to take up an academic post at Rhodes. That interregnum of eleven years was important for Buckland and the whole industry. During this time he devised and performed *The Ugly Noo Noo*, a ground-breaking physical theatre extrapolation on so-called Parktown prawns, a large species of cricket in the Highveld. The work was hilarious, touched a nerve in contemporary audiences and cleared the field for more, similar works.

In 1989, *Ugly Noo Noo* travelled to the Edinburgh Theatre Festival, and *Bloodstream*, *Feedback* and *The Well Being*, all crafted with the same physical theatre principles, had grown international legs, in Canada, America, the UK and Europe.[2]

'*The Well Being* gave rise to a whole awareness of this medium', said Lionel Newton, one of Buckland's most prominent collaborators and a drama graduate from the University of Cape Town. Speaking of his 28 years in the industry, Newton names Andrew Buckland as mentor, as well as the late Barney Simon.

> When you come into a room to make something that has never been made before, it is a miracle. This is what I got from Barney. But Andrew Buckland is God. I met Andrew at the National Arts Festival in Grahamstown when I was playing in *Thina Bantu*. He invited me to collaborate with him.

The rest is physical theatre history.

Buckland laughs with warmth at this compliment. 'It's been my life, not my career, but it's also been a rollicking horse coupled by bolts of good fortune, including the people I have worked with.' He speaks of the ego-less nature of the work. 'The actor in physical theatre is essentially dissolving the ego to find universal truths to connect with other human beings in collaboration. You leave your ego and your personal baggage far behind in order to be accessible to your audience.'

Many people who I have spoken to question physical theatre as a real discipline. They all agree that the genre is about storytelling. The threads defining performance art and physical theatre meld and knot together in a morass of values that become almost indistinguishable. And in many respects, it is also understood as the bridge between contemporary dance and so-called straight theatre. But one of its central impetuses is generous collaboration – in terms of the writing of scripts, but also and maybe more significantly, in terms of the construction of narrative or the layering of sequential movements. For this reason, in this chapter, I focus, not so much on the content of individual works, but on the underlying fabric of physical theatre, which defines them wholly or partially. For pragmatic reasons, the ambit of this chapter is not and does not claim to be comprehensive. I have not focused on work from Cape Town, where there, too, is a great blood vessel feeding the discipline, stemming from work by the Magnet Theatre, founded by Jennie Reznek and Mark Fleishman, as well as work by Alfred Hinkel and the Cape Town-based Jazzart Dance Company, to name but a few.

Gordon, considered the most significant source of much of physical theatre in South Africa, wrote in 1994 that explaining what physical theatre is 'fills me with dread. Definitions reduce the manifold possibility and multiplicity of opinions.'[3]

In this chapter, I attempt to fathom why the identity of this discipline, which has status within several South African universities, is disputed, but also consider how it has not only a history, but a present and a future. While this history formally begins in South Africa with Gordon at Rhodes, it draws threads from many time periods. There are touches of ancient oral traditions, as there are strong dance ties. It bears resonance with theatre emerging from amateur groups as it relates to conventions which embrace old European theatre styles that touch on masking, puppeteering and clowning.

The characters in this complicated narrative are diverse and many: too many, in fact, to all be done justice. Cherry-picking from contemporary and seasoned performers and those newly emerging into the linked fields of physical theatre, performance art and contemporary dance, this chapter, by way of personal interviews, attempts to engage with the impetus and substance of the medium, given limiting pragmatics.

In 1974, Gordon, armed with a qualification in what was then called Speech and Drama, from the University of Natal, was employed by Rhodes University. Eight years later, he qualified as a Cecchetti ballet teacher. In 1989, he did a teaching stint at London's Laban Centre for Movement and Dance, and was the first Standard Bank Young Artist Award recipient, that year, for contemporary dance.[4]

In describing the work he produced then, *The Anatomical Journey of a Settler Man*, Gordon writes of improvisation, 'silliness and pain … this anatomical journey contemplated struggle, humour, power, emptiness, aspiration and loss.'[5] After his time with Laban, he returned to Rhodes University in 1992, where he established physical theatre as a component of the drama degree. A year later, at the Grahamstown National Arts Festival, he launched the First Physical Dance Company.

Dance critic Adrienne Sichel refers to the company as having 'blazed a trail in choreographic research, training and conceptual performance'.[6] Physical Theatre became a taught discipline to masters level at Wits University in Johannesburg, the University of Cape Town and Rhodes, within their drama departments, but it has also exploded in pockets and bursts all over the disciplines relating to both drama and dance education and performance.

Rob Murray was born in 1973 in Zimbabwe, and grew up in KwaZulu-Natal, where he was educated at Pietermaritzburg University. Deeply influenced by Buckland's work in the 1980s, he realized he wanted to follow the physical theatre pattern. But it was at the Edinburgh Theatre Festival sometime after graduating that, as he relates, 'I saw a Russian "anti-clown" troupe, and they … blew my head to pieces. Some of the most savage, funny, poignant, violent, poetic and searing theatre work I have probably still ever seen. And I knew then I wanted to train further.' He went to Rhodes, reading for his masters degree under Buckland in 2000, with a focus on contemporary mime.

Some time thereafter with Remix Dance Project in Cape Town, which works with disabled dancers, he helped to develop Buckland's approach further:

> Working with deaf learners and later trainees and colleagues saw the birth of FTH:K (From the Hip: Khulumakahle). The company, during my time there, moved through three distinct phases: environmental theatre, which involved looking at socio-political concerns; integrated theatre, bringing together deaf and hearing performers onstage; and visual theatre where we moved beyond the previous two. It's been a journey. A process. It has led me to masks, puppets and other performing objects, and these, with a very physical entrance into a project, are the ones that make sense to me the most, and I suppose entering into one of the realms that have always captivated me, to quote Antonin Artaud: 'the truthful precipitate of dreams'.

This is a measure of most of the thinking around other performance genres in South Africa; in this respect, Cape Town-based dance scholar Sharon Friedman comments on the work of contemporary choreographers Mamela Nyamza and Dada Masilo, as starting from within a traditional balletic mould but redefining itself constantly. 'Choreographers were concerned with writing South African stories on the bodies of their dancers', she adds.

Ballet was also a starting point for performer/director Sylvaine Strike, who graduated in drama at UCT in 1993. She went on to do an intensive clowning and miming focus with Jacques Lecoq in Paris, which she completed twelve years ago.[7] She remarks on a kinship with Magnet Theatre's Jennie Reznek and Mark Fleishman, who taught her as an under-graduate: 'It was a little niche department, at the time.'

Expressing reluctance to refer to herself as a physical theatre practitioner, she is of the opinion that '[p]hysical theatre is a very broad term, which has become an umbrella for the more poetic work. I tend to work with magical realism. But Lecoq taught me to believe that I can be everything I can be. It is wrong to try and intellectualize a feeling. My greatest gurus are Lionel Newton, my father and Barney Simon.' She spoke of her portfolio of work, from *Black and Blue* in 2004 to *The Miser* in 2012, each an astonishing extrapolation that stretches theatre means and audience expectations. 'My philosophy is to never repeat myself in my work.'

A performer who trained in drama at Rhodes, but who is more recognized in dance circles, is Athena Mazarakis. For her, the body is a primary instrument to making physical theatre. 'Through the body the theatre unfolds, embracing all the kinds of contemporary dance we see in initiatives like the Dance Umbrella,[8] as well as the work that has come out of training under people like Jacques Lecoq.' She was in the first course in physical theatre at Rhodes in 1992.

Forty-year-old Craig Morris, who was also one of the 'guinea pigs' of that first course at Rhodes University in 1992, and who today is amongst the more prominent physical theatre practitioners in South Africa, says: 'My core understanding of physical theatre is still rooted in the same impulse that I was introduced to in my first year at university. While there have been many other approaches to physical theatre [naming Nicholas Ellenbogen's Theatre for Africa[9] and Durban's Loft Theatre Company as examples] in the early years, Gary was limited by the skill or the abilities of the performers, who were first year university students, coming unsuspectingly into the course. But it was also our strength. We were blank canvases.' Born in KwaZulu-Natal, Morris, like Buckland almost a generation earlier, had gone to university to avoid conscription in the South African National Defense Force, still compulsory for young white men at the time.

Morris cites *The Unspeakable Story*, a physical theatre work on the life of European surrealist artist René Magritte, as the debut work of First Physical.

'We were generating our own physical language. We were working from scratch. But we knew to want to create a balance between a dance ethos and everyday movement. Andrew instilled in us the understanding of the role of the performer in relation to the audience. The first instrument we have is our physical body.'

Taking on physical theatre professionally was not a hard decision for Morris:

> It gave me focus. Before I went to university, I had a little dramatic experience, drifting more towards comedic roles, instinctively. My experience at Rhodes gave my aptitudes focus. Rhodes was a beautiful incubator. It was a spring and a well of experiences that engendered performers like Mazarakis, PJ Sabbagha[10] and Juanita Finestone-Praeg.[11]

Long-time collaborator with Mazarakis and Morris, Gerard Bester was educated not at Rhodes but at Wits University, under Fred Hageman, which he considers 'a visceral experience': 'I was schooled in Bloemfontein and came in the early 1980s to movement classes at Wits, with tightly clenched hands. I couldn't embrace. What I learned in movement classes was emotional and physical. On a personal level, it was a major release for me.'

Bester was 'headhunted' in a sense by internationally respected South African-born choreographer, Robyn Orlin, and became part of her seminal work *Daddy I've Seen This Piece Six Times and I Still Can't Understand Why They Are Hurting Each Other*, which debuted in the early 1990s and travelled the world. 'I'm the narrator, or the ringmaster in this piece', he said, adding that 'I have always been full of fear in this type of work. Performing is bloody scary. I have always admired Robyn Orlin with her 150 stories to tell. It is important that one has something to say. Physical theatre should never just be about producing work for its own sake.'

In South Africa, at the moment, many large established theatres are losing audiences to smaller, more informal spaces. The works being hosted are more experimental. A number of key names are emerging with alacrity and a fierce sense of muscularity on the theatre circuit, including Jenine Collocott, playwright Nick Warren, James Cairns, Nina Lucy Wylde-Ferreira, James Cuningham, Tarryn Bennett, Tara Notcutt, Rob Murray and Helen Iskander, to name a few. They are white, they are aggressively creative, they are fuelled by enthusiasm for everything from Shakespeare to Paul Gallico, and they are making important new physical theatre.

Collocott trained in film at AFDA in Johannesburg but decided to specialize in the discipline of clowning in Italy at Helikos, a theatre school under Giovanni Fusetti, some years after graduating. 'With clowning, the audience is always there; you are complicit with them', she says. 'A clown character is developed through a performer's own idiosyncrasies. Every fold of yourself gets exaggerated. It is deeply, deeply personal, but through this, it becomes very funny as well.'

Collocott elected to study with Fusetti for several reasons. Lecoq had by that time passed away. Fusetti had been a graduate of Lecoq's school and is training new practitioners within a similar methodological mindset. 'In this kind of work, you can talk about things that you otherwise cannot. Nothing is holy.'

Collocott's work *High Diving* in 2009 made critics take note: a quirky, fresh play, involving several different disciplines relating to physical theatre, from shadow puppets to simple narrative, it involved the collaboration of veteran performance artist Toni Morkel, who cut her performance teeth in the 1970s in work by Robyn Orlin; James Cairns, who began his astonishing physical theatre career as a stand-up comic; and newcomer Roberto Pombo. The work was created on a tiny budget and debuted at the Fringe of the National Arts Festival in Grahamstown.

Born in 1986, Pombo grew up in Krugersdorp, west of Johannesburg. A graduate of Wits University's drama department, he was taught by Mazarakis, Bester and Iskander. Currently, he is enrolled to further his theatre education at Helikos. He writes:

> The three year course basically follows the Lecoq pedagogy – looking at the outside world as a source of inspiration for movement and creation through mimicry; working with masks, clown work, story telling and the exploration of theatrical genres. Fusetti has developed the clown work using his experience in Gestalt therapy and years at the Lecoq school. The clown work is fundamental in everything else we do at school.

Pombo, who before leaving South Africa had earned critical attention as a stage actor, adds that 'physical theatre is theatre where movement is the primary source of creation. It is a basis for everything – text, space, characters, voice.'

But there is another stream of physical theatre realities, trickling and splitting from the roots established at Rhodes University. According to one of the young lecturers at the Market Theatre Laboratory in Newtown Johannesburg, Khaylihle Dominique Gumede, physical theatre is 'about the body as a physical element given language issues'.

Gumede began his post-matric studies in law at Wits University. He switched to drama and rose to awareness in 2013 with his direction of a largely student-workshopped work, *Milk and Honey*, premised around the 1913 Land Act, which debuted at the National Arts Festival in Grahamstown in 2013, as a student work.

Milk and Honey is told in several indigenous South African languages, but it is underlined with an elegant understanding of a chorus and of mime, which makes it legible to any audience.

Also in 2013, Gumede staged a site-specific work, *Africartography*, involving Market Theatre Lab and Wits University students. 'Because we are so multilingual as a society, the body in motion conveys a message cluttering the baggage of meaning. The body is a three-dimensional chasm of memory; it's integral to my research.'[12]

David Alcock points out a practical problem in theatre of this nature. He cites Ian Steadman, Matsemela Manaka and Maishe Maponya on local political theatre of the 1970s and 1980s, much of which was workshopped. Their texts were thrashed out on rehearsal floors, and scant historical evidence exists as to their final versions. While this method averted the problems of translation, they created an archiving crisis.

Morris concurs on the issue of language: 'In physical theatre, the language expressed by the body enables the message to transcend limitations of translation.' He speaks of *Attachments 1–7*, conceived and performed with Mazarakis and directed by Bester, focused on the ebbs and flows of a relationship between a man and a woman.

'Is it dance? Is it theatre? I'm not sure. For me it is a harmony between pedestrian action and artistic innovation. I try to play between literal and abstract. Dance forms have been around so long they've become encoded and too abstract for an un-dance audience.'

'I believe *Attachments* enjoyed success because we used pedestrian everyday postures as a "hook" for the audience', says Morris, who, like several physical theatre practitioners, including Lionel Newton and Sylvaine Strike, earns much of his income through corporate or industrial theatre, specifically commissioned by the directors of big multinational companies, ports, banks, mines, to alert their staff to issues from safety on the job to AIDS awareness. 'Physical theatre is entertaining but it is also didactic – crossing language or literacy bars – without being preachy or boring', Morris adds.

Newton develops this further: 'The physicality in plays like *Bopha*, *Asinamali* and *Thina Bantu* were an answer to the cultural boycott at the time. If no one was prepared to play with us, we would play with ourselves.' He speaks of how physical theatre skills can avert the need for a set, even a cast, in a work.

At the time of being interviewed, Newton was working on a three-part monodrama called *Agreed*, to perform at the Market Theatre in early 2014:

> Some of the characters in this work I have developed with my industrial audiences, like Langballe, a belligerent clown who debuted in Uitenhage in the Eastern [Cape]. Industry theatre is a huge part of the physical theatre world kept alive by the actors. But the genre of physical theatre burgeoned from apartheid. There were no published words to be censored in these plays.

Mazarakis concurs with that idea of language being transmutable into physical movement: 'It is making bridges to and creating access.' Known for several pieces in which she examines homophobia and the so-called corrective rape of black lesbians in contemporary South Africa society, Mazarakis is currently employed as the education officer at the Forgotten Angle Theatre Collective. For several years previously, Mazarakis taught physical theatre at Wits University. In 2007 she debuted a piece at the Dance Umbrella and, later in the year, at the National Arts Festival in Grahamstown, called *Elev(i)ate*. The work was one part of a series of two, examining the burden of weight.

'My brief to myself was how to change the format of the encounter between audience and performer', she explains. In the Dance Umbrella manifestation of this work, she literally picked up audience members, in a spoof of a circus-based strong man.

In Mazarakis's work, the idea of the burden of weight was teased apart linguistically and literally, examining all the different connotations burden could represent, yielding a deeply poetic gesture. This, intertwined with her physicality on stage, has become a kind of signature for Mazarakis.

As a homosexual woman, the issue of homophobia in our society touches her directly. 'I can't switch off. There's lots of research and statistics; I became paralysed by it and by the gruesomeness of this phenomenon in our society. I had to start speaking through the narratives. I had to create a visceral response in my audience.' She introduced elements like the sounding of a shrill whistle, every 26 seconds in a work – indicating how frequently black lesbians are being attacked in township society.[13]

'It allowed me to take the intent of the performance and shift the performing body as a way to hold people to account. As a white homosexual woman, I could never dance that pain because it is black homosexual women who are being targeted. I can only be a by-stander. Hence the piece in question: *Standing By*.'

This question is broached by many performance artists, including Gavin Krastin and Alan Parker, who in 2013 debuted a work at the National Arts Festival in Grahamstown called *Rough Musick*, which according to Sichel is a requiem to victims of homophobia: one which engaged audience participation and response. Krastin's work casts a glance at the transgressiveness of South African-born performance artist Steven Cohen before him; similarly he uses his body to confront his audiences.

Both Krastin and Parker are graduates of Rhodes Drama Department. Parker became manager for First Physical in 2009, and Associate Artistic Director in 2010, when Gordon moved to Hong Kong.[14] Currently, he is a Cape Town-based freelance choreographer/performer, with teaching responsibilities at UCT School of Dance and AFDA Cape Town, specializing in contemporary dance and choreographic studies.

Parker, who originates from Benoni, east of Johannesburg, writes:

When I applied to Rhodes, I initially wanted to become a playwright and had never heard of physical theatre. On arrival at Rhodes, I was immediately taken by the movement and physical theatre courses that form part of the drama degree. By second year, I decided I wanted to be a physical performer and began attending after hours classes offered by First Physical. I had never been that interested in 'dance' but found the merging of dance and drama in physical theatre especially appealing.

On studying physical theatre at postgraduate levels, he adds:

One never felt confined to a particular style, or vocabulary or theme/ concept. The course really aimed to create idiosyncratic choreographers – with an emphasis on finding 'your' signature as opposed to replicating existing ones. I found the openness of this path very appealing – that one could 'choreograph' things other than bodies ... words, visual images, sounds and sensations. Gary's insistence that physical theatre should challenge, provoke and question rather than simply entertain or be aesthetically beautiful also really stayed with me.

I define physical theatre (and teach it) more as an artistic approach to making work than as a distinct genre or style. I think over the last two decades 'physical theatre' has become an easy way to define or categorise anything that is both physical and theatrical. Physical theatre has more to do with the way in which a performance is made than its realisation.

Collaboration and dialogue are physical theatre's fundamental characteristics. Each component has a relationship with the other; each contributes or problematises interpretation and representation. Physical theatre is thus also political and self-aware.

Krastin was born and educated in Cape Town. He too wanted to be an actor, but found himself following the physical theatre trajectories established by Gordon and Finestone-Praeg at Rhodes: 'It was a bodily mode of performance that I had never encountered before, one that enticed curiosity in me.'

Krastin completed his masters in drama at Rhodes in 2011, taught at the department for a year and held the job of researcher at the First Physical Company. He is now a freelance dancer/choreographer, based in Cape Town:

The open-endedness of physical theatre celebrates de-codification, idiosyncratic movement patterns and individuality of the body/body-type; it picks at the surface of representation, spectacle and 'for show' in exploration of the real and the personal. The training in physical theatre does not aim to manufacture 'cookie-cutter' exact replicas – where everyone has to look and move a certain way. One is afforded an experience of naivety of language when approaching a performative statement as physical theatre.

I find the experiencing or journey of creating a work very exciting, scary and full of surprises; works are devised in collaboration with the cast, where each body offers something different, in relation to the concept. That space creating hierarchy and distance is shortened: your aim is no longer to manifest a predetermined work scripted by a stranger or to learn a movement vocabulary verbatim from a choreographer who has made the language for/on his/her body specifically. For me the rehearsal process is like a collaborative becoming, resulting in a palimpsest. This mode of working promotes slippage and leakages and sets up a wonderful playground for experimentation with the collisions of the moving body and image, where visual statements don't have to mean or behave in a particular fashion, but assume a more ambiguous, abstract role.

When words, texts and logic fail, frustrate or aren't enough, physical theatre is a playground of provocation and re-discovery through posture, gesture, proxemics and touch, a process not mapped but instinctual and organic.

Another choreographer who cites the Rhodes trio of Gordon, Buckland and Finestone-Praeg in her evolution is Nadine Joseph, who graduated with a masters from Rhodes in 2012. 'I am interested in the memories embedded in the body and how our individual memories can speak to a collective memory in terms of particular traumas and atrocities', she writes, explaining that her personal pedagogy is to use physical theatre 'to encourage language/voice development; to use the body to find a different way of speaking and/or interacting with society; to find a different approach to the body, in particular contexts and with particular modes of representation'.

Wits-graduate Kieron Jina, of a similar age to Joseph, calls himself an independent artist and activist. Trained at Wits University, he adds that the discipline 'enables me to explore what it means to be African through performance, dance and technology. As a young South African, I feel a responsibility to let art be a voice for the youth. I focus on highlighting issues that would normally not get the attention they need to bring about positive change.' He, too, refers to physical theatre as an umbrella term: 'It is open-ended. We live in a diverse society – and being of mixed race myself – I am interested in exploring the results of mixing forms and mediums, physical theatre being a part of this merge.'

The roots of physical theatre in Johannesburg reach deeper than the confines of Wits University, however, and there is a field of informally grown physical theatre which is rich and fertile.

In 1968, thespian extraordinaire Barney Simon visited America, where, amongst other things, he came in contact with the work of the Young Lords, the Puerto Rican equivalent of the Black Panthers. 'I saw street theatre, raw alive and naïve', he told *Business Day* in 1986. This experience inspired what were called communication workshops, when he returned to Johannesburg in 1970.

He devised and directed health-education projects in Zululand and the Transkei. In Pat Tucker's *The Best of Company*, a history of the Market

Theatre, Simon comments 'It took a lot to make me do that work, and it was a conscious, political decision.' But he was shunned by the predominantly white theatre fraternity and was eventually compelled to start working at the Arena, a Doornfontein-based newly established informal venue subsidized by the apartheid government-supported Performing Arts Council of Transvaal. Under the direction of Mannie Manim and Francois Swart and backed by apartheid-infused anger for black performers and audiences not being allowed, The Company was established in 1974, breaking away from PACT and finding its permanent home at the old produce market in Newtown. And so the Market Theatre was born in 1976.

Daniel Robbertse has taught at the Market Theatre Laboratory for over twenty years. An adjunct to the theatre, the Lab evolved as a place of learning in the 1990s. Its students, on the whole, do not have university grounding; many work during the day and study part-time. He recalls collaborating with the likes of Buckland and Orlin on the teaching staff, with the goal of bringing diverse theatre skills to black youngsters.

Barney Simon, one of the founding directors of the Market Theatre, was sold on the idea of bringing physical theatre there. Orlin and works like her AIDS-focused *We Must Eat Our Suckers With The Wrappers On* that did the French/Belgian circuit in 1999/2000 represented a major influence in terms of maintaining links with more physical theatre stuff.

One of the Market Theatre Lab students during the 1990s was Mncedisi Shabangu, a performer who has distinguished himself on stages locally and abroad, with material from Shakespeare and Beckett to contemporary work. Two years after he graduated from the Lab, Shabangu came to teach; he became influential in communicating to the next generation.

'A work called *Bunju* devised by the Market Theatre Lab went to the National Arts Festival during the nineties', says Robbertse. 'It was quite unique and brought in critical comparisons with Grotowski's idea of "poor theatre". But it was not so much à la Grotowski, but a matter of making theatre by using what was at hand. Performers associated with the lab were invested with a sense of hyper-physicality. They were moving from realism.' He cites contemporary plays, including Omphile Molusi's *Itsoseng* and *Cadre* and Phillip Dikotla's *Skierlik*, which have taken audience imagination by storm and which significantly feature physical theatrical components that come out of paltry budgets for sets or large casts, but also out of intense rethinking of expression.

Gordon was aware of the potential for local, formerly unexplored stories in the 1990s. He commented on how elements of physical theatre were part of productions like *Woza Albert!*, but were not recognized as 'physical theatre'.

Choreographer Jeannette Ginslov writes that physical theatre

does not mean that the body expresses a stand or adherence to a political climate: This would entail supporting an ideology, master narrative or hegemony. Rather, the performing body reveals a personal politics. The mode of production ... requires that each performer express personal and experiential knowledge through the moving body. It is here, at this site, where the personal becomes political.'[15]

It may be seen that this work ethos applies to the phenomenon of physical theatre throughout South Africa.

But physical theatre is about more than staging or language or politics. It's about forcing the physical body into the confines of the play, and making it 'speak' in its own diction. It breathes choreographic soul into an otherwise so-called straight play, offering rich and often almost inarticulate reflection on the play's message.

Rob Murray adds: 'Bodies don't lie. Over 70 per cent of any communication is based on body language.' He paraphrases Lecoq: '"Just be quiet. Listen. Play, and theatre will happen". I adapted this for visual theatre and particularly FTH:K's tagline of "Listen with your eyes"'. On the other hand, Craig Morris has a completely pragmatic approach: 'In preparing for a new work, I train as though I was a professional athlete. As I age, I learn to develop physical intelligence and an economy of movement.'

Notes

1. Like many plays mentioned in this chapter, *The Well Being* has not been formally published. The context of this is twofold and has to do with the publishing industry as much as with the nature of the work. As scholar David Alcock says, 'theatre is ephemeral: the difficulty of recording theatre performance, particularly those with ... less reliance on text, is a problem which faces academics and historians' (Alcock, 'Somatic Emphasis in South African Theatre: Intervention in the Body Politic', in Marcia Blumberg and Dennis Walder (eds), *South African Theatre As/And Intervention* (Amsterdam: Rodopi, 1999), 49).

2. David Alcock (ibid., 51) says the unpublished manuscripts of most of these plays are in the archives of Rhodes' Drama Department; he considers these works part of the protest theatre tradition in South Africa.

3. G. Gordon, 'Physical Theatre: Weaving Together the Threads of the Curriculum', *South African Association of Drama and Youth Theatre Journal* (1994): 10–17.

4. Many of the characters in this story were Standard Bank Young Artist Award winners for either dance or drama. I have not mentioned this, or any other accolade, given space constraints.

5. Quoted in A. Sichel, 'Us and Them: Dance, Sport, Gender and Politics', in Chris Thurman (ed.), *Sport Versus Art: A South African Contest* (Johannesburg: Wits University Press, 2010), 167–8.

6. Ibid., 168.

7. Jacques Lecoq (1921–99) was an actor, mime and acting instructor. He is known for his methods on physical theatre, movement and mime. He taught at the school he founded in Paris, L'École Internationale de Théâtre Jacques Lecoq, from 1956 until his death in 1999. During the 1980s, many South African artists studied with him, including Buckland, William Kentridge, Strike, Jennie Reznek and Mark Fleishman.

8. Dance Umbrella in Johannesburg is an annual festival of contemporary dance, established in 1998.

9. This theatre company was established in Cape Town in 1989 and has spawned several award-winning productions, giving wing to the careers of practitioners like Ellis Pearson and Bheki Mkhwane.

10. Choreographer, artistic director and a founder of the Johannesburg-based Forgotten Angle Theatre Collaborative.

11. Senior lecturer at Rhodes University's Drama Department, with an academic and performative interest in physical theatre, Juanita Finestone-Praeg currently runs First Physical. As Sichel explains, the company, like many other arts companies nationally, is beset with funding problems. Indeed, their 20th birthday celebration in 2013 was in Sichel's words 'in skeleton mode' for this reason ('History Gets Physical', *The Star, Tonight,* 18 June 2013, 3).

12. On the issue of how dance and theatre are hand in hand, with particular reference to physical theatre, Gumede comments, 'I have a consistent and unashamed love affair with the Vuyani Dance Theatre works.' VDT, established by Gregory Maqoma, is a 15-year-old contemporary dance company based in central Johannesburg.

13. This evokes a physical theatre intervention by Peter van Heerden, which debuted at the Dance Umbrella of 2005, called *Six Minutes*, representing a disturbing reflection on brutality against contemporary women.

14. Gordon became Head of Academic Studies at the Hong Kong Academy for Performing Arts in 2010.

15. J. Ginslov, 'The Moving Body: A Political Minefield – The Body Politic in the Mode of Production of the First Physical Theatre Company', in *Enquiries into Physical Theatre* (Grahamstown: Rhodes University, 1999), 98.

Bibliography

Alcock, D., 'Somatic Emphasis in South African Theatre: Intervention in the Body Politic', in Marcia Blumberg and Dennis Walder (eds), *South African Theatre As/And Intervention* (Amsterdam: Rodopi, 1999), 49–57.

Bester, G., personal interview, Wits Theatre, 28 November 2013.

Buckland, A., telephone interview, November 2013.

Cairns, J., personal interview, Moema's, Parktown North, March 2013.

Collocott, J., personal interview, Croft & Co, Parkhurst, March 2013.

Friedman, S., 'Mapping an Historical Context for Theatre Dance in South Africa', in Sharon Friedman (ed.), *Post-Apartheid Dance: Many Bodies Many Voices Many Stories* (Newcastle upon Tyne: Cambridge Scholars Publishing, 2012).

Ginslov, J., 'The Moving Body: A Political Minefield – The Body Politic in the Mode of Production of the First Physical Theatre Company', in *Enquiries into Physical Theatre* (Grahamstown: Rhodes University, 1999), 98–104.

Gordon, G., 'Physical Theatre: Weaving Together the Threads of the Curriculum', *South African Association of Drama and Youth Theatre Journal* (1994): 10–17.

Gumede, K. D., personal interview, Kaldi's, Newtown, 30 September 2013.

Jina, K., email interview, November 2013.

Joseph, N., email interview, November 2013.

Kennedy, C., 'A Visceral Connection Through Theatre', *Business Day Live*, 13 September 2013.

Krastin, G., Facebook-based interview, November 2013.

Mazarakis, A., personal interview, Vovo Telo, Milpark, 8 November 2013.

Morris, C., personal interview, Mugg & Bean, Norwood, 18 December 2013.

Murray, R., email interview, November 2013.

Newton, L., personal interview, Norwood, November 2013.

Parker, A., Facebook-based interview, November 2013.

Pombo, R., email interview, November 2013.

Robbertse, D., personal interview, Kaldi's Newtown, 1 August 2013.

Sichel, A., 'Us and Them: Dance, Sport, Gender and Politics', in Chris Thurman (ed.), *Sport Versus Art: A South African Contest* (Johannesburg: Wits University Press, 2010), 157–72.

Sichel, A., 'History Gets Physical', *The Star, Tonight,* 18 June 2013, 3.

Sichel, A., 'Not So Medieval After All', *The Star, Tonight,* 23 July 2013, 3.

Stephanou, I. and L. Henriques, *The World in an Orange: Creating Theatre with Barney Simon*, ed. Lionel Abrahams and Jane Fox (Johannesburg: Seven Stories, 2001).

Strike, S., personal interview, De La Crème Café, Melville, October 2013.

CHAPTER 5
POPULAR COMMUNITY THEATRE
Emma Durden

The Seed; To Be Like This Rock (Umsindo Theatre Projects)
The Milk Factory; Fikile (Emuhle All Artists)

Introduction

During the apartheid era, as a predominantly white theatre scene grew and thrived in the towns, a separate strand of 'township' theatre emerged in the segregated black locations.[1] Zakes Mda notes that this predominantly musical theatre genre deals 'with the sensational side of life: prostitution, adultery, rape, and divorce'.[2] These popular plays reflected the reality of township life, in a melodramatic way, and from an apolitical stance. While these productions had many elements of Western theatre tradition, they were popular in that their audiences were drawn from all classes within the confines of the townships.[3]

In South Africa, this popular drama is often referred to as 'in the Gibson Kente style', after one of the most prolific theatre makers of the 1960s. In an interview in 1987, Kente described his own work as being inspired by the community around him, noting: 'I am an observer of life; I think this is the reason why my art has been successful. We have to relate to everything we see around us, and everything around us bears some meaning.'[4] He is very clear about the need for this work to be both reflective of the realities of life but also presented in an entertaining way, acceptable to its audiences. Kente's use of professional and popular jazz musicians and actors added to the entertainment value of his plays, and were partly responsible for their commercial success.

At the same time as the growth of this genre of popular melodrama, a separate strand of political theatre developed in the country. This political and protest theatre sought deliberately to highlight the conditions under which black people were forced to live. A further distinctive genre, which Mda calls *Theatre for Resistance*, grew, in the style of worker's theatre and agit-prop, and 'deliberately addressed itself to the oppressed with the overt aim of rallying or of mobilizing the oppressed to fight against oppression'.[5]

However, these productions, unlike their apolitical counterparts, were not always popular. Kente comments on the difference between his style of theatre and political work that was shown at the Market Theatre: noting, 'You often know the tone of the plays there in advance. How many of those plays can stand the test of township opinion? Very few actually.'[6]

While Kente's theatre was specifically created for the people, there was another strand of political theatre developed *by* the people: many ordinary working people became involved in theatre productions as a way of expressing themselves under an otherwise oppressive regime. This tradition of people coming together to create plays about what concerns them continues today as what is most often referred to as *community theatre*.

Defining South African community theatre

In many European countries, community theatre has developed as an applied theatre form, where professional theatre makers work together with community-based project participants giving voice to the social issues that affect a particular group. However, in South Africa this is different. Most community groups fit into the tradition of township theatre, the creation of popular theatre *for* and *by* township-based performers. This desire to create is more often motivated by a love of the arts than by a need to spread a message, although many groups combine the two.

There is an ongoing tension between the worlds of professional and community theatre in South Africa, with professional theatre being seen as more artistic and worthwhile, and community theatre as a lesser form. Despite this, community theatre is growing in stature and popularity, and is a recognized part of the arts industry. Some of the leading names in South African theatre have come from a community theatre background, including significant past and present theatre makers and directors, such as Mbongeni Ngema, James Ngcobo (Artistic Director of the Market Theatre), Prince Lamla (Standard Bank Young Artist Winner for Theatre, 2013) and many more. Community theatre festivals around the country are hosted by government bodies, mainstream theatres and non-profit organizations. These are often hotly contested competitions, with substantial cash prizes and kudos going to the winners.

Mainstream playhouses around the country have an element of mentoring, where community theatre groups are provided with artistic advice and guidance by a professional theatre maker. With this mentoring, many community theatre productions are changed in the process of collaboration, and become a blend of western theatre aesthetics and popular local drama. While a production's key themes (most often generated around pressing social issues affecting the community) usually remain the same, the script structure, form and staging often change after input from professionals.

There are divided schools of thought on this topic, with some feeling that this outside intervention interferes with the 'purity' of township theatre, and others who feel that for theatre to retain its audiences, it needs to improve its appeal and become more 'professional'. Most important is the fact that the groups themselves are actively looking for these collaborations and want to integrate into the broader industry. They want to be exposed to other forms of theatre and to continually be inspired. They feel that township theatre is an old-school form of community theatre that they respect, but are no longer part of.

With these opportunities, there is the possibility that young artists from community groups may break away from their groups to enter the professional theatre realm, and this could erode the essence of community theatre and its transformational potential. That said, community theatre practice is undoubtedly seen as a stepping stone into the professional industry.

By analysing the work of two rising community theatre groups from KwaZulu-Natal, investigating their background and some of their work, we see that their motives and the complexity of their works are closely linked. These groups, Umsindo Theatre Projects from Umlazi township, south of Durban, and Emuhle All Artists from the Gamalakhe township near Port Shepstone on the KwaZulu-Natal south coast, have both been through the programme co-ordinated by Twist Theatre Development Projects.

Twist Theatre Development Projects is a South African non-profit organization which recruits community theatre groups for involvement in its annual programme of workshops and festivals, matching these groups with mentors and professionals from the industry. This programme is designed in an attempt to help the community groups to develop their work and build their groups into more sustainable units that are able to earn an income, but also encourages them to continue to create theatre for their own communities and serve as a voice for change in their own areas.

Umsindo Theatre Projects

Umsindo Theatre Projects was started in Umlazi in 2002 by twins Siso (Musawenkosi) and Goso (Bongomusa) Shabalala, and Xolani Dlongolo (who has since left the group to start one of his own). The three had been exposed to the arts at their township high school, and to the Gibson Kente shows that toured Umlazi in the late 1970s, and wanted to continue with this passion after they finished school. They recognized that there was talent in Umlazi, but nobody to nurture it. Many school leavers had nothing to do, and the trio started the group as a way to keep young people busy and to express themselves creatively. As time went by, the group also started working with school-going children, running classes with them after school hours, as a way of keeping them off the streets. The group consists of 35–45 members, mostly children, who practise traditional dance and singing daily. The ten older members form a drama group that focuses on creating work for festivals.

The Umsindo founders are clear that their work is created for the community around them, commenting that 'those are the people who most relate to our work'.[7] Most of their performances are in an abandoned butchery in Umlazi, which they have kitted out with old seats and lights discarded from other theatres. They also perform in community halls around the township and further afield. Their shows are popular and play to capacity crowds. They have a policy of asking for contributions, so those who can afford to, pay something for entrance, while those who cannot, see the play for free.

The group has won awards at festivals around the country, and the founders (who take on the role of directors of all of the shows) have been exposed to theatre nationally and overseas, and have performed in Europe themselves in professional productions. The group have worked with international writers and actors, and their ambition is to tour international stages and festivals. However, they also want to build their own arts centre at home, offering courses in all arts disciplines to the young talents in Umlazi.

The twins feel that their mark of success is being able to reach people's hearts and change people's thinking. They feel that most people do not want to read to understand society's problems, but if they see it presented on stage they start to engage with these difficult issues. This desire to tackle social issues is reflected in their work, including *The Seed* (2011), a play that explores unfaithfulness and HIV infection, and *Brothers* (2013), which looks at corruption and crime. Xolani Dlongolo comments on why they are compelled to do this:

They think if HIV is not in my home it's not existing – they think 'so why should I bother?'… We want them to bother. We want them to face these issues, because they are scared. If they bother, then they can save lives.[8]

However, the way that the group tackles these issues is very different to how a strategically designed and considered applied theatre or educational programme might do so. *The Seed*, for example, talks about HIV in the context of migrant labour, and the script is sensationalized, with a big-city prostitute being the source of the HIV infection that destroys a rural family. Unmediated, it can be argued that this message reinforces stereotypes rather than communicates clearly about the problem. This use of sensationalism and stereotype is typical of the popular township theatre genre.

The Seed *(2012): Symbolism and sensationalism*

The Seed (2012) is developed in collaboration with writer Amy Jephta from Cape Town and director Monageng 'Vice' Motshabi from Johannesburg under the auspices of the Twist mentorship project. Much of the symbolic and poetic language comes from Jephta's pen, and some of the strong visual imagery is inspired by the partnership with Motshabi, and combines with Umsindo's graphic sensibility to make the show unique.

The play is based on the allegory of a seed that is planted and comes to fruit. One of the central characters is Mthobosi, a grave-digger and a gardener, tending to the trees in the graveyard. Mthobosi sets the scene for the play, commenting:

This tree started as a small seed, a very small seed. But not just any seed. This was a special one. One that started growing and spreading and causing all kinds of trouble. (141)

The notion of the seed and its fruit is very strongly represented, with one of the early images in the play showing Sbongile, a prostitute, in a room full of apples, which she unsuccessfully tries to put into some sort of order. Later we meet the character of Dingane, a migrant worker who has sex with Sbongile. When he comes home to his wife, Dingane has an apple tied to his body, which he passes along to his wife. Later in the play, a baby is born with an apple in its hand. Although never overtly stated, it is clear that this seed is HIV.

The script explores issues of love, trust, sex, infidelity and guilt. The apple is passed along this line and echoes biblical notions of the fruit as a symbol of man's greed and the reason for humanity's eventual downfall. There is no space for subtlety in this stark exploration of how AIDS affects families. Dingane's wife contemplates suicide, commenting:

> This poison that has made me sick, that has poisoned my blood and is feeding on my body. I won't let it take me slowly. I will rather take myself before it gets to me. Before this poison eats me away, one bite at a time, like I ate the fruit from that tree ... (148)

The final image in the show (not written in the script, but evident in the playing) is that of a train racing at speed along a track. The inference is that this mother will take her two children to stand with her in the face of the oncoming train. It is a bleak ending that suggests a fatalistic view of HIV and AIDS commonly held by many South Africans. Despite this dark subject matter, the symbolic staging of the work, with the use of living trees losing their leaves, the ever-present apples and use of shadow versus stark bright light, makes for fascinating viewing, and the play has been very popular with township audiences. Umsindo feel, however, that their most popular (and successful) show is the anti-human-trafficking play *To Be Like This Rock*.

To Be Like This Rock *(2011): A clear message in a gripping medium*

To Be Like This Rock (2011) was devised by the group and first performed at the Ishashalazi Women's Festival in 2009, where it took home first prize. The group then went on to work with mentors Neil Coppen and Debbie Lutge in 2010 under the auspices of Twist Theatre Development Projects, rescripting and restaging the work. It performed at community arts festivals around the country, as well as having seasons at professional theatres in Durban and Johannesburg and a successful run at the National Arts Festival fringe, where it won a Standard Bank Ovation Award in 2011.

Set in contemporary South Africa, the action shifts from an unnamed village to the outskirts of Durban. The plot is complex, a series of flashbacks and switches between different places and times. At the opening of the play, South African 'scouts' are in the audience, convincing parents that they should let their daughters travel to South Africa, where they will be given well-paid work in a restaurant. For many this is their chance to escape poverty. The notion of escape is one that recurs throughout the play: first escaping the prison of poverty, and later the entrapment of forced labour.

The first scene is between a mother and her young daughter, Tinny (pronounced Tiny), and creates an image of care and nurturing. The mother character is simply 'Mama' and an every-woman embodiment of the tender mother figure. Tinny, the main character, is representative of the small and vulnerable, but demonstrates a core of resilience as the plot unfolds.

Important theatrical choices include the colourful clothes worn in the opening scene at the market and the use of slow motion at crucial moments where Tinny loses her mother. This world is changed totally when after a long journey she ends up in a prison-like house filled with piles of stones that the girls grind down by bashing them against each other, when they are not servicing clients who come for sex. Despite being set to do heavy labour, the girls themselves are physically weak and lack any agency or personal power. They are simply tools for the men that control them. It is only the diminutive Tinny that is small enough to escape at the end of the play. The message is clear: no matter how small you are, you can make a big change.

The stage for *To Be Like This Rock* is dominated by a set of iron bars, symbolizing the prison. The dust from the rocks, the minimal set, the dim lighting, the rhythmic bashing of the stones and the haunting choral singing all help to build dramatic tension and lock the audience in a kind of nether-world which serves to emphasize the conditions that trafficked girls are kept under. Talking about what they have to endure, day and night, the relevance of the title becomes clear:

Grace   Yes Tinny, pray for God to turn us all into rocks.

Candy   Say: Lord, make of me a rock. (Closing her eyes) I want to be like this rock. I wish to be like this rock.

Grace   (She picks up one of her rocks and holds it forward in her palm.) It never feels anything. We break, we smash them but they never feel anything. They never cry or hurt or feel …

Tinny   (Rises on her knees and holds her rock forward.) Lord, I wish to be like this rock. I pray to be like this rock. (233–4)

The characters on stage pour themselves into dramatic songs that emphasize their hopeless situation. In an Aristotelian way, the storyline follows Tinny into the crisis where one of the girls that she is imprisoned with dies. This main storyline is beautifully woven through the girls' individual stories, how they were tricked or taken and are now trapped. They make a plan for Tinny to escape, which she finally does, in a final thrilling action scene.

The other girls teach Tinny a phone number, and the name of the road where they are kept. They tell her how she can escape after they come to take her away, and how to find a local shop-keeper who can call for help. Tinny makes a break and runs from the stage. The character of Tinny's mother stands at the side of the stage, and the three remaining girls stand up and throw down their rocks. The image of them rising is moving. The implication is that they are free. This final image is resonant of the South African woman's movement cry: 'You strike a woman, you strike a rock.'

Little is overstated, the script is sparse and what is left unsaid resonates as much as what is said. The staging is very graphic. This is typical of what has become Umsindo's trademark visceral presentation style and is a break away from the norms of community theatre, which often either rely on 'poor-theatre' staging techniques or on domestic plays in realistic settings.[9]

To understand how *To Be Like This Rock* is representative of a new wave of hybrid community/professional theatre, it is useful to know its origins. The group created an original work that was based on human trafficking. This piece was performed for a community arts festival in 2009. Mentoring with Coppen and Lutge resulted in the development of a tighter plot, with simpler dialogue and the envisioning of theatrical images and slow-motion moments in the blocking. This fusion changed the work in many ways.

To Be Like This Rock is a dramatic and well-crafted piece of drama, which may have the ability to move its audiences to action. It achieves what Umsindo sets out to do: placing an often unspoken subject firmly on the agenda, in a unique style.

Emuhle All Artists

Emuhle All Artists was started in 2000 by Bongani Baai, a self-taught theatre maker. He started Emuhle to provide township-based young people with an education and understanding of theatre and provide a platform for talented young artists: 'We have to be township reporters and educate people; to take up the issues in our society and tell them through stories.'[10]

Emuhle works predominantly in the south coast areas of KwaZulu-Natal, but travels to community festivals around the country when opportunities arise. Baai himself writes much of the group's new work, but says that some of their plays are devised through the workshop tradition. This involves the group talking about what is happening in their own lives and homes, and creating plays based on these stories.

Baai is clear that they do not see the local community as their only audience, commenting that 'We are making plays for everyone, not just the people in our townships. When I write I run away from writing a local play … I want to write about issues that touch people from everywhere.'[11]

The group has performed around the country at community arts festivals, and locally for festivals, at schools and community halls. Community halls are usually full to capacity, and their outdoor performances, for holiday-makers along the beachfront, draw large crowds.

Generating income is one of the important motives of the group, and they want to reach large audiences, but Baai is clear that their success is also measured in the way that the group provides a firm grounding for young people interested in the arts. After working with the group, one of the girls has been cast in the popular TV soap opera *Generations*, one in a television advert and others have been cast in outside productions working with recognized names in the theatre industry. Some have gone on to study drama at university. For Baai, this is the real success of the group, when the youngsters involved in it spread their wings and find professional work. The group does not see itself as predominantly political, bringing about social change, but wants to bring about change and opportunities for young people.

Much of the work by the group explores the contrasts between two worlds: between rural and urban life, between men and women, between good and evil. Their 2012 production of *The Milk Factory*, co-written by the group with Simphiwe Vilikazi, explores lies, betrayal and deception between rural villages and the new world.

The Milk Factory: *Where old meets new*

The Milk Factory explores the conflicts of people adapting to a way of life that is not what they are used to, and trying to come to terms with this change. The protagonist, Musa, refers to a traditional way of life and a bygone time when the people were connected with the land in a different way. He speaks of dreams and ancestors, and his words evoke an other-worldliness that is connected with this traditional belief system. This is in contrast with the more rational and modern Jabulani, who asserts, 'I don't believe in dreams, especially your nonsense' (94). Jabulani serves as the voice of reason in the play, contrasting with the hot-headed Musa.

The action of the play, with a plot to blow up a milk factory that has claimed the lives of two of Musa's family members, is set in an indistinct time. Reference to kingdoms and warriors abound, juxtaposed with talk of factories, schools and bombs. This switching between references to the historical world and the contemporary one serves to highlight the difference between an old way of life and a modern one.

The two central characters refer to the sale of milk, and to competition between villages to sell this cheaply to the biggest buyer. This sale of the milk creates a war between villages, reminiscent of the historical tribal wars of the Eastern Cape province of South Africa. These wars were centred on issues of land ownership and cattle and were exacerbated by colonialism. There is an oft-repeated question throughout the play – 'Who owns the milk factory?' – which is never answered, and highlights issues of land ownership which continue to be a contested area in South African politics.

Milk Factory is presented as a series of unanswered questions and inaction. The plan to blow up the factory is never carried out. The play opens and closes with scenes of people working together as a machine in the milk factory, highlighting the fact that despite a desire to bring about change for themselves, these villages are without the power to do this, as they have been throughout history.

The notion of contrast is also explored in what Baai thinks is one of their most successful productions, the 2011 presentation of *Anti-Christ*, a dark horror which explores the life of a young woman torn between her deeply Christian mother and devil-worshipping father. The script sets up these forces of good and evil against each other, embodied in the parents, and the daughter herself becomes possessed by these two different forces. It is a brooding, dark work, staged with red and black costumes and predominantly red lighting. Baai comments that the show garnered interest in their own community because of its very controversial subject matter, then went on to play at festivals in Durban and Cape Town. The Umsindo team worked with Baai on directing this work, which has the same graphic symbolic style as many of Umsindo's productions.

Some Teens (2012) is a work written by Baai that explores the differences in the lives of two teenage sisters dealing with adolescence. Both are representative of a generation that parents do not understand. Both have a different approach to how they see their own lives and deal with the challenges that they are confronted with.

Fikile *(2013): A romantic melodrama*

Fikile, continuing the group's common theme of contrasts, is created by the group through the Twist project with writer/mentor Neil Coppen. The script explores the turbulence of change for young South Africans, exploring issues of rural versus urban life and the options open to those with an education versus those without.

The play is set in the peri-urban area of Gamalakhe just outside Port Shepstone. The central character and narrator for the story is Fikile, whose name, in English, means 'arrived'. Fikile has left her rural community to study at university and returns home at the end of her studies to take up a job in a nearby town and marry her childhood sweetheart. She has travelled to a modern world and then journeyed back home. This dual journey is the central theme of the play. On her arrival, Fikile comments:

> I'm home … home? Even saying the word sounds different. (She repeats it to herself.) Home. Is Gamalakhe still my home? Can I make a life again here for myself? (14)

While Fikile has been exploring a new world, Sihle, the boyfriend who she left behind, buried both his parents, fell on hard times, developed an alcohol problem and got involved in petty crime. These hardships are representative of some of the problems that characterize the community that Sihle comes from.

As the story unfolds, we discover that Fikile met and fell in love with Colin, a boy at university. This use of an Anglicized name highlights the contrast with the home-boy Sihle. Colin represents a different way of life: privilege, education and the future. He is referred to in the script as a 'coconut' (brown on the outside, but white on the inside). Colin is also an artist, a photography student. Herein lies the conflict of the play: Does Fikile choose the old or the new man, the crook or the artist, the past or the future?

The structure of the play is a departure from the more common 'real-time' unfolding of many community theatre plays. The plot develops throughout a series of flashbacks: Fikile flying home, Fikile reminiscing with friends, remembering when she first fell in love with Sihle, remembering her first encounter with Colin. This structure serves to highlight the constant journeys and the difference between the two worlds or the rural poor and the urban elite. Fikile tells her best friend, Phumzile, about Colin:

> I often wonder where he is and what he is doing. What my life would have been like if I had stayed in Cape Town with him. Right now I am wondering if I made the wrong decision coming back home to be with Sihle. (Pause) Life is too full of choices. (23)

This consciousness of the choices that she has to make, and not knowing whether she has made the right one, highlights the difficulty for the audience of straddling two worlds, of leaving and returning. Phumzile comments: 'And it's those choices that make us who we are.'

As Fikile decides that Sihle, the old way of life, is the right choice for her, a parallel plot-line unfolds. An unnamed stranger arrives in the village, having been mugged and relieved of his valuables. He is helped by Zanele, Sihle's sister, who brings the stranger home to her brother's house. The man explains that he has come to propose to the girl he loves, but the ring was stolen along with his other possessions. This parallel story is underscored by the sister's comments:

> **Zanele:** My brother is getting married in two days' time. I know how important these jewels are to the ladies. We will take you to the police station in the morning. (27)

Sihle arrives home to find a strange man with his younger sister, and immediately becomes aggressive. The stranger is not given a chance to introduce or explain himself, and Fikile walks in.

> *The stranger rises from his chair as if he has seen a ghost.*
>
> **Man** Fikile.
>
> **Sihle** You know her?
>
> **Zanele** I thought you said ...
>
> **Fikile** *(Shocked, finally she says the words)* Colin!
>
> *Music ... Blackout.* (28)

This open-ended, soap-opera-like finale is extremely popular. The entertainment value of the piece is high, reminiscent of the popular melodrama and Kente's township theatre style.

The staging of *Fikile* is very simple, typical of the 'poor-theatre' style common in community theatre. Crates provide the seating arrangements and are moved around the stage to create different scenes and scenarios. Banana leaves and a wooden frame are used to suggest passing landscapes of the south coast and various vehicles. The bodies of the rest of the cast are used to create the aeroplane and other structures. Some of the characters carry simple props, such as Colin with his suitcase, symbolizing the transient outsider, and a hat for Fikile's father, signalling tradition and gravitas.

Singing is an important part of the production and is used to score various interlinking scenes and underscore the more emotional and dramatic material of the play. The music is sung by the company of actors and includes popular gospel and traditional songs, immediately recognizable to a local community audience. The songs serve to strengthen the idea that this play is representative of their shared community and shared experiences.

Fikile presents a recognizable scenario for many young, black South Africans, and in this sense is a great example of community theatre reflecting the concerns of the youth, something that the group deliberately sets out to do. This essence of community theatre is obvious, as is the influence of Coppen's hand in the economical dialogue and neat plot structure evident in the final version of the play. Again, we see an example of community and professional theatre makers coming together to create work that is both relevant and slick.

The future of a 'new' community theatre

Both of the groups mentioned in this chapter create theatre that is *by* and *for* a community of people. However, this community is not always fixed geographically. A broader audience can relate to topics of shared concern. The plays discussed in this chapter are indicative of issues that span the global and local. Local township audiences and audiences further afield can relate to these plays, which contain elements of both Western and African traditions and aesthetics. It is this transmutability that helps community theatre to thrive.

Contemporary community drama in South Africa may have grown from the Kente tradition of township musical theatre, but it has a more conscious role as message making rather than entertaining. However, it has clearly moved on from the apartheid-era protest theatre, as personal stories with less didactic messages are more often played out on stage. Today's community theatre plays an agenda-setting function for communities. The work itself is seen by its community-based creators as art, although this art is recognized as having functionality beyond being 'for art's sake'. This shift is where the real difference lies between the community theatre of the apartheid era and contemporary community work that must be popular and appealing to keep audiences interested.

Community theatre groups are claiming their territory in the mainstream theatre industry. Through collaborations and professionalization, this new wave of community theatre has a unique ability to move, entertain and educate communities with otherwise limited access to the live arts.

Acknowledgements: With thanks to Roel Twijnstra, Bongani Baai, Goso Shabalala and Siso Shabalala.

Notes

1. 'Townships' or 'locations' were demarcated densely populated urban areas developed under apartheid as dormitory suburbs for Black, Indian and Coloured populations, who moved closer to towns from rural areas for work, or were moved from their homes in what became 'whites only' areas.

2. Z. Mda, *The Role of Culture in the Process of Reconciliation in South Africa*, paper presented at the Centre for the Study of Violence and Reconciliation, Seminar No. 9, 30 November 1994, http://www.csvr.org.za/index.php/publications/1751 (accessed 20 September 2014).

3. The notion of popular theatre is twofold: one where it is conceived as theatre for the people and another where it is conceived as theatre by the people. Theatre for the people has been largely associated with Western theatre, and has been used as a controlling mechanism throughout the ages as a means of encouraging social stability and promoting a particular morality amongst the populace. Most often emanating from the dominant classes, this type of theatre has historically been deliberately overturned by workers' movements in many countries, who wanted to see their own values and interests represented on stage.

4. Gibson Kente, interview, 1987.

5. Mda, *The Role of Culture.*

6. Kente, interview.

7. Interview with Shabalala.

8. Xolani Dlongolo, interview, 2012.

9. Jerzy Grotowski's (1968) notion of Poor Theatre strongly influenced a stripped down theatre aesthetic in South Africa, with a reliance on physicality, the transmutability of objects and the minimal use of props, costumes or sets.

10. Bongani Baai, interview, September 2014.

11. Ibid.

Bibliography

Primary sources

Emuhle All Artists with Simphiwe Vilikazi, 'The Milk Factory', *New South African Scripts, 2011/2012* (Durban: Twist Theatre Development Projects, 2012).

Emuhle All Artists with Neil Coppen, 'Fikile', *New South African Scripts, 2012/2013* (Durban: Twist Theatre Development Projects, 2013).

Umsindo Theatre Projects with Neil Coppen, 'To Be Like This Rock', *New South African Scripts, 2010/2011* (Durban: Twist Theatre Development Projects, 2011).

Umsindo Theatre Projects with Amy Jephta, 'The Seed', *New South African Scripts, 2011/2012* (Durban: Twist Theatre Development Projects, 2012).

Secondary sources

Baai, Bongaini, interview, September 2014.

Davis, G. and A. Fuchs (eds), *Theatre and Change in South Africa* (London: Psychology Press, 1996).

Dlongolo, Xolani, interview, 2012.

Durden, E., *Dear Daughter, I want to tell you why I killed a man ... An investigation into crime and violence in the plays of community theatre groups*, conference presentation, Drama for Life Africa Research conference, University of Pretoria, December 2012.

Grotowski, J., *Towards a Poor Theatre* (Holstebro, Denmark: Odin Teatret Forlag, 1968).

Kente, Gibson, interview, 1987.

Kerr, D., *African Popular Theatre: From Pre-colonial Times to the Present Day* (London: James Currey; Portsmouth, NH: Heinemann, 1995).

Mda, Z., *The Role of Culture in the Process of Reconciliation in South Africa*, paper presented at the Centre for the Study of Violence and Reconciliation, Seminar No. 9, 30 November 1994, http://www.csvr.org.za/index.php/publications/1751 (accessed 20 September 2014).

Prentki, T. and S. Preston (eds), *The Applied Theatre Reader* (New York: Routledge, 2009).

Shabalala, Goso and Siso, interview.

Will, R., *The Role of the Artist in Society: 24 Interviews from South Africa* (Bloomington, IN: Xlibris Corporation, 1988).

CHAPTER 6
THE THEATRE MAKERS IN ONE-PERSON FORMAT
Veronica Baxter

Ronnie Govender, *At the Edge* and *1949*; Rajesh Gopie, *Out of Bounds*; Greig Coetzee, *The Blue Period of Milton van der Spuy*; Bheki Mkhwane, *Born Thru the Nose*; Omphile Molusi, *Itsoseng*; Philip Dikotla, *Skierlik*; Andrew Buckland, *Laugh the Buffalo*

Introduction

One-person or solo-performer shows are not uniquely South African, nor are performances that require the actor to play multiple characters. However solo, multi-character performances do require a physical dexterity or 'athleticism' for which South African actors have earned a formidable reputation.[1] This dexterity is more obvious in the South African style of what Paula T. Alekson calls a 'monopolylogue'[2] – that is, many characters played by one actor in the unfolding of a drama. The solo performance will be investigated through a selection of South African performances, focusing on the plays *At the Edge* and *1949* (Ronnie Govender), *Out of Bounds* (Rajesh Gopie), *The Blue Period of Milton van der Spuy* (Greig Coetzee), *Born Thru the Nose* (Bheki Mkhwane), *Itsoseng* (Omphile Molusi), *Skierlik* (Philip Dikotla) and *Laugh the Buffalo* (Andrew Buckland).

There are several iconic performances by South Africans that are not being considered in detail here, but some of these performances or performers are considered elsewhere in this book. For example, Pieter-Dirk Uys is probably South Africa's best known and most popular solo performer, especially for his character of Evita Bezuidenhout. This chapter will not consider Paul Slabolepszy's *The Return of Elvis Du Pisanie*, or Geraldine Naidoo and Matthew Ribnick's *The Chilli Boy*, or the multi-character performances of *White Men with Weapons* and *Breasts* from Greig Coetzee.

There may be fewer women than men in South African theatre working in the solo-performance genre, and even fewer performance texts with one woman playing multiple roles. I speculate that the solo genre works for women playing multiple *female* characters, but perhaps audiences do not read a woman playing male roles in the same way as they do a man playing female roles. I do not mean to imply that female performers are less adept than men in performing in multi-character solo performances, but rather to raise the question of whether, in the eyes of their audiences, women performers can only signify 'female' in South Africa – therefore playing male characters in a drama shifts their performance into caricature, whereas the same is not true for male actors. Most solo performances by women stay with either one character's biography or playing only female characters.

More recent work by women includes the autobiographical *Woman in Waiting* (Thembi Mtshali and Yaël Farber, 1999), as well as *Cheaper than Roses* (Ismail Mohamed, 1998), *A Coloured Place* (Lueen Conning, 1998) and *At Her Feet* (Nadia Davids, 2006). *At Her Feet* is a solo performance involving multiple characters, but is covered elsewhere in this book by Greg Homann. A different style of solo performance is Jemma Kahn's hit show *The Epicene Butcher and other Stories for Consenting Adults* (2013), narrated in the Japanese style of *kamishibai* or story picture (Moncho 2013).

According to Amy Pinney, the writer and performer of solo performances most often are the same person.[3] Pinney is most concerned with the role of director in making the performance, whom she suggests is also often the writer-performer. However, salient to this discussion is that Pinney argues that the solo performance is usually perceived to belong to the performer, and most people assume that the material is autobiographical. She argues that often the director's role is obscured or absent, which to some extent is true for the cases studied below.

Elspeth Tilley is persuasive when she argues that a 'polycharacter monodrama' (one actor playing many characters) is well-suited to representing post-colonial experiences, because it is by nature intercultural.[4] Citing Ric Knowles, she argues that a polycharacter monodrama provides 'contested, unsettling and often unequal spaces between cultures, spaces that can function in performance as sites of negotiation'. One actor embodying several characters creates a simultaneous reading of the actor, the character and the actor-as-character. Tilley cites Elin Diamond who argues that the actor is not subsumed by character, any more than the character by actor, allowing both to emerge in the drama.[5] The audience perceives both in time and space, seeing character and actor in a relationship to each other, and to themselves as audience. It is no wonder therefore that much solo performance reads as autobiographical.

The performances discussed below are selected for their ability to talk to their times – roughly speaking, the same time span as post-apartheid South Africa and the advent of democracy. Loren Kruger suggested that South African theatre was caught in a 'post-anti-apartheid' phase, where the stylistic elements of anti-apartheid theatre were recycled for the new era.[6] Perhaps only *Itsoseng* and *Skierlik* are similar to anti-apartheid protest pieces, but like the other works selected here for analysis, they too negotiate the identity formation of South Africans. Their non-realist mode of performance, while generating considerable empathy, still creates critical distance for the spectator.

Jonathan Kalb discusses solo performances that are specifically documentary in intention, discussing Brecht's *verfremdung* in the style of acting used by Anna Deavere Smith, for example.[7] Smith is famous for her quest to uncover the American character, through interviewing hundreds of people from whom she constructs what Kalb calls 'impressions'.[8] As Tilley suggests, her impersonations of selected people are not presented as illusory – Smith is always present underneath the character, providing a critical distance for the audience. In the work of several South African solo performances the nature of contradictions becomes clear – especially in a society where an obsession with race has characterized a painful history. Watching a single actor inhabit many characters, switching with seeming ease from one 'race' category to another, or perhaps across gender, gives South Africans an opportunity to resolve these contradictions, or at least to negotiate them through the eyes of a 'stranger'. Jill Dolan suggests that a monopolylogue 'models the fluidity of cultural identities' and offers an opportunity for 'a more hopeful dialogue about difference': that is, what she calls 'utopian performatives'.[9] While the work of South Africans here is not documentary (although some may be biographical), the solo performances do show the diversity of cultural identities in South Africa, and the element of distancing is common to the performances.

Andrew Buckland (based in the Eastern Cape for the past 30 years) had his initial success with *The Ugly Noonoo*. This play became iconic of early physical theatre in South Africa, and of socio-political critique infused with comedy that marks the solo performer work. Buckland followed this success with *Between the Teeth* (1991), *Feedback* (1994), *The Well Being* (1998), *Voetsek* (2007) and, in 2013, *Laugh the Buffalo*. In this time he also engaged with other performance and writing projects, working at Rhodes University, with the First Physical Theatre Company and UBOM theatre company.

Buckland's solo style and practice emerges from a strong mime background, where the audience has to work to complete the image being shown. This requires an active 'seeing' on the part of the audience, as well as exercising an imaginative leap into the multi-character world of the performance. He argues that the work of the theatre performer is not to present or represent someone on stage, but to embody them, as demonstrated in a TEDxRhodesU online talk.[10] The audience must work imaginatively to populate the stage with characters and props that are not actually there – Buckland pulling a rope or having an extended conversation with another character. In this TED talk, Buckland asserts that the theatre (and this type of theatre) is a fundamental human need, because it holds the key to our ability as humans to adapt to change through play. He argues that humans must play to learn, and theatre is the 'practice' our imaginations need.

His most recent performance was characteristic of his work and philosophy, with a story of a not very intelligent man who becomes embroiled in a secret service plot run by the 'Buffalo', who may be a whistle-blower. *Laugh the Buffalo* (directed by Janet Buckland) contains many allusions to the much-debated Protection of State Information Bill (that many read as an attack on civil liberties) and secrets and lies in government and business. Buckland depicts how the man must undergo 'training' in a ten-day silent retreat, and endure the ridiculous fidgeting and habits of his peers in order to prove himself worthy of a secret job.

The story was relatively incidental to the enjoyment of the performance, the physical and vocal clarity with which characters were created and the movement through what Richard Higgs describes as 'linguistic tricks and visual puns', where Buckland's body becomes 'a semantic object itself, pushing the boundaries of the very best in African storytelling art'.[11] It was billed as a performance that

> promises his characteristic combination of humour, an intense focus on the physicality of performance, clowning, satire, foolishness and dark consideration of the human condition, with serious doses of joy. (Baxter Theatre, 2013)

There is no doubt that Andrew Buckland[12] is the consummate physical clown, who sets the bar high for the solo form. He has one character that emerges strongly in many different performance pieces, arguably a 'stock' character that he has built on over the years. This character I am going to call the *dof ou*, meaning a slow-witted man, who is played with a heavy Eastern Cape accent. The *dof ou* is very literal in his understanding of the world around him, and incapable of nuance and symbolism. He is always the butt of the joke, even though he does not realize it. He is Andrew Buckland's foil – the *dof ou* is the mask that Buckland creates, through which much of the comedy is generated. This character is a stock character in the South African lexicon, recognizable in the 'boet and swaer' advertisements for a particular type of car oil, or the Corne and Twakkie show. The character generates humour because he is ponderous, literal and tries very hard. He aspires to be more than he is capable of, and has little insight into his own failings. His tragedy is very comic and is similar to the eponymous character in Greig Coetzee's *The Blue Period of Milton van der Spuy*.

Milton van der Spuy is one of Greig Coetzee's earlier characters, and is a tragi-comic *dof ou*. His tragedy is that he has been raised to aspire to artistic expression, without the intellect or skills for any accomplishment. His mother has married beneath her, her pregnancy ending her studies of art and the classics. Her aspirations are therefore focused on and through her children, naming them Milton (after John Milton) and Mona Lisa. Milton recounts a pitiful series of scenes in which Mona Lisa falls, his fantasies of flying and tree climbing giving way to the truth of her suicide from the eleventh floor of their flat building. His 'blue period' is in honour of her death, literally interpreted as needing to paint with blue, but unable to make a single mark on the canvas. Milton van der Spuy's comedy is his tortured artistic temperament, as he fails convincingly to paint, make a flying machine (like Leonardo da Vinci) or even cut off his ear with scissors (like van Gogh). His poetry is rejected. His failures are hilarious, as are his half-understood comments on Shakespeare's use of cliché and John Milton's bad rhyme. These comic asides belie the success he has had in killing his father in a puddle, which he now keeps in a bottle. His father has cheated them all it seems, causing Mona Lisa to jump, failing to appreciate his wife and telling Milton he has no talent.

Milton van der Spuy is an imaginary character for Greig Coetzee, but the play gestures towards a number of important ideas in contemporary South Africa. The play demonstrates the crisis of a white working-class family, trapped in poverty in a city high-rise; despite his mother's attempts to educate Milton, his lack of intelligence and the end of job reservation for whites mean that he will be unemployable.

Rajesh Gopie's *Out of Bounds* (published 2008) recounts the story of Lall, whose aspirations belie his origins in a working-class, extended family in Inanda and then Phoenix. The earlier action of the play takes place from 1985 in another time of conflict between black, Zulu-speaking and Indian South Africans, causing Indians to flee their homes in Inanda, near

Durban, and thus completing the forced removal of Indians to Chatsworth and Phoenix. Gopie's play focuses on a young boy, Lall, who grows up resenting his fate to share his life and bedroom with his grandmother and several cousins in their house in Inanda, and then to be moved to a humble flat in Phoenix. Desperate to escape his class origins he works his way to a university entrance and bursary, and then an international scholarship for the United States. Pretending that he is from somewhere other than Phoenix, constantly comparing his brown-suited father and smoking, sparrow-like mother to their rich, flamboyant relatives, his final snub of his parents is to publicly announce that his rich uncle Raj was his role model.

Similarly to Milton van der Spuy, Lall aspires to wealth and class mobility, something greater than what he has experienced growing up. The character shows a deep alienation from his origins in his actions, but the writer/performer's portrayal of the Inanda home, the connection between the soccer-loving brothers and the competing aunties is affectionate in the detail. Lall's love for his grandmother and the domestic worker Togo is a redeeming feature, and his sensitive recognition of his gay cousin, Amar, renders Lall likeable if somewhat confused. Lall is a typical product of a huge social upheaval, in this case the loss of stability and identity in Inanda, due to the attack on Indians by Zulu-speaking black Africans, and then the demise of apartheid a few years later. Two dramatic social changes in a short space of time created the type of crisis that simultaneously robbed Lall of his sense of self as Indian, part of an extended family and a 'Lallchand warrior'.[13] Gopie shows through Lall's story a traumatic upheaval which Hansen suggests is indicative of a 'deep and shared archive of fear',[14] but Lall's choice is to remove himself from home and become modern and Westernized. The play ends with Lall living in New York, receiving a call that his father has died.

Ronnie Govender's two plays for one actor, At the Edge (1987) and 1949, recount the stories of Cato Manor, Durban, South Africa in the mid-twentieth century – in particular, the painful, forced removal of the Indian community under apartheid and the 1949 conflict between black, Zulu-speaking and Indian South Africans. In some ways, these plays are reminiscent of anti-apartheid protest pieces, but they are largely constructed as memorials to the vibrant Indian community in Cato Manor. Vasu Reddy argues that 'memory is the active signifier in effecting the performance and staging of a self-consciousness',[15] that is, Govender as narrator/biographer is remembering a community that was fragmented, in his scripting and performance of the plays. While both these plays are quite old compared to others featured in this chapter, they have been regularly reperformed by female actors Leeanda Reddy (2000) and Jailoshni Naidoo (2010–14) in South African and Indian tours.

Govender's work is written in a vivid mix of formal English, as used by characters such as the principal of a school and a South African Indian *patois*. *At the Edge* is constructed out of four stories, 'Brothers of the Spirit', 'At the Edge', 'Paw Paw' and 'Over my Dead Body', each one a tale rich in community relationships and memory. All the way through each story there is a clear indication that an era is ending through the declaration that Cato Manor will be cleared and become white, after a forced removal of the Indian residents, but this is juxtaposed with often hilarious stories of characters that are larger than life, with nicknames like Cut-Throat-Bobby or Paw Paw. Hansen sees this as part of what he calls 'charou-dom', specifically part of the representation of the memory of an innocent time:

> Jokes, puns, and everyday mockery of the *charou* way of life consti-
> tuted an important medium for reflection on the past, the bewildering
> present, and a very uncertain future.[16]

Hansen argues that part of the post-apartheid Indian condition is a yearning for a time when Indian South Africans were set apart, when their position was protected and more secure by virtue of their Indian identity. He suggests that the longing for a previous time is 'a shameful yearning for a happy life in unfreedom'.[17] It is shameful because despite the apartheid oppression at that time there was a great sense of community, and people found ways to evade laws and manage unfair situations to advantage, much as Ronnie Govender's final character in the story 'Over my Dead Body' (2004).

Thunga Padayachee represents the defiant spirit of Cato Manor that is seen in other South African plays about forced removals (for example, *Sophiatown* or *District 6: The Musical*). He was what Govender terms a self-taught 'bush-awyer', the next best thing to a lawyer. In the early part of the story his expertise in side-stepping apartheid laws and creatively manipulating justice is made evident through his big-hearted and passionate defence of a school teacher and a poor family. When he is unable to evade the final piece of legislation – the forced removal of Indians from their homes in Cato Manor – the situation is filled with pathos. It is his disappointment in justice that makes his character's last stand against removal poignant. His belief in the law was undermined when he received a banning order under the Suppression of Communism, but after 180,000 people were removed to Chatsworth, including his children, Thunga loses regard for the law, and for the 'civilization' it supported. Already ailing he refuses to leave his home, and dies on the eve of his home being bulldozed, on his verandah. By 1968, Cato Manor was largely vacant, but ironically by 1980 some areas were re-zoned for Indian occupation again.

The play *1949* is also rooted in a storytelling tradition, only its last story dealing specifically with the violence of black residents of Mkhumbane against Indians in Cato Manor. The story makes evident how the violence is catastrophic for Indians and Zulus, but how it serves the apartheid agenda, providing justification for segregation legislation and forced removals. In the story, the black, Zulu-speaking Dumisane works in a garage whose white owner is vitriolic in his prejudice against Indians, and who actively incites his black African workers to attack the Cato Manor Indian residents. Dumisane tries to dissuade his work colleagues from becoming part of the violence, citing their Christian faith, and using the example of his landlord's family, the Manirams, who were poor but kind. While the mob violence erupts through Cato Manor, with houses and businesses burning, the Manirams have not run away but, at his bidding, hide in Dumisane's room. When they are discovered by the rampaging mob, Dumisane is killed because he is seen as a traitor.

Bheki Mhkwane performed his solo show as *Stickman* (2003) and then as more fully fledged, *Born thru the Nose* (2005), directed by Ellis Pearson. The play depicts a crisis faced by ordinary black South Africans who have jettisoned their cultural rites for the sake of a 'modern' and Westernized lifestyle. Mhkwane tells the story of Caiphus, a successful black executive, who is about to become a father for the first time. His wife has planned a modern hospital birth, to the disdain of his grandmother. When it seems as if the baby will never be born, a caesarean section seems imminent. His grandmother insists that this will be an inauspicious start if the child is 'born through the nose', and sends Caiphus on a journey to appease the ancestors. He is caught between the traditional world of his grandmother and his wife's modern demands, but embarks on his travels in order to bring peace to his homestead. On his journey he finds out the truth of his father and mother's lives and deaths on a farm in northern KwaZulu-Natal, subject to the cruelty of the white farmer, Van Wyk. Through much danger and strife, he is able to achieve peace by completing the traditional ceremonies to bring the spirits back to his home, and the baby is born safely.

Bheki Mkhwane brings a vigorous physical theatre style to the performance of the piece. He relates the story mostly as Caiphus, but seamlessly switches to play grandmother, white farmer and wife, through a subtle shift of weight and changes in voice and breathing. His move from confident but frustrated businessman to triumphant father is complex and layered, showing a panoply of South African characters through the body. The set lines of the racist farmer's jaw are reflected through the body; the cracks of the whip he wields are menacing. The contrast is with peace-loving Caiphus, initially wearing a business suit, but who becomes less Westernized in dress as he is pulled towards performing his traditional rites. He is trying to be the man of the family, but his manly assertiveness is humorously undermined by first his wife, bent over backwards by her enormous pregnant belly, and then his grandmother's indomitable will.

It is the invisible ancestors and traditional rites of passage of Zulu people that feature strongly in this performance. In some ways the piece is educational for its audiences, not all of whom may be familiar with the rites that preserve the role that the ancestors play in everyday life. Caiphus must fetch the spirit of his father home in order to release the next generation's birth. This he does by taking a branch of the *mphafa* tree (Buffalo Thorn) to the place of his father's death, and must carry his spirit to his own home. While the business of Caiphus fetching his father's spirit is wrapped in the high drama of realizing the truth of his death and avoiding Van Wyk's wrath, there are also moments of comedy with a farmworker, and the decision as to whether the *mphafa* branch will fit in his BMW, or if Caiphus is expected to walk all the way back to Durban.

The rites used to bring the ancestral spirit to the home of the living are not practised by all South Africans, but through this performance came to be understood and appreciated by the audience members. Jill Dolan invokes Benedict Anderson's 1982 concept of 'imagined communities', suggesting that during a performance she is

> reconstituting my own subjectivity and my own sense that time and space can be fluid and malleable. Something inexpressible flits before my eyes, resonates in my soul, a feeling of pleasure, a strong but inarticulate feeling of literally 'imagined community'.[18]

It is this experience of being part of an 'imagined community' that resonated strongly for audiences for *Born Thru the Nose*, and while Caiphus was in crisis at first, performing the rituals resolved the problems and gave him new respect for his traditions and family.

Solo performances written and performed by Omphile Molusi (*Itsoseng*, 2008) and Philip M Dikotla (*Skierlik*, 2013) are both extraordinary for their physical performances, but also for the narratives about splintered communities and the expression of disillusionment with South Africa's transformation.

Itsoseng was once a flourishing township in what was the 'homeland' of Bophutatswana. Molusi claims that his work is semi-autobiographical, in that Itsoseng is his home town. Omphile Molusi has been performing *Itsoseng* since 2006, staged at the National Arts Festival in South Africa, and it has garnered several awards since then, including a Fringe First at the Edinburgh Festival in 2008. His impetus for writing and performing the piece was frustration and disillusionment with his home town. In the play, the narrator figure is Mawilla, who is attending the funeral of his first love, Dolly. On the way he encounters the ruins of his town, the iconic places of his youth, including the shopping centre that was burnt down in protest during homeland rule. Along with Dolly, the ruined shopping centre represents Itsoseng's collapse into poverty, hopelessness and abandonment. Dolly has died from AIDS, after working as a prostitute. Mawilla recounts the promises made and broken by the politicians through the years, the improvements and rebuilding that never came.

The piece is evocatively performed, using minimal props made from rubbish from the site of the shopping centre. A discarded paper cup is folded on itself to become the mouth of a pimp warning Mawilla to keep away from Dolly; the limp flower becomes the ill Dolly, asking if she looks like a prostitute; a small box becomes her coffin. Memorable characters of Itsoseng are the young men who burn the shopping centre down. Although the shopping centre was the only one in the area, and represented the economic hub of the town, their actions are prompted by the blind belief that the new South Africa will build a bigger and better shopping centre. Even when this dream does not materialize, they cling to the same dogmatic political ideals. Freedom has failed to deliver on its promises in Itsoseng. In an interview, Molusi says 'we do not talk about those who are not benefitting from this freedom ... these guys do not have a voice to speak about their issues. This show for me was like a post-apartheid protest piece.'[19]

Itsoseng describes dystopian hopelessness and a narrative of loss. There is a suggestion of helplessness in the face of adversity, which is nothing like the protest theatre of the anti-apartheid movement. The play *Skierlik*, winner of the 2013 Zabalaza festival at the Baxter Theatre, and a Best New Play nomination from Fleur du Cap, is perhaps more angry than helpless. Written and performed by Phillip Dikotla, the play describes from Thomas's point of view how a young white man went on a shooting spree in the informal settlement of Skierlik (in 2008). The play initially describes how the settlement came into being with people who were forcibly removed from farmlands, who set up the shanty town *skielik* (Afrikaans for 'suddenly'). Thomas grew up there, built a home, married and had a child. Then he recounts how 17-year-old Afrikaner Johan Nel shot and killed four people, including his little family. He describes his reluctance to return to the place that holds these memories, and the difficulty of forgiveness and acceptance. The play is uncompromising, angry, in its indictment of South Africa's failure to transform and reconcile.

Tilley argues that polycharacter monodrama 'breaks down old, reified constructs of bounded subjectivity to make space for new, living, plural forms'.[20] This is especially important for reading solo performances with an optimistic eye – in that if an actor can play roles that interculturally transcend race, gender, age and class, the audiences can see in that moment of transcendence a type of utopia, the much desired non-racial South Africa. This echoes Jill Dolan's idea that the monopolylogue play 'performing across cultural identities in the formalized space of theatre might provoke utopian performatives that offer glimpses of how people might be together in a more respectful, care-full, loving human community'.[21]

Notes

1. Cf. David Alcock, 'Somatic Emphasis in South African Theatre: Intervention in the Body Politic', in Marcia Blumberg and Dennis Walder (eds), *South African Theatre and/as Intervention* (Amsterdam: Rodopi, 1999), Mark Fleishman, 'Physical Images in the Theatre of South Africa', *South African Theatre Journal* 11:1–2 (1997): 109–24.

2. Paula T. Alekson, '"A Cast of One": The History, Art and Nature of the One-Person Show', *An Iliad*, McCarter Theatre Center, 2010, http://www.mccarter.org/aniliad/html/5.html (accessed 20 December 2013).

3. Amy Pinney, 'Between a Director and a Cast of One: A Beginning Aesthetic', *Theatre Topics* 16:2 (2006): 183.

4. Elspeth Tilley, 'Staging a "Plurality of Vision": Diasporic Performance in Polycharacter Monodrama', *Modern Drama* 55:3 (2012): 304.

5. Ibid., 308.

6. Loren Kruger, *The Drama of South Africa: Plays, Pageants and Publics Since 1910* (London: Routledge, 1999), 191.

7. Jonathan Kalb, 'Documentary Solo Performance: The Politics of the Mirrored Self', *Theater* 31:3 (2001): 13–29.

8. Ibid., 18.

9. Jill Dolan, "'Finding Our Feet in the Shoes of (One An) Other": Multiple Character Solo Performers and Utopian Performatives', *Modern Drama* 45:4 (2002): 499 and 496.

10. Andrew Buckland, 'Theatre or Extinction – Choose!', Andrew Buckland at TEDxRhodesU, 16 August 2012, https://www.youtube.com/watch?v=C8DWMCbAyEs&list=PLa1ZB5Hy6werDq-k-U_f9PcHsfBrLHbEv (accessed 20 December 2013).

11. Richard Higgs, 'Andrew Buckland's Laugh the Buffalo', *Artspoken and Reviews*, 22 October 2013, www.artslink.co.za/news_article.htm?contentID=34146 (accessed 20 December 2013).

12. Buckland has been profoundly influential in his solo performances and the development of his physical style. It is beyond the scope of this chapter to discuss other solo performers that he has trained and collaborated with, inter alia Craig Morris (*Flicker, Hero, Blood Orange*), Tim Redpath (*Prodigal, Mouche*) and Rob Murray (*Conspiracy of Clowns* and former artistic director of FTH:K).

13. Rajesh Gopie, *Out of Bounds* (Cape Town: Junkets Publisher, 2008), 33.

14. Thomas Blom Hansen, 'Melancholia of Freedom: Humour and Nostalgia among Indians in South Africa', *Modern Drama: World Drama from 1850 to the Present* 48:2 (2005): 117.

15. Vasu Reddy, 'History and Memory: Writing by Indian Authors', in Nahem Yousaf (ed.), *Apartheid Narratives* (Amsterdam: Rodopi, 2001), 95.

16. Hansen, 'Melancholia of Freedom', 298.

17. Ibid., 299.

18. Dolan, 'Finding Our Feet in the Shoes of (One An) Other', 497.

19. Omphile Molusi, 'Omphile Molusi', Afrovibes Festival, Amsterdam, 30 October 2013, https://www.youtube.com/watch?v=scsI_Bfdsxg (accessed 23 May 2014).

20. Tilley, 'Staging a "Plurality of Vision"', 307.

21. Dolan, 'Finding Our Feet in the Shoes of (One An) Other', 496.

Bibliography

Alcock, David, 'Somatic Emphasis in South African Theatre: Intervention in the Body Politic', in Marcia Blumberg and Dennis Walder (eds), *South African Theatre and/as Intervention* (Amsterdam: Rodopi, 1999).

Alekson, Paula T., "'A Cast of One": The History, Art and Nature of the One-Person Show', *An Iliad*, McCarter Theatre Center, 2010, http://www.mccarter.org/aniliad/html/5.html (accessed 20 December 2013).

Brown, Duncan, 'Narrative, Memory and Mapping: Ronne Govender's "At the Edge" and Other Cato Manor Stories', in Taoufik Agoumy, Taieb Belghazi and

David Richards (eds), *Urban Generations: Post-Colonial Cities*, Conferences and Colloquia 126 (Rabat: Faculty of Letters of Rabat, 2005), pp. 297–313.

Buckland, Andrew, 'Theatre or Extinction – Choose!', Andrew Buckland at TEDxRhodesU, 16 August 2012, https://www.youtube.com/watch?v=C8DWMCbAyEs&list=PLa1ZB5Hy6werDq-k-U_f9PcHsfBrLHbEv (accessed 20 December 2013).

De Beer, Diane, 'Ex-stand-up Comic Stands up for Poor', *Tonight – Independent online*, 2014, http://www.iol.co.za/tonight/what-s-on/western-cape/ex-stand-up-comic-stands-up-for-poor-1.1663013#.U3iJSvmSzkA (accessed 20 December 2013).

Dolan, Jill, '"Finding Our Feet in the Shoes of (One An) Other": Multiple Character Solo Performers and Utopian Performatives', *Modern Drama* 45:4 (2002): 495–518.

Fleishman, Mark, 'Physical Images in the Theatre of South Africa', *South African Theatre Journal* 11:1–2 (1997): 109–24.

Gopie, Rajesh, *Out of Bounds* (Cape Town: Junkets Publisher, 2008).

Hansen, Thomas Blom, 'Melancholia of Freedom: Humour and Nostalgia among Indians in South Africa', *Modern Drama: World Drama from 1850 to the Present* 48:2 (2005): 297–315.

Hansen, Thomas Blom, *Melancholia of Freedom: Social Life in an Indian Township in South Africa* (Princeton, NJ: Princeton University Press, 2012).

Higgs, Richard, 'Andrew Buckland's Laugh the Buffalo', *Artspoken and Reviews*, 22 October 2013, www.artslink.co.za/news_article.htm?contentID=34146 (accessed 20 December 2013).

Kalb, Jonathan, 'Documentary Solo Performance: The Politics of the Mirrored Self', *Theater* 31:3 (2001): 13–29.

Kruger, Loren, *The Drama of South Africa: Plays, Pageants and Publics Since 1910* (London: Routledge, 1999).

Molusi, Omphile, 'Omphile Molusi', Afrovibes Festival, Amsterdam, 30 October 2013, https://www.youtube.com/watch?v=scsI_Bfdsxg (accessed 23 May 2014).

Moncho, Kgomotso, 'Five Female Theatre Makers in South Africa You Should Know', 2013, http://afripopmag.com/2013/07/five-female-theatre-makers-in-south-africa-you-should-know/ (accessed 17 May 2014).

Pinney, Amy, 'Between a Director and a Cast of One: A Beginning Aesthetic', *Theatre Topics* 16:2 (2006): 183–91.

Reddy, Vasu, 'History and Memory: Writing by Indian Authors', in Nahem Yousaf (ed.), *Apartheid Narratives* (Amsterdam: Rodopi, 2001), 81–100.

Snyder, Marilu, 'Megan Furniss Intrigues and Entertains in One-Woman Show', *What's on in Cape Town*, 2013, http://www.whatsonincapetown.com/post/megan-furniss-intrigues-in-innovative-one-woman-show/ (accessed 13 May 2014).

Thurman, Chris, 'Review: *Out of Bounds*', 2008, http://www.christhurman.net/art-and-culture/item/one-man-show-gets-to-heart-of-indian-identity.html (accessed 13 May 2014).

Tilley, Elspeth, 'Staging a "Plurality of Vision": Diasporic Performance in Polycharacter Monodrama', *Modern Drama* 55:3 (2012): 304–28.

PART II
PLAYWRIGHTS

CHAPTER 7
ATHOL FUGARD
Dennis Walder

(The) Blood Knot; Boesman and Lena; Sizwe Bansi is Dead; The Island; 'Master Harold' ... and the Boys; The Road to Mecca

Introduction

Athol Fugard is South Africa's most well known and prolific dramatist. As writer, actor and director, he has been a major influence upon the country's theatre for the last half century, an achievement that received fitting tribute when a theatre was established in his name in a renovated church hall in the former District 6 in Cape Town in 2010. Since the 1960s his plays have commanded audiences worldwide, although for many years they were premiered in his own country, in marginal, non-mainstream venues, with himself as director and, often, lead actor. His plays reveal a society in which the form of racist ideology known as apartheid created suffering of an intensity that shocked and which is yet depicted as potentially survivable. His is a dark vision of pain that never excludes the possibility of hope and dignity.

In the majority of his (more than thirty) plays, Fugard focuses upon two or three characters caught within a relationship of shifting power and dependency that simultaneously embodies the tensions, fears and hopes of their society. Simple, often circular plots, static settings and minimal props signal a dramatic language familiar from the work of Samuel Beckett – an obvious influence. Yet unlike Beckett, Fugard is always rooted in the local and particular, in what he refers to as the 'textures' of his 'one little corner' of the world.[1] This corner is the Eastern Cape region of South Africa, and it is a corner to which he remains attached through a house in Nieu Bethesda, a small village in the semi-desert Karoo near Middelburg, where he was born in 1932. In 1935 the family moved to Port Elizabeth, at the time a somewhat desolate, windswept, semi-industrial coastal town, where his mother kept the family going (his father was a disabled alcoholic) by running a boarding house and then a tearoom. His mother's strength lies behind a series of powerful female figures in his work.

The young Fugard was an omnivorous reader, which was just as well, given the limited opportunities offered by local schools. After technical college, he attended the University of Cape Town, where he studied social anthropology and philosophy; after three years he left without taking a degree to hitchhike north to the Sudan, where he signed on for a two-year stint on a tramp steamer bound for the Far East – an experience which he said cured him of the racism endemic among South Africans. He began writing while on board ship, an experience depicted in the memoir-play *The Captain's Tiger* (1997), although it was not until he and his wife Sheila began living in Johannesburg in the 1950s, near the soon-to-be-demolished (because multiracial) township Sophiatown, that his dramatic instincts found effective form, in two plays with black amateur casts. As a clerk in the court that sent black South Africans to prison for not having the right pass (to live or work in a given area), Fugard saw apartheid at first hand, although it was not until nearly two decades later that he created a form of theatre that effectively and brilliantly bore witness to the suffering of black people under that system – notably in two of the most renowned works associated with him: *Sizwe Bansi is Dead* (1972) and *The Island* (1973). But if the political thrust of these plays was obvious, as increased pressure upon the playwright and his collaborator-performers proved, his work has never been limited to protest. Rather, it was and is about offering a voice to the voiceless, the excluded and the marginalized, whatever their race or class, during and after the apartheid era.

Throughout his career, Fugard's work has revolved around a few fundamental themes: identity, pain, guilt and survival. He is not simply a 'liberal', although his work promotes liberal, humane values. Like Albert Camus, whom he resembles as well as admires, he comes from the underprivileged white sector of the population which formerly ruled the country; and like Camus, he remains pessimistic about the human condition, while optimistic about individuals. The central issue is what Hegel identified as the problem of recognition. For Hegel, all consciousness involves the desire to be recognized by other consciousnesses, which leads to a view of human relations as a perpetual struggle, a struggle which, says Camus, is absurd, since, in the event of one consciousness being destroyed by the will to power of another, the victorious consciousness 'cannot be victorious in the eyes of something that no longer exists'. Hence absurdity, rather than tragedy, is the end of human endeavour; hence, too, the yearning for meaning in an absurd or meaningless universe, which brings an emphasis on the immediate, concrete facts of existence.[2]

This emphasis, which in Fugard translates into an emphasis upon what he calls 'carnal reality',[3] is apt for a dramatist, since it involves a focus upon the body; and it is in live performance that his plays succeed best – their surface often opaque, written scripts for performance, rather than texts for close verbal analysis. Nonetheless, his dialogue captures the speech rhythms of his chosen characters with startling accuracy and humour; where he falters is when he adopts a more abstract idiom, as in the relatively unsuccessful, semi-mythological *Dimetos* (1975), an attempt to comprehend the role of the artist as maker, at a time when he was going through a radical self-questioning.

Fugard has always protested against the prevailing tide of opinion, which, in the era since Nelson Mandela's release in 1990, has meant resisting attempts to identify with the new, multiracial and democratic regime in his country while it has, in his view, shown distressing signs of corruption and neglect. His post-apartheid work – such as *Valley Song* (1996), *Sorrows and Rejoicings* (2002) and *Coming Home* (2009) – has tended towards a nostalgic return to the past, and, after living mainly in his own country, he has relocated to San Diego in the USA – where he has always received most acclaim, including a Lifetime Tony Award and a Yale doctorate, among many other honours and awards.

In addition to his plays, Fugard has written a prose memoir (*Cousins*, 1994), a novel (*Tsotsi*, 1980) which became a successful film (in 2005), and has collaborated in the cinematic reworking of several plays, while scripting two feature films (*The Guest at Steenkampskraal*, 1976, and *Marigolds in August*, 1979). His *Notebooks* (up to 1977) were edited by his close friend and anti-apartheid activist the late Mary Benson; extracts continue to appear in programme notes.

The plays

(The) Blood Knot *(1961, 1985)*

The Blood Knot was the first of a series of plays set in Port Elizabeth. It also marked the beginning of Fugard's reputation as a serious playwright, with the potential to affect audiences at home and abroad. He began writing this play while in London, where he and his wife had been vainly trying to find work in the theatre. On hearing news of the 1960 Sharpeville massacre (in which sixty-nine unarmed black protestors were shot dead by police, and many injured), he determined to return home. The time had come to acknowledge what was happening in his country. Yet his play was in the first instance about neither politics nor protest, although it clearly embodied the country's obsession with race. It was about the relationship between two mixed-race brothers, Morris and Zach, living together in a one-room shack on the grim city outskirts. Their sole possessions are a Bible and an alarm clock. Morris is light skinned enough to 'try for white'; Zach has no such hopes. Insecure in his identity, Morris tries to put on whiteness like a coat, while Zach eggs him on, until a final confrontation exposes the futility of his dreams.

When the play was first performed, with Fugard playing Morris and Zakes Mokae playing Zach, in a rundown former clothing factory in Johannesburg's central business district in 1961, the production lasted four hours and included much improvisation. Cut to a manageable length, it toured the country, the two performers obliged by law to travel separately. When it appeared on UK TV in 1967, the South African regime rescinded Fugard's passport, which was not returned until 1971, after a public petition to enable him to direct *Boesman and Lena* in London's Royal Court. Thereafter he was too well known internationally for further action to be taken against him directly.

By 1985, a more compressed version of *The Blood Knot* with the original cast appeared in New York, entitled simply *Blood Knot*. The opening image, which stunned its original, invited, multiracial Johannesburg audience, remained: not just a white and a black together on stage, but the former washing the feet of the latter in a nightly ritual. Before a word was spoken, the basic power relationship at the heart of their society was challenged. When the play first appeared in London in 1963, the influential theatre critic Kenneth Tynan remarked that it was merely about white guilt; but as Fugard wryly remarked thirty-four years later, 'Today Tynan is in his grave and the *Blood Knot* isn't.'[4]

The play is about guilt, certainly, as it is about such related emotions as anger, shame and envy. But who is to say these are not relevant themes, then as now? And the underlying, interpersonal dynamic between the two brothers enables audiences anywhere to identify with the two men. As the play proceeds, through imaginary games and role-playing, it emerges that although they had different fathers, they had the same mother: a washer-woman who, in one of the play's most troubling moments, they pretend to stone. This occurs at the start of the final exchanges, when Morris performs the role of the rude and arrogant white man so well that it provokes his brother into attacking him – almost. Earlier, Zach has pushed the reluctant Morris to be his substitute when, to their surprise, a white girl agrees to be Zach's 'corresponding penpal of the opposite sex' (Scene One, p. 64), and a meeting is arranged. But, as Morris points out, the girl and her policeman brother won't be happy to see Zach.

Zachariah   What have I done, hey? I done nothing.

Morris   What have you thought, Zach, that's the crime. I seem to remember somebody saying 'I like the thought of this little white girl.' And what about your dreams, Zach? They've kept me awake these past few nights. I've heard them mumbling and moaning away in the darkness ... All they need for evidence is a man's dreams. (92)

The play opens out momentarily into the contemporary world of detentions and interrogation, before returning to the relationship between the two brothers, and the problem they face: how to respond to Ethel Lange of Oudtshoorn, 'eighteen years old and well developed', who wants to contact 'a gent of sober habits and a good outlook on life' (68).

Zach proposes that Morris pretend to be such a gent, using his wages to buy a suit, and take on a new identity. But 'There's more to wearing a white skin than just putting on a hat' (103), objects his brother, in a turn of phrase that, as with all these all early plays (*Hello and Goodbye*, 1965, is another), carries an ironic weight beyond the laughter. Two dream monologues express the brothers' yearnings for acceptance and dignity, yearnings dispelled by the conclusion, when their final 'game' – as Morris pretends to be the white master while Zach plays his 'simple, trustworthy type of John-boy' – gets out of hand, and Zach rises up to hit his brother, before the sound of their alarm clock returns them to the present and an acceptance that 'we're tied together' by the blood knot, 'the bond between brothers' (121–3).

As Fugard's play anticipates, it was only by a recognition of mutuality and a shared inheritance that the country's transition to democracy became possible; equally, the play demonstrates the ever-present potential for violence.

Boesman and Lena *(1969)*

In *Boesman and Lena*, Fugard took his Port Elizabeth family dramas a stage further, towards an extreme of poverty and despair, which, nevertheless, allows for a glimpse of transcendence. The Coloured (mixed-race) couple at its centre are houseless wanderers, even further beyond the pale than the brothers of *Blood Knot*. Fugard was inspired to write the play by observing a number of itinerants, including a woman on the banks of the Swartkops River on the outskirts of Port Elizabeth, walking 'like a somnambulist', her face 'shrivelled and distorted by dissipation, resentment, regrets'. She represented a 'demand that the truth be told', he said, noting 'the texture of that place – the mudflats'.[5]

As Stanley Kauffmann observed of the first American production, with James Earl Jones, Ruby Dee and Zakes Mokae in New York in 1970, 'On this mud, out of which we all come, Boesman and Lena make their camp.'[6] This encapsulates almost the entire action of the play – except that an elderly black man comes out of the surrounding darkness to share the fire belonging to the couple on the mudflats, and then dies. Boesman and his partner Lena take up their burdens again and move on. The minimal setting, sparse action and pared-down dialogue suggest an extreme beyond which human endurance cannot go.

But for Fugard, telling the truth of the situation he has witnessed is uppermost, and that is rooted in the time and place of its telling. This time we know where we are, politically speaking: the two squatters' *pondok* (makeshift dwelling) has been razed by the white man's bulldozer, and they carry on their shoulders the burden of centuries of colonial, racist exploitation as well as the more immediate impact of apartheid re-zoning. *Boesman and Lena* is the only one of his plays in which the word 'apartheid' appears; but, as always with Fugard, he avoids polemic, preferring to probe below the socio-political surface of his chosen setting in the search for truth – a truth which includes elements of yearning, as it includes the bitter laughter of the desperate.

'Now's the time to laugh', exclaims Lena at the beginning of the play, as she sarcastically recalls Boesman's impotent laughter when the bulldozers knocked their dwelling down. She looks up and curses the bird whose ability to fly in the sky overhead represents a freedom she yearns for –

Lena ... (... *scrambles to her feet and shakes her fist at it*)

Jou moer! [you cunt] ...

So slowly … ! Must be a feeling, hey. Even your shadow so heavy
you leave it on the ground.

(*She sits down again, even more exhausted now by her outburst. She
cleans the mud from between her toes as she talks.*)

Tomorrow they'll hang up there in the wind and laugh. We'll be in
the mud. I hate them. (194–5)

The two-act play is replete with curses, which led to it being banned by the
Cape school board in 1984 (copies were burnt). The censors were perhaps
unaware of its implications. Lena speaks the language of the dispossessed,
through which there shines a desire for freedom.

To begin with, Lena cannot remember where she has been; and her
partner cruelly taunts her by adding to her confusion. He is about to
attack her physically when the elderly Outa ('uncle', as Lena calls him)
appears, to be abused in his turn. His presence provokes Boesman's
futile jealousy, but Lena turns to him to bear witness to her sufferings
– the beatings, the miscarriages in the dark. Outa cannot understand
her language; he talks only his own, Xhosa (the local African language,
varied in performance). It is a weary, melancholy monotone, another tale
of endless travails. When Boesman returns to their makeshift hovel at
the end of the Act One, Lena remains outside with Outa, companions in
suffering.

An hour later, in Act Two, Lena suddenly transcends her earthbound,
mortal existence, stamping her feet down on the river mud in a wild song:

Korsten had its empties
Swartkops got its bait
Lena's got her bruises
Cause Lena's a *Hotnot meid* … (234)

Most critics see no hope for the disoriented, abused Lena, but her dance
has a transfiguring effect on stage, especially as it was first performed by
Fugard's remarkable Cape actor Yvonne Bryceland (1925–92). Her song,
which lists the various places through which she and her partner have
wandered, and whose names she struggles to recall throughout the play,
represents an affirmation of identity, while defying her outcast status as a
bruised and battered '*Hotnot meid*' – an insulting term derived from the

settler naming of the first inhabitants of the Cape. She effectively throws her abuse back into the face of authority and the audience, as well as towards her partner, Boesman (his name another term of racist abuse), whose bullying has reduced her to a childless cipher.[7]

Boesman hates Lena because he hates himself: she is defined by her pain, he is defined by his shame; both of them are caught between the white man who rejects them and the black man who sympathizes while residing in his own world of even deeper, incomprehensible agony. Yet again, there is more to their lives than the dark mud from which they have emerged and to which they return at the end. For Alan Shelley, they are at least obliged to admit that they have a relationship as strong as the blood knot that binds Morris and Zachariah; for Albert Wertheim, Lena finds a freedom in her celebration of the basics of life – a fire, a mug of tea, a piece of bread – that has religious overtones.[8] While crucially, as Marcia Blumberg pointed out in noting the casting of black South African Nomhle Nkonyeni as Lena for the 1993 Market Theatre production, the choice of actor performing Lena will also always have significant implications.[9] All agree that this is one of Fugard's greatest plays.

Sizwe Bansi is Dead *(1972) and* The Island *(1973)*

On the completion of *Boesman and Lena*, Fugard expressed 'nagging doubts' about its socio-political content. Despite its indictment of the system, was it explicit enough, he asked himself, or had he failed to align himself with the forces of change and resistance in the country?[10] In a sense, he need not have worried: not only did his plays articulate the ground for an alternative vision of the country from that proposed by the government, but his drive to bear witness to the lives of the victims of apartheid soon created a remarkable group of experiments with play making that placed his chosen actors' experiences at the centre of the stage, challenging through production and performance the very divisions upon which the state relied.

It all began when Fugard was approached by a group of township residents who had heard of *The Blood Knot* and who wanted the playwright's help in developing a drama group – this, in a country without drama schools for black people, and a long history of keeping the races apart, right down to the laws forbidding interracial sex – which Fugard attacked head on in a play developed with Yvonne Bryceland. The play was *Statements After An Arrest Under the Immorality Act* (1972). The key to this play and, to a varying degree, the other two so-called 'Statements' plays is the fraught issue of identity in a context in which who you are and how that is defined is a matter of everyday experience – as it was, for example, for Jews during the Nazi era. As Jeanne Colleran remarked, while many plays by Fugard (and other South African dramatists) present the effects of the race laws then governing his country, few presented the very core of the issue: the prohibition against skin contact. She went on to make a persuasive case for the continuing validity of *Statements After An Arrest*, a work which takes actors and audiences into a nightmare world of nakedness of body and soul as it explores the impact of transgressive desire.[11]

For all that *Statements* indicates the playwright's interest in the 'sub-textual' dimension of staging; hovering as it does between realism and dream, it marks a difficult, tendentious phase in his obsessive struggle to express the 'carnal reality' of life during the apartheid era, lacking the grip of the more accessible theatre he found himself working on with the Serpent Players – the group of township residents who approached him to help satisfy their 'hunger' for expression.[12] Two Serpent Players formed an abiding creative partnership with him: John Kani and Winston Ntshona, whose naturalistic performances drawing on personal experience provided the bedrock for *Sizwe Bansi* and *The Island*. Both plays deal explicitly with race legislation – the former the pass laws, the latter the island prison to which political offenders were sent (Nelson Mandela was there for 27 years); both plays initially brought police harassment; both have survived the disappearance of the laws they challenged.

The unique combination of Fugard's push towards a Grotowskian emphasis upon the actor's creative resources and Kani and Ntshona's ability to draw on the immediate, everyday experiences of black people in South Africa resulted in a uniquely powerful form of witnessing in the theatre. The 'mandate' or origin of *Sizwe Bansi* lay in a studio photo of a black man smiling: this was workshopped into a complex web of interwoven monologues, from the opening (initially improvised) account of the arrival of 'Mr Henry Ford Junior number two' at the local Ford plant, prompting the departure of Styles to set up his own photo studio, a 'strong-room of dreams. The dreamers? My people. The simple people, who you never find mentioned in the history books.' Such a person arrives in the shape of the hesitant 'Robert', who desires a 'snap' to send his wife. As the camera flashes, the stage blacks out, a single spot remaining on 'Robert' as he dictates a letter to his wife, revealing his true name, Sizwe Bansi, and his story, of being unable to find work without a valid pass, until his friend Buntu (the same actor who plays Styles) persuades him to take on the identity of the dead Robert they have stumbled across in the street outside a shebeen. Fugard recorded a 'near-riot' in the township during a performance there, people reacting with 'disbelief, panic and fear' when the actors exchanged Robert's photo for the dead Sizwe's.[13]

In both plays, acting is a means of survival, even celebration. The 'mandate' for *The Island* was a two-man version of *Antigone* performed by political prisoners on Robben Island. The four-scene play begins with an extended mime, two shaven-headed prisoners in shorts digging sand, each in turn filling a wheelbarrow and emptying it where the other is digging, a Sisyphean task parodying the struggle of the Greek heroine to bury her brother, just as black South Africans were struggling to deal with the unnumbered victims of the state. All the ensuing action takes place in a small space on the bare floor, a metaphor for imprisonment. The two men decide to relieve their suffering by presenting their version of the ancient Greek play to the warders and their fellow inmates. When John (first performed by John Kani) instructs Winston (Ntshona) to play the heroine, he laughs at the burly man in the makeshift wig and false breasts, who tears them off in disgust:

Winston   You call laughing at me, Theatre? Then go to hell with your Theatre! ...

John   Sure I laughed ... But just remember this, brother, nobody laughs forever! There'll come a time when they'll stop laughing, and that will be the time when our Antigone hits them with her words. (209)

The play-within-the-play climaxes as Winston stands before the imagined prison audience as Antigone, pleading guilty to infringing the laws of the state, but then instead of committing suicide, tears off his Greek disguise to go to his 'living death' unrepentant. The play concludes by echoing the opening mime of the prisoners shackled together, running, as a siren wails and darkness descends. Some critics saw this as implying an acceptance of the status quo, predictable from a privileged white perspective. But it could more persuasively be seen as reflecting the solidarity in suffering that eventually brought down the regime. Either way, unlike the drearily one-dimensional 'protest' theatre of the time, Fugard and his collaborators successfully articulated the demand of the voiceless to be heard. Probably no single South African play has had such a powerful impact upon international opinion.

'Master Harold' ... and the Boys *(1982)*

Fugard has always maintained that his plays come as 'appointments' to be met. The longest wait involved the incident that became the autobiographical *'Master Harold'*. When he was a teenager helping his mother in the St George's Park Tearoom in Port Elizabeth, Fugard and Sam Semela, a waiter and the 'most significant – the only – friend' of his boyhood, had 'a rare quarrel'. In a 'truculent silence' they closed the café and set off, the boy following the man and, 'as I rode behind him I called his name'; he turned, and 'as I cycled past, I spat in his face. Don't suppose I will ever deal with the shame that overwhelmed me the second after I had done that.'[14] Audiences were shocked and divided by the onstage representation of this incident – some arguing that Sam should have hit back after the boy spits in his face, others that passivity shames the perpetrator all the more. What the play seeks is an understanding of the roots of violence in feelings of guilt and betrayal. Like all his plays, *'Master Harold'* focuses closely upon a nexus of personal relationships in a way that has larger implications. For many, this is Fugard's masterpiece.

Initially banned from production in South Africa, *'Master Harold'* was the first of Fugard's full-length works to be premiered abroad, at the Yale Repertory in New Haven in 1982, before transferring to New York and, finally, a year later, to the Market Theatre in Johannesburg. The tearoom setting is more realistic in detail than in any of the previous plays. As the play begins, Willie is mopping the floor while Sam leans nonchalantly against a table, advising his workmate how to conduct himself in the forthcoming New Brighton (township) dancing championships. Willie is as clumsy as Sam is graceful. Sam imagines a world of happy dancers, while Willie's thoughts run on a more brutally physical level – a variation on the theme of the contrasted brothers of *The Blood Knot*. When the young white 'master' Hally (Fugard's boyhood nickname) arrives, the closeness of the two 'boys' and their 'master' is invoked through shared memories, until a telephone call from Hally's hospitalized father breaks the spell. The boy is tormented by the thought of his crippled father coming home, and when Sam – his surrogate father – tries to divert him, he repeats an ugly racist joke about black 'arses', upon which Sam tears off his jacket, pulls down his trousers and presents his backside *'for Hally's inspection'* (45). The boy cannot look; and when Sam puts a forgiving hand on his shoulder, he spins round and spits in Sam's face.

This was a moment of theatrical shock that had audiences react in horror and disbelief, followed by feelings of guilt (among whites) and anger (among blacks). Early productions in America and South Africa had audience members shouting out, or stunned into silence. But as John Kani remarked of the Market Theatre production in Johannesburg in 1983, while playing Sam was 'something hard and hurtful', yet he did it 'for a vital lesson to be learnt'.[15] The lesson remains relevant. We are invited to identify with Hally's rejection of his surrogate father, clearly the outcome of his loneliness and anger, but also to understand the response of the older black man, who, with awful self-control, wipes his face and suggests they 'try again'. The play ends with the white boy watching as the two servants dance together, an image suggestive of black empowerment.

In a later work, *Playland* (1992), Fugard developed the theme of reconciliation: set in a travelling amusement park on New Year's Eve 1989, a young white veteran of the Angolan border war (1966–89) encounters a middle-aged black night watchman to whom he reveals his involvement in an atrocity. The result is a shared revelation of past violence, and an attempt to suggest that only mutual forgiveness will suffice. The play is marred by the moral imbalance between the white veteran's engagement in a war crime and the black watchman's murder of his wife's rapist. But it was timely in suggesting that violence only breeds further violence, as the country fell ever deeper into bloodshed during the 1980s.

The Road to Mecca *(1984)*

Fugard's interest in female characters is evident throughout his career. Lena in *Boesman and Lena*, Hester in *Hello and Goodbye* (1965), Milly in *People Are Living There* (1968), Frieda in *Statements After An Arrest*, Gladys in *A Lesson From Aloes* (1978) are all older women; but there are also the younger women at the centre of *Dimetos*, *My Children! My Africa!* (1989), *Valley Song* (1995) and *Sorrows and Rejoicings* (2001). Taken together, these characters represent variations upon the theme of survival in terms of gender difference in the context of an overtly masculine, authoritarian society. There is one play in particular which has demonstrated Fugard's awareness (conscious or not) of a growing feminist politics in South Africa: *The Road to Mecca* (premiered at Yale in 1984).

Conceived (as many of these plays were) initially as a vehicle for the extraordinary talent of Yvonne Bryceland – who first performed it, on stage and screen – *Mecca* takes place in the glass-encrusted living room of a reclusive, eccentric sculptress in Nieu Bethesda, Miss Helen. Frail and a widow approaching seventy, Miss Helen is marginalized by the small, rural, conservative Afrikaner community in which she lives, because of the wilful individuality of her life and art. She is confronted by two other characters, a powerful Dutch Reformed (Calvinist) minister Marius Byleveld (originally played by Fugard), who wants to persuade her to give up her art and enter an old folks' home, and Elsa Joubert, a young liberal social worker from Cape Town. For Albert Wertheim, Miss Helen's vision can be read as Fugard's, that is, 'not the vision of a revolutionary or iconoclast', but the 'constructive' vision of an artist who can 'move others so as to effect change' without bloodshed.[16] There are only three characters on stage, and their developing relationships are explored in terms of a shifting kaleidoscope of emotions resulting in a final revelation – embodied in a stunning theatrical coup, which has the widow Helen light all the candles in her home, brilliantly illuminating the glass-studded walls, before exclaiming:

> The road to my Mecca was one I had to travel alone … This is as far as I can go. My Mecca is finished … (*She blows out a candle.*) … Just as I taught myself how to light candles, and what that means, I must teach myself now how to blow them out … and what that means. (*She attempts a brave smile.*) The last phase of my apprenticeship … and if I can get through it, I'll be a master! (78)

Aware of the approaching end of her life (the original Miss Helen committed suicide), she is committed to exerting what control she can over what she does, as a means of resisting the various calls upon her: from the insistent, overbearing yet well-meaning minister, who it emerges has been secretly in love with her, to the equally well-meaning and loving Elsa, who has aborted the result of the only love she has had, a child with a married man.

In the somewhat schematic, Ibsenesque setting-up of a debate between conservative and liberal positions, Miss Helen's art and life are clearly intended to demonstrate the potential for spiritual, if not political, freedom, through the dogged pursuit of her personal vision of light, against the surrounding darkness threatening her and, by implication, the society in which she lives. The well-chosen epigraph, from Emily Dickinson's 'The soul selects her own society', is powerfully embodied in the frail central character, whose Mecca of sculpted mermaids, peacocks and wise old owls represents, as she says, her true self, her identity (34–5). As she says to Elsa, it has a logic of its own; that logic is not far from her creator's, either – she, too, awaits inspiration, which has to come in visual images, and light up the imagination, before it can be realized.

The play is not without its difficulties: originally entitled 'My English name is Patience', after the 'good old South African story' recounted by Elsa, of a destitute black woman whom she envies for having given birth to a child, and yet whom she has left to walk her way on the Karoo road, the image remains as a challenge ignored, rather than, as Wertheim insists, transformed into an allegory of 'undaunted progress' and 'survival'.[17] Yet Wertheim is right in identifying Fugard's overriding interest in searching for a means to survive the barren landscape of the desert in people's hearts so long evident in the history of his country.

That Fugard did not feel he had finally found a way of articulating this is evident in the plays which have succeeded *Mecca*, several of them with, once again, women playing key roles: in *Valley Song*, his first 'post-apartheid' play, the central figure is a young Coloured girl, Veronica, who wants to escape her small Karoo village and her pious grandfather 'Buks' to sing in the big city. A third character, played by the same actor who plays her grandfather (Fugard, again, in early productions), is a white man (a metatheatrical Author) who wants to own the land Buks has worked all his life. The girl's desire for release from her past is undermined by the conflict between the two men for the land, implicitly picking up the question raised by the end of apartheid: how and when will ownership be restored, and how far, if at all, is that relevant to the youth of the country?

If there is in this and later plays an unwillingness to face the future, and a tendency to revisit the past, it seems that the Author expresses Fugard's feelings when he remarks at the end that, while admitting the future belongs to the young woman, he wishes the valley could stay 'the unspoilt, innocent little world it was ... I am not as brave about change as I would like to be' (53). This yearning, nostalgic note is struck again in the plays which follow, including *The Captain's Tiger* (1997), *Sorrows and Rejoicings* (2001), *Exits and Entrances* (2004) and *Coming Home* (2009). This is not Fugard's last word, however. In *The Train Driver* (2010), as in so many of his earlier works, two characters of different racial complexions argue their differences while eking out an existence on the edge of society, and indeed at the end of life, showing once again the enduring power of a dramatist concerned to show what theatre can do, to seek out the truths to survive the trials of the present.

Summary

Fugard's theatre has had a profound impact upon his country, and the wider world. It has always been radical in form if not significance, regarding the mainstream, established theatre at home and abroad with suspicion, while bearing witness to the lost and disinherited in South Africa, but also, by implication, to all those excluded from power by race, class and/or poverty. The form of his plays reflects his long-standing interest in a stripped-down theatre, a theatre of basic essentials: a small cast of characters in a circling, at times repetitive, yet passionately close relationship embodying the tensions of their society, often first performed by actors directly involved in its creation, in fringe or at least non-mainstream venues. The potential to interpret this kind of theatre making in terms of encouraging fruitless passivity is there, as is the sense in which, initially at least, the racial as well as (more common) class gap between audience and representation can be thought of as undermining its implicit challenge. A vision of life as relentless, even absurd, in which unrelieved suffering appears to be the lot of humanity may seem to offer little cheer, so much so that the humour of his characters and their frequently comic turns of speech always come as a surprise. But Fugard offers an approach to theatre which suggests that it is in the everyday detail of local people's lives and speech that the roots of awareness may be found – if not a political awareness, then at the least a celebration of the lives of others, of those on the edge, who struggle with the fear not only of neglect but of extinction. The desire to use the theatre as a means of exploring and affirming the need for a sense of self-worth in a context of subjugation and humiliation is fundamental.

Hence the significance of his chosen themes – identity, pain, guilt and survival. At the risk of damaging simplification, it may be said that critics generally divide into those who see these as universal themes, and who, like Vandenbroucke, Shelley and Wertheim, consider his achievement a moral and humanist one; and critics such as Colleran, Kruger and myself, who argue for a more historically and politically aware critique, while always acknowledging his sense of the suffering of the oppressed. Several critics have over the years effectively attacked Fugard's 'liberal humanism' from within his own country, including Martin Orkin's *Drama and the South African State* (1991) and the remarks of black playwright-critics like Zakes Mda.[18] Yet it was the exiled ANC activist-poet Mongane Serote who highlighted the lasting historic role of Fugard's theatrical intervention from *The Blood Knot* to *Sizwe Bansi* and *The Island*: this kind of theatre, Serote insisted, represented a form of resistance at a time when explicit political resistance seemed futile.[19] Fugard's collaborator-performers were effectively keeping the flame of freedom alive, even as they enacted the suffering imposed upon them by the state and its adherents. Alongside many other, lesser-known local theatre groups, Fugard has forged a conspicuous form of dissent, a role overtaken by events which have obliged him, like them, to look for new ways of dealing with the present – and the past, which is where his more recent work has focused.

Fugard's work continues to fill the theatres in which it appears, where audiences acknowledge by their presence and enthusiasm his fundamental and continuing appeal, whatever the limitations of particular plays. Certainly his creative energy is phenomenal. More recently, he has begun translating his own work into Afrikaans, a language which has always provided a suggestive layer within the richly hybrid South African dialect of his plays.

Notes

1. Athol Fugard, *Notebooks 1960/1977*, ed. Mary Benson (London and Boston: Faber, 1983), 172.

2. Albert Camus, *The Rebel*, 1951, transl. Anthony Bower, 1953 (Harmondsworth: Penguin, 1977), 108–9. See also *The Myth of Sisyphus*, 1942, transl. Justin O'Brien, 1955 (Harmondsworth: Penguin, 1977), *passim*. Camus' words and phrases turn up repeatedly in Fugard's *Notebooks*.

3. Fugard, *Notebooks*, 171.

4. In Charles Fourie, 'Interview with the Outsider', *Electronic Mail & Guardian* (15 August 1997), http://mg.co.za/article/1997-08-15-interview-with-the-outsider (accessed 20 April 2014).

5. *Notebooks*, 166.

6. Stanley Kaufmann, '*Boesman and Lena*', *New Republic*, 25 July 1970.

7. See Errol Durbach, '"No time for apartheid": Dancing Free of the System in Athol Fugard's *Boesman and Lena*', in Marcia Blumberg and Dennis Walder (eds), *South African Theatre As/And Intervention* (Amsterdam and Atlanta: Rodopi, 1999), 61–74.

8. Alan Shelley, *Athol Fugard: His Plays, People and Politics* (London: Oberon, 2009), 83; Albert Wertheim, *The Dramatic Art of Athol Fugard: From South Africa to the World* (Bloomington and Indianapolis: Indiana University Press, 2000), 62.

9. Marcia Blumberg, 'Re-Staging Resistance, Re-Viewing Women: 1990s Productions of Fugard's *Hello and Goodbye* and *Boesman and Lena*', in Jeanne

Colleran and Jenny Spencer (eds), *Staging Resistance: Essays on Political Theatre* (Ann Arbor: University of Michigan Press, 1998), 139–41.

10. See *Notebooks*, 178–81.

11. Jeanne Colleran, 'Re-Situating Fugard: Re-thinking Revolutionary Theatre', *South African Theatre Journal* 9:2 (September 1995): 39–50.

12. For details, see Dennis Walder, 'Introduction', in Athol Fugard, *The Township Plays* (Oxford: Oxford University Press, 2000), xxiii–xxxiv.

13. Athol Fugard, 'When Brecht and Sizwe Bansi met in New Brighton', *The Observer Review* (London), 8 August 1982, 22. Repr. as '*Sizwe Bansi is Dead*', *A Night at the Theatre*, ed. Ronald Harwood (London: Methuen, 1983), 26–32.

14. *Notebooks*, 5–6.

15. Quoted in Anne Fuchs, *Playing the Market: The Market Theatre Johannesburg 1976–86* (Philadelphia: Harwood Academic, 1990).

16. Wertheim, *The Dramatic Art of Athol Fugard*, 157.

17. Ibid., 166.

18. Zakes Mda, 'Politics and the Theatre: Current Trends in South Africa', in Geoffrey V. Davis and Anne Fuchs (eds), *Theatre and Change in South Africa* (Amsterdam: Harwood Academic, 1996), 201.

19. Mongane Serote, *On the Horizon* (Fordsburg, Johannesburg: Congress of South African Writers, 1990), 45.

Bibliography

Primary sources

Plays by Athol Fugard
The Road to Mecca (London and Boston: Faber, 1985).
Playland (London: Faber, 1993; New York: Samuel French, 1994).
Valley Song (London and Boston: Faber, 1996).
The Captain's Tiger: A Memoir for the Stage (New York: Samuel French, 1999).
Interior Plays, with a preface by Fugard, edited with an introduction and notes by Dennis Walder (Oxford: Oxford University Press, 2000). [Includes, amongst others, *Statements After An Arrest Under the Immorality Act* and *Dimetos*.]
Port Elizabeth Plays, with a preface by Fugard, edited with an introduction and notes by Dennis Walder (Oxford: Oxford University Press, 2000). [Includes *Blood Knot, Hello and Goodbye, Boesman and Lena, 'Master Harold' … and the Boys*.]
Township Plays, with a preface by Fugard, edited with an introduction and notes by Dennis Walder (Oxford: Oxford University Press, 2000). [Includes, amongst others, *Sizwe Bansi is Dead* and *The Island*.]

Sorrows and Rejoicings (New York: Theatre Communications Group, 2002).
The Train Driver and Other Plays (New York: Theatre Communications Group, 2012). [Also includes *Coming Home*.]

Prose by Athol Fugard
Notebooks 1960/1977, ed. Mary Benson (London and Boston: Faber, 1983).
Cousins: A Memoir (Johannesburg: Witwatersrand University Press, 1994; New York: Theatre Communications Group, 1994).

Secondary sources

Amato, Rob, 'Fugard's Confessional Analysis: '*Master Harold*' ... and the Boys', in M. A Daymond, J. U. Jacobs and M. Lenta (eds), *Momentum: On Recent South African Writing* (Pietermaritzburg: University of Natal Press, 1984), 198–214.
Barnard, Rita, 'A Man's Scenery', in *Apartheid and Beyond: South African Writers and the Politics of Place* (New York: Oxford University Press, 2007), 95–118.
Blumberg, Marcia, 'Women Journeying at the South African Margins: Athol Fugard's *The Road to Mecca*', *Matatu* 11 (1994): 39–50.
Blumberg, Marcia, 'Re-Staging Resistance, Re-Viewing Women: 1990s Productions of Fugard's *Hello and Goodbye* and *Boesman and Lena*', in Jeanne Colleran and Jenny Spencer (eds), *Staging Resistance: Essays on Political Theatre* (Ann Arbor: University of Michigan Press, 1998), 123–45.
Colleran, Jeanne, 'Re-situating Fugard: Re-thinking Revolutionary Theatre', *South African Theatre Journal* 9:2 (September 1995): 39–50.
Durbach, Errol, '"No time for apartheid": Dancing Free of the System in Athol Fugard's *Boesman and Lena*', in Marcia Blumberg and Dennis Walder (eds), *South African Theatre As/And Intervention* (Amsterdam and Atlanta: Rodopi, 1999), 61–74.
Fourie, Charles, 'Interview with the Outsider', *Electronic Mail & Guardian* (15 August 1997), http://mg.co.za/article/1997-08-15-interview-with-the-outsider (accessed 20 April 2014).
Kruger, Loren, 'Space and Markets', in *The Drama of South Africa: Plays, Publics and Pageants Since 1910* (London: Routledge, 1999), 154–70.
Mda, Zakes, 'Politics and the Theatre: Current Trends in South Africa', in Geoffrey V. Davis and Anne Fuchs (eds), *Theatre and Change in South Africa* (Amsterdam: Harwood Academic, 1996), 193–218.
Seymour, Hilary, '*Sizwe Bansi is Dead*: A Study of Artistic Ambivalence', *Race and Class* 21:3 (1980): 273–89.
Shelley, Alan, *Athol Fugard: His Plays, People and Politics* (London: Oberon, 2009).
Vandenbroucke, Russell, *Truths the Hand Can Touch: The Theatre of Athol Fugard* (New York: Theatre Communications Group, 1985).
Walder, Dennis, *Athol Fugard*, Macmillan Modern Dramatists (Houndmills, Basingstoke: Macmillan, 1984).
Walder, Dennis, 'Resituating Fugard: South African Drama as Witness', *New Theatre Quarterly* 8:32 (November 1992): 343–61.

Walder, Dennis, 'Crossing Boundaries: The Genesis of The Township Plays', in Jack Barbera (ed.), *Twentieth Century Literature: Athol Fugard Issue* 39:4 (Winter 1993): 409–22.

Walder, Dennis, *Athol Fugard*, Writers and Their Work (Horndon, Tavistock: Northcote House, 2003).

Walder, Dennis, '"On the threshold of the future?": Interview with Athol Fugard', in David Kerr (ed.), *African Theatre: Southern Africa* (Oxford: James Currey, 2004), 68–78.

Wertheim, Albert, *The Dramatic Art of Athol Fugard: From South Africa to the World* (Bloomington and Indianapolis: Indiana University Press, 2000).

Film

Falls the Shadow: The Life and Times of Athol Fugard, dir. and ed. Tony Palmer, Portobello Pictures, 2012 (includes numerous extracts from historic performances as well as interviews with the playwright, actors and critics).

CHAPTER 8
REZA DE WET
Anton Krueger

African Gothic; Crossing; Breathing In; Three Sisters Two

Introduction

Reza de Wet (1952–2012) has won more awards for her scripts than any other playwright in the history of South African letters.[1] Her darkly comic masterpieces have enthralled (and perplexed) audiences with their idiosyncratic mix of magic, realism and fantasy counterpoised with menacing erotic undercurrents. After her astonishing debut in 1985 with *Diepe Grond* (*African Gothic*, 2005) she was instantly hailed as a 'playwright of the major league'[2] and 'a powerful new South African voice'.[3] Even those who found her work 'too literary'[4] still maintained that she had a 'rare talent'.[5] Little more than a decade later, she had come to be 'regarded by many as [South Africa's] best playwright'.[6]

For over twenty-five years, Reza de Wet had a unique presence in the national consciousness. Her characteristic style was often at odds with contemporary trends in South African drama. Her work is recognizably part of a Western theatrical tradition, and has been compared to that of Chekhov,[7] Strindberg,[8] Lorca[9] and Genet,[10] as well as Tennessee Williams,[11] Sam Shepard and William Faulkner.[12] And yet, many of her texts also draw on a particularly African sensibility. De Wet has often described her worldview as drawing on an African philosophy, since she sees the Afrikaners as also being an indigenous tribe, using a language and a culture which had been moulded by their experiences in Africa. Via their close proximity to black African culture over many centuries, she felt that (white and brown) Afrikaners had been imbued with, for example, beliefs in ancestral spirits, and that many of them accepted the mysterious presence of other-worldly forces to a greater extent than their English counterparts.

Reza de Wet was born in the small town of Senekal and went to school in Bloemfontein, a city she described as 'the heartland of the Afrikaner nation'.[13] She studied drama and English literature at the University of the Free State (*Universiteit van die Vrystaat*), after which time she embarked on a career as an actress with the Performing Arts Council of Transvaal (PACT), where she was awarded a number of leading roles, mostly for the experimental Arena theatre. She later completed her postgraduate studies at the University of Cape Town and the University of South Africa. After working as a professional actress for a number of years, she moved to the small university town of Grahamstown in 1982 with her husband and daughter. She was to spend the rest of her life in the Eastern Cape Town, working at the Department of Drama at Rhodes University until her early retirement in 2007. She continued writing award-winning play texts up until a year before her death from leukaemia in 2012.

Her fascination with theatre began when she first saw her mother singing in an operetta when de Wet was only three years old. She also spoke of the formative influence of her first encounter with a circus at the age of five. This was a 'world of magic and the non-verbal tradition'[14] to which she would return time and again for inspiration. De Wet often drew on her childhood imagination, saying that in all of her plays she was 'dependent on the knowledge' of what she had experienced as a child:

> When you're a child, everything has a lyrical quality ... the world outside is so wonderful ... your own experience of your own body and its functions is intense and erotic ... many of our repressions are the result of growing up.[15]

Similarly, she told Riaan de Villiers that 'When you're small ... [t]here are so many possibilities. Then suddenly other norms are forced down on you and the rich inner world becomes impoverished.'[16] For de Wet, the imaginative world of childhood was associated not only with innocence, but also with primal drives and polymorphous erotic explorations. Many of her childlike characters come across as both brutal and innocent, and they're caught up in a curious muddle of naivety and cruelty. There was also something childlike about the way in which de Wet approached her work, saying, for example, that writing was an opportunity for her 'to really play'[17] and that getting awards was 'like a child getting presents'.[18] There are a great many interviews with de Wet in which one gets the impression that she felt herself to be living within an almost ethereal world, saying that she was 'constantly experiencing the magical'[19] in everything she did, and that she had 'a strong mystical bent'.[20] Amongst her more eccentric beliefs was her conviction that Chekhov was helping her to write her plays,[21] and that she could sense the presence of her deceased grandmother while she wrote.[22] In other interviews she claimed that both her mother and her grandmother communicated with her from beyond the grave.[23] Given this numinous *weltanschauung*, it is little wonder that so many of her texts are permeated by supernatural events.

Reza de Wet first came to prominence as an Afrikaans playwright, but besides her prodigious output in her home language, she also published twelve plays in English. She started writing in English for a number of reasons, claiming that she wanted to reach a wider audience, but also because she wanted to be 'free from peer group pressure'.[24] Also, she said that she did not want to become a figurehead for Afrikaner nationalism.[25] Some plays, like *Nag Generaal* (1991), were completely reworked into English (*Breathing in*, 2005), whereas other plays were first written in English (*The Brothers*, 2007) and then translated into Afrikaans (*Die Broers*, unpublished).[26] She also wrote texts for physical theatre pieces, such as *The Unspeakable Story* (1996) and *Heathcliff Goes Home* (2007), which have not been published.

Many of her plays could be seen as grotesque parodies of staunch Afrikaner society, whereas two plays commissioned in English are direct attacks on English colonialism in South Africa and its patronizing attitude towards both Afrikaner and Black cultures (*Worm in the Bud*, 1990, and *Concealment*, 2004). De Wet claimed that the irony of using the English language 'to launch an attack on the colonial attitude'[27] pleased her immensely. Whether she was satirizing the English colonial attitude or the repressive forces within her own heritage of Afrikaner Calvinism, her plays have evoked as much laughter as they have aroused a sense of disquiet.

The plays

African Gothic *(1985, 2005)*

Reza de Wet's 1985 debut, *Diepe Grond* (*African Gothic*),[28] was a stinging critique of the myths entrenched in traditional views of Afrikaner identity. The play was, somewhat ironically, first performed at a student festival designed to promote the selfsame Afrikaner culture.[29] One of the first reviews about the play called it a 'grotesquely entertaining, bizarre tale',[30] and when it was first performed in the United States a few years later, it was seen as 'both lively, hilarious comedy and horrific, Gothic drama'.[31]

Some of the shocking scenes[32] in the play include public urination and a vicious, blood-spattering whipping, as well as allusions to incest. The unsettling ambiguity with which these scenes are treated was perhaps even more scandalous than their content. Despite a minor backlash from conservative Afrikaans communities, de Wet was quickly heralded as a brave new voice and the play was almost immediately granted a professional run at the Market Theatre where it won a string of accolades.

African Gothic was seen by many as representing 'the coming of age of Afrikaans theatre'.[33] Its story may have seemed 'simple enough',[34] but it was 'layered with cultural and historic significance'.[35] It has been described as a reflection of

> the collective psyche of the Afrikaner ... or more specifically the things which make it difficult to be an Afrikaner: the moralism ... the ritual forms of behaviour, the authoritative religious approach ... the claustrophobia.[36]

The play was written as a parody of an Afrikaans pastoral novel by Alba Bouwer, *Stories van Rivierplaas* (*Stories from River Farm*), written in 1957. In an interview with Barrie Hough, Reza de Wet said that the original work had 'created a mythical and idyllic South African'[37] past, but that in her play she had 'portrayed the destruction of this derelict paradise'.[38] Instead of portraying Afrikaners as peacefully communing with nature and enjoying the well-earned respect of their children and their (Black) servants, in de Wet's version two incestuous children respond to years of Calvinist repression by murdering their parents as well as the lawyer who comes to seek them out. In the midst of their tumultuous daily round, the brother and sister re-enact role-playing games using fragments of scenes they'd played out with their parents when they were still alive. The adult woman (Sussie) veers between playing 'the demented child-like sister and at times the terrifyingly puritanical *Volksmoeder*',[39] while her brother (Frikkie) displays 'random brutality combined with a sort of primal innocence'.[40] In this way, both children are continuously 'flipping from fantasy to reality as they live out their tragic little lives'.[41]

One of the things which is so disconcerting about the play is its sense of familiarity (the setting on the farm, the tightly-knit family structure) juxtaposed with bizarre cruelty played out with the careless frivolity of a children's pastime. Simon Lewis describes the play as 'a critical re-examination of Afrikaner myth and mentality ... an incestuous, confined parody of '30s Afrikaans drama aimed at forging a national identity'.[42] The play mixes familiar elements of Afrikaner culture and idiomatic expression and yet it also arouses a disconcerting sense that dark currents are at play within this collective unconscious, primarily in terms of an unchecked erotic desire which has been heightened by years of suppression. For example, Sussie has been taught to believe that, because Grové (the lawyer) has a wife with 'red nails and a red mouth', she must be 'bad', because her own mother told her that 'women who want to improve on God's work are wicked and damned'. This unnatural repression of the sensual plays a large part in unleashing the violence which eventually erupts into murder.

Some of the visual, visceral elements of the play are indeed shocking and none of de Wet's subsequent works were ever quite as brutal as this one; yet, as Pieter R. Botha points out, 'All the elements which characterise Reza de Wet's work are evident here.' These include:

> the total move away from realism, and towards the naïve and grotesque, the puritanical [as] contrasted with the sensual and most of all, the possibilities of transformation in all the characters.[43]

With this first play, Reza de Wet attracted the media attention and the academic interest in her work which would follow her for the rest of her life.

Crossing *(1994, 2000)*

Crossing forms part of a thematic trilogy with the plays *Missing* and *Miracle*, and they were published together in the collection *Plays One* (2000). For Reza de Wet, this cycle of plays contains 'a mixture of the naïve, the grotesque and the wonderful'.[44] Following on from the furore caused by *African Gothic*, she began to develop a more fairy-tale and fabulist style. She said:

> My work has changed a lot since [*African Gothic*]. It's more evocative, it has more of a magical quality, it's not so emphatic. *Trits* [the trilogy translated as *Plays One*] has a whole other texture and style, it no longer presents the Afrikaner as angst-ridden. There are still dark undercurrents, but they're more mysterious, indefinable.[45] [my translation]

When the play was performed in London in 2000, it was described as featuring 'elements of the old-fashioned mystery and of ghost stories, of magical realism, of Gothic hysteria, and of the Genet style power play'.[46] Although it was once again set deep within the territory of the Afrikaner psyche, Theresa Biberauer claimed that it displayed universal themes 'such as the inter-relationship between power and freedom, the past and the present, reality and appearance … rather than specific Afrikaner issues'.[47] And yet, even though it might have been lighter in tone, *Crossing* still creates a sense of foreboding, disharmony, unease. For de Wet, mood was always more important than character, and she said that for her, 'atmosphere is the most important aspect'[48] in a play. The specific sounds in her plays – howling wind, rain, the rush of the river – all serve a perpetual apprehension. Hannes van Zyl writes that for de Wet the 'social framework in the piece is less important … than the texture of dream and play'.[49]

Crossing centres on a stern sister (Hermien) who bullies her psychic, hunchbacked sister, who is also called Sussie, like the character in *African Gothic*. They live in an old house situated at a river crossing, and they see it as their vocation to warn people against attempting to cross the river while it is in flood. It has also become their self-imposed duty to fish the corpses of those who did not heed their warning out of the river, and to give them a decent burial. The departed are formally buried so that their ghosts will not return to haunt their house, but the sisters can only complete this ritual if they know the full names of the dead, which sometimes necessitates their holding a séance in order to recall restless spirits so as to determine their real names. When Maestro, a sinister, Svengalian hypnotist, enters the house with his slavish consort (Ezmerelda) the hunchback sister falls under his spell. At the play's end she opens wide the doors of the house and flees headlong into the night, towards the sound of the rushing river.

The play provides many examples of de Wet's characteristic juxtaposition of the crude with the lyrical. For example, the hunchbacked sister presents a grotesque spectacle, and yet Maestro tells her that she only seems to be misshapen because she has wings hidden inside her hump. The image of a deformed girl is transformed in one sly stroke into that of an angel. Similarly, in *Missing* a stern mother and her fearful daughter package animal manure for a living, but a mysterious stranger seduces the daughter away to the circus her mother had tried to keep her away from. In this way, there are often intimations of the magical within the harsh reality of almost unbelievably grim domestic circumstances.

The plays in this cycle are all inspired by medieval miracle plays, each of them featuring an innocent young ingénue (possibly based on Maria von Nijmegen) who is seduced. In all of these plays a mysterious stranger intrudes upon the suffocating isolation of a nuclear hub of characters, culminating in the destruction of the young woman. The role of the seducer, however, also serves a liberating role since he frees the young girl from a cruel matriarchal figure and assists her in escaping oppression. This liberation is often connected to the refining powers of a devotion to art, beauty and the imagination; and yet, in contrast to many of the medieval plays, there is no redemption at the end. Instead, they unbalance the pursuit of freedom with the aggressive domination of erotic drives. Even though the plotlines may at times appear to be almost simplistic, similar to those of a fairy tale, the puppet-like characters appear to allude more to archetypes than to stereotypes. This duplicity in de Wet's writing was described by Marthinus Basson in a famous metaphor: what appears to be an innocuous surface of a pond nevertheless holds 'tremendous depth, filled with currents and hidden creatures; sometimes even the dangerous, the dark, the ominous, the crude, and the erotic'.[50]

Breathing In *(2004)*

Originally written in English, *Breathing In* is a play in which 'Realistic, Magical-realism and fantasy elements are freely mixed together'.[51] The 'strong gothic and erotic elements remind one of *African Gothic* and *Crossing*'[52] although the piece has a tone all its own. De Wet achieves intimations of the uncanny in a 'phantasmagorical play'[53] set in a world that seems both familiar and frighteningly strange. There is a recognizably naturalistic setting (a farm house during the Anglo-Boer War), and yet the central action revolves around the ghoulish notion that a beautiful young girl has maintained her youth by breathing in the last breath of the dying men her mother persuades to be murdered for her. In the play, a mother (Anna) is a 'life-sucking, death-defying scavenger'[54] who lives for a daughter described as embodying both 'fragility and duplicity'.[55] Robert Greig sees Anna as a 'witch with an androgynous voice, a seductive manner and a presence that is always ambiguous ... the treatment lays paving stones over moist, undulating ground'.[56] In many ways, this is an anti-romantic play, which ridicules the romanticist notions of a man giving his life for a country or a woman, mocking notions of sacrifice: a parody of Plato's myth of the soul mate. Instead of representing the dream of pure love, it presents the fatal power of seduction.

Anna deftly manipulates a young soldier (Brand), turning his ideals of loyalty and self-sacrifice against himself. She eventually persuades him to turn against his general and everything he has ever believed in (duty, patriotism, fatherland) for the sake of his love of – and desire for – a beautiful young woman. The play seems to be about a kind of domination women might be able to exercise over men by means of their powers of persuasion. It deals with the power inherent in the pull of attraction rather than the force of brute strength. Anna and her daughter are cut loose from commitments towards a collective identification, and the play does not appear to have a particular moral perspective. Without the censure of a politically correct view, it explores ways in which love can make the world grow smaller, how an obsession with caring for one's kin can bring the borders in, how an ostensibly valuable human emotion, such as a mother's love, can contribute towards an insular world which thrives on egocentric self-interest. A sinister undertone of matriarchal domination which informs so much of de Wet's work is clearer here than in any other of her plays and this seems to be the crystallization of a theme she had already been toying with in all of the plays in *Plays One*, namely the incurable pull of individual desire as it resists the flow of a social consciousness.[57]

Marthinus Basson's name has become synonymous with the plays of Reza de Wet, very successfully directing 11 of them to great acclaim. Basson talks about *Breathing In* as concerning 'the eternal struggle between submissive and oppressive forces'.[58] In many of de Wet's plays she explores ideas of masculinity and femininity in terms of Jung's definition of *animus* and *anima*,[59] and in this play, Anna embodies 'the masculine principle'.[60] De Wet said that she finds 'this masculinity more macabre than seeing it in a man, and also more treacherous'.[61] It is important to bear in mind that de Wet found it patronizing to be referred to as a 'woman writer' and consistently avoided being classified as a feminist. Instead of presenting a play as a form of argument, she was more interested in creating a mood, a dark atmosphere in which to play. Derek Wilson writes that, 'Followers of de Wet's plays are familiar with her uncanny ability to plumb the depths of the unfathomable and still seep her plotlines in the mysterious, the eerie and the bizarre.'[62] The setting of *Breathing In* is a world in which spirits and dreams are as substantial as flesh, a world Guy Willoughby depicts as 'a dark, fetid, time-suspended continuum in which the usual responses … just don't apply'.[63]

Three Sisters Two (1997, 2005)

Three Sisters Two forms part of a cycle of three plays published together as *Russian Trilogy*. These are all inter-texts, sequels to Chekhov's major works, and they are written in an uncannily similar form and style, using four acts and Chekhovian dialogue and precisely the same carefully measured rhythm as the originals. *Three Sisters Two* follows the later life of the characters in *Three Sisters*, while *Yelena* follows *Uncle Vanya*, and *On the Lake* takes place a few years after *The Seagull*.

For many who had been following de Wet's career, this project seemed to be a natural culmination of her long-standing fascination (some might say obsession) with Chekhov. She claimed that her enthralment with childhood experience was shared by the Russian writer, saying that like Chekhov she yearned 'for a time of simplicity and beauty when there is no awareness'.[64] When she saw her first Chekhov play at the age of fifteen, de Wet said that 'it seemed so magical and evocative. At the same time it seemed so familiar; it had the quality of a memory for me ... I seemed to feel Chekhov very, very deeply'.[65] She was subsequently taught by the Chekhov-philiac Robert Mohr at UCT, and auditioned as Nina (from *The Seagull*) for her first professional work in the theatre. De Wet later claimed that she had been assisted in the writing of her plays by Chekhov, saying, for example, that she was 'an apprentice of Chekov' and that she 'learnt a lot from him, as if by osmosis'.[66] Elsewhere, she has written about Chekhov even more intimately: 'He's my friend and I think he's been helping me out of the kindness of his heart'.[67] For her the process of writing *Three Sisters Two* and the other plays in this trilogy came more easily than her other subsequent plays, due to the close connection she felt and what she described as the 'force field'[68] she shared with Chekhov. It was almost as though the play 'wrote itself'.[69]

Although these works are set in Russia and remain faithful to the culture and form of Chekhov's dramas, curiously enough, one might consider these three plays as being the closest that de Wet ever came to socio-political commentary about South Africa during the 1990s, since each of these plays is about 'the end of an era'.[70] *Three Sisters Two* is set during the Bolshevik Revolution, when the Russian Empire was crumbling. It invites comparisons between the recently disenfranchised Afrikaners in post-apartheid South Africa and 'the consequences facing a ruling party when a change of regime takes place and the old dispensation disintegrates'.[71] All three of these plays reflect the waning strengths of a people who have lost power, and their attempts to come to terms with the new dispensation characterized by 'diminishing circumstances' and 'irrevocable change' as a result of 'an impending crisis which threatens to disrupt and destroy their old way of life'.[72] The Afrikaans version of *Three Sisters Two* (*Drie Susters Twee*) won de Wet her second Hertzog prize, the highest accolade in Afrikaans literature.

Summary

In contrast to the strong trend of realism in South African theatre – fostered by Athol Fugard and sustained by writers like Mike van Graan and Craig Higginson – Reza de Wet not only rejected realism as a style, but went as far as to say that 'Realism is just an illusion … it's a distortion of reality.'[73] For Reza de Wet, 'reality has just as much to do with the psyche and fantasy.'[74] In her view, the attempt to create realism in theatre could have a negative effect in that it might destroy or divert attention away from the underlying myths which were considered by her as more real than the material world itself.[75] She saw theatre as ritual, as dream, as exorcism.

Her plays take place either in the 1930s, or the Anglo-Boer war, or, in the case of her Russian trilogy, in the first few decades of the nineteenth century. As Marthinus Basson puts it, 'Reza always works in the past, and the past is a strangely familiar place.'[76] Her themes frequently include explorations of masculine and feminine archetypal forces and the erotic subconscious drives repressed by Calvinism. Her dramas are played out in fabulist fairy-tale worlds which seem to be, on the one hand, familiarly naturalistic, while also belonging to an uncanny kingdom. Her plays enter into 'areas of private experience which, you realise later, have a wider, mythic … dimension.'[77] Guy Willoughby criticized the repetition of some of these themes in her early work, saying that her plays were becoming an 'increasingly fraught and cloying series of Calvinist exposes.'[78] However, de Wet soon proved her versatility in addressing a broader range of concerns, while maintaining her own idiosyncratic style.

Reza de Wet's plays share a reverence for the fantastical and the marvellous, and never attempt to make outright socio-political statements. In fact, she has repeatedly and emphatically eschewed the demands of a political theatre, claiming that she has always written instinctively and about individual concerns, saying that she feels 'terribly strongly that the theatre should not be used as a political platform … it has to have an integrity of its own … It should reflect a personal vision.'[79] Elsewhere, de Wet has said that 'theatre should not be permitted to fulfil a didactic function, it must rather present an alternative world, an imaginary realm wherein the audience can live.'[80] She speaks of her experience of writing as sometimes being like 'an hallucinatory experience … almost like going into a trance.'[81] And yet there are also plays such as *Worm in the Bud* and *Concealment* which are clearly satires, and which appear to have emerged from a more rational place. Then, her Chekhovian trilogy was also an experiment largely in form and style, a postmodern response to her favourite author. A number of her other plays are also intertexts, such as *African Gothic*'s commentary on the novel by Bouwer, and work informed by her grandmother's diaries. Some of her plays form intertexts with each other, indicated by the use of the same character names in different plays, and hints that characters might be related to others in different plays. And yet, de Wet distanced herself from postmodern writing and aligned herself rather with what might seem a more old-fashioned tradition: one drawing on medieval miracle plays and archetypal characters, rather than the more cerebral realms of deconstruction. In this sense, de Wet's writing, as well as her personality and worldview, appear to be caught up in a number of contradictions and paradoxes. She was devoted to a writer famous for having heralded an era of realism in theatre, and yet found in his works a world immersed in myths and dreams.

When she passed away in 2012, Reza de Wet was eulogized as one of the greatest writers in South African literature. During the course of her career, all of the major theatre critics of her generation had sung her praises, including Guy Willoughby, Robert Greig and Adrienne Sichel. Sichel wrote that:

> For decades her plays have resonated with ancient premonitions, poetic imaginings and spiritual transcendence ... work sets out to 'evoke the marginal world which exists between the known and the unimaginable'.[82]

According to Temple Hauptfleisch, founder of the *South African Theatre Journal* and long-time head of the Drama Department at the University of Stellenbosch, de Wet had written 'compelling and imaginative works which are highly regarded by academics for their literary qualities and loved by audience and performers for this sparkling vitality in performance'.[83] De Wet's long-standing friend and director, Marthinus Basson, said that:

> Playwright Reza de Wet has crafted magical tales with an earthy humour and archetypal characters that seem quite simple on the surface. Yet her plays resound deeply with not only mystery but also a complexity of meanings and associations that has everything to do with the power of the imagination.[84]

In some way, Reza de Wet's refusal to write overtly about contemporary political events might, ultimately, contribute towards her plays being read and performed for longer than those whose popularity at the present moment is due to their resonance with a specific historical time and place. She will be remembered as one of the finest South African playwrights of the late twentieth century and her 'imaginative richness and meticulous craftsmanship'[85] will no doubt continue to be appreciated for a long time to come. Her works have been translated into many languages and performed on four continents, and as her English plays and translations continue to find audiences abroad, it seems likely she will fulfil the promise Adrienne Sichel predicted for her in 1985 on the occasion of her debut, namely that she might one day still come to be regarded as 'a major force in theatre worldwide.'[86]

Notes

1. Her accolades include a CNA prize (1992), five FNB Vita awards (1986, 1987, 1989, 1994, 1998), four Fleur du Caps (1993, 1994, 1997, 2004), the Dalro award (1986), the Rapport prize (1986), AngloGold Ashanti/Aardklop-Smeltkroesprys (2009) and a Kanna (2009). She has also twice won the most distinguished award in Afrikaans literature, the Hertzog prize (1994, 1997).

2. Daniel Raeford, *Weekly Mail*, 19 October 1986, 19.

3. Adrienne Sichel, '"Grond" is Deep Indeed', *The Star*, 2 April 1985, 12.

4. Helize van Vuuren, '"Diepe Grond" 'n Onbeholpenheid en Oordaad, maar Duidelike Belofte', *Die Burger*, 1987, 9.

5. Ibid.

6. Diane de Beer, *The Star*, 25 August 1998, 4.

7. Barry Ronge, 'An Unreal Escape from Reality', *Sunday Times*, 30 July 1989, 33.

8. Hannes van Zyl, 'Reza Skryf 'n "Sprokie"', *Insig*, April 1993, 35.

9. Derek Bond, 'The New Boer Wars of Modern South Africa', *First Act* (*Times Cultural*), May 2007 (n. p.).

10. Ibid.

11. Ibid.

12. Sichel, '"Grond" is Deep Indeed'.

13. Erika Terblanche, 'Reza de Wet (1952–2012)', *Litnet*, 24 February 2012, www.litnet.co.za/Article/reza-de-wet-19522012 (accessed 17 March 2015) (own translation).

14. Patricia Handley, 'A Pond Reflecting the Sky', *ADA Magazine* 13 (1995): 12.

15. Barrie Hough, 'Kleintyd die Groot Invloed' (Interview with Reza de Wet), *Beeld*, 20 March 1987, 2 (own translation).

16. Riaan de Villiers, 'In gesprek met Reza de Wet', *Die Suid-Afrikaan* 10 (1987): 47 (own translation).

17. Laetitia Pople, 'Galgehumor werk in Afrikaans' (Interview with de Wet), *Beeld*, 3 July 1992, 3 (own translation).

18. Ibid.

19. Handley, 'A Pond Reflecting the Sky'.

20. Marcia Blumberg, 'More Realities' (Interview), in *South African Theatre as/and Intervention* (Amsterdam: Rodopi, 1999), 251.

21. Roline Norval, 'Reza se Stuk Goed Oorsee Ontvang', *Beeld*, 27 March 1997, 5.

22. Sarie (only name given), 'Stille Water, Diepe Grond', *Die Burger*, 18 May 1994, 1.

23. Chris Barron, 'Obituary: Reza de Wet: Playwright who sought Hidden Truths', *Times Live*, 5 February 2012, www.timeslive.co.za/opinion/commentary/2012/02/05/obituary-reza-de-wet-playwright-who-sought-hidden-truths (accessed 17 March 2015).

24. Adrienne Sichel, 'Colonial Hypocrisy is Reza's Target', *The Star*, 1 February 1990, 1.

25. Rolf Solberg, *South African Theatre in the Melting Pot: Trends and Developments at the Turn of the Millennium* (Grahamstown: Institute for the Study of English in Africa, 2003), 181.

26. Her only published text which was completely translated by another person is *Missing* (*Mis*), which was translated by Steven Stead. De Wet worked together with Stead on translating *Miracle* (*Mirakel*), but since then translated all of her own works and went on to write numerous pieces only in English.

27. Anja Huismans and Juanita Finestone, 'Unwilling Champion – an Interview with Reza de Wet', Introduction by Temple Hauptfleisch. *Contemporary Theatre Review* 9 (1999): 61.

28. The title of the play would be translated literally as 'Deep Ground'. It was performed in America as *Dearth*, then later as *Deep Ground*, but it was eventually published as *African Gothic*, the name which continues to be used.

29. The Kampus Toneel (lit. 'Campus Stage') contest was organized by the ATKV: *Afrikaanse Taal- en Kultuurvereniging* (Afrikaans Language and Cultural Association).

30. Sichel, '"Grond" is Deep Indeed'.

31. Cited in Roline Norval, 'Reza se Stuk Goed Oorsee Ontvang', *Beeld*, 29 August 1991, 8.

32. When it was performed in Los Angeles in 2005 it was described as opening with 'the heroine urinating noisily into a chamber pot in full view of the audience' and ending with 'someone being noisily flayed alive with a *sjambok*' (Charlene Avis, 'African Gothic (or Diepe Grond) – a Dark Comedy', *Juluka*, February 2005, 5.)

33. Wilhelm Snyman, 'Classic Afrikaans Play gets New Treatment at the Nico', *Cape Times*, 16 April 1996, 11.

34. Ibid.

35. Ibid.

36. De Villiers, 'In gesprek met Reza de Wet'.

37. Terblanche, 'Reza de Wet (1952–2012)'.

38. Ibid.

39. Sichel, 'Colonial Hypocrisy is Reza's Target'.

40. Owen Williams, 'Primeval Force in Diepe Grond', *The Argus*, 6 March 1995, 2.

41. Wilhelm Snyman, *The Cape Times*, 7 March 1995, 14.

42. Simon Lewis, 'Review of David Graver *Drama for a New South Africa*', *HAfrLitCine, HNet Reviews in the Humanities and Social Sciences*, May 2000, http://www.revolution.hnet.msu.edu/reviews/showrev.php?id=4088 (accessed 17 March 2015).

43. Pieter R. Botha, 'Teater kom Kimberley toe!', *Die Volksblad*, 15 September 1999, 4.

44. Pople, 'Galgehumor werk in Afrikaans'.

45. Sarie, 'Stille Water, Diepe Grond'.

46. Theresa Biberauer, 'Platteland Spinsters Give London Audiences Plenty of Food for Thought', *Sunday Independent*, 1 October 2000, 10.

47. Ibid.

48. Dorothea van Zyl, 'Reza wil Gehoor Beheks', *Die Burger*, 30 June 2004, 14 (own translation).

49. Hannes van Zyl, 'Reza Skryf 'n "Sprokie"'.

50. In Handley, 'A Pond Reflecting the Sky', 12.

51. Dorothea van Zyl, 'Kellerman die Bindende Factor in *Breathing in*', *Die Burger*, 17 July 2004, 8.

52. Ibid.

53. Pople, 'Galgehumor werk in Afrikaans', 12.

54. Adrienne Sichel, 'Taking in Reza de Wet's New Play', *The Star*, 6 July 2004, 11.

55. Ibid.

56. Robert Greig, 'Blurring the Boundaries', *Cue*, 2 July 2004, 3.

57. Some of the ideas in this paragraph come from a similar one in a chapter on de Wet in my book *Experiments in Freedom: Explorations of Identity in New South African Drama*. (Newcastle: Cambridge Scholars Publishing, 2010).

58. In Andrea Buchanan, 'Double Direction', *Cue*, 1 July 2004, 8.

59. See Marisa Keuris, 'Die Rol van die Sprokie in Reza de Wet se *Op Dees Aarde* (1987)', *Stilet* 8:1 (2006): 41.

60. In Anja Huismans and Juanita Finestone, 'Anja Huismans and Juanita Finestone Talk to Reza de Wet', *South African Theatre Journal* 9:1 (May 1995): 92.

61. Ibid.

62. Derek Wilson, 'Bizarre Play Captivates', *Cape Argus*, 19 July 2004, p. 1.

63. Guy Willoughby, 'Sucking on the Female Life Force', *This Day*, 23 July 2004, 12.

64. In Blumberg, 'More Realities', 245.

65. Ibid.

66. Dorothea van Zyl, 'Kellerman die Bindende Factor in *Breathing in*' [own translation].

67. Norval, 'Reza se Stuk Goed Oorsee Ontvang' [own translation].

68. In Blumberg, 'More Realities', 242.

69. Ibid.

70. Paul Boekkooi, 'Met Hertzog Prys vir Reza is Geskiedenis Gemaak', *Die Burger*, 26 June, 1997, 4.

71. Marisa Keuris, 'Found in Translation: Chekhov Revisited by Reza de Wet and Janet Suzman', *Journal of Literary Studies* 20:1–2 (2004): 155.

72. In Juanita Perez, 'Reza de Wet in Conversation with Juanita Perez', in *Russian Trilogy* (London: Oberon, 2002), 8.

73. Boekkooi, 'Met Hertzog Prys vir Reza is Geskiedenis Gemaak'.

74. Ibid.

75. Johan Botha, 'Meisie van Senekal bring 'n Mirakel na Kaapse Verhoog', *Die Burger*, 12 March 1993, 6.

76. In Buchanan, 'Double Direction'.

77. Robert Greig, 'Precise Lesson in Language', *Business Day*, 25 July 1989, 8.

78. Guy Willoughby, 'Not so Cloying', *Financial Mail,* 13 April 1990, 35.

79. Celia Wren, '"Colonial Dream" versus Africa's Spirit in New Play', *Weekly Mail*, 9–15 March 1990, 21.

80. Pople, 'Galgehumor werk in Afrikaans'.

81. Sichel, 'Colonial Hypocrisy is Reza's Target', 2.

82. Sichel, 'Taking in Reza de Wet's New Play', 11.

83. Temple Hauptfleisch, 'Introduction', in Anja Huismans and Juanita Finestone, 'Unwilling Champion – an Interview with Reza de Wet', *Contemporary Theatre Review* 9 (1999): 53.

84. In Handley, 'A Pond Reflecting the Sky', 10

85. Hauptfleisch, 'Introduction', 56.

86. Sichel, '"Grond" is Deep Indeed'.

Bibliography

Primary sources

Plays by Reza de Wet
Plays One: Missing, Crossing, Miracle (London: Oberon, 2000).
Russian Trilogy: Three Sisters Two, Yelena, On the Lake (London: Oberon, 2002).
Plays Two: African Gothic, Good Heavens, Breathing In (London: Oberon, 2005).
The Brothers (London: Oberon, 2007).
Two Plays: Concealment and Fever (London: Oberon, 2007).

Secondary sources

Avis, Charlene, 'African Gothic (or Diepe Grond) – a Dark Comedy', *Juluka* (February 2005): 5.

Barron, Chris, 'Obituary: Reza de Wet: Playwright who sought Hidden Truths', *Times Live*, 5 February 2012, www.timeslive.co.za/opinion/commentary/2012/02/05/obituary-reza-de-wet-playwright-who-sought-hidden-truths (accessed 17 March 2015).

Biberauer, Theresa, 'Platteland Spinsters Give London Audiences Plenty of Food for Thought', *Sunday Independent*, 1 October 2000, 10.

Blumberg, Marcia, 'More Realities' (Interview), in *South African Theatre as/and Intervention* (Amsterdam: Rodopi, 1999).

Boekkooi, Paul, 'Met Hertzog Prys vir Reza is Geskiedenis Gemaak', *Die Burger*, 26 June 1997, 4.

Bond, Derek, 'The New Boer Wars of Modern South Africa', *First Act* (*Times Cultural*), May 2007 (no page number given).

Botha, Johan, 'Meisie van Senekal bring 'n Mirakel na Kaapse Verhoog', *Die Burger*, 12 March 1993, 6.

Botha, Pieter R., 'Teater kom Kimberley toe!', *Die Volksblad*, 15 September 1999, 4.

Buchanan, Andrea, 'Double Direction', *Cue*, 1 July 2004, 8.

Daniel, Raeford, 'A Fledgling Debuts in the Major League', *Weekly Mail*, 19 October 1986, 19.

Daniel, Raeford, 'Of Death and Claustrophobia', *The Citizen*, 22 July 1989, 14.

De Villiers, Riaan, 'In gesprek met Reza de Wet', *Die Suid-Afrikaan* 10 (1987): 44–8.

Greig, Robert, 'Precise Lesson in Language', *Business Day*, 25 July 1989, 8.

Greig, Robert, 'Blurring the Boundaries', *Cue*, 2 July 2004, 3.

Handley, Patricia, 'A Pond Reflecting the Sky', *ADA Magazine* 13 (1995): 10–13.

Hauptfleisch, Temple, 'Introduction', in Anja Huismans and Juanita Finestone, 'Unwilling Champion – an Interview with Reza de Wet', *Contemporary Theatre Review* 9 (1999): 53–63.

Hough, Barrie, 'Kleintyd die Groot Invloed' (Interview with Reza de Wet), *Beeld*, 20 March 1987, 2.

Huismans, Anja and Juanita Finestone, 'Anja Huismans and Juanita Finestone Talk to Reza de Wet', *South African Theatre Journal* 9:1 (May 1995): 89–95.

Huismans, Anja and Juanita Finestone, 'Unwilling Champion – an Interview with Reza de Wet', Introduction by Temple Hauptfleisch. *Contemporary Theatre Review* 9 (1999): 53–63.

Keuris, Marisa, 'Found in Translation: Chekhov Revisited by Reza de Wet and Janet Suzman', *Journal of Literary Studies* 20:1–2 (2004): 148–64.

Keuris, Marisa, 'Die Rol van die Sprokie in Reza de Wet se *Op Dees Aarde* (1987)', *Stilet* 8:1 (2006): 39–50.

Krueger, Anton, 'Fear of the Hybrid in the Plays of Reza de Wet', in *Experiments in Freedom: Explorations of Identity in New South African Drama* (Newcastle: Cambridge Scholars Publishing, 2010), 171–82.

Krueger, Anton, 'Keeping it in the Family: Incest, Repression and the Fear of the Hybrid in Reza de Wet's English Plays', *Literator* 31 (2010): 45–60.

Lewis, Simon, 'Review of David Graver *Drama for a New South Africa*', *HAfrLitCine, HNet Reviews in the Humanities and Social Sciences*, May 2000, http://www.revolution.hnet.msu.edu/reviews/showrev.php?id=4088 (accessed 17 March 2015).

Norval, Roline, 'Reza se Stuk Goed Oorsee Ontvang', *Beeld*, 29 August 1991, 8.

Norval, Roline, 'De Wet en Tsjechof Lankal "op dieselfde Golflengte"', *Beeld*, 27 March 1997, 5.

Perez, Juanita, 'Reza de Wet in Conversation with Juanita Perez', in *Russian Trilogy* (London: Oberon, 2002), 7–13.

Pople, Laetitia, 'Galgehumor werk in Afrikaans' (Interview with de Wet), *Beeld*, 3 July 1992, 3.

Pople, Laetitia, 'Ouer Garde wys sy Slag', *Die Burger*, 3 July 2004, 12.

Ronge, Barry, 'An Unreal Escape from Reality', *Sunday Times*, 30 July 1989, 33.

Sarie (only name given), 'Stille Water, Diepe Grond', *Die Burger,* 18 May 1994, 1.

Sichel, Adrienne, '"Grond" is Deep Indeed', *The Star*, 2 April 1985, 12.

Sichel, Adrienne, 'Colonial Hypocrisy is Reza's Target', *The Star*, 1 February 1990, 1–2.

Sichel, Adrienne, 'Taking in Reza de Wet's New Play', *The Star*, 6 July 2004, 11.

Snyman, Wilhelm, 'Classic Afrikaans Play gets New Treatment at the Nico', *Cape Times*, 16 April 1996, 11.

Solberg, Rolf, *South African Theatre in the Melting Pot: Trends and Developments at the Turn of the Millennium* (Grahamstown: Institute for the Study of English in Africa, 2003).

Terblanche, Erika, 'Reza de Wet (1952–2012)', *Litnet,* 24 February 2012, www.litnet.co.za/Article/reza-de-wet-19522012 (accessed 17 March 2015).

Van Vuuren, Helize, '"Diepe Grond" 'n Onbeholpenheid en Oordaad, maar Duidelike Belofte', *Die Burger*, 1987, 9.

Van Zyl, Dorothea, 'Reza wil Gehoor Beheks', *Die Burger*, 30 June 2004, 14.

Van Zyl, Dorothea, 'Kellerman die Bindende Factor in *Breathing In*', *Die Burger*, 17 July 2004, 8.

Van Zyl, Hannes, 'Reza Skryf 'n "Sprokie"', *Insig*, April 1993, 35.

Williams, Owen, 'Primeval Force in Diepe Grond', *The Argus*, 6 March 1995, 2.

Willoughby, Guy, 'Not so Cloying', *Financial Mail*, 13 April 1990, 35.

Willoughby, Guy, 'Sucking on the Female Life Force', *This Day*, 23 July 2004, 12.

Wilson, Derek, 'Bizarre Play Captivates', *Cape Argus*, 19 July 2004, 1.
Wren, Celia, '"Colonial Dream" versus Africa's Spirit in New Play', *Weekly Mail*, 9–15 March 1990, 21.

CHAPTER 9
PAUL SLABOLEPSZY
Adrienne Sichel

Saturday Night at the Palace; Mooi Street Moves; Pale Natives

Introduction

In his introduction to *Mooi Street and Other moves,* a collection of six Slabolepszy plays, critic Robert Greig describes this quintessentially South African dramatist as 'the cartographer of the white male soul facing the abyss'.

This is only one facet of this award-winning actor, playwright, screen-writer and director's ability to capture, articulate and voice aspects of the South African psyche rooted deeply in apartheid and post-apartheid society. Under-rated, enigmatic and prolific are also descriptions which apply to this master of tragi-comedy.

To a great extent Paul Slabolepszy's personal history[1] has defined his art making, as well as his ability to access various aspects of South African life and verbal textures. The eldest of four children, he was born in Bolton, England, on 10 February 1948 to Polish Royal Air Force Spitfire pilot Henryk Slabolepszy and his English wife Margaret. The family emigrated to South Africa when Paul was three years old. The reason for their departure was due to parochial attitudes experienced by his Polish father 'who found it extremely difficult being a foreigner' in post-war England. Wanting a new life for his young family, Henryk Slabolepszy pulled the name of their new homeland out of a hat. South Africa won over the United States, Australia, New Zealand and other destinations.

As a result, young Paul grew up not in Chicago, or Perth, but in small towns – in Modderfontein at the dynamite factory near Johannesburg; in the Eastern Transvaal coal mining town of Witbank (post-1994 renamed eMalahleni – place of coal, in the province of Mpumalanga) and further north in Messina (now Musina in the Limpopo Province) where his newly skilled father was employed as a production engineer. This was also the environment where the playwright-in-the-making was exposed to the Afrikaans language and the *platteland* way of speaking English.

His childhood would also have exposed him to the inequalities between black and white South Africans and how English-speaking citizens tended to be discriminated against in Afrikaner communities. His countryside context also fuelled his enduring passion for sports which he later used as springboards for several of his plays, notably *Over the Hill* (set in a rugby locker room in Nelspruit, Eastern Transvaal), *Under the Oaks*, *Once a Pirate* (about an Orlando Pirates soccer fan), the smash hit rugby farce *Heel Against the Head*, *Life's a Pitch* (cricket) and *Whole in One* (golf). This environment also empowered him to authentically capture the small-town ethos which informs *The Return of Elvis Du Pisanie – A Monologue*. The suicidal, Elvis-obsessed, middle-aged Edward Cedric du Pisanie returns to his hometown of Witbank and relives his childhood, which began in Modderfontein.

The actor and playwright's first memory of having an audience was as a 12-year-old performing under a giant baobab tree in the primary school grounds in Messina telling original, improvised, stories. These tales about the fictional Gonas and his bicycle gained a loyal following. The storytelling boy scout and his troop also put on concerts in the Messina MOTH (Memorable Order of Tin Hats) Hall. These shows also whetted Slabolepszy's appetite for entertaining.

His formal debut as a writer was writing flamboyant soccer reports about the school games at the College of the Little Flower in Pietersburg (now Polokwane), where he was a high school boarder. The science teacher would post them on the laboratory window. When he was 16 he wrote reports on the Far Northern Transvaal Soccer League which were published in the *Northern Review*. His acting skills originated in 'wildly enthusiastic' soccer commentaries which he recorded on a tape recorder while sitting on the touchline at school matches.

Being a sports commentator was his dream. Young Paul persuaded his father, who was determined that he study engineering at the University of Cape Town, that one route was to first enrol for a Bachelor of Arts degree (he chose the BA in Broadcasting) in 1967. The radio commentating mission was derailed after the wide-eyed student saw Robert Mohr's highly dramatic production of *Seppuku*, which was the first piece of professional staged theatre he had ever seen. The die was cast. He entered the drama programme (hiding this from his family), where his teachers were the legendary Rosalie van der Gucht and Mavis Taylor. Taylor was 'not concerned' about Slabolepszy's non-standard English, Afrikaans-tinged accent, and cast him in numerous productions, including *Oh, What a Lovely War* in which he played the MC.

The ambiguities of being an insider-outsider, which inform so much of his writing, were derived from his experiences growing up as a *rooinek* (red neck) in staunch Afrikaner communities and as a *soutie* (a very derogatory term for English-speaking South Africans derived from the Afrikaans word *soutpiel* – roughly translated as salt penis). Ironically when Slabolepszy arrived at UCT Drama School he says suddenly he was called a 'rock' (short for rockspider, which is a derogatory word for Afrikaners used by English-speaking South Africans).

His British birth exempted him from military conscription. If Paul Slabolepszy had gone to the army, fought in the Border wars, as well as serving out his military duty in the townships, his playwrighting might have been very different. As it is, he focused on slices of South African life as he saw it and heard it. Language is key to Slabolepszy's plays, which are marked by an easily recognizable earthy vernacular. In her review of *Heel Against the Head* in *Business Day* of 6 May 1995, critic Mary Jordan describes Slabolepszy as

> the contemporary custodian of our popular culture. As an intelligent observer, he draws attention to our whole way of life. We have relaxed modes of leisurewear that are uniquely our own; and Calvinistic thought patterns that accept friendliness as a reality of polite behaviour. Slabolepszy's dramatic work has both clout and merit because he perceives the old fashioned values behind the provincial loutishness. He has our speech patterns and inflexions exactly right.[2]

In 1971 he left drama school (graduating from UCT in 1979 with a BA in English and Drama after completing a final subject) to work at Pieter Fourie's CAPAB (Cape Performing Arts Board) Afrikaans drama company where he acted in productions such as *A Flea in her Ear* alongside legendary Afrikaans actors Cobus Rossouw, Sandra Kotze and later Anna Neethling-Pohl. The big draw card for the young actor was 'the so-called communist' German director Dieter Reible 'who was doing subversive theatre'. The Nico Malan, where this state-funded company was based, was segregated. This wasn't the case at the University of Cape Town's Little Theatre. 'There were mixed students, open casting, open audiences. When I moved to the Nico the Whites Only set-up hit me like a brick.'

At CAPAB (which also ran an English company) Slabolepszy befriended photographer Brian Astbury, who photographed productions which included his wife Yvonne Bryceland.

> Brian was pissed off because CAPAB Drama didn't like Yvonne too much because of her strong South African accent. At the end of 1971 Brian said 'Fuck this! I'll find a studio where we can do what we want to do – mixed casts, mixed audiences, the works.' I said: Fok, I'm there.

This is how the small-town dreamer, as Slabolepszy likes to describe himself, became one of the founder members of the ground-breaking, non-racial Space Theatre along with Astbury, Bryceland, Athol Fugard, Jacqui Singer and Bill Flynn, who became his best friend and collaborator until he died, aged 58, in 2007. Towards the end of 1972, writer and director Barney Simon (with Pact Drama's Mannie Manim) paid a visit from Johannesburg:

> Barney seduced me under Brian's nose. He said to me 'Listen, we are going to do alternative theatre and tell our own stories.' He inspired me so much. He had a different way of working from Athol. I made an immediate connection with Barney – he tapped into my exploratory nature and my desire to write, but I couldn't articulate that. Barney opened a door for me with his unique research process which was unlike anything I'd ever encountered before.

Asked about the influence of Fugard and Simon on his theatre making, which, although always a written text, has a workshopped, experimental ethos, Slabolepszy explained:

> I had more contact with Barney. I met Athol at the Space when we started it. I watched rehearsals of *Statements after an Arrest under the Immorality Act*. Athol was far more private. Barney [was] more outgoing and he drew things out of you. With Barney you connected, with Athol there was a screen. Barney was affirming and nurturing, tapping into my story-telling instincts; while with Athol (inspiring as he was) I felt I was simply a performer breathing life into his creations.

In Johannesburg, in 1974, Slabolepszy became a founder member of Simon and Manim's collective The Company, where he earned his first DALRO

(Dramatic, Artistic and Literary Rights Organisation) best actor award (1976) for the role of Smitty in *Fortune and Men's Eyes* staged at the Wits Nunnery, directed by Barney Simon. The Company opened the Market Theatre in 1976 where this production was restaged to great acclaim.

The actor-playwright has had five world premieres at The Market, starting with *Saturday Night at the Palace* (1982), *Pale Natives* (written in 1993, staged in 1994) and *Fordsburg's Finest* (1997). *Pale Natives*, a portrait of South African white male middle-aged angst at the birth of democracy, was restaged as a 20th anniversary production by the Market Theatre in 2014.

He wrote his first play, *Renovations*, in 1979 and it was presented as a play reading for Pieter Fourie at CAPAB Drama. The only one of his thirty-three plays never to be produced is set in a digs shared by a white and a Coloured student. The white parents visit with dramatic consequences. 'This was a story springing from real life. It is about renovating the father's racist mind. I wish I could find that script.'

His second play, *The Defloration of Miles Koekemoer*, the story of a country bumpkin bank clerk who throws a fancy dress party in his city flat, was staged at the Baxter Theatre in 1980 with the three characters played by Richard E. Grant, Fiona Ramsay and Marcel van Heerden, at the start of their very illustrious careers. This one-acter is now performed by schools under the new title *Miles from Machadadorp*.

Paul Slabolepszy's prowess as an experienced, virtuoso actor cannot be underestimated in its contribution to the creation of his most iconic characters: Vince in *Saturday Night at the Palace*, Pa in *Smallholding*, Eddie in *The Return of Elvis du Pisanie* and Crispin in *Heel against the Head*. He also performed all these roles at the plays' premieres. In recent revivals (mainly at student level) of *Palace* and *Elvis*, it has struck me that like Shakespearian metre, Slabolepszy's language has specific textures and rhythms. Body language and socio-political/cultural contexts are crucial to the gritty characterization. For example, Vince doesn't merely walk, he prowls like a ducktail fuelled by white superiority, arrogance and ignorance.

All of Slabolepszy's plays are period pieces, time capsules, capturing aspects of South African life. In her review of *Pale Natives*, headlined 'Nothing pale about this study of masculinity' (*Business Day*, 27 January 1994), Mary Jordan observed:

> As five old school mates meet after a quarter of a century to anticipate the third marriage of one of their number, he tests their moralities as

each seeks personal knowledge and individual truth. Slabolepszy's intuitive ideas and images collide in a full and rich text. Words are used with Elizabethan vigour, humour and conviction.[3]

As is the case with so many experienced South African theatre professionals, financial circumstances and the absence of post-apartheid repertory companies and other resources have forced this playwright to write commercially. While his body of work contains several classics in their own genres, tragically the script of *Making Like America* (1986) has been lost. This five-hander plugs into growing white security-conscious paranoia. The main characters are the Buys brothers Wesley (played by the author), who welds burglar bars for his two-bit Johannesburg security company, and his former cop and ex-con brother Cowboy (Marius Weyers). Barry Ronge rated this play in *The Sunday Times* as 'a show that puts Paul Slabolepszy among the best … He now occupies the same position in relation to our theatre and society that Arthur Miller and Tennessee Williams did in America in the 50s.'

South African adoration of American popular culture and television pops up in other Slabolepszy plays. What this playwright and actor did achieve in the wake of the introduction of television in January 1976 was to take audiences beyond sit-com comfort zones with highly entertaining yet engaging, thought-provoking subject matter. Slabolepszy's ability to tune into, reflect, even predict socio-political undercurrents and political change is also evident in *Smallholding*, *Braait Laaities*, *Mooi Street Moves* and *Pale Natives*.

His love affair with theatricality and acting is at the core of *Freak Country*, a satiric political thriller and tragi-comedy of cross-cultural errors, set in an unnamed Southern African airport interrogation room, in which a drunken politically incorrect South African actor finds himself at the mercy of unamused customs officials.

Pure comedy business is ever present in the sports plays, notably *Under the Oaks*, *Over the Hill* and *Heel against the Head*. Yet, the audience's laughter generated by the characterizations, subtexts and the language is not always escapist, as it is often used as subterfuge to convey a deeper meaning.

The plays

Saturday Night at the Palace *(1982)*

Saturday Night at the Palace owes its genesis to a news report Paul Slabolepszy read in the *Rand Daily Mail*. The headline 'Bizarre Attack on Roadhouse' triggered his curiosity and imagination which synthesized with his sense of the ugly complexities of the country and society he was living in.

This play was written as an entry for the 1981 Amstel Playwright of the Year Award (1978–94). As the winning entry, *Saturday Night at the Palace* went into production and premiered upstairs at the Market Theatre on 6 May 1982. This was the beginning of director Bobby Heaney's long association with Slabolepszy as a writer and actor (Heaney has birthed the majority of this playwright's plays). The cast comprised Fats Dibeco as the waiter September who is closing up Rocco's Burger Palace – described in the script as 'A run-down drive-in road-house somewhere between Benoni and Brakpan, South Africa' – before he visits his family in the homelands. Bill Flynn played Forsie, the not-so-bright hospital orderly, and the author took the role of his macho friend Vince, a failed soccer player with a giant racist chip on his working-class shoulder.

The levels of violence and betrayal underpinning the authentic dialogue, vibrant characterizations and all-too-familiar situations appealed to audiences. The critically acclaimed play and production put Slabolepszy on the national radar, winning Vita and Fleur du Cap awards. He also received the 1983 Standard Bank Young Artist's Award for drama.

International exposure followed when *Palace* travelled to the Old Vic in London in April 1984. Michael Billington observed in *The Guardian*:

> In a sense, Mr Slabolepszy is making a similar point to Fugard in *Master Harold*, that racial antagonism often has its roots in self-hatred. But the best thing about his play is his easy, natural depiction of the relationship between the two white men: Forsie is the born stooge who worships the macho values of Clint Eastwood, while Vince is the insecure tail chaser who needs someone to dominate.[4]

The unpredictability of that relationship and the pathetically misplaced sense of superiority of the characters themselves, paired with September's dignity under enormous fire, combine to present a gritty portrait of apartheid society.

Unlike Pieter-Dirk Uys and Fugard, Slabolepszy's plays were not banned, nor was he harassed by the security police. Perhaps the slice-of-life nature of his work spared him. The playwright recalls the presence of the security police in the audience at the Market after a performance of *Saturday Night at the Palace*. One of them was in the bar. 'We asked him: "Does this happen?" He said "yes". The play had got to him, had made a connection.'

But in Bloemfontein the rector of the University of the Free State stormed out of the performance. 'He was screaming: This doesn't exist.' The rest of the country disagreed. The production was seen by 40,000 South Africans and toured for two years. The innate, mirrored, truths and metaphors for a diseased society rang true and, post-apartheid, continue to do so. Yet now there are issues of hate speech.

While Forsie refers to September as an oke (bloke), Vince uses the K word liberally. He tells Forsie 'He doesn't own it poephol. How can a kaffir own a road-house?' (47). There were no official objections to Vince's racist rantings. That wasn't the case when Slabolepszy, directed by Henry Goodman, performed the Barney Simon monologues *Joburg, Sis!* in Cape Town in 1978. This production in the Baxter Theatre Studio was briefly banned by the Publications Control Board on 12 February. Among the offensive words were *shit, piss, pissed, fuck* and *fucked*. Also prohibited was 'use in the dialogue of the word "kaffir"'.

These same monologues were previously performed by Pact Drama at the Old Arena in Doornfontein, in Johannesburg, seemingly with no official complaints or response. In his correspondence to the University of Cape Town's Registrar, Baxter Theatre director John Slemon explained that a review in the *Cape Times*, 'precipitated the attention of the censors'. Headlined 'Crudity Mars the Show', the review was written by Geoffrey Tansley and published on 11 February. Most interesting, in terms of Slabolepszy's own writing, was the critic's comment that 'an intrinsically fine piece of theatre writing was marred by an insistence on too much realism driven home for an inartistic effect'.[5]

It is exactly that heightened realism which fuels *Saturday Night at the Palace* and the rest of the playwright's artistic arsenal. Could it be the veracity of the language and the skilfully crafted characters, the culturally spiked humour, which spared Slabolepszy from such critical lambasting and earned such public support?

The audience not only sees and hears Vince but understands where he's coming from when he lashes out to a panicked Forsie:

Whose side are you on? Your whole life you've had it made! I'm nine years old they skop my old man out of the mines to give bastards like this work. Huh? Scaling tins of baked beans from the corner Greek. You get caught once, just once – it's with you for life (*Tapping his forehead*) you carry it here. Huh? Then you got your child psychiatrists – their moffie advice. 'Go write some poetry, Vince, you'll feel better.' Poetry! For fuck's sake, man. The times I've been in for a job – the bastards take one look at your face; you know what the answer's going to be. 'Sorry, no vacancies.' I tell you I've had it, my mate … A man's got his pride, man. (66)

Issues of class, race and job reservation flow in a stream of vernacular steeped in hurt and prejudice.

In *Saturday Night at the Palace* and the rest of his plays, Slabolepszy proves to be a crafty eavesdropper on pockets of South African life. He excels at being the chronicler of the seemingly ordinary, the normal, in both abnormal apartheid and shifting post-apartheid contexts.

Mooi Street Moves *(1992)*

A decade after Vince, Forsie and September unleashed their tragic lives into the annals of South African theatre history, Stix Letsebe and Henry Stone made their entrance, not at an East Rand road-house but in the heart of Hillbrow, a Hillbrow as pock-marked by social transition and under threat of survival as apartheid South Africa itself. *Mooi Street Moves*, a one-act play in three scenes, premiered at the Great Hall in Grahamstown in June 1992. The Market Theatre premiere followed in January 1993.

In a reversal of the South African classic film *Jim Comes to Joburg*, Henry (a role created by Martin le Maitre), a naive country boy, travels to the big city to search for his brother Steve. At two o'clock in the morning, in what was his brother's flat in the once genteel Cumberland Mansions, he finds the soccer mad, Zulu-speaking Stix (Seputla Sebogodi), who is eating a plate of pap. Stix is generous with his meal but Henry refuses. At home, down in Richard's Bay, this porridge may be acceptable at a *braaivleis* but it is not white man's food (certainly not without meat). As the two young men interact, those cultural and racial divisions and value systems are on trial. These differences soon dissipate as the two men encounter each other as human beings in a crisis.

This play, as with so much of Slabolepszy's oeuvre, serves as a time capsule. It surfaced six months after the start of the Convention of Democratic South

Africa negotiations between South African stakeholders at the World Trade Centre in Kempton Park. This historic meeting of diverse political parties to formally end apartheid was commonly called Codesa. Shortly after the gullible Henry walks into his life, Stix tells the country bumpkin that he can 'Codesa-desa' (bargain) prices of TV sets and other obviously hot goods (254).

Stix (real name Sipho), the smooth operator, explains the transforming urban landscape, and arrival of slum lords, to his visitor: 'This explains, you see, why when you come in this building – you see some people are making fires in the electric stove. 'n Boer maak 'n plan, but a Black Man – he goes all the way' (257). The dramatic change has happened because 'Mandela is free, my bra. Soweto has come to town. Things are different, jong' (258).

The changes aren't just happening in parliament or at Codesa, but at ground level. Families moving into town from Soweto bring their cultural belief systems and practices with them, whether to the elite Northern suburbs or Hillbrow flatland. Slabolepszy's observant, informed, newspaper reading eye incorporates these social shifts into the dialogue. An astonished Henry tells Stix the next day:

This morning – when you gone out – I check outside here, there's this big noise … they chopping a sheep. On the stairs! All this blood and guts … and they … they selling it in chunks! In big … chunks! Bladdy … sacrifices …!! No I'm telling you this place! (278)

Stix is teaching this man, who has a dream of making a living drilling boreholes for water, the art of selling (stolen goods) on the street. His own philosophy has kept him alive: 'You must know the play. You are never the same thing twice … like a chameleon, you are what you want to be, but – you make the sale. Lesson number one. Sidewalking' (279).

This emblematic survival strategy got him to Hillbrow in 1988: 'that's how we live here in Jo'burg. Like the crab … Ghwack – ghwack – you sidewalk. Side-walking, bra (*Dancing sideways*) the walk of the people. Stix' Walk. Stix Letsebe.'

That stage direction, 'dancing sideways', is not as straightforward or simple as it appears to be. In fact it is riddled with complexity. In the original production, Sebogodi combined the jazzy slink of a *tsotsi*, a township clever, with the slither of a chameleon. The way Slabolepszy's characters move are just as important as the way they speak 'South Africanese'. The characters all have built-in choreographic/movement texts which enhance, amplify and ultimately validate their identities.

Mooi Street Moves is another example of this playwright's ability as a conjurer of moral conscience and socio-political consciousness.

Pale Natives *(1993)*

Masculinity has been a major theme in Paul Slabolepszy's plays. Male characters dominate his writing – women are referred to mainly as mother figures. When they do appear (in works such as *Over the Hill* (Lynette the ex-Citrus Queen) and *Under the Oaks* (Beatrice)), they aren't substantial. The rebellious Evie in *Smallholding* and Thandi in *Fordsburg's Finest* are the few exceptions.

Pale Natives made its debut at the Market Theatre on 25 January 1994, four months before the first democratic elections. The atmosphere was volatile, to say the least. No one knew if the country was on the brink of a civil war or at the dawn of democracy. In the cast were Bill Flynn (as the buffoonish Eddie), Tim Plewman (Ashley), Danny Keogh (Kyle), the author as Roux and director Bobby Heaney as the paralytically drunk groom-to-be Dave.

The five middle-aged men meet for a stag party in a seedy sports club hall in the south-east of Johannesburg. They make constant references to the new South Africa. Kyle, the get rich quick loser whose good looks are deserting him, is the most vitriolic. 'Legacy', the rabid Afro-pessimist tells his mates after the hi-fi won't work and they are complaining about bad light bulbs and non-functioning toasters, '[a]fter three hundred years, this is what you left with, this is the result. Third World Fucken Circus ... Tin-Pot ... One-Horse ... Lame Brain ... Banana fucken Republic!' Eddie chips in later with 'I'm telling you. This country is finish' – echoing what was going through the minds of the (mainly white) audiences.

As these old school friends, who were in a band called Pale Natives, share their lives, this play becomes a soundtrack, a darkly comic requiem, for white, apartheid privileged society. In the *Financial Mail* (in a review titled 'Mates under the sun'), Guy Willoughby observed:

All Slabolepszy's recurrent themes resurface deepened and extended: the nature of male bonding; lower middle-class (white) fears for the future; the jock whose youthful glory days are over. But Slabolepszy's greatest strength – an ear for the rhythms and phrasing of everyday speech – is at its best. His affection for the nondescript members of society – neither the rich nor the homeless – and his delineation of their middling works is brilliant. There is the darker aspect [of] the cheery male camaraderie that goes beyond political pressures (and one senses the writer turning with relief from the necessity of political comment). Slabolepszy is picking at the homo-erotic roots of male friendship – which makes for a certain gingerly aspect to the writing.[6]

The review concludes that 'Ultimately, *Pale Natives* interrogates the middle-class white predicament – we're pale natives in a sunburnt land – with wit, pathos and insight.'[7]

Those qualities of sharp, culturally tinctured wit, aching pathos and piercing insight elevate *Pale Natives*, as well as Slabolepszy's other weightier plays, from mere entertainment into works of enduring dramatic art.

Notes

1. Interview conducted with Paul Slabolepszy in Johannesburg on 19 September 2013.

2. Mary Jordan, 'Slabolepszy Shows that He Understands Rugger Buggers', review of *Heel Against the Head*, *Business Day*, 26 May 1995.

3. Ibid., 'Nothing Pale About this Study of Masculinity', review of *Pale Natives*, *Business Day*, 27 January 1994.

4. Michael Billington, 'Saturday Night at the Palace (Old Vic): Review', *The Guardian*, 12 April 1984.

5. Geoffrey Tansley, 'Crudity Mars the Show', review of *Joburg, Sis!*, *Cape Times*, 11 February 1978.

6. Guy Willoughby, 'Mates under the Sun: Review of *Pale Natives*', *Financial Mail*, 1994.

7. Ibid.

Bibliography

Primary sources

Saturday Night at the Palace (Johannesburg: AD Donker, 1985).
Over the Hill, in *South Africa Plays New Drama from Southern Africa*, selected and introduced by Stephen Gray (London: Nick Hern, 1993).
Mooi Street and Other Moves, introduced by Robert Greig (Johannesburg: Wits University Press, 1994). Plays: *Under the Oaks*; *Over the Hill*; *Boo to the Moon*; *Smallholding*; *Mooi Street Moves*; *The Return of Elvis du Pisanie*.

Secondary sources

Barrow, Brian and Yvonne Williams-Short (eds), *Theatre Alive!: The Baxter Story 1977–1987* (Cape Town: The Baxter Theatre at the University of Cape Town, 1987), 53–5.

Billington, Michael, 'Saturday Night at the Palace (Old Vic): Review', *The Guardian*, 12 April 1984.

Jordan, Mary, 'Nothing Pale About this Study of Masculinity', review of *Pale Natives*, *Business Day*, 27 January 1994.

Jordan, Mary, 'Slabolepszy Shows that He Understands Rugger Buggers', review of *Heel Against the Head*, *Business Day*, 26 May 1995.

Slabolepszy, Paul, interview, 19 September 2013.

Tansley, Geoffrey, 'Crudity Mars the Show', review of *Joburg, Sis!*, *Cape Times*, 11 February 1978.

Willoughby, Guy, 'Mates under the Sun: Review of *Pale Natives*', *Financial Mail*, 1994.

CHAPTER 10
ZAKES MDA
Kene Igweonu

And the Girls in their Sunday Dresses; The Final Dance; The Mother of All Eating; You Fool, How Can the Sky Fall?; The Bells of Amersfoort

Introduction

Zakes Mda is one of Southern Africa's most respected, innovative and audacious playwrights, artists, poets and novelists. Through his works, Mda challenges the appalling social and economic conditions of millions of black South Africans during apartheid, much in the same vein as the popular anti-apartheid movements of that period, but at the same time he 'goes against the grain of the performance traditions and politics of the same movement [i.e. the Black theatre movement of the apartheid era]'.[1] Even though Mda focuses mainly on the experiences of black people in his works, depicting the harsh realities of their existence under apartheid for instance, he does not shy away from criticizing what he perceives as the failure of post-apartheid South Africa in addressing some of the socio-economic inequalities that remain in the society. In fact, most of his plays, written in the period before the end of apartheid, are 'prophetic' in their articulation of the socio-economic inequalities that persist in post-apartheid South Africa and in much of post-independence Africa.

Zanemvula Kizito Gatyeni Mda was born to Ashby Peter Solomzi and Rose Nompumelelo Mda on 6 October 1948 in Sterkspruit, Herschel District, in the Eastern Cape Province. He is the first of four children and has two brothers and one sister. Soon after his birth his father relocated the young family first to Johannesburg and then later to Soweto, where the young Mda spent his early childhood. Mda's father, a lawyer by profession, was one of the founding members of the Pan Africanist Congress (PAC), a breakaway faction of the African National Congress (ANC), which was formed on 6 April 1959 at Orlando Community Hall in Soweto with Robert Mangaliso Sobukwe as its founding president. Sobukwe and other prominent PAC leaders were soon arrested, and later jailed, for organizing the 21 March 1960 protest against the 'pass laws'. The pass laws, which led to the protests, were used to enforce racial segregation in apartheid South Africa and to effectively restrict the movement of the black population in certain areas. The outcome of the protest led to what later became known as the 'Sharpeville massacre' when the police opened fire, killing sixty-nine protesters and injuring close to 200 people.[2] Following his release on bail in 1963, Mda's father fled South Africa and went into political exile in neighbouring Lesotho. In 1964, Mda and the rest of the family joined his father in Lesotho, where he completed his high school education in 1969.

Mda followed briefly in his father's footsteps and studied law for a while, 'but then decided to change direction, pursuing instead a course in the arts and humanities'.[3] Mda completed his Bachelor of Fine Arts (BFA) degree by correspondence at the International Academy of Arts and Letters, Zurich (Switzerland). He then went on to obtain a Master of Fine Arts (MFA) in theatre and an MA in mass communication, both from Ohio University, USA. In 1989, Mda completed his PhD at the University of Cape Town, South Africa, and later published his thesis in book form as *When People Play People* (1993). This book, which explores the use of theatre as a vehicle for social development, has since become a standard text for the study of applied and community theatre in Africa.

Mda has won several awards and worldwide acclaim for many of his works. In 1978 he received a special merit award at the first Amstel Playwright of the Year Award in South Africa for his play *We Shall Sing for the Fatherland*. He went on to win the Amstel Playwright of the Year Award in 1979 for *The Hill*. Written in 1978, *The Hill*, directed by Rob Amato (with Nomhle Nkonyeni as assistant director), had its first production in 1980 at the People's Space Theatre in Cape Town. *The Hill* is set in Lesotho, and uses flashbacks and play-within-a-play to present a bold exploration of the dilemma of migrant workers in South African mines, as well as the irony of their losing all the economic benefits accrued from working in dangerous and dehumanizing conditions in the mines to prostitutes on their return. Mda also won the Christina Crawford Award of the then American Theatre Association in 1984 for his play *The Road* (1982). Writing about Mda as a playwright, Victor Ukaegbu observes that:

> Mda's theatrical style has resonances of Bertolt Brecht's epic theater and of absurdism, with his techniques being developed through the integration of traditional African theatrical and modern European

dramatic forms. Characters and actions are presented and interpreted with typical Brechtian detachment and criticism. Mda's integration of flashbacks and his use of the play within the play link the past, present, and future and provide a wider socio-cultural context to the characters and their environment.[4]

Mda now spends most of his creative energy in writing novels for which he has won several awards including the 1997 M-Net Book Prize for his first novel, *Ways of Dying*, which was first published in 1995. In 2001, Mda won a number of awards for his novel *The Heart of Redness* (first published in 2000), including the Commonwealth Writers' Prize for Africa, the Hurston/Wright Legacy Award and The Sunday Times Fiction Prize. *The Madonna of Excelsior* (published in 2002) was voted as one of the Top Ten South African Books Published in the Decade of Democracy in 2004. Other novels include *She Plays with the Darkness* (first published in 1995), *The Whale Caller* (2005), *Cion* (2007), *Black Diamond* (2009), *The Sculptors of Mapungubwe* (2012) and his memoir *Sometimes There is a Void: Memoirs of an Outsider* (2012).

The plays

And the Girls in their Sunday Dresses *(1988)*

And the Girls in their Sunday Dresses was first performed by the Meso Theatre Group at Springwell House as part of the 1988 Edinburgh Fringe Festival. It was directed by Teresa Devant and had Tokoloho Khutsaone and Gertrude Mothibe as The Woman and The Lady, respectively. *And the Girls in their Sunday Dresses* is a two-character play that is set in an unnamed post-independence/post-apartheid southern African nation that could well be Lesotho or South Africa. At the time of its first production in 1988, Lesotho had been independent for just over two decades, but South Africa was still under apartheid. However, this audacious play can be easily considered as one of Mda's most prophetic works about a post-apartheid South Africa in which the poor masses continue to be marginalized and disadvantaged by the political and economic elites, who use their positions of power to perpetuate some of the socio-economic inequalities and injustices of the past.

The play centres on the lives of two women, The Lady and The Woman, who have been in a queue at the government food aid depot for days in the hope of purchasing some of the rice donated to the poor of the country by the Italian government at a bargain. It is in this situation that The Woman, a domestic worker, and The Lady, a prostitute who had been forced out of business by much younger competition and thus fallen on hard times, strike up an unlikely alliance. They find that they have to depend on each other to survive the long days and hours of queuing for rice at the government office. Anticipating a lengthy wait, both women had arrived at the government office prepared for the wait in their own ways. The Lady does not have any money to buy food but comes prepared with a chair with which to sit out the long wait. For her part, The Woman comes with enough money to buy food to eat while waiting for the government bureaucrats to distribute the bags of rice. The Woman is content just to sit on the ground and wait; however, she is unable to continue in this way after the ground is muddied by rainfall.

When we first encounter the two women, it is to discover that The Lady had secured a deal with The Woman to share her food in return for taking turns to sit on her chair. The women are determined to wait for their share of the rice. Even after The Woman observes the rice being loaded onto a truck and driven away, The Lady is quick to try and reassure her:

Woman   Look, they are loading it into the trucks!

Lady   What?

Woman   The funken rice we are waiting for. They are loading it into those trucks.

Lady   Don't worry. They'll surely leave something for us.

Woman   It's not fair! We have been waiting here for days, and those trucks just drive in and get loaded with rice. It's not fair!

Lady   They'll leave some bags for us, I tell you. I am sure they have counted the number of people in the queue and they'll leave some bags for us. (13–15)

However, Mda goes on to show that such faith in the humanity of those in government and in positions of power is futile. From the nonchalance of the government ladies in their summer dresses, to the unscrupulous government officials who sell the aid rice that is meant for the masses, and the rich contractors who buy up the aid rice to sell the same later on the open market, and the masses who buy the rice knowing full well that it is meant to be received free, Mda portrays a society in which everyone is complicit in the corruption. Despite The Woman's indignation at having to wait endlessly in a queue while, as she puts it, 'Wholesalers, general dealers and jobbers' (14) buy up the aid rice cheaply from the corrupt government officials, only to resell it at much higher prices, Mda argues that everyone is complicit in the corruption as further exchanges between the women show:

Woman   If it's food aid it must be given to the poor for free. And in many cases it helps to keep them where they are – poor.

Lady   The poor, yes, and you and I don't qualify. Let's face it, you came because you heard it's a bargain. You knew before you came that the countries that donated it meant for it to be distributed among the poor for free. But you came to buy it still. You shout at those big guys, but you are not different from them.

Woman   Do you have to bundle me with them?

Lady   All we need is patience, and our turn will come. (14–15)

However, as the women soon discover, patience is not all that it takes. As they wait, they exchange stories about their previous relationships with foreign men and of being abandoned by these men. Mda utilizes the opportunity presented by the women's swapping of stories to argue that the struggle against corruption 'is not just South African. It is Southern African' (26). Also, in the fashion of agitprop theatre, The Woman sermonizes and challenges The Lady to decide not to 'take abuse from anyone' (27), and that 'It is now time for us to change things. To liberate not only ourselves, but the men themselves, for we are all in bondage!' (ibid.). As a result, when they eventually receive the call to move forward with the queue, The Lady appears hesitant, which allows Mda to draw on the idea of play-within-a-play, in which they both play the roles of customer and office girl respectively, to convey the futility of the process. And, as they soon find out, if you are patient and make it to the front of the queue, the corrupt bureaucrats still try to frustrate you by demanding you fill in endless forms with bizarre details including the colour of your eyes and hair, your height and weight, the number of teeth in your mouth, and so on.

In his usual fashion, Mda does not give answers to the issues raised in the play except to mark the point of departure for both women, by refusing to accept the status quo, which is seen in their combined resolve not to contribute to the corruption and attendant dehumanizing treatment of waiting endlessly in the queue:

Lady   I am not going through with it.

Woman   You are not?

Lady   No. I am not. I am going home now, and I am not taking the chair.

Woman   What about the rice?

Lady   To hell with the rice! I am going home, and I know that never again will I need the food aid rice, and my chair of patience. Are you coming or not?

Woman   (*excitedly*) You know what? I love you. I think you are a great human being. Of course I am coming. I am coming.

Lady   Let's go then. (27)

By ending this play with both women refusing to participate in the corrupt practice of buying the aid rice that is meant to be distributed free to the poor, Mda articulates the view that each of us has a part to play in bringing an end to the endemic corruption that plagues most of post-apartheid and post-independence Africa.

The Final Dance *(1993)*

The Final Dance is described by Mda as 'a script for a cinepoem'.[5] The work is written for the camera and is seen from the points of view of the audience, Old Man and Girl. The way the action moves from one scenario to another, showing different angles, alternating, repeating and resonating perspectives, situate the audience as voyeurs in the events that unfold in the work. The entire story is 'told' in silence, without dialogue, and focuses on the life of its two main characters: Old Man and Little Girl. According to Mda, *The*

Final Dance 'is a powerful contemplation on the age-old themes of social discrimination and the need for a humanism that overrides the short-sighted differentiations that we impose in our relations with "others".[6] Like most of Mda's plays (*Joys of War*, *The Bells of Amersfoort* and *You Fool, How Can the Sky Fall?*, for instance) that divide the stage into three acting areas using platforms placed at varying levels – representing different places, periods in characters' lives and, importantly, different levels of power or social existence – *The Final Dance* utilizes three spheres or spaces in its narrative. These are the outdoors space, the Old Man's shack and the mansion belonging to the Little Girl's parents. The outdoors represents a middle ground where both the rich and the poor meet: the mansion and those encountered in it represent the elite of society, while the shack is representative of the struggling masses. In this way Mda denies race the vital role it plays in other works, and instead situates the 'oppressors' and the 'oppressed'/the bourgeoisie and the proletariat within the various racial divides in southern Africa and elsewhere. That *The Final Dance* moves beyond race to articulate the unequal human and social condition of living in general is a point acknowledged by Peterson who queries:

> Does the Old Man's poverty within the Southern African context suggest that he is African [black] and the Little Girl white? Then what do we make of his penchant for improvising a clownish dance to Kabalevsky's 'Comedians' Gallop'? Or the fact that their moment of reconciliation and celebration is an appropriation of the waltz to Strauss's 'Tales from the Vienna Woods' that we initially associate with her haughty parents?[7]

The disdain with which those that control political and economic power treat the poor, the weak and the vulnerable in society transcends race to a great extent, and this seems to inform Mda's decision to deliberately obscure the racial origin of the characters in *The Final Dance*. In its place he privileges a post-colonial and post-apartheid, but distinctly imperial, mindset that he sees as sustaining these inequalities in society – this is seen in the Victorian costumes and manners of the characters encountered in the mansion and the Little Girl's 'resolve to shock their Victorian graces',[8] as opposed to the Old Man's ragged '1990s' (read: post-apartheid era) clothes which render him out of place in the mansion environment.

However, it is also worth noting that the Old Man is also not free from oppression within the 'middle ground' of the outdoors space, as is seen in his unfair treatment at the hands of the Man at the recycling centre who underpays him for the aluminium cans gathered from long hours of scavenging the outdoors. In fact, Mda suggests ironically that the outdoors is not the middle ground that it ought to be, but a place where the unequal power relationships from the margins (represented by the mansion and the shack) are played out. For instance, at the opening of the 'cinepoem' we are introduced to the Dog's (a co-resident of the Man's shack) palpable sense of unease and trepidation at the outdoors – possibly as a result of past experiences and dealings in that environment. The cinepoem starts with the view of a filthy street with overflowing garbage cans, one of which had fallen over:

Closer angle – the fallen garbage can

There is a dog inside which causes the can to rock from side to side as it tries to select what is and is not worth eating. It finds some juicy morsel and, in its enthusiasm rocks the garbage can so much that it rolls and knocks against one of the upright garbage cans. The resulting clanking sound startles the dog which runs out of the garbage can.

Follow – **DOG**

It is scared to death and runs up the street whining. (40)

It seems it is only in his shack that the Old Man feels at home – at one with himself and his fellow residents (and fellow scavengers) the Dog and the Cat. Here we first encounter the Cat 'peacefully sleeping under the makeshift table' (41) and later the Dog, whom we saw earlier at the opening of the cinepoem, 'coils itself on the doorstep' (41). It is also in the shack that we see both animals, which are generally considered 'natural enemies', eating happily together from the same bowl. Using the character of the Little Girl, Mda sets out to challenge, and in the process propose, in the didactic style of Theatre for Development interventions, the vision of a new society that is accepting of everyone and that is free from discrimination.

The Mother of All Eating (1992)

The Mother of All Eating was first performed in 1992 at the Sechaba Hall, Victoria Hotel, Maseru, Lesotho. That production was directed by Mda and had Gonzalez Mosiuoa Scout as The Man. Set in 1980s Lesotho, *The Mother of*

All Eating is a scathing monologue about greed, materialism and corruption, known metaphorically as 'eating', and their tragic effects on the individual and society at large. The one-character play centres on The Man: a corrupt principal secretary to a government minister who considers it the norm to defraud the government and his co-conspirators at every opportunity.

The play opens with The Man returning home from a business trip only to find that his eight-months pregnant wife is not at home. Next, he receives a phone call from Jane who we understand is Joe's wife – Joe has been The Man's friend from their days in high school and university. His conversation with Jane, like all his encounters with the other unseen characters in the play such as the Chief Engineer, Director of the Department of Tenders and Messenger, is cleverly constructed so that even though the audience never actually hears the voice of these characters, the play still retains the sense of unfolding 'dialogue' between The Man and Jane or other characters. With the opening conversation between Jane and The Man, Mda immediately establishes The Man's character as conceited, immodest and corrupt. He simultaneously worries about his absent wife, complains about Joe's refusal to 'eat' like everyone else and ultimately makes a pass at Jane whom he admits to lust after. From the outset, Mda's clever portrayal of The Man leaves the audience in no doubt that he is irredeemably corrupt. The events of the play portray the man as greedy, deceptive and self-centered – particularly in the way he venerates corruption in government, schemes to undercut his fellow accomplices, brags about the wealth he has accumulated and dares the audience to see anything wrong with what he was doing.

He takes a long look at the audience.

The Man   (*frantically*) Come on! Don't be so judgmental against me. Don't look at me as if I have killed someone! I have told you already that I am not doing anything that others are not doing … we are doing it in the interest of this country. For the development and economic growth of our beloved country … Why do you expect Lesotho to be different? It is in the interest of this country that you should have some millionaires like us, so that you can proudly point us out to the world and say, 'We too, in our country, we are developing, we have our own millionaires.' (29)

However, by introducing the element of 'waiting' in the play, Mda succeeds ultimately in confronting the audience with the shocking realization that they are inadvertently complicit in The Man's corruption by revealing his humanity. Throughout the events of the play, we find The Man waiting anxiously for his wife's return and contemplating whether to call the police to report her missing. Waiting for something or someone that never arrives is a recurring theme in much of Mda's works, as seen in the earlier play *And the Girls in their Sunday Dresses*. However, unlike Samuel Beckett's *Waiting for Godot* in which the characters Vladimir and Estragon opt to return the next day to continue their waiting for the ever-elusive Godot, Mda's characters find some kind of closure to their waiting. For example, in *And the Girls in their Sunday Dresses* The Lady and The Woman resolve to leave and stop contributing to corruption by queuing to buy aid rice from the corrupt government officials who sell it. Likewise, The Man in *The Mother of All Eating* discovers that his wife and baby had died in a car crash while trying to get to the hospital and were never coming back. In both of these cases there is a palpable sense of closure: a determined sense of direction or glimmer of hope that we do not find in *Waiting for Godot*.

The Man's response to the sad news and his vulnerability from that moment onwards reveal his humanity and ultimately expose him to the audience as 'one of us'. While still trying to come to terms with the realization that his 'waiting' for both his wife and baby is truly over, The Man is besieged by those he cheated out of what they perceive as their 'fair' share of the proceeds of their latest corrupt deal. These co-conspirators, The Messenger, Chief Engineer, Director of Public Works, Director of Tender Board and Director of the Hydro-Electric Scheme, all confront and attack him at his most vulnerable, leaving the audience to empathize with him due to their shared humanity. It is also at this moment of denouement that Mda, in a manner that is characteristic of the didactic approach deriving from Theatre for Development, offers his audience a point of departure from the status quo by urging them to rise up and take action against corruption. Compelled by the Messenger, The Man ultimately accepts that the power to bring change resides with the masses on the streets of Lesotho and not the few in government:

> **The Man** ... Okay, okay, I admit. One day the people shall rise. The people have the capacity to rise! The people are not blind! They may seem to be docile now, but it will take a very small thing to spark action in them, and to arouse them to anger that has not been seen before ... (35)

Mda consequently leaves The Man's final words, in which he clearly identifies with the audience/masses, before eventually receiving '*a last kick on the stomach which finally shuts him up*' (36), to continue to echo in the mind of the audience: 'So you can beat me up now, but *our* time will come too …' (36, emphasis mine).

You Fool, How Can the Sky Fall? *(1995)*

The first production of *You Fool, How Can the Sky Fall?* (1995) was directed by Peter Se-Puma and had the following cast: Gamakhulu Diniso as The President; Anton Dekker as The General; Themba Ndaba as The Minister of Culture; Theresa Iglich as The Minister of Health; Darrill Rosen as The Minister of Justice; Ernest Ndlovu as The Minister of Agriculture; and Desmond Dube as The Young Man. The play is described as 'an unbridled study in grotesquerie'[9] and is certainly a surrealist piece that finds parallels in the post-independence governments of Lesotho and Zimbabwe. In this regard, *You Fool, How Can the Sky Fall?* can also be seen as a cautionary tale to the new black majority government that emerged in post-apartheid South Africa in 1994. The play uses life in an illusory prison as a metaphor for the life of members of the cabinet in a corrupt and inept government headed by The President, who is addressed by his cabinet ministers as 'the Wise One, His Excellency the Father of the Nation'.

By setting the play in a prison, Mda signifies the remoteness of post-independence/post-apartheid government politicians and leaders from the very people they are meant to serve. Cocooned and shielded, as it were, from 'real life' as experienced by ordinary citizens, these politicians make and enact diktats and laws without considering their impact on the lives of ordinary people. Moreover, while in this state of denial and isolation, the occasional encounters they have with the 'outside world' are seen as torturous and humiliating by these deluded politicians and leaders. Like most of Mda's plays, action in *You Fool, How Can the Sky Fall?* takes place on three planes or stage areas. The first of these is a dimly lit upstage area which Mda refers to as 'the shadows' and designates as the weakest plane where the characters go to rest, albeit in grotesque positions. The second plane is the downstage area, which is the main acting area where most of the action of the play takes place, while the third space, and by far the most potent, is the plane beyond the unseen metal doors. It is in this third plane that the rest of the citizens can be found. It is the site of the revolution that swept away the erstwhile colonial government in Lesotho and Zimbabwe for instance, but which ultimately produces dictatorial governments that soon abandon the ideals of the revolution and mortgage the future of the citizens for selfish gains. The play is a full-on satirical portrayal of the idiocies of dictatorship by those who inherit state power through revolution, only to turn around and deny the masses the same rights that they fought so long and hard to attain.

At various points in the play, between the dingy cell or cabinet chamber and the third plane, the audience can '*hear the sounds of chains, of keys, and of a heavy metal door opening*' (50) to reveal the '*grotesque and menacing shadow*'[10] of their supposed jailor and torturer. It could be considered that in Mda's conception, it is the cabinet members' encounter with this menacing shadow and the citizens beyond the metal door that frames the entire events of the play. The cabinet ministers who venerate The President and obey him unquestioningly are summoned and tortured individually by their jailors, represented by the grotesque and menacing shadow. At the same time the entire cabinet, particularly The President, is distressed by the news that the Daughters of the Revolution had successfully undermined their authority by holding a beauty contest in protest against the government. However, in true absurdist fashion, the cabinet resolves to counter the impact of their supposed trouncing at the hands of the Daughters of the Revolution by conferring The President with divine titles as 'The Anointed One' and 'Chosen One', as well as the degree of Doctor of Philosophy (90–1).

In true Mda fashion, *You Fool, How Can the Sky Fall?* uses the idea of 'waiting' to generate and sustain the dramatic tension in the play. Soon after the opening of the play, we learn that the cabinet is awaiting the return of the Minister of Works, who is the only one other than The President that is held in awe by members of the cabinet due to his resourcefulness in devising corrupt means of pilfering the coffers of government.

President   ... Anyway, has no one of you heard from the Honourable the Minister of Works yet?

Justice   No one, sir ... since they took him away.

Agriculture   They took him, and never brought him back. (46)

Occasionally, throughout the play, we find the members of the cabinet recalling the exploits of the Minister of Works, while they continue to wait for his return. As in other plays explored here, Mda brings closure to the waiting near the end of the play when we discover the jailors/torturers had killed the Minister of Works in 'a most ignominious' way (85). Also, Mda portrays the members of the cabinet anxiously awaiting their turn to be tortured, as well as the opportunity to discover who the traitor among them is. However, at the end, it takes the Young Man, who is evocative of the ordinary citizens, to unravel the mystery of the traitor's identity and bring that waiting to an end. By using the Young Man's revelation of The President's treachery to bring about a startling denouement to the play, Mda calls attention to what he perceives as society's role in creating the sort of tyrannical, inept and self-absorbed leaders represented by The President, who warns as he is spat on by Health, the only female member of the cabinet:

President   You spit at me now. But I am your own creation.

All the others join in the spitting.

President   What you enjoy doing is building gods, putting them on a pedestal, worshipping them for a day, and then throwing stones at them and knocking them down. You have a very short attention span in the admiration of the gods that you create!

Lights fade to black as they repeatedly spit at him, mustering as much phlegm as possible, and plashing him all over with it. (108)

The Bells of Amersfoort *(2002)*

In a note to the publisher, Mda describes *The Bells of Amersfoort* (2002) as 'the most recent of my plays. It tries to rehabilitate the Afrikaner in the imagination of South Africa.'[11] Ironically, *The Bells of Amersfoort* remains Mda's latest play to date. He was commissioned to write it by the Netherlands-based De Nieuw Amsterdam Theatergroep. The play's first performance in March 2002 was a joint production with actors from the De Nieuw Amsterdam Theatergroep and South Africa's Sibikwa Community Theatre. It was directed by Aram Adriaanse, with music composed by Mda, and opened at the Theatre De Balie in Amsterdam, Netherlands, on 29 March 2002, and transferred to the National Arts Festival, Grahamstown, South Africa, later that year.

The Bells of Amersfoort is about the only play by Mda in which the characters are not entirely symbolic but realistic (*Banned* also utilizes a mixture of symbolic characters and realistic character types). Unlike other plays with symbolic characters such as The Man, The Lady, The Woman, Young Man, and so on, the characters in *The Bells of Amersfoort* are realistic and have names that identify them as distinct individuals. The play revolves around the life of its main character, Tami Walaza, a black South African exile living in Amersfoort in the Netherlands. Even though Tami, like Johan Van Der Bijl and Katja, and other characters in the play are realistic, they nonetheless bear the burden of representation. Tami for instance is forced to take on the weight of representing blacks in general, and is expected to conform to Katja's stereotypical view of black Africans when she challenges her by asking, 'What kind of a black person are you who knows nothing about drumming?' (128). Katja goes on to ask, 'Black people are storytellers, aren't they?' (ibid.). For her part, Katja represents the stereotype of the 'spoilt' European who has never experienced hardship:

> **Tami** Don't you dare preach to me. Did the comrades send you
> here to reform me? Did they? To preach to me? What would you
> know about it? What experience do you have of it? Damn nothing,
> I bet! You are just a spoilt little girl who grew up in the protective
> cocoon of a caring society. You wouldn't know a thing about
> hardship. You wouldn't know a bloody damn thing about the things
> that have happened to me. (118)

Though set, for the most part, in the Netherlands, *The Bells of Amersfoort* deals specifically with the themes of home and exile in the context of a post-apartheid South African society. Tami, who fled South Africa in the days of apartheid, feels isolated in the Netherlands, and longs to go home to the new South Africa to fulfil her dreams of healing the land with her fiancé, Luthando, whom she left behind. Her isolation is compounded by a palpable sense of unease about going home, which manifests itself in bouts of pain triggered by the sound of the bells of Amersfoort when they toll. Even though Tami longs to go back to South Africa and to Luthando, she feels unable to leave the town of Amersfoort until her demons are exorcized. Responding to Luthando's enthusiastic call to return home, Tami pledges to come once she has expelled her demons:

> **Luthando** We are free, Tami, we are free. After almost four
> hundred years we are free. The burden of humiliation has been

removed from our shoulders ... Is that not what you and I fought for, Tami? Now we have got it. Come back, Tami. Come back.

Tami   ... The demons continue to eat my insides. I am a seeker, Luthando. I have always been a seeker. Perhaps that is why I am here. I am a seeker, but I do not know what I seek.

Luthando   How will you know when you find it?

Tami   When I find it I will not seek anymore. And the demons that are eating me shall disappear from my life .... (129)

As the play progresses we discover that the bells of Amersfoort incarnate Tami's torture at the hands of Johan Van Der Bijl in apartheid South Africa – and, that it was Johan who led the police offers that disrupted her wedding, and arrested and tortured her for her role in the struggle against apartheid. In this sense Johan represents white South Africans who participated in the injustices meted out to blacks during apartheid. Mda uses a scene that re-enacts Johan's appearance at the Truth and Reconciliation Commission to bring healing to Tami, even though she does not recognize it at that time and confronts Johan accusingly: 'You got something. You got amnesty ... What did I get? What did the victims get for their stories?' (151). However, although she didn't know it at that time, that experience of the Truth and Reconciliation Commission, even though cursory, had delivered her of those demons she spoke to Luthando about, as evidenced when the bells toll again at the end of Scene Ten without the pain that accompanied the previous tolling.

With her freedom from the demons that tormented her for years, Tami was able to return to South Africa. However, she finds that things have changed and that the ideals of the struggles had been betrayed by the likes of Luthando. Through the character of Luthando, Mda takes a swipe at erstwhile freedom fighters who have not only abandoned the promise to heal the land, but have embraced corruption as a way of life.

Summary

One way of understanding Mda's dramaturgy is to go back in time to one of his earliest plays, *We Shall Sing for the Fatherland* (first performed in

1978). In writing about what he perceives as the principal defining features in Mda's works, Ukaegbu notes that 'His plays explore and articulate victims' feelings, and as political theater they empower the victim and echo Mda's own anguish at events in his society.'[12] Ukaegbu also observes that 'the symbolic use of character and setting and the dynamism of his plays demonstrate Mda's unique theatrical style.'[13] This defining feature in Mda's dramaturgy is evident in the works explored in this chapter and can equally be traced to *We Shall Sing for the Fatherland*.

We Shall Sing for the Fatherland focuses on the lives of two veterans of the liberation struggle who had been abandoned in the post-apartheid dispensation. Their abandonment on the attainment of the liberation they fought to achieve as freedom fighters eventually results in their destitution. Betrayed, oppressed and marginalized by the very people they fought alongside in the quest for a new society, the veterans contemplate the true meaning of freedom and what it means to be a citizen of the new South Africa. The works explored in this chapter show, as any serious study of the works of this audacious playwright, artist, poet and novelist will demonstrate, that, to borrow Ukaegbu's words, 'Mda's work stands out for its use of a variety of theatrical devices, for its imagination, and for its urgency of thought.'[14]

Notes

1. Bhekizizwe Peterson, 'Introduction', in Zakes Mda, *And the Girls in their Sunday Dresses: Four Works* (Johannesburg: Witwatersrand University Press, 1993), vii.

2. (*SAHO*, n.d.)

3. Zakes Mda, *And the Girls in their Sunday Dresses: Four Works* (Johannesburg: Witwatersrand University Press, 1993), viii.

4. Victor Ukaegbu, 'Zakes Mda', in *Contemporary Dramatists* (Detroit, MI: St James Press, 1998), 465.

5. Mda, *And the Girls in their Sunday Dresses*, 39.

6. Quoted in Peterson, 'Introduction', xxii.

7. Ibid., xxiii.

8. Mda, *And the Girls in their Sunday Dresses*, 44.

9. Rob Amato, 'Introduction', in Zakes Mda, *Fools, Bells and the Habit of Eating: Three Satires* (Johannesburg: Witwatersrand University Press, 2002), xi.

10. Ibid.

11. Quoted in ibid., xviii.

12. Ukaegbu, 'Zakes Mda', 465.

13. Ibid.

14. Ibid.

Bibliography

Primary sources

Works by Zakes Mda
And the Girls in their Sunday Dresses: Four Works (Johannesburg: Witwatersrand
    University Press, 1993).
Fools, Bells and the Habit of Eating: Three Satires (Johannesburg: Witwatersrand
    University Press, 2002).

Secondary sources

Amato, Rob, 'Introduction', in Zakes Mda, *Fools, Bells and the Habit of Eating:
    Three Satires* (Johannesburg: Witwatersrand University Press, 2002).

Graver, David, *Drama for a New South Africa* (Bloomington: Indiana University
    Press, 1999).

Peterson, Bhekizizwe, 'Introduction', in Zakes Mda, *And the Girls in their Sunday
    Dresses: Four Works* (Johannesburg: Witwatersrand University Press, 1993).

'Police kill 69 people during the Sharpeville Massacre', *SAHO: South African
    History Online*, http://www.sahistory.org.za/dated-event/police-kill-69 people-
    during-sharpeville-massacre (accessed 13 August 2013).

Ukaegbu, Victor, 'Zakes Mda', in *Contemporary Dramatists* (Detroit, MI: St James
    Press, 1998), 464–5.

CHAPTER 11
LARA FOOT
Loren A. Kruger

Tshepang; Hear and Now; Karoo Moose; Solomon and Marion; Fishers of Hope

Introduction

Lara Foot has been Director and CEO of the Baxter Theatre Centre at the University of Cape Town since 2010, having worked there as associate director since 2000. After receiving her BA Honours in Drama from Witwatersrand University in 1989, she worked in Johannesburg as a director, especially at the Market Theatre where she was resident director from 1996 to 2000. She has staged plays by international playwrights such as Beckett, Büchner and Arthur Miller as well as plays by South Africans Fugard, Slabolepszy and Susan Pam-Grant. While at the Baxter, she began to write and direct her own plays. These include *Tshepang* (2003, published 2005), *Hear and Now* (2005), *Karoo Moose* (2007, published 2009) and *Solomon and Marion* (2011, published 2013), as well as the as yet unpublished *Fishers of Hope* (2014).

The plays

Foot's writing first reached audiences in 1999, when she directed an adaptation produced in workshop with the cast of Zakes Mda's first novel, *Ways of Dying*, at the Market Theatre. The adaptation revised the novel's focus on Toloki, self-styled professional mourner (played by Bheki Vilakazi, who went on to do research for Foot's later productions), by creating vivid dialogue for interlocutors such as former beauty Noria (Naledi Rakane) and Toloki's rival, coffin maker Nefolovhodwe (Mncedisi Shabangu, who went on to perform again for Foot, most recently in *Fishers of Hope* 2014). In the novel, Toloki initially dismisses Noria as a 'beautiful stuck-up bitch from his village ... grown old now ... but still beautiful,[1] even though he later comes to appreciate her advice on life and death in the squatter camp they both inhabit. Foot's adaptation, however, challenged his view; she cast Nomsa Nene, who had her debut at the Market Theatre in 1978, as the first and most powerful of four narrators, and thus used an older woman to shape the audience's perception of the action. Although Mda leaves time and place unspecified, the burning tires and the death of youth suggest that Toloki finds his vocation in the pre-post-apartheid interregnum around 1990, when violence between political and barely political rivals was killing bystanders as well as activists. By 1999, Foot's amplification of the role of Nene's 'Storyteller one' as wise adviser and sassy narrator encouraged audiences, albeit without explicit radical alteration of the text, to see the story as one depicting changes in ways of dying wrought by AIDS.

Tshepang *(2003)*

Foot's first original play, *Tshepang*, tackled an even more controversial subject: the 'twenty thousand child rapes in South Africa per year' (55).[2] The play did not directly represent Baby Tshepang (Hope), the child so named by the media who rushed to the village of Louisvale where she had been abused by her mother's partner in 2001, but the spare one-act drama narrated and re-enacted mostly by a single speaker, Simon, depicted the village people whose lives had been wasted by poverty, hopelessness and drink. Simon's account, witnessed by his silent companion Ruth, did not exonerate the perpetrator, Ruth's partner whom Simon calls Alfred Sorrows, but portrayed him and his fellow villagers as surplus people abandoned by the South African state. Although his phrase was once used by activists to denounce the apartheid government for hounding black people from their homes, it now sadly applies to those left behind by the new black elite who have presided over a wealth gap that has left the poor even worse than under apartheid.

Simon's narration, performed in Cape Town and Johannesburg by Shabangu, with Nonceba Didi as Ruth, begins by showing the town's inhab-itants, or at least a representative sample, battered by drought, poverty and thirst quenched by *valwyn*, wine made from rotten grapes that wine farmers still give – albeit illegally – to workers in lieu of wages, and by random sex with multiple partners. Shabangu impersonates Alfred and other male neighbours in turn, while talking about Ruth and other women. Although he tries to engage Ruth's attention, she focuses on the labour of curing animal skins and appears to pay little mind to his stories of injuries incurred while drunk or to his call, in the direction of the audience, for Sarah, the daughter of the owner of the bar where he drinks. When he brings out the hand-carved nativity figures that he hopes to sell to passers-by, Ruth looks briefly at the figure of Mary but 'does not touch it' (15) or otherwise react to him, even when he says to the audience, 'Don't worry about her. She doesn't talk, not any more' (17). Instead, Ruth stares out into the distance, as if waiting for someone to bring back the child who was taken first to hospital and then to an orphanage, while Simon recounts formative moments in his adolescence, including sex with Sarah supervised by her brother who forced Simon, Alfred and other boys to finish 'inside a half-loaf of white bread' (24). He also recalls Alfred's abuse at the hands of his stepmother, whose beatings with a broom Simon re-enacts until the broom breaks to show Albert's broken bones (28).

When Simon eventually mentions Baby Tshepang by name, Ruth turns to 'lash out at him' (39), but she lapses again into silence when he spells out the state of the nine-month-old found lying in the veld with a 'gooey' red mass between her legs: 'raped, sodomized, disembowelled' (40). Using a loaf of bread to stand in for the child raped in Ruth's shack while she was allegedly out drinking, Foot makes an unsettling connection between the infant raped and the abuse of bread in Alfred and Simon's sexual initiation. Recalling the media frenzy that followed the rape, Simon remembers a blonde journalist whose 'painted ugly fingers pointing at the town' provoked him to yell 'this town was fucking gang-raped a long time ago' (49) before passing out from the effort and the drink. This story is bleak indeed, but at the end, after Simon recounts one sensationalized headline after another culminating in the statistic about national rates of child rape cited above, Ruth allows him to rest his head on her shoulder and, after three years of silence, speaks the last words of the play: 'Baby Tshepang' (56). While very far from reconciliation, personal or public, this ending shows a fragment of dignity restored to damaged people in a damaged land, while also setting the stage for Foot's future representation, with minimal drama, of lives hidden behind national headlines.

Hear and Now *(2005)*

For her next play, Foot collaborated closely with Gerhard Marx, the sculptor and installation artist who had designed the set for *Tshepang*. Marx's sketches in response to stories by renowned Afrikaans writer Jan

Rabie inspired the play *Hear and Now*. This was co-written by Foot and her partner, Lionel Newton, who also played the central character, introduced simply as a 'man', in the State Theatre premiere in 2005 and in subsequent performances abroad. The sketch by Marx featured on the cover of both book and programme shows a foreshortened figure of a standing boy who appears to be carrying around his neck a hospital bed with the outlines of stunted legs under the covers. His 'notes on design' call for the actor to wear 'a set of wooden legs, the size of a young child's' around his waist and to 'move around on his knees' (5) and put this figure and his able-bodied female companion ('woman') in a built environment whose skewed dimensions resemble a three-dimensional rendering of an M. C. Escher lithograph. Raised performance levels upstage were connected to lower levels with ladders festooned with strange, apparently organic, outgrowths. The raised areas also featured doors that appeared to be propped up by piles of books. Together these fixtures created a space full of obstacles to highlight the handicapped man's struggle with the space around him. On the main level, a window lies flat like a prop, which the man picks up on occasion, looks through and puts down again, suggesting that his view of the world is shaped not only by his handicap but also by his imagination. The pun in the title highlights this balance between the performance of physical disability and the conjuring of imagined spaces and actions free from the obstacles that limit the character's movement.

The dialogue between the man (Newton sometimes on his knees but more often on crutches) and the woman (Denise Newman in an ordinary late twentieth-century dress and cardigan) dramatizes a relationship under strain, as the man begins by asking 'for how long' has she returned and the woman responding by saying 'as long as I can stand it' (12). This is an exchange that recurs at several points to punctuate dialogue from the past or to announce the woman's entrance or exit through one of the prop doors, occasionally held up for her by the man. She accuses the man of making things up but she joins him nonetheless when he recalls scenes from his childhood, setting the scene by telling the audience that he came from 'a town of certainty' and 'Church steeples' which South Africans might identify as any one of many Afrikaner Calvinist settlements or perhaps recognize as the town satirized in Rabie's novel *Ons die Afgod* (*We the Idol*, 1958). The character in this play makes this tribal history personal by remembering his 'huge and hairy' father (20) who played with his sister when he was in a good mood but dismissed the boy's nocturnal fears as mere imaginings, turning words of comfort into a sharp command 'you hear nothing!' (21).

The father still uses a sharp tone commanding his son to 'stand up!' (27), even when the boy's legs collapse under him. The man recalls that his father became 'more and more angry' (41) over time and that he left the boy in an institution, despite promising to return after the boy finished the book his father gave him. This last recollection provides the final scene with a kind of explanation for the man's obsession with the books that surround him in the present space (59).

In between these memories of childhood trauma, the couple also recall the more recent event of their meeting in the block of flats where they both live. The conversation includes not only jokes about the various noises emerging from their neighbours' flats but also the woman's recollection of farm life, comments on her ailing mother who apparently wants 'her ashes to be scattered in the duck pond' (36), and her later disconcerting discovery of stubble on her mother's chin as she washes the latter's dead body. The play comes to a close with the couple exchanging stories about the decay of a beloved city park that appears to locate the scene in present-day Pretoria, where the play premiered. The woman feels unable to scatter her mother's ashes in the duck pond because the hobos have 'eaten the fuckin' ducks' (51) but rubs them into a nearby Jacaranda tree that reminds her of a 'cradle' (60) and which would recall for the audience the Jacaranda-lined avenues that still distinguish central Pretoria, even though the tree hails originally from South America. The man returns to a story he told the woman too many times about his home town sinking into the mud – 'stone walls and trees leaning into the sponge-like earth' – as a kind of punishment for 'not helping the wounded' (54) to which she previously responded with sharp facts – 'Jan, you were abandoned' (54) – but in the end she assents to his story even if, as his final words suggest, 'there is always more' (61) – she will hear it again and again.

Although it does not depict the sort of South African story that might grab headlines abroad, *Hear and Now* deserves note for its experimental transformation of its source material. As the character's name suggests, this story hints at autobiography but Foot and Marx resist any treatment that might be bounded by a single life or any exemplification of Afrikaner family history. Marx is Afrikaans but his expressionist scenography favours a stylized treatment of biography that is less interested in a naturalist representation of an individual Afrikaner than in using this story as material for a multi-media experiment in dialogue with international trends in performance art. Foot also complicates the biography by putting critical words in the mouth of a woman who, despite her rural background, does not appear to speak Afrikaans, and thus encourages the audience, including the Afrikaans audiences that frequent the State Theatre even in the post-apartheid period, to see this story through the eyes of an outsider even if they hear occasional lines of Afrikaans from the male character. Thus, while *Hear and Now* may seem to lack the overt political theme of *Tshepang*, both the text – lyrical and vulgar by turns – and the experimental scenography show the prison of Afrikaner patriarchy as well as the horizon beyond this confinement.

Karoo Moose *(2007)*

The lives of these in-between people come to the fore in *Karoo Moose*, which had its premiere in September 2007, a few months after *Reach*, but this time at Aardkop, a smaller South African festival. Set in an isolated and impoverished village in the Karoo, the harsh plateau roughly inland from the setting of *Tshepang* whose fishermen suggest proximity to the coast, the play depicts women and children and the men who prey on them, in better-off as well as dirt-poor families. As Thami Mbongo, one of several performers named in the published text who shared the role of narrator while also playing other roles, notes at the outset, Noxton 'is a village where children don't stay children for very long and where adults cannot really afford to be adults' (9–10). At the centre of the drama is Thozama, a girl not quite 15. Foot borrows the name from Thozama Jacob, her collaborator on this occasion, to whom, along with her children and Jacob's, Foot dedicates this play. In the absence of her mother, who died when she was run over by a drunken white farmer, Thozama is burdened with a derelict drunk of a father Jonas whom another narrator (Mdu Kweyama) describes as a 'man without' (12). Since he provides only intermittently for the family, Thozama has to stay home to help her grandmother Grace (Jonas's mother) while her younger siblings go to school. Her place at home does not, however, protect her from Khola, a thug to whom Jonas owes money. Khola rapes Thozama in exchange for Jonas's alleged debts and later, after the birth of the child, briefly kidnaps the infant by buying off Thozama's younger sister with sweets.

The rape of the 14-year-old Thozama both echoes and transforms the plot of *Tshepang*. Whereas in *Tshepang*, sexual violence is the occasion of a play whose central subject is, despite the horror of infant rape, above all about the wasted lives of perpetrator and victim alike, in *Karoo Moose*, Thozama's rape follows a more conventional if no less reprehensible narrative, in that Khola uses the adolescent Thozama as an object of exchange and an instrument to exert power not only over his female victim but also over other men: Thozama's father Jonas and Khola's own henchman David and any other village man who might challenge him. Despite his earlier hapless resignation, Jonas rises to the occasion near the end to strangle Khola as the latter is about to kill Thozama, but Jonas fades from view in the concluding image which shows Thozama and the village children boarding a truck driven by Brian van Wyk, the younger white partner of the two policemen in the village, on the way to 'somewhere better' (62) even though, as Thami says in conclusion, 'we do not know where somewhere better is or even if it exists' (63). Despite the absence of hard evidence for this utopia, however, Chuma Sopotela (stepping out of her role as Thozama) says in the last words of the play, 'a truck crammed with children drives along the highway … We see each of their beautiful faces as they wave goodbye to us' (63). This final image – as the ensemble of adult performers mimes the movement of the truck and, by holding up small brightly coloured suits of clothes, represents without merely mimicking the children on the outing – highlights the power of the imagination to conjure hope.

More concretely, this moment and the play as a whole demonstrate the capacity of the human body and voice, aided by a few portable props, to represent both the specific reality of a small South African village and a story of universal dimensions. Directed by Foot with Bongile Mantsai providing lyrics and musical direction for songs in Xhosa, *Karoo Moose* broke out of the interior sets of both *Hear and Now* and *Reach* and the monologue/duologue format of all her plays to draw on forms and practices that would be familiar to South African audiences. African story-telling forms, in this case the Xhosa *intsomi*, traditionally feature an elder narrator, often a woman, aided by choral responses from listeners, often children. These traditional forms and the customary vocal responses they prompt in African audiences have been transformed, especially since the re-emergence of independent South African theatre in the 1970s, by theatre makers drawing also on a range of European methods. *Karoo Moose* shows the impact of several of these, in particular the poor theatre techniques of Grotowski, the mime techniques of Le Coq and other schools, and Brecht's techniques of estrangement, quotation and musical punctuation in epic theatre. Epic theatre, as Brecht defines it, is best understood not as theatre about national heroes on a grand scale, but as *narrative* theatre: performance that tells stories of common people with social-critical intent and point of view. *Karoo Moose* undoubtedly carries a political message, an unspoken indictment of the newly powerful who neglect the poor, especially the rural poor who still make up 40 per cent of the population, but the fusion of forms, techniques and the story of Thozama and her community creates a drama that is magical as well as realistic, intimately moving as well as politically stringent.

Even before the text introduces the villagers to the audience, the performance begins with a scene that consecrates the space. The six performers enter 'ritualistically', each carrying a prop identified with one of the several characters that each will play, except for Chuma Sapotela, who plays only Thozama and whose entrance, carrying a cabbage 'proudly' on her head (7), highlights the charm and vulnerability of her adolescence. Thami brings on the net, beer bottle and belt associated with Khola, who will later use them to subdue Thozama, but here he bangs on the bottle to prepare the ritual, calling forth the climactic response from Mdu, who shakes the horns of the moose until he 'leaps into the air and becomes a frightened animal' (7). The unlikely presence of a North American animal in the Karoo is initially explained by Brian as an 'accident on the freeway', which freed the moose supposedly intended for a 'zoo or a game park' (11). However, this account by a white character – played like his mother by a black performer – quickly gives way to the black characters' perception of the moose as an uncanny embodiment of the evil roaming their world. The Van Wyks may appear better-off insofar as they have a solid house and enough to eat, but they are also troubled by bad memories: Brian's sister committed suicide because her father raped her. However, while this ghost haunts Brian and his mother only in their heads, Thozama, her family and her friends and enemies are convinced that they see the moose as a 'wild and unimaginable terrifying beast' roaming the village. Yet this beast is not just a supernatural visitation: in the opening ritual, Mdu shows a creature more terrified than terrifying, and Thozama assures her sister that the moose 'doesn't eat children' (14). But it is she who takes the lead and delivers the death blow when a group of children and dogs surround the moose, despite the 'terrible scream' that may be either the moose or Thozama herself (32), and it is she who strips the horns and cooks the meat. This act of appropriation provokes the black policeman Malokwe to arrest her despite his partner Brian's hesitation and despite Grace's attempt to explain that this is the first meat that her family has eaten since Khola came to consume Jonas's chicken and violate his daughter.

This tension between unspecified supernatural threats and everyday torments like hunger, embedded in the overall tension between hope and exhaustion, pervades the play and invites comments in response. When Thozama gives birth in a vehicle identified as the police car, possibly the same one in which she was carried to prison for stealing and eating the moose, the narrators juxtapose the magical image of the 'moon hang[ing] like a cradle in the sky' with Thozama's 'exhausted and desperate' struggle after two days of labour (46). Mdu beats a cowhide drum to announce the birth and then places it on the ground where it frames Chuma's 'infant-like' re-emergence as Thozama's baby through this narrow opening (46). After Thozama names the child Liqhawe (hero), Thami interjects with a meta-theatrical comment: 'Here our story insists on taking a new turn ... Should birth not bring hope? Desperate for new beginnings [the play] plots a new story for Brian and Thozama' (47). This interjection highlights the dangers of 'superficial optimism' in theatrical fictions and the artificiality of fictional solutions to real social problems, as Brecht warned his critics in 1953.[3] In this case, the entangled problems of poverty, misogyny, AIDS and government incompetence, to name only a few, may appear overwhelming, but rather than presuming to offer global solutions, the play more modestly suggests the potential power of individual and collective agency in society as in the theatre. While Brecht may have been sceptical of attempts to represent the impossible or the magical, *Karoo Moose* suggests in its very title the possibility of grasping the impossible. When Thozama 'takes on the power of the beast' to attack Khola (61), the vivid image of the girl crowned by the moose horns lifted into the air rests literally on the shoulders of the ensemble member who carries her (see image, *Karoo Moose* 60), and Thozama's rescue in turn depends on Jonas, who emerges from the shadows to kill Khola and thus becomes more than the 'man we expected him to be' (61). The final picture, the truck carrying Brian, Thozama and the children on the way to 'somewhere better', may seem to outsiders superficially optimistic but to local audiences it represents tenacious commitment in the face of impossible odds to changing their world step by step.

Solomon and Marion *(2011)*

Solomon and Marion began as a play called *Reach*, which dramatizes misunderstandings and attempts at understanding in a series of encounters between Marion Banning, an elderly English-speaking South African, and Solomon Xaba, adult grandson of Thozama, Marion's former housekeeper, who has come to her belatedly to expiate his guilt as an accessory in the death of Marion's son Jonathan. *Reach* had its premiere at the Theaterformen

Festival in Hanover in June 2007 but achieved more impact with the local premiere in July at the National Arts Festival in Grahamstown, South Africa's largest and most influential festival, and later on national tours with the same cast. The production was directed by Clare Stopford and featured the veteran Afrikaans actor Aletta Bezuidenhout, who had been acting in English since her work with Barney Simon at the Market Theatre, and Mbulelo Grootboom, who showed an exceptional ability for portraying suppressed rather than emphatic emotion in keeping with the 'brooding' threat in the script. Its distinctive quality emerges clearly when compared to a more famous play on national tour in 2007, which also dramatizes conflict between an older white South African and a younger and angry black man. Athol Fugard's *Victory* (2006), directed by Foot, focused on a cranky old white man lecturing two intruders and would-be thieves – his former domestic servant's daughter, the ironically named Victoria, and her petty criminal boyfriend – about the inspiration to be had from books, an unrealistic response to young, impoverished South Africans. Whereas Fugard's text is typically garrulous, Foot's dialogue between the elderly white woman and the young, black man, keeper of ambiguous company with criminal associates whom we never see, is strongest when it follows her characteristic pattern of spare, apparently low-key interaction with an undertone of tension building slowly to full-blown crisis.

While the text as published in both versions (2009 and 2013) begins with Marion thinking aloud a letter to her estranged daughter in Australia, the Grahamstown festival performance in 2007 followed an earlier unpublished draft ('Reach MS') to open with the encounter between Solomon and Marion, as Grootboom entered to discover Bezuidenhout lying dusted with red leaves in a wind-swept house. As Solomon, he asked himself out loud why he bothered with 'this old woman' whom he initially does not name, but when he finds Marion he revives her and introduces himself as the grandson of Marion's former domestic servant. Marion initially reacts to Solomon's overtures with bouts of suspicion and rudeness, expressed for example in her tendency to call Solomon 'my boy' and to defend the epithet as an 'endearment' (27) when Solomon rejects the label as racist. Solomon reacts with a somewhat 'threatening' reminder that Marion's house is exposed to danger – 'Someone could kill you and no one would hear' (28). But over the course of the play she comes to accept his concern as genuine and his presence as a surrogate for her son Jonathan, who has been dead for seven years. As they interact over several weeks, these two people separated by age and gender as well as race reach a tentative truce. On the day that she prepares a special meal for both of them, Solomon confesses to having enabled Jonathan's death by distracting him at an ATM long enough to allow the gang whom he had been helping to abduct, torment and kill their victim. He asserts that he has returned to tell her how her son died so as to face his responsibilities 'as a man' (58). The revision has Solomon add that he had recently undergone traditional Xhosa initiation, but the simple gravitas of the original confession does not need either this ethnographic note or the rather graphic account of Jonathan's murder, which smacks of the 'exhibitionist' elements that South African writer Njabulo Ndebele regretted in anti-apartheid protest writing and which he hoped would wither away with a 'rediscovery of the ordinary'[4] in stories of everyday life. Although this exchange ends with Marion thanking Solomon and sending him on his way with a pot, she collapses after his departure and confides in a letter to her absent daughter that she does not expect him to return. Nonetheless, Solomon does return after two weeks and the play ends with Solomon helping Marion up and defending his use of the apparently 'subservient' term 'Mies Marion', in language that echoes Marion's earlier defence of 'my boy', as an expression of 'caring' (64).

The production of *Reach* in Grahamstown concentrated the action in a single act rather than the published two and brought out elements in the relationship between Marion and Solomon that may not immediately strike the reader of the text alone. Birrie Le Roux's set featuring drifting red leaves and greying well-worn wood furniture reflected the age and isolation of the inhabitant, while Bezuidenhout's performance highlighted Marion's fragility. In contrast, Grootboom's brooding and laconic presence suggested a Solomon whose attitude to Marion remained more equivocal than his vocal emphasis on caring implied. Even though he gives her physical help as well as care, lifting her up at the end, for which she offers 'thank you!', the last words of the play, Solomon's line that follows his avowal of care just beforehand, 'I'm not sure what I'm saying, Mies Marion' (64), expressed with reticence, implied not only linguistic uncertainty but also emotional ambivalence.

The 2011 revision as *Solomon and Marion* highlighted the two characters rather than the incomplete gesture towards intimacy that links – and also separates – them. The author's note suggests for the first time that the play had its source in the apparently random murder of actor Brett Goldin in 2006, and in the author's 'empathy' with his mother and with her response to the 'heartache and resilience' of expatriate Janet Suzman, who was rehearsing *Hamlet* with Goldin at the time (*Solomon and Marion*, 7).

Press responses to the play suggested that the role of Marion was made for Suzman[5] but, while Suzman may well have been the better choice to play an English speaker, Foot's attempt to magnify the play's links to topical events, such as South Africa's shocking murder rate and the AIDS crisis, has the opposite effect. These additions tend to clutter up the essential story of Marion and Solomon, which was vividly rendered in the first draft even if it left Solomon's motivation unexplained.

Directed by Foot herself, *Solomon and Marion* in 2011 featured Suzman, who, after decades in Britain, made Marion decidedly more English in bearing as well as voice, and Khayalethu Antony, who played a younger and friendlier Solomon. This combination gave the conclusion a softer tone, which, along with the presence of Suzman, prompted critics to recall Goldin's murder and incorporate it into their reviews. The most detailed review by Corrigall suggests that 'Foot wanted to get behind the headlines … The result was a play called *Solomon and Marion*.'[6] This comment reflects the more detailed account of the death of Jonathan in the revised play, but Corrigall goes on to highlight Solomon and his unknown accomplices, suggesting that this play, like *Tshepang*, allows us to 'probe the psyche of perpetrators'. Even more importantly, I would argue, it encourages readers and spectators alike to reflect on people like Solomon, caught between perpetrator and victim, whose plight is largely ignored by the newly powerful in South Africa.

Summary

Although there are several women directing in South Africa, and others, such as director-writer Yael Farber, who work partly in South Africa but live abroad, Lara Foot remains one of very few female playwrights in a culture that is still thoroughly misogynist. Living in a society in which men rape, maim and kill women and girls with impunity, she has had ample provocation to foreground stories of women's suffering and resistance. Her most recent play, *Fishers of Hope*, extends this range by portraying a fishing family along the shores of Lake Victoria in Kenya, whose livelihood is threatened by overfishing and other forms of environmental degradation, as well as stubborn patriarchal prejudices against women fishing. Nonetheless, all her plays from *Tshepang* to *Fishers* deserve critical acclaim not merely because they tackle the troubling persistence of violence in South Africa, especially against women, but also because they treat these themes with restraint and grace and so capture the attention of audiences who might not be drawn by topical content alone. Moreover, these plays, especially *Karoo Moose* and *Fishers of Hope*, Foot's richest and most dramatically complex texts to date, transcend conventional distinctions between magic and realism, wonder and analysis, affect and politics, and thus show the power while also acknowledging the limits of theatre to create compelling stories for these dark times.

Notes

1. Zakes Mda, *Ways of Dying* (Cape Town and Oxford: Oxford University Press, 1997), 11–12.

2. Child rape forms part of a larger pattern of sexual violence in South Africa. According to the South African Institute for Race Relations (SAIRR), 200,000 women suffer sexual assault in South Africa every year. In this context, some have argued that the media's focus on the rape of children may be disproportionate; for further discussion of these debates and their relevance to *Tshepang*, see Lucy Graham, '"Save us all": "Baby Rape" and Post-apartheid Narratives', *Scrutiny 2* 13:1 (2008): 105–11.

3. Bertolt Brecht, 'Kulturpolitik und Akademie der Künste', *Werke: Große kommentierte Ausgabe* 23 (Frankfurt: Suhrkamp, 1998), 258; idem, 'Cultural Policy and the Academy of Arts', in *Brecht on Theatre*, trans. John Willett (New York: Hill and Wang, 1991), 268.

4. Njabulo Ndebele, *The Rediscovery of the Ordinary: Essays on South African Literature and Culture* (Johannesburg: Congress of South African Writers (COSAW), 1991), 38.

5. Mary Corrigall, 'Lara Foot digs beneath the headlines', *Corrigall on Culture*, 21 November 2011, http://corrigallculture.blogspot.com/2011/11/lara-foot-digs-beneath-headlines.html (accessed 30 April 2014).

6. Ibid.

Bibliography

Primary sources

Works by Lara Foot
Biography on Baxter Theatre website, www.baxter.co.za (accessed 17 March 2015).
Hear and Now (London: Oberon, 2005).
Tshepang (London: Oberon, 2005).

Karoo Moose (London: Oberon, 2009).

Reach, in Greg Homann (ed.), *At this Stage: Plays from Post-Apartheid South Africa* (Johannesburg: Wits University Press, 2009), 31–67.

Reach MS, Director's script in the National English Literary Museum, Grahamstown. 2009: 21.36.

Solomon and Marion (London: Oberon, 2013).

Secondary sources

Brecht, Bertolt, 'Cultural Policy and the Academy of Arts', in *Brecht on Theatre*, trans. John Willett (New York: Hill and Wang, 1991), 266–9.

Brecht, Bertolt, 'Kulturpolitik und Akademie der Künste', *Werke: Große kommentierte Ausgabe* 23 (Frankfurt: Suhrkamp, 1998), 256–61.

Corrigall, Mary, 'Lara Foot digs beneath the headlines', *Corrigall on Culture*, 21 November 2011, http://corrigallculture.blogspot.com/2011/11/lara-foot-digs-beneath-headlines.html (accessed 30 April 2014).

Graham, Lucy, '"Save us all": "Baby Rape" and Post-apartheid Narratives', *Scrutiny 2* 13:1 (2008): 105–11.

Kruger, Loren, 'South African Theatre in the Age of Globalization', *Theatre Journal* 64 (2012): 119–27.

Mda, Zakes, *Ways of Dying* (Cape Town and Oxford: Oxford University Press, 1997).

Ndebele, Njabulo, *The Rediscovery of the Ordinary: Essays on South African Literature and Culture* (Johannesburg: Congress of South African Writers (COSAW), 1991).

South African Institute for Race Relations (SAIRR), 'Press Release: Pistorius's alleged murder victim is one of 2,500 adult women murdered every year', 15 January 2013, http://www.sairr.org.za/media/ (accessed 30 April 2014).

CHAPTER 12
MIKE VAN GRAAN
Brent Meersman

Green Man Flashing; Some Mothers' Sons; Brothers in Blood

Introduction

For the first decade of the twenty-first century, Mike van Graan has been South Africa's most prolific dramatic playwright with a new play every year since 2003. Most of these have had national exposure, the scripts professionally realized in productions in both Johannesburg and Cape Town, and on South Africa's lively festival circuit. His plays have won awards for best new South African play at the country's two major theatre awards – the Fleur du Cap Theatre Awards (Cape Town) and the Naledi Theatre Awards (Johannesburg).

Michael Paul van Graan was born in 1959 in Cape Town, where he still resides. His tertiary education is theatre related with a BA (Hons) in Drama (1986) at the University of Cape Town. He also obtained a Higher Diploma in Education. His Honours dissertation was on international models of popular and political theatre, its principles, functions, forms, techniques and creative methods, and their possible relevance to political theatre in South Africa.

When in his mid-twenties, a Theology Exchange Programme afforded him the opportunity to travel for 11 months to the USA, Nicaragua and Brazil, learning about liberation theology and popular culture.

His cultural activism started early: van Graan participated in the Towards a People's Culture Festival in 1986, and then served as director of the Community Arts Project (CAP) from 1988 to 1991. Throughout his adult life, he has remained active in senior management positions and as a consultant for cultural institutions and for numerous arts festivals and conferences.

During South Africa's transition to democracy and during the first phase of the new dispensation, van Graan worked actively towards shaping the country's future cultural institutions, from 1993 to 1996 as elected General Secretary of the National Arts Coalition, the country's largest arts and culture lobby, and then as special adviser to Dr Ben Ngubane, the Minister of Arts, Culture, Science and Technology in the first cabinet of the new democracy.

In January 1996, van Graan launched Article 27, a consultancy specializing in cultural policy, the name referring to the Universal Declaration of Human Rights Article 27: 'Everyone shall have the right freely to participate in the cultural life of the community and to enjoy the arts'.

He also researched and co-edited (with Tammy Ballantyne) the second edition of *The South African Handbook on Arts and Culture* (2002). Van Graan therefore has a deep inside knowledge of the theatre industry in a way few playwrights ever have.

It would be fair comment to say that over time, frustration and some disillusionment with how the new government was handling cultural policy set in. By the year 2000, cultural institutions in South Africa were in a crisis, and numerous organizations were either failing or folded. Van Graan became a reliable and crucial commentator with his exposés and sharp analyses of things cultural in his weekly columns for artslink.co.za, later Artwatch, and Artwit, and as arts columnist for the national weekly *Mail & Guardian* from 2003 to 2005, where he regularly put the spotlight on corruption and incompetence in various state institutions.

Van Graan is a patriotic and committed democrat who has through his playwriting extended his cultural and civil society activism into any number of societal problems challenging the country, its people and its fledgling democracy.

The plays

Early plays (1980–92)

As a playwright, van Graan started with sketches in high school as part of a church youth club. Throughout his twenties, he wrote, directed and acted in numerous sketches and plays performed by members of student organizations affiliated with the anti-apartheid civil society movement (broadly known as the UDF, the United Democratic Front). These scenes and playlets were performed in community halls and other civic centres, staged at political rallies and gatherings, and were also used for educational workshops.

Prisoners of Conscience juxtaposed a political detainee with a conscientious objector; *Tricameral Blues* was a satirical piece exposing the absurdities of the apartheid constitution; *Boetie, hy gaan border toe* (Brother is going to the border) denounced military conscription; and *Passing by the other side* was a piece of street theatre protesting against the migrant labour system and the pass laws (the performers were arrested by the apartheid authorities).

As democratic space freed up in the cultural landscape, van Graan began to participate in the mainstream, starting on the Fringe at the National Arts Festival with works such as *The Dogs Must be Crazy* (1991), a set of seven satirical sketches about politics, and *Some of our Best Friends are Cultural Workers* (1992), a two-hander satirizing funding in the arts.

Green Man Flashing *(2004)*

Van Graan's breakthrough as a dramatist came with *Green Man Flashing*, the work for which he is justifiably best known. It is his most realized work. It started life in 1999 as a radio play with the title *The Reunion*, the South African Broadcasting Corporation's entry for Worldplay 2, the BBC World Service's international festival of radio drama. Nigel Vermaas, a veteran radio producer, commissioned it and mentored van Graan through the process of writing his first radio play.

Van Graan adapted *The Reunion* for the stage as *Slippery Slope*, which had its first airing as one of several new South African scripts given staged readings at the Baxter Theatre Centre in 2002. *Slippery Slope* in turn was rewritten in dialogue with director Clare Stopford as *Green Man Flashing*. It was entered into competition with five other scripts at the 2003 UCT Drama School/PANSA Festival of Reading of New Writing, another festival of staged readings, this time directed by Liz Mills. It won the Jury Award for Best Script with a citation for its 'courageous and insightful tackling of contentious, contemporary South African themes through believable, full-blooded characters'.

Green Man Flashing then premiered on the Fringe of the 2004 National Arts Festival in Grahamstown under the direction of Stopford as a fully-fledged production with a professional cast, where it was picked up by the Market Theatre, where it had a run in 2005. It went on to be widely performed and critically acclaimed.

The title refers to the traffic light signals at a pedestrian crossing. Its catchy title is somewhat quirky, since in South Africa the green man light never flashes but is a solid light followed by a flashing red man. As suggested by its former title, *Slippery Slope*, it serves as a warning sign that all is not well with democracy in the new South Africa.

It is worth examining the plot and characters in some detail as it exemplifies van Graan's playwriting, his major themes and style. The play opens as a courtroom drama, with the inquest into the death of one Luthando Nyaka. It has the feel of a thriller, and is filmic in structure with rapid scene changes – 13 scenes in the first 29 pages of script – and many of these scenes themselves split into two juxtaposed scenes. The last three scenes are more sustained. Van Graan has said that he was 'influenced by the storytelling style of the Brazilian movie *City of God*.'[1]

Set in 1999, six weeks before the country's second democratic elections, Gabby, a white activist with an impeccable anti-apartheid struggle record, is now personal assistant to a black government minister, Comrade Khumalo, tipped to be the next deputy president of the country after the election. She alleges he has raped her, and we as audience never doubt her story. The party sends a two-member delegation, consisting of Luthando, ANC ruling party security chief, and Gabby's estranged black husband and party fixer Aaron Matshoba.

Aaron and Gabby lived in exile in Germany during the apartheid years. We learn that their estrangement is partly caused by the racialized societal pressures still lingering in the new South Africa. As Gabby puts it, 'So many of the couples we knew in exile split up after they came back. It's bizarre. Like, apartheid kept us together. And freedom … our freedom seems to be driving us apart.'

But the real reason for their separation is the death of their son, Matthew, stabbed in a mugging incident when Aaron was on party business in Angola surrounding the peace settlement. Gabby cannot bring herself to forgive him. She feels he has been neglecting her and the family for years. Aaron typifies the detachment of the political cadre who has given himself to a cause.

Aaron   (*Quietly.*) Children die, Gabby. It's terrible whenever it happens. It's devastating when it happens to be yours. But it happens.

Van Graan takes the violent nature of South African society head-on.

Gabby   I know. It's bizarre. We came back here when apartheid was dying. Now apartheid's dead. My son's dead. My marriage is dead. And I'm carrying a gun.

When Gabby is raped, Aaron once again chooses the party over the rights of individuals. As Aaron puts it, 'sometimes justice has to be sacrificed for the greater political good'. He and Luthando are on a mission to have Gabby sign a non-disclosure agreement and accept a diplomatic post, essentially in order to exile her for five years. But Aaron says he is doing it for her own good: a rape trial with such high political stakes would destroy her.

As Aaron tells Gabby's best friend and lawyer, Anna:

Aaron   But there's a taxi coming down the road at 80 km an hour. And it's not going to stop, despite the traffic lights being red and the green man flashing in your favour. Would you still cross the street?

Anna   Of course not.

Aaron   But why not? It's *your* right to cross the street!

Part of the appeal of this play is that what motivates the characters is muddied, something not always as developed in van Graan's other works. Aaron calls Anna's motivations into question. Does she want a case with such publicity for her career, or is it really to put the issue of violence against women in South Africa on the national agenda? He also worries the matter will hit the press, as Anna's ex-husband is a parliamentary reporter, Graham Richards, whom she calls 'the original useless man' (possibly an intertextual reference to the Junction Avenue Theatre Company's anti-apartheid play *The Fantastical History of a Useless Man*).

An added layer of complexity is introduced with the investigating Inspector Abrahams of the violent crimes unit. At one point in the play, we see his confession before the Truth and Reconciliation Commission (TRC) for participating in the torture and rape of a female activist. His testimony is interwoven with a parallel scene, Gabby's account of Khumalo raping her. This is classic van Graan – making the connection between the injustices of the apartheid period and today's travesties in the democratic era.

Van Graan asks whether the amnesty and forgiveness given to the apartheid perpetrators for the greater political good and the country should not also be extended to Khumalo. Charges brought against him could reignite a civil war in parts of the country, even endanger the Constitution.

A further irony is that former apartheid perpetrator Abrahams is now meant to uphold the side of justice by prosecuting and arresting a key figure in the liberation movement. In real life, South Africa abounds with such ironies, and the play resonated with audiences.

Luthando's approach to Gabby is brutal. Her wish for justice is labelled as white entitlement when it comes to threats against the powerful. Her accusations are framed in racial terms:

> **Luthando** You [Gabby] can't resist, can you? Feeding the
> stereotype that black men can't keep it in their pants ... that all black
> men are rapists!

He throws aspersions on her story as a dirty tricks campaign against Khumalo and politically motivated. Such refrains would become familiar to South Africans when deputy president Jacob Zuma was dragged to court on rape charges.

But after Aaron briefly reconnects with Gabby, things change unexpectedly. When Aaron leaves the room to take a call on his mobile phone, Luthando pressurizes and threatens Gabby. Since her son's murder she has been carrying a gun. Not in a rational state of mind, she pulls it on Luthando who in an effort to wrestle it from Gabby ends up being wounded in the shoulder. Aaron returns and finishes him off in cold blood with two shots to the chest.

> **Aaron** Let's just say the world is a better place without 'Comrade'
> Luthando. For here lies a police informer, a thug, a murderer with
> no conscience. May his victims now rest in peace. (Pause.) It's not
> legal. It's not constitutional. But no one can say that justice has not
> been done.

Unbeknown to them the police inspector has secretly and illegally recorded everything. Revelations of such illicit surveillance have become a regular occurrence among South African public figures. In a further twist, the police in the end collude, and Abrahams confirms Aaron's story at the inquest.

The final scene is ambiguous. Gabby has not pressed charges, and she has opted for the diplomatic post in Australia. The play closes with her about to give testimony. We do not know if she will tell the truth.

> **Anna** In your own words, then, Ms Anderson, please tell us what
> happened on the morning that Mr Nyaka was shot.

(Lights come up on AARON and GABBY at the same time. AARON wears an anxious look.)

Gabby *(As if she is physically at the inquest, takes in ABRAHAMS and finally AARON, then looks away from AARON.)* Where shall I start?

(Slow fade to black.)

It is a strong and effective ending theatrically as it leaves the audience with the same moral dilemma – would they speak the truth?

Although written long before, the play made a tremendous impact when a number of productions of it were staged around the country and life, it seemed, had started to imitate art. There was the corruption trial of Shabir Shaik implicating Jacob Zuma, and sensationally Zuma was charged with rape. *Green Man Flashing* suddenly appeared uncannily prescient.

Professor Njabulo Ndebele observed that 'Mike van Graan's *Green Man Flashing* brilliantly lays bare the difficult paradoxes South Africans have to confront in achieving the real promise of our inspiring constitution: our ability to live it.' More than any other of van Graan's works, the play enters the moral miasma and the complex emotional quandary created between political principles and personal conscience, between often pragmatic actions and South Africa's promise of a human rights culture. It was an immediate hit with audiences. Stopford managed to control its potential for melodrama – a play with the death of a child, a rape, a punishing divorce and a murder all in one sitting.

Another crucial element for audiences and critics was that the play was breaking new ground. South African theatre at the time was awash with comedies and revivals of old work. Playwrights it seemed were either struggling or unsupported in trying to get to grips with the new realities of the country.

The critics generally agreed:

Protest theatre has struggled to come to terms with itself after 1994 … The good news is that even though it's taken ten years, protest theatre is evolving again. In *Green Man Flashing*, van Graan's writing and Stopford's direction conspire to infuse the stage with the kind of subtlety a country and era as complex as ours should demand of its theatre. It's about time.[2]

Mike van Graan's *Green Man Flashing* achieves what none of the main shows do in pushing new boundaries … It provides an acute dissection of many of the most pressing contemporary political issues … The scripting is tight, and deals with these large issues in a manner that remains gripping and, at times, moving.[3]

Some Mothers' Sons *(2005)*

Van Graan's next morally complex dramatic work was *Some Mothers' Sons*. It returns to the theme of politics and justice, but this time not in the murky world of the deep state, but within the recognized existing legal dispensation of the new South Africa.

In 1996, van Graan had had his professional debut as a playwright with a trilogy of two-handers, *Dinner Talk*, a reference to the chattering classes, a response, he has said, to the oft-asked question at that time, what will you write about now that apartheid has gone? *Some Mothers' Sons* is a play fleshed out from one of these *Dinner Talk* scenes. He also changed the white character from an English-speaking South African called Steve to an Afrikaner called Braam Visser (explicitly alluding to the legendary activist lawyer Bram Fischer, playfully referenced in the actual dialogue).

My review of the original version was critical:

Although strong on theme, when compared to his other works, it lacks the dramatic bite of *Green Man Flashing* or the riskiness of *Hostile Takeover*. The problem is its all too perfect symmetry – two equal halves, two equally matched characters. This encourages a soft spot in van Graan's theatre as dialectic. At times, it feels like a debate with dramatic trimmings – even though it is complex, layered and the situations themselves are riveting.[4]

Based on similar critical feedback he received in London after a two-and-a-half-week run at the Oval House Theatre, van Graan rewrote the play primarily to restructure it.

In the telescoped space of two prison visits, two men –Vusi Mataboge and Braam Visser – confront their differences: first in the mid-1980s during apartheid, where Vusi is a detainee undergoing torture and Braam a leftward-leaning human rights lawyer-activist; then 20 years later, under the new democratic dispensation where multiple murders end in a reversal of their situation.

Vusi has gone on to be a top human rights lawyer himself, and Braam has been arrested after he shot dead two men and wounded a third while they were standing in the dock in a courtroom. Vusi, who used to justify killing during the liberation struggle, is now in the position of upholding the right to life even of murderers. Braam, who had 20 years earlier convinced Vusi that revenge was wrong, who had never owned a gun, campaigned against the death penalty and avoided active combat in the military service, is now a remorseless, vengeful killer.

Braam and his wife Renee had experienced several burglaries. Then in a hijacking his wife was killed while six months pregnant. In an extra twist to the story, we learn that Braam had approved of his wife having an abortion early on in their marriage.

As in *Green Man Flashing*, where rape as torture during apartheid is juxtaposed with the rape in post-apartheid South Africa, torture during detention under the old regime is juxtaposed with rampant violence and murder in the new South Africa.

The play's central theme is about trying to hang on to one's humanity in a society under an onslaught of endemic violence:

Vusi   Don't become like them, Vusi!

Braam   Is that what I used to tell you?

Vusi   Don't let them take way your heart …

Braam   Sure. I remember saying that.

Vusi   When they take your heart …

Braam   … they take your soul …

Braam is losing himself:

Braam   … I'm more scared of living than of dying. I've never felt so helpless. Never. So out of control of my life. Every time I see a black person, I think, 'is he a hijacker, a mugger? Does he have a gun?' It wasn't like that. I'm becoming a racist. After apartheid! I see it happening to me! And it angers me! It angers me that I cannot do anything about it! What kind of life is this? The pacifist? He's dead.

The non-racist? He's dying. The human rights lawyer? He's just …
committed suicide.

In the final lines, we learn that Braam does commit suicide in his cell by
hanging himself by his shoelaces, echoing the staged suicides the security
police engineered to kill activists in detention during apartheid.

Although the play deals ostensibly with the meaning of justice as
opposed to the law, the hot-button issue at the time was the reinstatement
of the death penalty. Its abolition was the first act of the new Constitutional
Court after the first democratic election. That ruling remains a very contentious issue, particularly as authorities struggle to get violent crimes under
control, and where polls have shown that a referendum on the issue would
probably favour bringing back the death penalty.

The play shows van Graan's knack as a dramatist for creating
predicaments that allow him to wring out every ambivalence, shade,
contradiction and aporia in the issue under focus. As one critic wrote:
'*Some Mothers' Sons* … is an ingenious public vehicle for a public issue
that most would rather not talk about in public.'[5] In such a violent
society as South Africa, numbness towards human life leads criminals to
kill as easily as their victims find it to howl for the death penalty. It is a
testament to van Graan's handling of the issue that theatre patrons were
divided – *Some Mothers' Sons* was seen as a closet pro-death penalty piece,
while others read it as unambiguously probing from the opposite premise.

Brothers in Blood *(2009)*

In a more ambitious work, *Brothers in Blood*, van Graan returns to
justice and death. It is set in Cape Town in 1998 at a time when a grass-
roots, militant, anti-drug community group was most active – PAGAD,
People Against Gangsterism and Drugs, a militant organization, largely
Muslim-led, that made headlines for mob justice and executing drug lords.
The play opens with images of one of their marches.

To explore the nexus of race and religious ignorance and prejudice, van
Graan sets up his stage with characters from the three dominant faiths in
Cape Town: Abduragman Abrahams, a Muslim high school principal, and
his daughter Leila; Reverend Lionel Fredericks, an evangelical Christian
pastor on the Cape Flats; Dr Brian Cohen, a Jewish doctor working on
the Cape Flats; and Fadiel Suleiman, a young, black Muslim refugee from
Somalia.

Abubaker is interrogated by Brian, who is serving on the neighbourhood watch for a Jewish community that feels under siege. To complicate matters, Brian is now living in an area from which Abubaker's family were forcefully removed during apartheid. In a later scene, ironically, Abubaker calls the police to check out Fadiel when he spots him lurking around his neighbourhood.

Van Graan puts his purpose for this scene in the stage directions:

> *There are constant shifts in power/status between Abubaker and Brian during their sequences together. While one may have physical power, another has moral power, with shifts taking place between each.*

Van Graan plays a reversal of the famous Shylock scene (Act Three, Scene One of *The Merchant of Venice*):

Abubaker   What do you see?

Brian   What do you mean?

Abubaker   Standing in front of you, what do you see?

Brian   (*Beat*) A man …

Abubaker   What kind of man?

Brian   Just a man …

Abubaker   A man like you?

Brian   I suppose.

Abubaker   A man with feelings?

Brian   Mr Abrahams …

Abubaker   When you treat me like a criminal, what do you think I feel?

Abubaker then quotes the speech by Shylock.

In van Graan's theatrical universe the characters are usually overtaken by unexpected events and twists of fate. The plot does not develop because of the characters' nature, but the characters develop because of what happens to them. The moral dilemmas they face are not based so much on their own doing and their weaknesses, but on the situations in which they find themselves. The deus ex machina of this world does not come to resolve an intractable situation and save the characters; instead it is usually malevolent and comes in aid of the themes the play is exploring. In *Brothers in Blood*, van Graan takes this further than in any other of his works. The style is again filmic, with short scenes (29 in 60 pages), some further interspliced into two centres of action.

There is also a fair amount of monologue (the play ends with three monologues, one from each father of each faith) and soliloquy, with each character confiding in the audience via some device: Abubaker talks to his late wife; Brian to his therapist (invisible to the audience); Fadiel in a video diary (modelled on suicide bomber videos); Leila also has a diary; and Reverend Fredericks says prayers and gives sermons. Dramatically it is a risky device, but it serves to isolate each of his characters in their worlds, a thematic point van Graan wishes to make.

Symmetry of character is necessary for such a dialectic and didactic purpose. Therefore van Graan constructs his characters as follows: Fadiel's father survived the war in Somalia by fleeing to South Africa, only to be killed in a xenophobic attack; Leila lost her mother and toddler sibling (and so Abubaker his wife and daughter) in the crossfire of drug-related gang violence; in turn, Fredericks lost his son to drug addiction, and he 'lost' his daughter when she married a Muslim and converted to Islam; and Brian lives in a similar state of post-traumatic fear after a bus of Jewish children is stoned, caught up in a violent march of PAGAD.

Fredericks, perceiving a threat from the Muslim-led anti-drug militants, preaches of Christian missionaries martyred in Somalia. As a born-again fundamentalist Christian, he sermonizes against homosexuality, abortion and the abolition of the death penalty, all issues that have brought various faith groups into conflict with South Africa's Constitution since 1994.

Leila is in rebellion – listening to dance music, smoking cigarettes, dressing sexily, dating boys. She applies for a job with Fredericks. Leila reminds him of his late daughter. She then hooks up with Fadiel and falls pregnant; she breaks off the relationship and threatens to have an abortion – what's more, an abortion to be performed by a Jewish doctor. Fadiel is now a character who will also lose his child. Fadiel decides to petrol bomb the clinic and take Brian hostage. In the end, his plan is thwarted by Abubaker and Leila arriving with Fredericks whom she called for help after receiving Fadiel's video tape.

The play was well received and won van Graan the 2010 Naledi Award for Best South African Play. The point it makes is that tolerance is the superglue of South Africa's fragile democracy. The issues raised invigorated audiences and the redemptive message and ending pleased the public.

As critic Zingi Mfeka wrote:

> If the subject matter is one considered to be taboo ... you can be certain that playwright Mike van Graan will at some point think to himself, 'Hmm, wouldn't that be a delightful play for South Africans to see on stage? ' ... The script confidently stands its own ground, so little embellishment is required. It's all in van Graan's writing, making this probably one of his strongest to date.[6]

Van Graan had managed to dance in a minefield of highly explosive subject matter. This was partly because he chose to focus on events and situational challenges of lived reality, drawing his characters into behavioural rather than moral dilemmas. They have prejudices to overcome, but the play doesn't bring into question religious belief itself, whether traditions and cultural practices are right or wrong, good or bad, or to what extent religious and cultural rights should be limited by constitutional and human rights.

Van Graan shows no sign of flagging and, at the time of writing, he has three new scripts in the pipeline: *Elusive Spring*, *Rainbow Scars* and *Writer's Block*.

Experimenting with style (1999–2009)

After 2000, van Graan firmly entered the mainstream of theatre with professional productions on the main stage at the major festivals and numerous runs in pivotal theatres – mostly at the Market Theatre, Artscape and the Baxter. Many of these plays were commissioned works.

Van Graan has always been drawn towards controversy and injustice, and he chooses the hot-button topics of the day. He has worked rapidly through many societal issues. In *Just Business* (2012), a reworking of his earlier play *Hostile Takeover* (2004), he focused on Black Economic Empowerment and corruption. *Iago's Last Dance* (2009) was a trilogy of playlets (the titles of which make the acronym HIV: ***Heartbreak Medea***, ***Iago's Last Dance*** and

Valiant Spartacus) dealing with HIV/AIDS through the lens of betrayal. Van Graan linked the betrayal within sexual relationships with the ultimate betrayal of the Mbeki government to treat the infected. *Die Generaal* (2007) took on a range of issues including land claims, language and the position of Afrikaners, and the downtrodden lumpenproleteriat.

Stylistically, van Graan has tried his hand at various theatrical genres in order to pursue his dramatic activism. With *Bafana Republic* he created a comedy brand, using satirical sketches and comic revue. The first instalment was launched shortly before the FIFA 2010 World Cup when there was still a dearth of sharp political commentary, and theatre seemed dominated by work with 'entertainment value' and politically correct conformism to the new order. Critics and audiences welcomed a new voice besides stalwart Pieter-Dirk Uys, who had been soldiering on alone in the world of political satire, feeling increasingly let down by the lack of satirical voices, especially from Black writers and performers.

As a columnist, van Graan knows how to produce pithy vignettes, and his revue sketches are at their best when they have a dramatic vehicle to deliver them – in the first *Bafana* production these were a roller coaster ride, a Bafana Idols TV show, a match commentary and a climactic farewell song, a relyricized version of 'De La Rey'.

In *Mixed Metaphors*, a play about youth in the new South Africa, van Graan used performance poetry and rap song rhythms.

In *Mirror Mirror,* a performance piece for students, he turned his hand to Brechtian alienation. South African politics was allegorized around a Disney-style faux castle. Apartheid days were recast as feudal times; a white queen and her foppish royals rape and plunder the country; the sans culottes are led by the palindromic Okib (soon tortured to death); and when the peasants' revolt succeeds, the peasant leader starts the cycle all over again in a battle for power with his bribe-taking Number 2. What van Graan achieved with *Mirror Mirror* was to get students to think about their position politically as artists, something they probably had never done.

Essentially *Mirror Mirror* was an allegorized polemical column. But there are severe limitations with such a technique. The democratic state cannot be lampooned in the same way as the apartheid state, where the state exerted total control and people believed a simplistic received mythology, a Bible-story past. The political stance to take then was far clearer, and there was a well-defined call to action. The project was to debunk with bunk, and the transgression was akin to burning the flag. In the new South Africa, it is personal conscience and morality that must be put to the screw. And that kind of introspection is the natural province of dramatic theatre. Van Graan was better served by the eclectic style he developed for his major dramas surveyed here above.

Summary

Van Graan has not limited himself to particular issues. Although most of his work is broadly considered political, he has also written about martial relationships (*Two to Tango*) and terminal illness (*Is it because I'm Jack?*).

Rather than a writer of a particular theme, van Graan has emerged as a progressive activist-playwright. He appears to start with an issue, outline the areas of conflict, create characters to represent these various angles, complicate these characters by exposing their contradictions for ironic effect, place them in a scenario where they must confront each other and then plot a chain of events that explores and puts the issues at hand to the test.

His characters therefore must straddle the fault lines in society. Sometimes relationships are allegorical, such as the black and white marriage of Sizwe and Anna in *Die Generaal*. Symmetry and juxtaposition of character and circumstance are therefore intrinsic devices, hence the filmic treatment, short scenes often parallel and interspliced. Other filmic techniques adopted include an action-packed pace, guns and violence on stage and rapid time shifts often reaching into the past.

Van Graan built himself a strong brand at a time when very few playwrights were tackling the issues of the day, and were even less keen to criticize the new democratic government and the ruling party, not least because of a dependence on funding from the state. Although the state has always maintained its funding is at arm's length, fame and fortune for most clearly depend on towing the line.

Something easy to overlook is that van Graan was one of the forerunners in the new democratic age to break the apartheid mould of theatre. There were not that many dramatic works in the traditional mode with fully realized character parts for black actors when van Graan broke onto the scene.

Van Graan's work has its roots in the protest theatre of the apartheid period, but he has managed to bring politically engaged theatre to maturity in the democratic age. As critic Robert Greig put it '[b]y speaking out, he creates spaces for others to follow suit'.

Notes

1. Van Graan at a Great Texts talk at the Gordon Institute for the Performing Arts, 16 April 2013.
2. Max Rayneard, *This Day*, 6 July 2004.
3. Matthew Wilhelm-Solomon, *Mail and Guardian*, 9–15 July 2004.
4. Brent Meersman, *Mail and Guardian*, 28 April–4 May 2006.
5. Percy Zvomuya, *Mail and Guardian*, 13–19 October 2006.
6. Zingi Mkefa, *Sunday Times*, 7 June 2009.
7. Play list courtesy of Mike van Graan.

Bibliography

Primary sources

Works by Mike van Graan[7]

The Dogs Must be Crazy (1991).
Some of our Best Friends are Cultural Workers (1992).
Dinner Talk (1996).
Not Exactly PC! (1996).
The Tables Trilogy (1999).
Hostile Takeover (2004).
Mixed Metaphors (2005).
Two to Tango (2005).
Mirror, Mirror (2006).
Die Generaal (2007).
Bafana Republic (2007).
Bafana Republic: Extra Time (2008).
Odysseus van Holland (2008).
Ramiz and Julio (2008).
Bafana Republic, Penalty Shootout (2009).
Some Mothers' Sons (2005), in Greg Homann (ed.), *At This Stage: Plays from Post-Apartheid South Africa* (Johannesburg: Wits University Press, 2009), 69–110.
Green Man Flashing (2003), Playscript Series No. 11 (Cape Town: Junkets Publisher, 2010).
Iago's Last Dance (2009), Playscript Series No. 13 (Cape Town: Junkets Publisher, 2010).
Is it because I'm Jack? (2010).
Brothers in Blood (2009), Playscript Series No. 19 (Cape Town: Junkets Publisher, 2012).
Just Business (2012).

Secondary sources

Gaylard, Rob, 'Brothers in blood', *South African Theatre Journal* 26:1 (2012): 93–7.
Meersman, Brent, *Mail and Guardian*, 28 April–4 May 2006.
Mkefa, Zingi, *Sunday Times*, 7 June 2009.
Rayneard, Max, *This Day*, 6 July 2004.
Wilhelm-Solomon, Matthew, *Mail and Guardian*, 9–15 July 2004.
Zvomuya, Percy, *Mail and Guardian*, 13–19 October 2006.

CHAPTER 13
CRAIG HIGGINSON
Michael Titlestad

Dream of the Dog; The Girl in the Yellow Dress; Little Foot

Introduction

Craig Higginson is an award-winning, internationally renowned theatre director, playwright and novelist. He is also a widely respected teacher of creative writing in all its genres, and has facilitated the work of many emerging South African playwrights in his capacity as the Literary Manager of the Market Theatre in Johannesburg.

Higginson began his directorial career with the Royal Shakespeare Company as the co-director of his adaptation of Nabokov's novel, *Laughter in the Dark* (2000). The play was subsequently adapted for radio and broadcast on BBC3, winning the Gold Sony Radio Academy Award for 2004–5. Since 2000 he has directed seven major productions, including highly innovative and widely applauded adaptations of *Grimm Tales* (produced at the Market Theatre in 2007) and Rudyard Kipling's *The Jungle Book* (which was derived from a version by Tim Supple, adapted by Higginson, and which was nominated for four Naledi Awards and is published by Oberon). His range is exceptional: he has directed four Shakespeare plays, a number of canonical and iconoclastic contemporary works and also productions intended to increase the reach of theatre to young South Africans. The last combine acting, storytelling and puppetry with mesmerizing effect, and reveal a willingness to dwell on the darker, less saccharine, aspects of folk memory, narratives of childhood and children's subjectivity.

Despite his remarkable achievements as a director and teacher, Higginson is signally identified as an author. He co-authored *Ten Bush* with Mncedisi Shabangu (who also directed the production at the Market Theatre, which subsequently toured Sweden in 2009 and Germany in 2010). The play, which reinterprets a tale from Swazi folklore to address indirectly a variety of post-apartheid concerns, was nominated for five Naledi Awards. In addition to *Grimm Tales* and *The Jungle Book*, he has also authored an elegant South African contextualization of *The Lord of the Flies* (2006) directed by Greg Homann and co-adapted a version of *Brer Rabbit* (2009) with Gina Shmukler who directed the play.

Higginson's theatrical reputation, though, rests on his five sole-authored plays: *Dream of the Dog* (2007), *The Girl in the Yellow Dress* (2010). *Little Foot* (2012), *An Imagined Land* (2015) and *The Red Door* (2015). Each of the first three plays has had a long life of production and revision (Higginson is an inveterate editor of his work), and each was widely reviewed in the South African and European media. Many of the reviews register the novelty of the plays: that each, in a variety of ways, challenges the ossified gestures of South African theatre by disrupting accepted national narratives and using broader, more ambitious strokes on a much larger canvas than is commonly the case. *Dream of the Dog* and *The Girl in the Yellow Dress* represent milestones in the last decade of South African theatre: both raised the stakes for local drama by opening the terrain to previously unimagined possibilities and through their capacity to speak to a range of audiences across the country and the world.

The literary fiction scene in South Africa is underfunded, lacks a significant readership and suffers from an overinvestment in a small number of writers who are held, for various reasons (not many of them linked to merit), to represent the nation's literary capital. Higginson has published five novels – *Embodied Laughter* (1998), *The Hill* (2005), *Last Summer* (2010) and *The Landscape Painter* (2011), and *The Dream House* (2015) based on his play *Dream of the Dog* – in this generally unreceptive environment. *The Landscape Painter*, which links narratives set during the South African War and the austerity years in Britain after the Second World War, was shortlisted for the M-Net Literary Award and won the University of Johannesburg Literary Award, one of the country's three pre-eminent literary prizes. It has also been a university set work in South Africa. Read in conjunction with his plays, it is evident that Higginson's fiction and drama are subtly dialogic, and anyone drawn to consider his plays should certainly read his novels. The fact that his fiction continues in something of a critical limbo – despite paperback reissues of his two most recent novels – reflects poorly on the South African cultural institution, attesting as it does to our obsession with a narrow definition of a 'national literature' (that every work should, in whatever coded form, tell the sanctioned story of the rise and fall of apartheid or stage one of the postures of post-apartheid despondency or ennui).

The plays

Dream of the Dog *(2007)*

Dream of the Dog began life as a radio play broadcast on SAfm, a national station, in August 2006. It premiered on stage at the Grahamstown Arts Festival in 2007 and had a successful run at the Market Theatre in Johannesburg, before a new production, starring Janet Suzman, opened at the Finborough Theatre in London. It transferred directly from there to the Trafalgar Studios in the West End. The play was nominated for four Naledi Awards, including 'Best New Play' (the Naledi Awards are the foremost theatrical awards in South Africa). The script exists in two versions: an economical, perhaps slightly clipped, script was published by Oberon (2010), and an expanded one with an alternative ending appears in *At this Stage: Plays from Post-apartheid South Africa* (2009). Both have particular merits, but it is difficult not to prefer the elaborated version, which seems more at ease with its political ambiguities, less reticent about engaging the inner-life of characters and develops a fuller, more compassionate portrait of each.

Dream of the Dog represents one of the most accomplished debuts in contemporary South African theatre. It concerns four enmeshed lives: Richard and Patricia Wiley, an aging couple on the verge of leaving their desultory farm in the Natal Midlands to live in Durban; Beauty, their quiet and respectful domestic worker of many years; and Look Smart (whose isiZulu name is Phiwayinkosi Ndlovu), a post-apartheid entrepreneur who grew up on the farm. We realize at the outset that Richard is suffering the steady encroachment of Alzheimer's disease. His memory is undependable: characteristic of sufferers, certain recollections are vivid and specific, but his sense of chronology is disjunctive and disruptive. As they are packing up the accumulation of their lives, Patricia dispatches Richard to recover the remains of their stillborn daughter, Rachel, buried on the farm.

It is into the domestic chaos of their pending departure that Look Smart arrives. The interaction between Patricia and Look Smart reveals a contested past. Patricia remembers with deep fondness the minutiae of their intimacy: witnessing his birth, his naming, teaching him to fish, paying for his education at a boarding school and the clay animals he made for her, which she displayed on her mantelpiece. Look Smart's memory of these details is, in each case, somewhat different, either in content or register; certainly his memories are less complicated, less sentimental than

Patricia's. What overshadows all of his memories, though, is the trauma that led to his departure from the farm. We discover from his account that Richard habitually had sexual relations with the black women working on the farm. Look Smart believes that Grace, a young worker whom he loved and intended to marry, was raped by Richard. Endeavouring to escape, she forced Richard off her and fled into the yard, where she was attacked and ravaged by one of the vicious farm dogs. She died from her injuries en route to the hospital after, Look Smart believes, Patricia hesitated for fear of getting blood on the back seat of her car. His most scathing accusation, however, is that Richard unchained the dog and set it after Grace so that she would be unable to reveal his guilt. Despite this shocking revelation, as Patricia and Look Smart recollect some of the more benign aspects of the past, they begin to rediscover a relationship of shadow parenting, marked by reciprocal, understated love.

Richard returns with the rough headstone, the coffin and body of Rachel having decomposed into the mud, and places it on the mantelpiece where Look Smart's clay animals once stood. When Look Smart leaves, disgusted by Richard's overt racism and combination of real and strategic oblivion, Patricia speaks to Beauty about the past. Beauty has lived in silence despite apparently knowing the facts of the matter, having personally witnessed Richard's actions on the fatal day. Grace never loved Look Smart in the way he loved her, and had no intention of marrying him. She regularly had sex with Richard, who paid her to do so, and she was pregnant with his baby when she was killed by the dog. It was when Grace declared her desire to keep the child that Richard loosed the dog on her in the full knowledge that it might well kill her.

The play's conclusion is provocatively ambiguous. Patricia realizes that there is no real point in continuing to confront Richard with his racist, violent past – in which he has lost one child and killed another – in that his mind comprises only fragments of congealed prejudice and rationalization. He is now too damaged, his memory too unreliable, to offer any meaningful admission or confession, or to seek expiation. The past cannot be recovered – neither within him nor by those around him.

Look Smart, who is developing the farm into a luxury gated community, plans to leave the house standing and replicate it (with minor differences) in a number of simulacra. At one level, he has taken ownership of history by replacing Patricia and Richard and diminishing their home to a blueprint for future economic redress. At another, his reasons for and way of recuperating the farm are ambiguous. Although motivated by his anger at Richard (based in the myths of Grace's fidelity and intention to marry him), he also exhibits nostalgia for his childhood on the farm. While the fulcrum of his identity is what he needs to believe, his approach to the future is merely the replication and multiplication of a past from which he cannot recover.

Patricia and Beauty share a resigned sense of being folded into histories from which they cannot extricate themselves. They share a prudential worldliness: life, with all its intersections, ambiguities, contradictions and violence, has to be endured. We live with the limitations and blindness of those around us. In the shorter version of the play, Beauty accepts Look Smart's offer of employment and intends to remain working on the estate. In the longer version, the play concludes with her on the verge of leaving for Durban with Patricia and Richard, unwilling to sever the deep intersection of her and the Wiley's worlds.

The farm is a primary site of the South African imaginary, and the generative site of the signal Afrikaans literary genre, the *plaasroman* ('farm novel'), which proliferated between the 1920s and the 1940s. *Plaasromane* offered a symbolic solace for dispossessed Afrikaners who, after defeat in the Second South African War, were reduced from agrarian republicans to an impoverished, urbanized proletariat. Farms, in the post-apartheid dispensation, commonly signal the history of colonial dispossession. Patricia's quaint Welsh-pony breeding is a diminished version of colonization ('colony' derived from the Latin word for 'farm'). Look Smart's gated community suggests the late-capitalist 'development' of the land; it is a reduced, commercial reclamation largely evacuated of post-colonial resistance or restitution. *Dream of the Dog* suggests that old political and individual mythologies are simply giving way to new ones: that we would be remiss and politically unrealistic to think that there is a self-evident connection between history, land ownership and belonging.

Perhaps the most significant contribution of the play is its complication of the conceit of the Truth and Reconciliation Commission. Based on the ecclesial teleology of confession, expiation and forgiveness, the TRC assumed that the past was recoverable and could be conspicuously and publically engaged. This was an essential 'political theology'[1] to service notions such as 'nation building' and 'social cohesion'. It became doctrinal in South African literature and theatre in the late 1990s. *Dream of the Dog* stages not only the opacity of the past, but the fact that we encounter irreconcilable versions at every turn: memory is generated out of contingent individual, social and political necessities. In addition to a fading, fractured past (a reality not unlike a national Alzheimer's disease), our history is also one of complex overlaps, intersections and compromises. In reality, the lives of black and white South Africans have always been interwoven and inextricable, which complicates the Manichean mythology so generally accepted as the basis and legacy of apartheid. The various constituencies of the nation, Higginson's play suggests, have a far more complicated and entangled history than can be expressed by the obvious, instrumental binaries invoked by activists, historians, artists and authors working in the long shadow of the protest tradition.

The Girl in the Yellow Dress (2010)

While *Dream of the Dog* was an auspicious debut, *The Girl in the Yellow Dress* has to date been Higginson's spectacular success. It also debuted in Grahamstown, but travelled, in rapid succession, to the Baxter in Cape Town, the Traverse Theatre at the Edinburgh Festival, Live Theatre in Newcastle, the Citizen's Theatre in Glasgow and the Stadtsteater in Stockholm. There have also been new productions in Chicago, Salisbury and London. The play had two successful runs at the Market Theatre in Johannesburg, the second of an exceptional 11 weeks. It was widely acclaimed (it was nominated for six Naledi Awards, won 'Best New South African Play' and was enthusiastically reviewed in the local and international press) and (like *Dream of the Dog*) it is now prescribed for study at several South African and overseas universities.

South African theatre, such as that of many metropolitan and postcolonial contexts, inclines to parochialism. *The Girl in the Yellow Dress*, inspired by Ovid's *Echo and Narcissus*, eschews narrowly South African preoccupations as well as the architecture of nationalism more generally by presenting a series of beautifully crafted dialogues between Celia, a trust-funded, young English woman living in Paris, who teaches English as a foreign language, and a French student, Pierre. Each session reveals more about the history of each character, dramatically (and wittily) combining the roles of teacher and student and the intricacies of English grammar to reflect on the ways in which we construct ourselves and one another in the languages we know and those we are struggling to learn.

It is evident at the outset that Pierre wishes not only to learn English, but to acquire a European 'habitus' (that is, a set of social dispositions that would facilitate unqualified acceptance): he is striving to become an insider in a context in which he contends with the alienation of being a migrant. He spotted Celia putting up notices at the Sorbonne and began to follow her, in the course of which respectful, polite predation she has become his aspirational ideal – at once the person whom he believes will usher him into the fullness of European identity and could potentially become his lover. He admits quite early in the process of the lessons to his preoccupation with her, which the troubled Celia considers at once sinister and flattering. The lessons are regularly interrupted by calls from Celia's mother, which she usually ignores. Her mother is relentlessly pressuring Celia to return to England to attend her brother's wedding, the prospect of which leaves Celia visibly shaken. Indeed, she experiences simply the ringing phone as jarring.

Slowly Pierre and Celia's respective histories of harm emerge. At a point, Pierre describes himself being brought to France as a child by Médecins Sans Frontières after a violent attack by Hutu *interahamwe* on his east Congolese village. It transpires that this is not his, but his mother's story; he tells it because he imagines it to be the story Celia wants to hear from him: a tale of trauma on 'the dark continent'. In fact, Pierre grew up in France, a second-generation immigrant, but continues to feel yoked to his family's past and confined to the various roles he is expected to play as an African student at a French university. He feels continually reduced or, at best, inter-pellated by the Europeans he encounters. He hopes, through Celia and the English lessons, to remove the masks that obscure his selfhood and stunt the fullness of his desires.

Celia, on the other hand, is socially isolated by an incestuous desire for her brother. There are intimations of a sexual relationship in the past: that her brother has moved on while Celia remains trapped by her memories and, now, a stunted, misdirected sexuality. As a radical outsider to her involuted emotional life, Pierre presents an opportunity for Celia to reach out into the world. Following an initial, explosive consummation of their relationship, each of them retreats back into the damage and alienation to which they have become accustomed. Yet, rather than presenting anything as ponderous as divided worlds that cannot connect, the play concludes on a delicate, hesitant recognition of possible mutuality, still in the mode of a grammar lesson.

Pierre The future tenses. We never got to them. You think there's time for one more lesson before I go?

Celia We may, we might. We can, we could. We should, we shall. We would, we will. These are all subjunctives. You can plot them on a graph. Each expresses a degree of uncertainty.

They regard each other.

Celia   Or certainty.

Blackout.

The true accomplishment of *The Girl in the Yellow Dress* is its assertion that human experience and potential is 'secular'. This is an unfashionable use of the term, but it is uniquely apposite to Higginson's vision. It implies that human experience, in all of its varieties, is – despite the formidable obstructions of culture, race, class and gender – ultimately communicable, at least in significant part. This might seem uncontentious (indeed an obvious prerequisite of authorship per se), but South Africa is mired in a tyrannous guilt and a politics of blame that has inclined playwrights to hypostasize, even sanctify, social-historical positions. This tendency could be interpreted as a hyperbolic expression of global identity politics that have made the primal sin the recuperation of the voice or experience of 'the other'. The result is a representational anxiety that assumes that the experience of any group (class, race, gender or culture) is unique, and beyond the legitimate territory of the playwright or author of fiction (other than as a humble but violent proclamation of irreconcilable difference). Higginson has been unflinching in challenging this script, not, as others have done, with ham-fisted sentimentality, but rather with a refined sense that, not only can we endeavour to share our realities across the boundaries that divide us, but that existence compels us to do so.

The Girl in the Yellow Dress is no leaden allegory dramatizing relations between the metropole and the post-colonial world, just as *Dream of the Dog* is not an allegory of the history and damage of apartheid. Both are subtle engagements with the limits of allegorical thinking, as well as the social fixities and the politics of representation on which it depends. If the predominant tendency in colonialism is a Manichean organization of society, post-colonialism risks its simplistic inversion. Apartheid and anti-apartheid theatre rested on a particular nationalist eschatology: a political theology endlessly rendered or subverted in didactic allegories. Higginson's first two sole-authored plays propose the prudential possibility that, in striving to reach the experience of others, we may – albeit provisionally and contingently – be able to identify and build upon the foundations of a common, secular humanity.

Little Foot *(2012)*

Little Foot was commissioned by the Royal National Theatre, London, for performance at the 2012 Connections Festival. That version is published in the Methuen anthology of Connections plays for 2012. A radically reworked version opened at the Grahamstown Arts Festival that year, before a run at the Market Theatre in Johannesburg. This version has been published by Oberon.

The play takes its name from the *Australopithecine* remains discovered in Silberberg Grotto of the Sterkfontein Caves, outside Johannesburg. Is seems that the nicknamed 'Little Foot' is neither an *Australopithecus afarensis* nor an *Australopithecus africanus*, but a new species altogether. It has been conjectured that Little Foot died falling down into the cavern because he was being pursued (the position of his remains suggests he died with his head resting poignantly on his arm). The play presents – in tableau, movement and as a chorus – a group of *Australopithecines*, larger in stature and more threatening than Little Foot, who speak to our biological, linguistic, social and emotional evolution: our journey out of darkness into the rather dim, flickering light of modernity and contemporary subjectivity. This louring presence of choral prehistoric forms and mythic utterance is the background against which the contemporary action of the play unfolds.

A group of friends, having just left school and now living in various cities, attending different universities or, in one case, catching up on incomplete school studies, meets in Sterkfontein Cave – as they have done regularly in the past – to celebrate New Year's Eve. Each year they creep in unseen through one of the countless entrances into the dolomitic labyrinth. Wizard has just returned from London, bringing with him, into the scared circle of shared pasts, his partner, Rebecca, who, though born in South Africa, grew up in the UK. The other friends, Coco, Braai and Moby, resent her presence and are also surprised to discover how little she knows about Wizard's recent past (including the fact that his father was shot and killed), his friends and their binding rituals or the cave, which she misconstrues as a goldmine.

Listening to the group's banter, recollections and their discussions regarding the possible circumstances of Little Foot's death, the audience becomes increasingly aware of seething resentments among them, centring particularly on their past treatment at the hands of Wizard. Coco cruelly describes the gay Moby's obsession with Wizard, and reveals to the group (or invents) the occasions on which Wizard publically betrayed his trust with the intention of humiliating him. It transpires that Coco and Wizard were lovers at school, and that Coco has never muted or managed her devotion. When Moby attributes Wizard's peculiarities to witnessing the shooting of his father – which he narrates graphically – Wizard attacks him. The group in turn ties his hands tightly behind his back and pushes him to the ground; later Braai and Moby kick him hard and repeatedly, venting years of repressed anger.

When Coco speaks of university lectures concerning the evolution of ethics, the *Australopithecine* chorus and the present are explicitly articulated. Tying up and assaulting Wizard, followed by his disappearance in the cave, is linked to the death of Little Foot (in the next scene, the two lie alone on stage together in injured silence). The friends, still carrying their burden of anger and humiliation, have to make a fundamental decision: Should they endeavour to find Wizard? In this lies the crux: Have we evolved beyond an ethics in which the group – the majority – should push home its advantage over the isolated and vulnerable individual? And, we are asked, is the friends' hatred of Wizard not their failing rather than his? The play ends with a tableau of the group united and Wizard safe.

Little Foot represented a significant effort to break the social-realist mould, which has long been the default option in South African theatre. Taking pre-history as a distant mirror to reflect an interpersonal, contemporary ethical conundrum displaces 'the political' in its narrow, national sense. At the same time, the play's combination of classical and contemporary elements (the chorus and an ethical rites of passage social drama) was a brave and controversial decision, which made unexpected demands on audiences, to which reactions ranged from fascination to outrage and irritation. Yet the unfamiliar and unlikely revivify a theatrical tradition and make for new possibilities: *Little Foot* was an important play in terms of its formal and philosophical discrepancy, as well as its ambitious staging. Watching it, one had the impression that anything was possible.

Summary

Two of the primary manifestoes for post-apartheid art are Albie Sachs's 'Preparing Ourselves for Freedom' (1991) and Njabulo Ndebele's 'Rediscovery of the Ordinary' (1991).[2] It would be wrong to elide their differences, but both imagined an artistic practice beyond type, struggle, opposition, resignation, triumphalism or didacticism. Both approve, in prospect, of art that would complicate the grand narratives of nation and world: that would unyoke the political imperatives of the nation and individuality, and be open to the fullness of our hesitant, mobile subjectivities and demeanours, and our inherent contradictions. Neither of these scholars (both of whom were anti-apartheid activists and key players in crafting the post-apartheid dispensation) seeks to mute the social and political role of art, but rather to liberate it from the habitual imperatives of hydraulic resistance and the mode – which Fredric Jameson ascribed to all 'Third World' literature[3] – of 'national allegory'.

Interviewed in the *Cape Times* (16 July 2010) about the success of *The Girl in the Yellow Dress* and *Dream of the Dog*, Higginson commented: 'There are huge swathes of our experience that remain unwritten. Theatre has a vital function and it is as urgent as it ever was during apartheid ... We can't simply repeat the methods and forms of previous writers like Fugard, but must find new forms and new subject matter' (13). Reviewing *The Girl in the Yellow Dress* (*Sunday Independent*, 'Life', 31 October 2010), Mary Corrigall suggests:

> This is the ultimate writer's play for not only does it meditate on the function of language but of fiction. In the final scene Pierre adamantly rejects creating fictions – he is unable to see the use of refashioning the self for the pleasure of others. In response Celia suggests that this is a useful exercise as it allows one to dream. Consequently, Higginson proposes that masks allow people to reimagine themselves, permitting them to project themselves into a future society. (3)

The intersection of these two comments – by Higginson and Corrigall respectively – is productive. It suggests a contemporary imperative: that theatre needs to engage new modes, techniques and discourses in order to come to terms with the swirling potential of post-apartheid society and subjectivity. Precisely because we are not confined to apartheid's political eschatology and have acknowledged that only the naïve invest in myths of miraculous transformation, writers in all genres have to contend with the complex construction of selfhood and acts of discursive 'worlding'.

In Higginson's plays, these processes of construction occur in dialogue between aspects of the self or with others, but always in the light of history and registering the complexity of the dynamics of meaning. His plays are most centrally about the ways in which his characters – in relation to their psychological pasts and political histories – are in the process of fashioning their subjectivity. They are plays about making selves, projecting ourselves onto others, but also discovering in others the echoes and reflections that keep the self in check, and make possible the ethics on which social coexistence and collaboration depends.

This far more fluid, less programmatic understanding of politics, ethics and subjectivity means that Higginson's drama (like his novels) breaks the frame of protest theatre or the theatre of reconciliation (or its failure), which have dominated our stages from the late 1960s to the present. Instead, his lithe, artful writing prises open the relation between nation and narration, between individual meaning and collective responsibility. It is defensible to argue that Higginson, in Sachs's and Ndebele's senses, is one of the few truly post-apartheid dramatists.

This humanist rebellion comes with certain dangers. With few exceptions, the reviews of Higginson's plays and novels resort to plot synopsis and general thematic descriptions. Perhaps the demeanours and dispositions of reviewers and critics of post-apartheid theatre and literature are persistently anachronistic. The anticipation of national allegory haunts local and international commentary, making it, with few exceptions, belated and, therefore, banal. Only the future will reveal the possibilities that Higginson's drama intimates, but we can be assured that *Dream of the Dog*, *The Girl in the Yellow Dress* and *Little Foot* point towards the remarkable potential of South African theatre.

Notes

1. The phrase 'political theology' derives from the juristic-political writing of Carl Schmitt. See: Carl Schmitt, *Political Theology: Four Chapters on the Concept of Sovereignty*, trans. George Schwab (Chicago: University of Chicago Press, 2005).

2. For further reading, see Albie Sachs, 'Preparing Ourselves for Freedom: Culture and the ANC Constitutional Guidelines', *TDR* 35:1 (Spring 1991): 187–93, as well as Njabulo Ndebele, 'The Rediscovery of the Ordinary: Some New Writings in South Africa', in *Rediscovery of the Ordinary: Essays on South African Literature and Culture* (Johannesburg: COSAW, 1991), 37–57.

3. Frederic Jameson, 'Third World Literature in the Era of Multinational Capitalism', *Social Text* 15 (Autumn 1986): 65–88.

Bibliography

Primary sources

Plays by Craig Higginson
Dream of the Dog (London: Oberon, 2010).
The Girl in the Yellow Dress (London: Oberon, 2010).
The Jungle Book, adapted by Craig Higginson from a version by Tim Supple
    (London: Oberon, 2011).
Little Foot (London: Oberon, 2012).

Secondary sources

To date, the secondary literature on the plays of Craig Higginson is limited to
press reviews, interviews and comments. For contextualization and references to
Higginson, the following sources are indispensable:

Attwell, David and Derek Attridge (eds), *The Cambridge History of South African
    Literature* (Cambridge: Cambridge University Press, 2012).

Chapman, Michael and Margaret Lenta (eds), *SA Lit Beyond 2000* (Scottsville:
    UKZN Press, 2011).

Cornwell, Gareth, Dirk Klopper and Craig MacKenzie, *The Columbia Guide to
    South African Literature in English since 1945* (New York: Columbia University
    Press, 2010).

Jameson, Fredric, 'Third World Literature in the Era of Multinational Capitalism',
    Social Text 15 (Autumn 1986): 65–88.

Kruger, Loren, 'Theatre: Regulation, Resistance and Recovery', in David Attwell
    and Derek Attridge (eds), *The Cambridge History of South African Literature*
    (Cambridge: Cambridge University Press, 2012), 564–86.

CHAPTER 14
MPUMELELO PAUL GROOTBOOM
Muff Andersson[1]

Relativity: Township Stories; Foreplay

Introduction

Playwright and director Mpumelelo Paul Grootboom is one of the midnight children of South African culture in that he was born in Meadowlands, Soweto, in 1975, on the cusp of the student uprisings. Meadowlands itself is a famous place, struggle-wise. The community was resettled by the apartheid regime in the mid-1950s and never forgotten thanks to Strike Vilakazi's song made famous by Nancy Jacobs: Meadowlands.[2]

Thus Grootboom, child of the mid-1970s, grew up witnessing tremendous violence and traumatic shifts and changes within his society. His work is evidence of both the terrors and marvels he encountered on the township street. Despite the inevitable grim hunger pains growling from within his plays, there is always that ticklish belly laugh on top: township song and humour that infuses his art with tiers of entertainment, spectacle and action. He sweeps his work with strokes of absurdity and, like Rushdie's midnight children, an 'abracadabra' factor; hence sheer entertainment outlives, for audiences, whatever appalling images they might have witnessed or possibly the sense of voyeurism they felt. Audiences can be assured that despite the violence in which they will undoubtedly participate within a typical Grootboom play – not for nothing has he been called the township Tarantino[3] – there will ultimately be magic.

Grootboom, going to primary and secondary school in first Meadowlands and then Garankuwa, a township outside Pretoria, must have seen the struggle intensifying even as he fell in love with Shakespeare at school. In this passion he was like many black South African literati before him – H. I. E. Dhlomo,[4] Sol Plaatje[5] and even the Bard-quoting former South African president Thabo Mbeki, who would become the topic of one of Grootboom's own plays, *Rhetorical.*

Grootboom spent all of three months enrolled as a medical student at the University of the Witwatersrand before dropping out and switching to the arts. His initial mentor was Percy Langa – a playwright, director and television producer – and she taught him to write scripts.[6] Through Langa he met John Rogers of Bateleur films in 1993, another major influence, friend and mentor to both Grootboom and his frequent co-writer Aubrey Sekhabi. Collaborations between the two began in 1997, when Sekhabi encouraged Grootboom to write *Enigma*, and have continued until the co-written production of the most recent play *Rhetorical* (2011), which played at the Kunstenfestivaldesarts in Brussels.[7]

The year *Enigma* (1997) made its appearance, Grootboom was appointed 'resident writer' by the North West Arts Council (now the Mmabana Foundation). Here his interest in training young actors developed through work with the then North West Arts Council Youth Theatre Groups, the Mmabana Youth Ensemble and Badiragatsi Youth Theatre Group.[8]

In 2002 he worked as Development Officer at the South African State Theatre, continuing his developmental community theatre work and expanding his writing for stage and television. Early television writing credits include *Young Vision* (a drama on SABC 2, 1994); *Suburban Bliss* (a sitcom on SABC 1, 1995); *Isidingo* (a soapie on SABC 3, 2000); *Soul City* ('edutainment'[9] on SABC 1, 2000); *Orlando* (a detective drama on SABC 2, 2001); *Mponeng* (a sitcom on SABC 2, 2005); and *Healside* (a medical drama on SABC 2, 2005).[10]

The mix of genres is not only a marker of writing agility. South African TV uses an audience rating system created by Unilever called 'listenership standard measurements' (LSMs). It is based on literacy rates, and by extension poverty rates, since LSMs 2–4 represent viewers without much education or literacy whereas the highest LSMs, 8–10, refer to the most educated and elite audiences. Hence working for a sitcom like *Mponeng*, aimed at lower LSMs, at the same time as *Healside*, aimed at higher LSMs, shows considerable understanding of audiences.

Grootboom has also ventured into the world of television directing, directing three episodes in the second 39-episode season of the medical TV Drama *Healside*.

Grootboom's theatre writing credits include *Enigma* (1997) and *Not With My Gun* (1998), co-written with Aubrey Sekhabi; *Urban Reality* (1998); *Messiah* (1999); *The Stick* (2000), co-written with Aubrey Sekhabi; *Dikeledi* (2000), an adaptation of Sophocles' *Electra*; *Cards* (2002), a rewriting of Mothusi Mokoto's script; and *In this Life* (2004), co-written with Presley

Chweneyagae[11] (this was later reworked and retitled *Relativity: Township Stories*). His other plays are *Telling Stories* (2007); *Interracial* (2007), co-written with Aubrey Sekhabi; *Maru* (2008), an adaptation of the Bessie Head novel; *Welcome to Rocksburg* (2009); and *Rhetorical* (2011), co-written with Aubrey Sekhabi (about the fall from grace of Thabo Mbeki).

Perhaps it is no surprise that Grootboom has picked up a spate of national awards. He won the 2005 National Standard Bank 'Young Artist Award' for theatre. This is one of the most prestigious South African awards for excellence. The same year he picked up the Naledi Theatre Award for best directing of a play/musical for *Relativity: Township Stories*. In 2008 he won the Herald Angel Award at the Fringe Edinburgh Festival for *Relativity: Township Stories*. In 2009 he took the Naledi again, this time for best director of *Foreplay*.

Unquestionably Paul Grootboom has 'made it', and despite the controversy inevitably surrounding his plays, including the nudity and sex in *Cards*, themes that make audiences giggle and clap but censors frown, he had made it so big that by 2002 he was employed as resident director at the State Theatre in Pretoria. Although this was a major leap towards transformation by the theatre, it was not without precedence in South Africa where at the time, as Jyoti Mistry has pointed out, there was 'the relocation of the marginal culture to the centre'.[12]

The plays

The Grootboom plays that have received the most acclaim (and reaction) have been *Cards*; *Relativity: Township Stories*; *Foreplay*; and *Rhetorical*. Of these I have chosen to focus on *Relativity: Township Stories* and *Foreplay* because their scripts are easily available. However, I will make reference to the other two when observations or aspects of reviews apply equally to the other two plays, or to moments of theatre that are similar to what we experience in the other two plays.

Relativity: Township Stories *(2006) (with Presley Chweneyagae)*

Grootboom has explained that *Township Stories* was inspired in part by Austrian playwright Arthur Schnitzler, whose work he first discovered through the film *Eyes Wide Shut*.[13]

However, Grootboom's adaptation has used melodramatic techniques in a structure mimicking that of the soapie *Isidingo*, which as a writer he would have become familiar with. The *Isidingo* structure sees four interwoven stories making up a single episode. Each story then reveals its backstory (the past) which intersects with events in the present to create tension for the future of the combined stories.[14] Four stories are interwoven into *Relativity: Township Stories*. The 'G-string' strangler, a serial killer targeting young women, is on the loose. A young abused girl who has run away from home pairs up with a violent gangster. Her father hires a contract killer. A father brutalizes his son, who is having an affair with a shebeen owner, and the cops beat up everyone.

But where a soapie is never resolved and the backstories can unravel indefinitely, Grootboom's four-parter had to be resolved in two acts and he used every possible soapie trick to bring it to a climax that would leave audiences gasping. As Robert Greig of the *Sunday Independent* wrote in *Cue*, *Relativity* was a 'panorama of extreme emotions and violence'.[15] There were mixed reactions from the beginning to seeing black people as violent on stage – an apparent reversal of anti-apartheid theatre in which audiences had become used to seeing cruel white people abusing black people. However, asked Jacqueline Keevy, did Grootboom's perpetuation of the image of the black person as violent or attaching these signifiers of extreme violence challenge the colonial imposition of identity through the human body?[16]

To give an idea of what Greig and Keevy were referring to, add into the mix of domestic violence and assaults in the four stories spoken about above a team of bungling detectives – including the cop Rocks who flirts with his woman colleague as they examine a dead woman's body, sniffs at the corpse's panties, goads his male colleagues with Rabelaisian marketplace rudeness because their surnames Molomo and Ranko[17] are body parts and tortures a suspect by setting fire to his balls – and you get an idea of the shock value of this play. Abuse, rape, incest, brutality and violence might indeed be part of everyday life in South African townships, but they have certainly not been represented much in theatre, let alone graphically.

Grootboom clearly sees a cycle of abuse operating within the violence that is evident in this play. One of the characters, psychologist Mantoa Nkhatho, gives a long-winded (two-page) explanation about the relationship between the abused and becoming the abuser:

> [M]ost serial killers were exposed to some sort of trauma in their formative years. Direct trauma, such as emotional, physical and sexual abuse. And to escape the memories of their horror, they

develop fantasies … violent fantasies where they see themselves as aggressors instead of the victims they actually were. (11)

At the heart of this monologue is an educational message that sounds less as though it emerged from the pen of an inspired artist and more as if it might have been cut and pasted from a website with a few key words pinned into a Google search, such as 'sexual abuse + perpetrator + victim'.

The downside of Grootboom's writing is that in sections the characters tend to talk for too long, and dialogue becomes stilted. Like every writer, Grootboom needs a good editor. Still, his stages are busy, Orlinesque, with choreography and lots of activity besides: so much so that a long speech, or a weak actor with a so-so accent in a part requiring, say, the voice of a 'coconut',[18] or a thin piece of the plot, can be carried by many other distractions.

On the plus side, Grootboom's writing is frequently clever, funny and raw, using 'homie' slang and expressions. Local audiences will chortle from lines of *scamto*[19] mixing several languages like Mavarara, '*Watte cherrie is daai?*' [originally Cape Afrikaans slang, now used broadly in townships as *tsotsi* slang meaning literally 'who is that cherry?' (girl in the sense of 'chick')] (23, italics in original), or Dario, 'and daai *moegoe* says to me' [a mix of Afrikaans *tsotsi taal* and English meaning 'and that moron says to me'] (24, italics in original), or Dario again, '*Hae, nnyo hae ganiwe, bafo, ya jewa! Ya jewa daai ding! Ee, die man! That's why o bolaiwa ke go iskomora so!*' (25, italics in original). In this sentence we find elements of Sotho, Tswana, Zulu, Afrikaans and English with a meaning approximating, 'C'mon, you don't shoot a pussy, brother, you fuck it, you fuck that thing. Hell, this man … that's why you wank so much.'

However, his work is also peppered with intertextual references intended to reach more than faithful fans. Elite audiences from overseas as well as LSMs 8–10 will not fail to miss the music from Rossini's *William Tell Overture* used in the sex scene in Kubrick's *A Clockwork Orange* during the violent sex scene, Mamiki's comment about J. D. Salinger and *The Catcher in the Rye* (32) or Dan's 'lend me your ears' from Shakespeare's *Julius Caesar* (58).

On the other hand, popular audiences in both South Africa and countries around the world will appreciate Dario's comment that 'They were hugging and laughing as if they're in *The Bold and The Beautiful*' (23), or Pelo's 'I know you ntanga. Jean Clodi van Deim [sic]' (24), or Thabo's reading preference, *Jack and the Beanstalk* (31), or Mamiki's reference to Bill Cosby (ibid.).

It has to be pointed out that no two performances of the play have been the same, with the violence and comedy levels shifting as well as unequal usage of local languages[20] and the printed play being different from the play performed at the State theatre. Presumably many of the local languages vanish in overseas performances.

In one dress rehearsal at the Market in 2006 there were wisecracks in the form of light heckling from a seeming audience member and a moment when one or two actors suddenly leapt into the audience with pens and paper, randomly asking audience members to write down an answer to a question. I asked an individual near me who had scribbled something down what the question was. He said it was 'What do you think is going on?' The person, incidentally a visiting scientist from the US with scant knowledge of local languages but sitting next to someone who was translating for him, wrote, 'I think they were both abused', referring to the characters Thabo and Thuli (which turned out to be true). I have no idea what questions other audience members were asked or what suggestions they made. But the moment produced a postmodern element in that it provided audience members with the idea that they too were playing a part in the producerly process of the play. It suggested that the actors might improvise according to audience suggestions. The action was a reminder that within South African popular TV and theatre productions the focus group of audience members is almost always used to assess audience readings of a text in advance of performance or airing.[21]

Foreplay (2008) (after Arthur Schnitzler)

In turn, *Foreplay* (2008) was an adaptation of *Reigen*,[22] the *fin-de-siècle* play with which Schnitzler scandalized bourgeois Vienna in around 1900. The play, branded at the time as obscene and pornographic, reveals the intimacy and hypocrisy of the society through ten love scenes linking various classes of the society through sex. Thus the nobleman, prostitute and poet are linked through the bedroom though they would normally be divided through what are perceived as regular power relations.

Grootboom freely adapted Schnitzler's play into *Foreplay*, using locally specific scenarios – central Pretoria and townships – and (stereo)types easily recognizable to audiences and changing certain structural aspects but keeping the rough cyclical design of the play. The use of Schnitzler's name as co-author on the screenplay presumably prevents copyright infringements or plagiarism charges.

When the play premiered in Amsterdam, Grootboom said:

Schnitzler is fascinated by the instincts that fuel many people but unavoidably cause much damage. The fact that this makes love and sex unemotional is something many South Africans recognise. It is my hope that my staging will get people thinking about their sexual morals.[23]

Only two years later, his director's note in the Pretoria programme had an entirely different tone to it: 'What can be more fun than watching ten people having sex with each other, talk about crap and give each other STDs?'[24]

Had he changed his mind about his project and decided it should just be read as entertainment or was his comment ironic? It is hard to say. *Foreplay*, beyond its salacious talk and circular carnal connectivity, is structured as a play about playacting and theatre, and as such creates another aspect of both postmodern and African traditional theatre: the concept of the internal audience commenting on the structure and play within the play as well as auto citation.[25] We see, incidentally, something similar in *Rhetorical*, which finds Presley Chweneyagae as Dada Mogkoane, a youth leader and Julius Malema sound-alike, narrating the story of the fall from grace of President Thabo Mbeki, played by Fezile Mpela. Dada's fiery populist speeches talk about Mbeki's better known intellectual speeches, such as his 'I am an African' speech, and pit these against Mandela's speeches and snippets of Jacob Zuma's trademark *Umshini Wam* ('Bring me my machine gun').

Whereas *Foreplay* is structured as a play about a play, *Rhetorical* is a play with an orator giving a speech about speeches. In both we find women who are the wives versus the women of easy virtue and their respective interactions with powerful men; a circular nature and structure of the play; the interweaving of several stories; and the mechanism of the internal audience used by soap opera producers.

In *Foreplay*, six actors – three women and three men – perform 'the lovers' in ten roles: the prostitute and soldier, to the soldier and waitress, to the waitress and youth, to the youth and the priest's wife, and so on.

Grootboom's sex scenes focus on what happens before sex. Grootboom has said this moment intrigues him because it shows 'how people are vulnerable, or become strong, or trick each other'.[26] In each case there is one desirous and one unwilling participant, followed by a dance in which desire overcomes resistance and ends with a pop of bubble-gum balloons. As one reviewer noted, the 'Wicks and Chappies[27] bubblegum bubbles and later blown up balloons' reflected a 'masterfully communicated, wordless reference to HIV' which by the end of the play had infected the entire cast.[28] Certainly the popped balloons represented consummation between the lovers.

'Couples' or 'couplings' might be more accurate than 'lovers' since sometimes the infidelity, trickery and deceit surrounding the encounters, the alcohol-fuelled sex including anal rape and attendant violence and even killing, are fairly far away from romantic love. The events surrounding sexual encounters speak rather to the manipulation of power, moral degeneration, hypocrisy and political corruption represented by both male and female characters.

Starting with the men, the represented playwright (played by Mandla Gaduka) is the narrator and youth who utters the words that caused a walkout by Christians at its Pretoria opening: 'God is a f... pervert' and 'all mankind is nothing but his whores' [surely a line reminiscent of Shakespeare?]. Sello Zikalala played the soldier/preacher Ray, who has sex with a teenager while talking to his Almighty and Holy Spirit, complaining to them about his neglectful wife and the weakness inside him that makes him seduce young girls. He cries out as his sexual act comes to an end, 'Hallelujah!' Boitumelo Shisana played the politician/freedom fighter who anally rapes a prostitute after killing her pimp. He says, 'You are like many other women in this country ... nothing but ignorant ... incapable of understanding what my mandate is ... my mandate is to lead you, you ignorant bitch'. He also calls her 'a capitalist bitch'.

The women are Koketso Mojela who played the bartender/waitress and schoolgirl; Ntshepiseng Montshiwa, the preacher's wife and actress; and Excellentia Mokoena, the prostitute in the local version.

'As in the Vienna of Freud, so too in the Pretoria of today is the merry-go-round of desire a metaphor for the power relations and taboos underlying society everywhere. Foreplay looks at a South Africa seemingly obsessed with sex and violence, where AIDS is still taking far too many lives', wrote a reviewer at Kunstenfestivaldesarts (Brussels) in May 2009.[29]

In the local version at the Laager theatre at the Market much was made in the opening scene of men picking up women – or would that be women soliciting men? – in a brothel. What particularly shocked and titillated South African audiences beyond the sexual escapades and violent rape scene was seeing Excellentia Mokoena as the tough, independent and conniving whore Leocardia stripped stark naked: this from the State Theatre, with its past history of chained, conservative apartheid theatre.

In keeping with past traditions, censors slapped on an age restriction of 16. Yet again, Grootboom's work on prostitutes slots into a well-explored trope from the African canon. From the perspective of African literature, Grootboom's scene could be compared to one in the novel by Meja Mwangi, *Going Down River Road* (1976), in which the protagonist Ben humiliates a prostitute. He strips off her clothes and leaves her vomiting and naked in a bar. He comments abusively that she looks like a hippo.

Since the local media kept returning to the theme of prostitution it is worthwhile at this juncture to look at another function prostitutes play in African literature, particularly popular forms. While Ngugi treats his prostitute as a respected figure who represents the most honest and free-spirited soul, the person prepared to talk in a straightforward way about the chaos that is around whereas everything else must be told in allegory, in most other instances in African literature prostitutes represent immorality and corruption, especially when written by male authors. In contrast, men in representation remain unjudged even if they are criminals or drink to excess.[30] Stephanie Newell argues that good-time girls offer 'interpretative strategies'[31] to audiences:

Perhaps the repetition of certain female character types occurs because female morality is more manageable than political corruption in Africa, and narrators can criticise women's behaviour more readily (and safely) than that of the national political class.[32]

Tiisetso Tlelima wrote in *Arts Review* (2009) about *Foreplay*:

There is a curious scene where nobody has sex with anybody but the tutor-playwright character gratifies himself by pressuring the schoolgirl to divulge her personal tragedy: 'You're not going to become an actor if you're not honest … you see, if a part demands you to be a bitch, you have to realise what a slut you are to play it … as an actress you have to recognise what you do or how you once felt like that and use it.'[33]

With Grootboom we find that the men are judged too in that there is comment about hypocrisy and violence. But where Grootboom's work again resonates with a common trope in African literature is that there is a tendency by male authors to 'justify or excuse' the behaviour of men: 'They had good reasons in their personal history to define men as unloving and unreliable.'[34] Pastor Ray, for example, who sleeps with a teenage girl, justifies his actions thus:

> priests who [engage] in inappropriate physical involvement outside marriage ... People call it moral failure and in turn demand that those preachers step down from moral leadership ... but I call it proof of pastoral humanness.

Marcia Blumberg cites Greg Homann referring to theatre in democratic South Africa as falling into three phases: pre-post-apartheid (1990–6); early post apartheid (1996–2002); and post-apartheid (2002–8).[35] Blumberg sees the pre-post-apartheid theatre as reflecting euphoria and peace. From there she sees a downward slope towards the post-apartheid theatre and what she calls 'restorative' theatre, a term she claims to have coined herself, linked to the notion of 'restorative justice'.[36] These ideas, however, are sadly not Blumberg originals. They resonate with well-worn African literature theory first articulated by Chinua Achebe that understands the post-colonial canon in three phases: the first euphoric nationalist phase, in which authors tell their stories of struggle, the triumph of their revolution and the new-found national peace; the second reflective stage in which there is a tentative acknowledgement that not everything is well, especially with the poor; and the third stage of post-colonial disillusionment in which writers highlight the way in which what was deemed immoral and excessive within the previous regime has been repeated by the new. In this third phase the protagonists inevitably find agency to expose corruption or topple dictator-ships in what is called the process of 'restorative justice'.

It could be argued that *Foreplay*'s prostitute looks beyond gender, race and class when she states that everyone 'is a fucking whore' (78) and that this moment of post-colonial disillusionment is yet another instance showing that Grootboom is not disturbing the foundations of the canonical African literature framework any more than Marechera, Ngugi, or even Achebe or Ousmane – but in the case of the latter two without the graphic language – before him.

Summary

What is perhaps unusual for a young black South African playwright is the unprecedented European interest in his work. Grootboom's *Relativity:*

Township Stories toured the world, to London and Berlin and festivals like Kunstenfestivaldesarts in Brussels and the Noorderzon Performing Arts Festival in Groningen. *Foreplay* had its world premiere in The Hague at the Afrovibes Festival and played at the Theatre Royal in Stratford. Grootboom's most recent production, *Rhetorical*, attracted sponsorship from Siemens Stiftung, Festival Iberoamericano de Teatro de Bogotá and the Museum of Contemporary Art Zagreb. This is rare indeed for a playwright from a country where fellow scribes are considered lucky devils if they manage to get their plays staged at an off-fringe venue at the annual Grahamstown festival.

So what is it that European audiences love so much about Grootboom? His is clearly daring theatre by any standards, but as an offering from South Africa it is a world apart from, say, the linear telling of Mbongeni Ngema's *The Zulu* (2013), a viewing of which is not unlike sitting through an animated history lesson back in the apartheid years when Zulus were taught as warlike and proud and male. It is also light years away from the musical retellings of the apartheid struggle that are timed to appear on national holidays – *You Strike the Women, You Strike a Rock* or *Asinamali* – and even though Grootboom makes use of both song and dance, 'musical' does not hit the right note to describe his work. Then too it is not a modern version of a workshopped Barney Simon-style production with that well-loved human train of two, toot-tooting in synch, nor is there simply brilliant, lean writing tripping off the actors' lips, lines delivered with perfect timing and loving attention to the details in a myriad of accents as we have seen recently at the Market with Atandwa Kani and Nat Ramabulana's *Hayani* (2013).

And to what extent is Grootboom simply giving Western audiences another version of the 'exotic' and 'erotic' African? Jacqueline Keevy questions whether Grootboom's 'use of the carnal, the raw, the sex, perpetuate[s] a vicious cycle of colonial prejudices within South African audiences within what should be a postcolonial theatre arena'.[37] Within the framework of Jonathan Schroeder's comments about the colonial gaze and the black performing body, whereby the gaze signifies 'a psychological relationship of power, in which the gazer is superior to the object of the gaze',[38] she argues that in post-colonial performance the performing body should become a key site of resistance.[39]

Citing Gilbert and Tompkins,[40] Keevy asks if Grootboom's work is

that the roles into which he has placed his black performers are within racist discourses 'with perhaps even more emphasis on their supposed violence and sexuality' [and] whether or not Grootboom in casting the Other, the Black performing bodies, as corporeal, carnal, instinctual, raw ... with his use of full nudity, simulated sex, simulated rapes, violence, explicit language, misogyny, obscenities, murder, drug use and religious rhetoric – has introduced colonial ideologies and stereotypes? Is his theatre 'black Black humour'? Reinforcing colonial ideologies of the savage?[41]

On the other hand, asks Keevy, does Grootboom's theatre (unconsciously) aid the location of the (sometimes) nude, sexual, black performing body in the arena/site of resistance in order to fracture the colonial gaze to further the aims of post-colonial theatre: 'Seeing the black performing body being attached to notions of extreme violence begs to ask the question: Does this subvert the colonial gaze or does it feed into a stereotype of the violent, savage black?'[42]

Hoxworth on the other hand believes that Grootboom, like Brett Bailey and Yaël Farber, tried to answer the question 'What now?' in post-apartheid South Africa, and began working with 'idiosyncratic theatrical forms experimenting with notions of "authentic" South African identity, both theatrically and culturally', forming a canon akin to 'museums of plays' or a tourist culture for global spectators around 'particular South African performance traditions'.[43]

Where Grootboom's work clearly excites, one might add to this idea, is in the *movement* of his actors, and here his use of professional choreographers has clearly paid off.

Hoxworth argues that the international theatre market places great value on 'authentic' cultural objects and suggests that what is viewed as authentic will find both overseas funding and large overseas audiences. Curiously, between 2003 and 2008, all three dramatists – Bailey, Grootboom and Farber – premiered new works that directly reimagined European source material (*MoLoRa*, *Orfeus* and *Foreplay*).

Such appropriation of 'Western' cultural material raises important questions concerning the long-term trajectory of South African theatre. With both textual sources and productions tending towards Euroamerican spectators, South African theatre faces the threat of becoming 'South African' product shaped primarily by international beliefs of and demands for 'South Africa'. Thus, the international traffic and travel of South African theatre over the past two decades begs the very question of South African theatre's putative 'South Africanness'.[44]

Less concerned about the Euroamerican construction of 'South Africanness', Craig Higginson in his Foreword to *Relativity: Township Stories* questions whether Grootboom's plays represent, along with other plays like Mike van Graan's *Green Man Flashing*, 'a new dialogical form more appropriate to a democracy'.[45]

Certainly the heteroglossia and busy-ness of the plot creates a vast difference from the monologue of an earlier era – Higginson refers to the monologue of apartheid propaganda being answered with 'an equally partisan voice of opposition'.[46]

Perhaps part of Grootboom's popularity is to be found in Anton Krueger's 2007 review of *Cards*, set in a Hillbrow brothel. Here Krueger alludes to the audience participation in the play, again authentically African and hardly 'AmericanEuro':

> The programme to this second run of this popular play promises sex, nudity, violence, swearing and drugs – and the show doesn't disappoint. It's a grand-scale sex spectacle of the first order, using multiple levels, blaring music (of a quite extraordinary range) and gratifyingly large dollops of complete nudity and simulated sex … In this crowd, people arrived well into the play and cell phones chimed out agreeably throughout the show. A constant interplay of commentary between audience and stage went on, with frequent cheering, clapping, and chirping. I loved this crowd. I love black audiences. This is what theatre should be, a communal event, something shared, not a movie where you're sitting there alone in the dark; and also not a preachy lesson in politics or high culture.[47]

Notes

1. With research help from Oscar Marleyn.

2. Gwen Ansell, *Soweto Blues: Jazz, Popular Music, and Politics in South Africa* (New York: Continuum, 2005), 80.

3. See Jos Shuring, 'Mpumelelo Paul Grootboom: Theatre Climate in South Africa Has Many Taboos', *The Power of Culture*, 2008, http://www.krachtvancultuur.nl/en/current/2008/september/mpumelo-paul-grootboom (accessed 17 March 2015).

4. Bhekizizwe Peterson, *Monarchs, Missionaries and African Intellectuals* (Johannesburg: Wits University Press, 2000), 200.

5. Tim Couzens, 'Introduction', in Sol T. Plaatje, *Mhudi* (Oxford: Heinemann, 1978), 20.

6. http://www.sahistory.org.za/people/mpumelelo-paul-cosmo-grootboom (accessed 17 March 2015).

7. http://archive.kfda.be/projects/companies/mpumelelo-paul-grootboom (accessed 17 March 2015).

8. http://www.zoominfo.com/p/Mpumelelo-Grootboom/864943956 (accessed 17 March 2015).

9. In which educational messages are built into entertaining popular forms like soap opera.

10. http://paulgrootboom.com/about (accessed 17 March 2015).

11. Star of *Tsotsi*, Gavin Hood's Oscar-winning film.

12. Jyoti Mistry, 'Conditions of Cultural Production in Post-Apartheid South Africa', *Extraordinary Times, IWM Junior Visiting Fellows Conferences*, Vol. II (Vienna: n.p., 2001), 3.

13. Shuring, 'Mpumelo Paul Grootboom'.

14. Muff Andersson, 'Isidingo: Between Memory Box and Healing Couch', MA thesis (University of the Witwatersrand, 2002), 38.

15. Robert Greig, 'Relatively Dark Creation of the World', *Cue* 8 (June 2005): 1.

16. Jacqueline Keevy, 'Interracial Mumbo Jumbo: Mpumelelo Paul Grootboom and Brett Bailey's Theatre', MA thesis (University of KwaZulu-Natal Pietermaritzburg, 2008), http://researchspace.ukzn.ac.za/xmlui/handle/10413/1012 (accessed 17 March 2015), 33.

17. In Sotho *Molomo* means 'mouth', also used as slang for vagina, whereas *Ranko* is presumably an Anglicization of *maraho*, buttocks.

18. Derogatory term for a black person who is considered black on the outside and white inside. The term is often used for people with posh English accents or accents from expensive schools.

19. Township slang composed of elements of different local languages with some words in English. It is relatively easy for South Africans to follow.

20. Mostly North Sotho with snippets of Afrikaans.

21. Andersson, 'Isidingo', 61; Muff Andersson, *Intertextuality, Violence and Memory in Yizo Yizo: Youth TV Drama* (Pretoria: Unisa Press, 2010), 3.

22. Also known as *La Ronde*.

23. Quoted in Shuring, 'Mpumelelo Paul Grootboom'.

24. Quoted in Loren Kruger, 'Foreplay (Review)', *Theatre Journal* 62:3 (2010): 453–4.

25. Andersson, *Intertextuality, Violence and Memory*, 20.

26. http://www.english.rfi.fr/culture/20100530-variations-sex-and-hypocrisy (accessed 17 March 2015).

27. Wicks and Chappies are two famous brands of bubble-gum, often used as small change in townships by vendors.

28. Cf. http://fleshisgrass.wordpress.com/2009/05/31/foreplay (accessed 17 March 2015).

29. http://archive.kfda.be/2009/en/node/212 (accessed 17 March 2015).

30. Nici Nelson, 'Representations of Men and Women, City and Town in Kenyan Novels of the 1970s and 1980s', *African Languages and Cultures* 9:2 (1996): 150–1.

31. Stephanie Newell (ed.), *Readings in Popular Fiction* (Oxford: James Currey, 2002), 6.

32. Ibid., 7.

33. Tiisetso Tlelima, 'Foreplay', *Arts Review*, 31 May 2009, http://paulgrootboom. com/home (accessed 17 March 2015).

34. Nelson, 'Representations of Men and Women', 155.

35. Blumberg refers to Greg Homann, 'Preamble', in Greg Homann (ed.), *At This Stage: Plays From Post-Apartheid South Africa* (Johannesburg: Wits University Press, 2009).

36. Marcia Blumberg, 'South African Theatre Beyond 2000: Theatricalising the Unspeakable', *Current Writing: Text and Reception in Southern Africa* 21:1–2 (2009): 246.

37. Keevy, 'Interracial Mumbo Jumbo', 11.

38. Jonathan E. Schroeder, 'Consuming Representation: A Visual Approach to Consumer Researcher', in Barbara B. Stern (ed.), *Representing Consumers: Voices, Views and Visions* (London: Routledge, 1998), 208.

39. Keevy, 'Interracial Mumbo Jumbo', 29.

40. Helen Gilbert and Joanne Tompkins, *Post-Colonial Drama: Theory, Practice, Politics* (London: Routledge, 1996), 203–8.

41. Keevy, 'Interracial Mumbo Jumbo', 11.

42. Ibid., 79.

43. Kellen Hoxworth, 'Tour(ist)ing Post-Apartheid South African Theatre: The Works of Brett Bailey, Yael Farber, and Mpumelelo Paul Grootboom in (Inter) National Production', Master thesis (University of Pittsburgh, 2012).

44. Ibid.

45. Craig Higginson, 'Foreword', in Mpumelelo Paul Grootboom and Presley Chweneyagae, *Relativity: Township Stories* (Johannesburg: Dung Beetle Dramas, 2006), 4.

46. Ibid.

47. Anton Krueger, 'Grootboom's Cards: A Tenderly Violent Sex Spectacle', 2007, http://www.joburg.org.za/index.php?option=com_content&view=article&id=4289 (accessed 17 March 2015).

Bibliography

Primary sources

Grootboom, Mpumelelo Paul, *Foreplay* (London: Oberon, 2009).
Grootboom, Mpumelelo Paul and Presley Chweneyagae, *Relativity: Township Stories* (Johannesburg: Dung Beetle Dramas, 2006).

Secondary sources

Andersson, Muff, *Music in the Mix: The Story of Popular South African Music* (Johannesburg: Ravan Press, 1981).
Andersson, Muff, 'Isidingo: Between Memory Box and Healing Couch', MA thesis (University of the Witwatersrand, 2002).
Andersson, Muff, *Intertextuality, Violence and Memory in Yizo Yizo: Youth TV Drama* (Pretoria: Unisa Press, 2010).
Ansell, Gwen, *Soweto Blues: Jazz, Popular Music, and Politics in South Africa* (New York: Continuum, 2005).
Blumberg, Marcia, 'South African Theatre Beyond 2000: Theatricalising the Unspeakable', *Current Writing: Text and Reception in Southern Africa* 21:1–2 (2009): 238–60.
Couzens, Tim, 'Introduction', in Sol T. Plaatje, *Mhudi* (Oxford: Heinemann, 1978).
Gilbert, Helen and Joanne Tompkins, *Post-Colonial Drama: Theory, Practice, Politics* (London: Routledge, 1996).
Greig, Robert, 'Relatively Dark Creation of a World', *Cue* 8 (June 2005).
Higginson, Craig, 'Foreword', in Mpumelelo Paul Grootboom and Presley Chweneyagae, *Relativity: Township Stories* (Johannesburg: Dung Beetle Dramas, 2006).
Homann, Greg, 'Preamble', in Greg Homann (ed.), *At This Stage: Plays From Post-Apartheid South Africa* (Johannesburg: Wits University Press, 2009).
Hoxworth, Kellen, 'Tour(ist)ing Post-Apartheid South African Theatre: The Works of Brett Bailey, Yaël Farber, and Mpumelelo Paul Grootboom in (Inter)National Production', Master thesis (University of Pittsburgh, 2012).
Jones, Megan, 'Township Textualities', *Alternation* 20:1 (2013): 26–51.
Keevy, Jacqueline, 'Interracial Mumbo Jumbo: Mpumelelo Paul Grootboom and Brett Bailey's Theatre', MA thesis (University of KwaZulu-Natal, Pietermaritzburg, 2008), http://researchspace.ukzn.ac.za/xmlui/handle/10413/1012 (accessed 17 March 2015).
Krueger, Anton, 'Grootboom's Cards: A Tenderly Violent Sex Spectacle', 2007, http://www.joburg.org.za/index.php?option=com_content&view=article&id=4289 (accessed 17 March 2015).
Kruger, Loren, 'Foreplay (Review)', *Theatre Journal* 62:3 (2010): 453–4.
Mistry, Jyoti, 'Conditions of Cultural Production in Post-Apartheid South Africa', *Extraordinary Times, IWM Junior Visiting Fellows Conferences*, Vol. II (Vienna: n.p., 2001).

Mwangi, Meja, *Going Down River Road* (Nairobi: Heinemann, 1976).

Nelson, Nici, 'Representations of Men and Women, City and Town in Kenyan Novels of the 1970s and 1980s', *African Languages and Cultures* 9:2 (1996): 145–68.

Newell, Stephanie (ed.), *Readings in Popular Fiction* (Oxford: James Currey, 2002).

Peterson, Bhekizizwe, *Monarchs, Missionaries and African Intellectuals* (Johannesburg: Wits University Press, 2000).

Schroeder, Jonathan E., 'Consuming Representation: A Visual Approach to Consumer Researcher', in Barbara B. Stern (ed.), *Representing Consumers: Voices, Views and Visions* (London: Routledge, 1998), 193–230.

Shuring, Jos, 'Mpumelelo Paul Grootboom: Theatre Climate in South Africa Has Many Taboos', *The Power of Culture*, 2008, http://www.krachtvancultuur.nl/en/current/2008/september/mpumelo-paul-grootboom (accessed 17 March 2015). http://www.sahistory.org.za/people/mpumelelo-paul-cosmo-grootboom (accessed 17 March 2015).

Tlelima, Tiisetso, 'Foreplay', *Arts Review*, 31 May 2009, http://paulgrootboom.com/home (accessed 17 March 2015).

CHAPTER 15
BRETT BAILEY
Kevin J. Wetmore, Jr

---

iMumbo Jumbo; ipi zombi?; Heartstopping; The Prophet; Big Dada: The Rise and Fall of Idi Amin; Voudou Nation; House of the Holy Afro; Orfeus; Exhibit A: Deutsch Sudwestafrika; Exhibit B; Exhibit C

Introduction

Brett Bailey is one of the most celebrated contemporary theatre artists in South Africa, yet his work is often controversial, both in terms of content as well as his own identity as a white South African working primarily with black artists and culture. His work has been performed outside of South Africa, with several notable European tours and Australian festival appearances, but he has yet to achieve any major success in the Americas. His work is inherently rooted in South African identity, history, politics and culture.

Bailey was born in 1967, a third-generation British South African, and grew up in Tokai, a white suburb of Cape Town, attending first a local co-ed prep school and then a prestigious all-boys secondary school. After taking a degree in drama at the University of Cape Town in 1991, he subsequently spent a year in India in 1994, 'questing for direction and meaning in life'.[1] Bailey's formative years as an artist were thus during the State of Emergency and the subsequent rapid political transition of the late 1980s and early 1990s, and his training, most notably with Mavis Taylor at Cape Town, focused on experimental theatre. After returning to South Africa from India, as Anton Krueger states, 'he decided ... to identify himself as an African, and to explain the traditional indigenous spiritual traditions of the land of his birth'.[2] Bailey then spent parts of 1996, 1997 and 1998 studying with Xhosa *sangomas*. He then completed a postgraduate diploma in performance studies at the DasArts Master of Theatre programme at the Amsterdam School for the Arts.

The major themes and elements of Bailey's work include ritual, journey and transformation, as well as play – especially in his first three plays, collectively known as (and published under the title of) *The Plays of Miracles and Wonder*, itself a playful reference to Paul Simon's song 'The Boy in the Bubble' (in which the lyric is, 'these are the days of miracle and wonder'). Yet Bailey's appropriation is appropriate, as his plays are also concerned with and consumed by miracles and wonders, both spiritual and visual. Third World Bunfight productions feature real *sangomas* performing rituals on stage and off.

Almost all of Bailey's narratives contain multiple journeys, featuring a character travelling from one location to another, and also require the audience, rather than sitting and passively watching, walking through a site-specific performance. Bailey's plays contain multiple transforma- tions – everyday objects take on new meaning and form: black umbrellas become the wings of birds in *ipi zombi?*, for example. Lastly, his productions are postmodern performances that play with language, image and idea. He embraces the paradoxical and the hybrid. Audiences are encouraged to laugh, even as they react in horror at the events being depicted: 'In his determination to move away from what he called "message theatre" towards a more savagely entertaining medium he believes to [represent] the grotesque ironies and contradictions of contemporary Africa, Bailey indulges raucously in repeating history as farce.'[3] His work embodies that spirit of hybridity, play and interplay between Africa and the West.

Bailey's theatre is one of spectacle. Ashraf Jamal argues, correctly, that the 'driving power' of Bailey's work is 'not textual but visual'.[4] Indeed, one could make the argument that he 'rewrites' texts through direction and design, such as in his production of Verdi's *Macbeth* in 2002. Without changing any of the lines in the opera, Bailey's *mise-en-scène* clearly resets the narrative in Africa. His plays are also experiential and sensual – sound, smell and even taste and touch are engaged during Third World Bunfight produc- tions, from the burning of herbs to the singing, drumming and chanting, to the actual experience of sitting in the theatre. Bailey often forgoes chairs when performing in non-theatre spaces, having audiences sit on hay bales or crates or even walk through the piece, rather than sit.

His productions are site-specific. *ipi zombi?*, staged at the 1998 Grahamstown National Arts Festival, was not only presented in an abandoned power station out in the desert outside of Grahamstown, but audiences rode to it in the 'Heebie Jeebie Express' – a bus designed to begin the experience of the production from the moment one began the journey to the theatre. Bailey's work is full of journeys, oftentimes the literal made metaphorical and the metaphoric made literal. At the same festival, Bailey and Third World Bunfight staged a second work called *Heartstopping*, which consisted of the audience meeting Bailey at the Grahamstown train station (itself a literal starting point for journeys) and walking to a nearby graveyard, which held the remains of white colonial settlers, for the first performance, and to the 1820 Settlers' Monument for the second performance in which performers wearing Xhosa initiation ceremony body paint performed wordless actions. In *Orfeus*, audiences physically followed Orfeus on his journey through the Underworld. In *Exhibit A*, audiences moved through a museum in which actors were featured within the exhibits. The audience is as likely to move as the performers in Bailey's productions.

Bailey founded Third World Bunfight (TWB), an all-black company (save for Bailey himself), in 1996.[5] 'Bunfight' is British slang for a formal tea party or an official function that has come to mean a petty squabble of no importance except to those directly involved. By titling his company 'Third World Bunfight', Bailey demonstrates a playful self-awareness – the formal social occasion that is also a 'Third World' squabble of no importance to the First or Second worlds, proud and satisfied in its place in the world and not concerned with things outside its own context, that Bailey and TWB seek to confront and transform through theatre. The company is also dedicated to the training of actors from impoverished backgrounds.

The paradox of TWB is that their plays are ensemble works created by an auteur who is credited as director, writer and designer. While TWB celebrates the power of the collective, it is Bailey's vision, ideas and texts that guide the company. Plays are developed by a process of workshopping led by Bailey over the course of weeks and months, in which the entire company lives isolated and improvises, interacts and uses source material to develop the pieces. Bailey trains his performers in acting, improvisation, mime, movement and yoga. For *ipi zombi?* the cast spent two weeks living and rehearsing in *sangoma* caves in the Eastern Cape.

Rising from his theatre work, Bailey has also engaged in the creation of other types of art and in leading the development of public art. In 2009, 2010 and 2011, Bailey has been the curator of Africa Centre's *Infecting the City* in Cape Town. The festival takes place annually in February, in public spaces. Each year the organizers propose a socially relevant theme and groups are encouraged to develop pieces for public exhibition, site-specific performance, installations or other engagement with the public. Bailey wrote and directed a biographical performance for Nelson Mandela for his 90th birthday party in Qunu, Eastern Cape, in 2008. He served as the director of the opening performance at the World Summit on Arts and

Culture in Johannesburg in 2009, and also developed the opening concerts for the Harare International Festival of the Arts (HIFA) in Zimbabwe from 2006 to 2009 and again in 2011. His work has also received numerous national and international awards. In 2001 he was named Standard Bank Young Artist of the Year for drama. In that same year he was given Fleur du Cap's Rosalie van der Gught Award for Best Young Director.

In analysing Bailey's work, one must take caution. Although three plays have been published, as Bailey himself states, the plays 'were never envisioned as pieces of literature separate from the rich and multi-layered non-verbal elements which make up the language of living drama: the music, the dramatic form, the spectacle, the ritualistic rhythm, the atmosphere.'[6] In other words, the written script barely begins to encapsulate the audience experience of a TWB production. Similarly, the site-specific adjustments made to each of the productions, even if performed previously, means that the plays change from location to location. Although his work is always about Africa, Bailey attempts to ensure that the work also speaks to the location of performance.

The plays

Johann van Heerden identifies Brett Bailey's work as part of a larger trend in post-1994 theatre in South Africa: 'Theatre makers ... started to explore the powerful theatrical elements of black (South) African cultures, history, mythology, symbolism, performance traditions and even (often sacred) rituals on stage.'[7] Keith Bain identifies the other trend in post-apartheid theatre: 'hypertheatricality', in which productions rely upon strong visuals, immersive *mise-en-scènes* and a strong sense of metatheatricality in which to affect an audience.[8] Bailey's first post-university shows were experimental pieces: 'dada cabarets and township happenings'.[9] These pieces also reflect Bailey's continuing interest in non-linear drama, popular culture and interactive performance. Bain sees the early works, especially the *Plays of Miracles and Wonder* trilogy, as 'filter[ing] the genuine ritualism of indigenous performance cultures through postmodern design aesthetics which emphasizes surrealistic theatricality, spectacle and dramatic surprise'.[10]

iMumbo Jumbo (1997)

Although technically an earlier version of *ipi zombi?*, Bailey's first major work, *iMumbo Jumbo*, was the first fully mounted production to be presented at a national forum, in this case the Grahamstown National Arts Festival. The play recounts the real 1996 journey of Chief Nicholas Gcaleka to the United Kingdom to retrieve the skull of King Hintsa, killed by the British in 1836. Gcaleka claimed he learned in a dream that the strife and conflict in post-apartheid South Africa was caused by Hintsa's spirit, which would not allow for peace until it was returned to South Africa. Coca-Cola and South African Breweries sponsored Gcaleka's trip to recover the skull, which received a good deal of media attention. The fact that the skull brought back by Gcaleka was determined to be that of a white female made Gcaleka a laughing stock, but the overall story and journey appealed to Bailey as a 'clash of cultures, symbols, beliefs, historical eras' and personalities.[11]

After recording several hours of conversation with Gcaleka, Bailey spent three months improvising with TWB to develop the piece, which then played in Recreation Hall in the Coloured neighborhood between Grahamstown and the nearby township – 'an apt location', states Bailey, 'for this drama of cultural collisions'.[12] The show was a huge success and was invited to be remounted at the Market Theatre in Johannesburg, where a more streamlined version with a smaller cast and some textual changes ran for two months. The play was then remounted in 2003, performed at the Baxter Theatre in Cape Town before travelling to London.

The production was theatrically inventive while also providing commentary and insight into the European perception and construction of 'Africa' and the African construction of 'Europe', not to mention the clash of the modern and the traditional and their mutual exploitation. When Chief Gcaleka arrives in the United Kingdom, for example, reporters wore masks of television cameras; faces became lenses. This technique had multiple effects. It suggested African masks, while also establishing the metaphoric mask of the media, journalists hiding behind cameras in order to escape being a part of the events occurring around them. McCallum also suggests that the camera masks imply that the media seems alive.[13] At another moment, Queen Elizabeth appears, played by a black actress wearing Xhosa ceremonial face paint, carrying a plaster corgi statue and a cell phone, alongside a character clearly intended as a parody of Nelson Mandela.

Judith Rudakoff reported on the revival of *iMumbo Jumbo* in 2003 at the Baxter Theatre in Cape Town, calling it a 'cultural divide' between Bailey and TWB on the one hand and the white urban audiences on the other. During the final performance, at the end of the show, a live chicken was sacrificed on stage, which caused a huge national controversy.[14] Animal rights activists objected, and several in the theatre that night fled in disgust.

Bailey himself weighed in, saying in a letter to the *Cape Times* that while he was 'sorry that the event offended some people, I do not regret that it was performed'.[15] The role of the artist is to 'push boundaries' and the world is 'over-sanitised', he claimed. It was a real moment in a complex and multi-layered performance that engaged ritual, which exposed the 'cultural divide' – a predominantly white audience (including those who were not present but heard about the event afterwards) objected to a genuine ritual moment in a performance that many thought was for 'entertainment'.[16]

ipi zombi? *(1998)*

ipi zombi? premiered at the 1998 Grahamstown National Arts Festival, and subsequently toured the Transkei, KwaZulu-Natal, Cape Town and Zimbabwe. Based on a series of events in KwaZulu-Natal, *ipi zombi?* was a theatrical tour de force that blended ritual with show business to explore traditional belief in modern South Africa while also featuring performers who go in and out of character, commenting on the nature of what they are presenting. On Friday, 29 September 1995, a *kombi* (minibus) carrying fifteen boys from Carl Malcomess High School crashed 28 kilometres outside the town of Kokstad, killing twelve. A survivor reported that he saw 'fifty naked women' by the side of the road before the crash and immedi-ately rumors of witchcraft began circulating.[17] The schoolboys subsequently held the women of Bhongweni Township responsible and went on a literal witchhunt, killing two elderly women and interrupting the mass funeral for the accident victims, whom the boys insisted had been replaced by 'witchmeat'. The bodies were stored for six weeks while *sangomas* attempted to find the witches and reunite the boys' souls with their bodies. When a second funeral was attempted in December, a mob of schoolboys again attacked, opening the caskets and hacking the corpses with *pangas*. The police intervened this time and the bodies were successfully interred later that day.

Loren Kruger argues that the boys' violent reaction was 'in part a response to their own disempowerment as their political authority gained by direct action during the 1980s passed to older and better educated people in the communities in the 1990s'.[18] Kruger also sees the 'scapegoating of women' in the original events and a critique of the same in Bailey's play.[19] Her assertions, accurate though they are, do not negate the genuine fear of the supernatural, of witches and of the dead that are also present in these events. It is that genuine fear and the use of *sangomas* to combat the supernatural that also interested Bailey, who went to Kokstad and Bhongweni and interviewed both those involved in the incidents and other community members.

In 1995, Bailey noticed there was no township drama at the National Arts Festival, so he began working with amateur actors from Rini Township and involving Xhosa *sangomas*. They improvised, they rehearsed and eventually, at the 1996 Grahamstown Festival, a version simply called *Zombie* was performed, the first work of the recently formed Third World Bunfight. In 1998, however, the full version was presented as one of the major performances at the festival. In an abandoned power station in the desert, a makeshift performance space was created. Lit by construction lights and a bonfire in an oil drum, the cast remained onstage for much of the performance, which did not simply narrate the Kokstad witch story but instead used a variety of theatrical techniques to create a larger journey. Using an amateur cast of 60, Bailey did not present a straightforward narrative of the Kokstad witch scare but instead offered a visual and experiential meditation on fear, magic, loss and show business.

The full title of the piece is *Intombi 'Nyama and The Natives in 'ipi zombi?'* The title, itself a reference to an old exploitive musical entitled *Ipi Tombi?* ('Where Are the Girls?'), also frames the event as rural 'natives' performing for urban sophisticates, although the production features a 'star': Intombi 'Nayma, a 1.2-metre-tall actor in a dress who lip synchs to Doris Day's 'Shaking the Blues Away' and flirts with the women in the cast in a parody of celebrity-starring musicals. The entire show is narrated by 'Viva', who serves as master of ceremonies, shaman and bridge for the audience.

As the *sangomas* in the production begin to work their rituals, Viva informs the audience, 'These things have power for our people, whether you believe them or not.'[20] As I have argued elsewhere, this statement is an inversion of the modernist's ordering of traditional culture in a modern world.[21] The 'believer' is not the traditional culturalist but the modern audience member. The West is free to believe that the *sangomas* have power or not, but the amaXhosa know that the power is real for their society and therefore a reality. This idea is a major theme in Bailey's work: the reality and efficacy of the spiritual beliefs of the amaXhosa people. Even in later plays, less overtly ritualistic, spirituality plays a role, even in its noticeable absence, as in *Big Dada*, discussed below.

Heartstopping (1998)

In *Heartstopping*, which also took place at the 1998 Grahamstown Festival, the audience was brought from the train station to a nearby cemetery containing the remains of colonial white settlers. The cemetery became the site of a wordless performance by black actors wearing body paint made to resemble Xhosa initiation ceremonial designs, removing tinfoil hearts from their chests and releasing them in the wind. It was a stunning series of images that was both theatrical journey and also a haunting of sorts – the Xhosa spirits whose hearts were broken by the colonial whites who came and even in death occupy what used to be their land. Complaints about grave desecration led to subsequent performances being held at the 1820 Settlers' Monument (which, not so coincidentally, was also the festival headquarters).

Also in 1998, Bailey published an essay about his ideas and process in the *South African Theatre Journal* entitled 'Performing so the Spirit May Speak'. Not quite a manifesto, like his theatrical works it is an exploration of his ideas about theatre, spirit and the purpose of his work. Observing that '[t]heatre may be a fountain of spirit' he discusses how *sangomas* are themselves performers 'using performance techniques and her role as initiated authority to inflame the spirit of her congregation and lead it into a state of heightened reality'.[22] In a sense, that is also what Bailey attempts in his theatre: to lead an audience into a state of heightened reality through performance. In that sense, he is a sort of 'theatrical *sangoma*'. He also notes that his work 'centers around mythology, dream, folklore'.[23] Thus, myth and dreams form the subject matter and ritual performance techniques through which that heightened reality is achieved. Both *ipi zombi?* and *Heartstopping* bring the audience into a 'heightened reality' while also presenting a constantly shifting reality on stage, as image replaces image, mode shifts into new mode, mood shifts into new mood, and the experience is not merely visual but experiential.

The Prophet (1999)

The Prophet was also performed at the Grahamstown National Arts Festival at the power station, the same location used for the previous year's *ipi zombi?* Less playful and less pop culture-oriented than his previous work, *The Prophet* narrated the story of the Xhosa cattle killing of 1856–7, instituted at the suggestion of Nonquwase, a teenage Xhosa girl who prophesied the return of the ancestral spirits and the defeat of the British if the cattle were sacrificed. Instead, the amaXhosa starved. Bailey's dramatized recounting again took the shape of a ritual re-enactment, a priestess and a priest leading a ceremony with traditional Xhosa singing, children dramatizing the historic events and five men playing 'The Dead', individuals possessed by the spirits of the ancestors. Combined with *ipi zombi?* and *iMumbo Jumbo, The Prophet* completes his early trilogy of ritual drama.

Big Dada: The Rise and Fall of Idi Amin *(2001)*

Big Dada: The Rise and Fall of Idi Amin, a 'postcolonial cabaret' satirizing Ugandan dictator Idi Amin, although dedicated to Zimbabwean president Robert Mugabe, was a 'turning point', according to Bailey.[24] First performed at the London Barbican Centre, in Amsterdam and at the National Arts Festival, all in 2001, followed by performances in Vienna, Brussels, Berlin, Johannesburg and Cape Town in 2005 and again in Cape Twon in 2007, this play marked a return to experimental cabarets of his post-university work, as the title suggests both Amin's surname of Dada as well as the twentieth-century avant-garde art movement Dadaism. Whereas the previous trilogy focused on spirituality and featured *sangomas*, *Big Dada* did not. 'I saw Amin as the destroyer of everything spiritual or sacred', Bailey observed, 'so [I] made this an anti-spiritual/anti-ritual work.'[25] It was developed at around the same time as *Safari*, a production developed for a Dutch festival about C. G. Jung's excursion to Kenya and Uganda in 1925 but that Bailey calls 'my least satisfactory work', due to its perpetuating stereotypes about Africa.[26] At the same time, he also developed *medEia*, a retelling of the Greek myth of Medea written by Dutch writer/performer Oscar van Woensel, at the Spier Wine Estate in Stellenbosch, where TWB took up residency in 2004.

Voudou Nation *(2004)*

Bailey began his programme of postgraduate studies at DasArts in 1999, and his final project concerned Haiti. He worked with dancers, musicians and actors in Port-au-Prince to create a wordless history of Haiti, historically the first post-colonial black-led nation, that mixed real history with mythology. The work then toured the United Kingdom for three months. Bailey admits to reservations about the project initially, as he 'knew nothing about Haiti' and 'had serious concerns about just barging in and misrepresenting a country which has suffered so much misrepresentation', but the appeal of a nation in the African diaspora and the Americas whose culture also features a performative heavily ritualized spiritual component as well as a history of an oppressive political regime allowed him to find common ground.[27] He used the *loa*, the *orisha*, the spirit gods of Haitian voudou as the central characters to allegorize Haitian history using image and music. He created a series of *tableaux vivants* to the songs of the Creole Haitian rock group RAM. Bailey's own summation is that the producers asked for a commercially viable linear drama, while he wanted to create a non-linear series of images without a narrative and so he 'made something somewhere between the two, a compromise, a series of very vivid scenes with a story of colonialism and slavery and revolt and liberation and dictatorship and supernatural Vodou intervention … It was quite baffling to anyone watching it. Narrative is definitely aided by text is the moral of this tale.'[28] Nevertheless, the production was well reviewed in the United Kingdom when it toured there, though it has not been remounted since.

House of the Holy Afro (2004)

His other work from that year, *House of the Holy Afro*, was first staged in Bern, Switzerland, and has subsequently been performed in Europe, Africa and Australia with productions at the Vienna Festival, Berlin and Brussels in 2005, at Melbourne for the Commonwealth Games in 2006, at the Edinburgh Fringe, Harare, Zimbabwe, and Umea, Sweden, in 2007, in Sydney and Zurich in 2008, at festivals in Perth, Adelaide, Linz and London in 2009, and finally in South Africa at the Market Theatre in Johannesburg in 2010. Odidi Mfenyana, a drag queen and cabaret performer, plays the high priestess of the titular holy house, combining nightclub performance with religious ritual and ceremony with tunes spun by DJ Dino Moran. The piece was designed as a collaboration between Mfenyana, Moran and TWB to be performed in nightclubs. Although seemingly a move away from his ritual and Xhosa spirituality-based work, the music for the piece consisted of traditional Xhosa and gospel songs set to house beats or reworked as hip hop. The title is both playful and representative – it is clubbing as ritual experience.

Orfeus (2006)

Orfeus was first performed in 2006 at the Spier Wine Estate in Stellenbosch, then reworked for the Grahamstown Nation Arts Festival in 2007, the

Vienna Festival in 2009 and the Theaterformen Festival in Hannover, Germany, in 2011. A retelling of the Greek myth of Orpheus, a musician who entered the Underworld to recover his wife Eurydice, Bailey transformed the narrative into a shamanic passage through an African Underworld where the sins of the nation are punished. Chained people are tortured, chained children are forced to make sneakers and the King of the Underworld is presented as a businessman with a laptop, organizing it all. Piles of burning tyres, broken rubble, platforms with Christmas lights and cattle skulls nailed to the front become the landscape of the literal journey, in which audiences follow Orfeus on his quest to find his lost bride. The soundscape of the play is as important as the landscape, with rhythms, chants, silence and screams shaping the experience, not to mention the music of Orfeus himself.

Present on the journey are prostitutes and sex workers, child soldiers, sweatshop workers, the aged, the sick and the tormented, all of the lost and exploited members of society who are not valued and whose suffering modern, polite society ignores. The experience of *Orfeus* 'offers up a compendium of Bailey's dramaturgical techniques to date, combining the ritual with the political, the meditative and the provocative, dreamlike surrealism and worldly reference, concentrated spectatorship and site-specific wandering'.[29] Orfeus himself can also be seen as a metaphor or stand-in for Bailey himself, guiding the audience through the nation's Underworld in a quest for something innocent that has been lost.

Exhibit A: Deutsch Sudwestafrika *(2010)*, Exhibit B *(2014)*, Exhibit C *(2015)*

Exhibit A: Deutsch Sudwestafrika was first staged in the Museum of Ethnology in Vienna's Hofburg Palace in 2010 and subsequently at the 2012 Grahamstown National Arts Festival. In both cases, black South African performers were part of the 'exhibits' next to colonial artefacts. The audience walked through the 'performance' as an installation. Each room's display was increasingly violent in nature, colonial era bibles and farming implements giving way to weapons, nostalgia for an imagined past being replaced by an indictment of the inherent violence of colonialism. In each room, black and Coloured performers stared back at the audience. The overall effect was to remove the bloodless, emotionless effect of a museum display and remind the audience of the human beings affected (and hurt and killed) by this history, by these implements.

At Grahamstown, the final room contained 'Congolese Immigrant' and 'Coloured Woman, Grahamstown', linking both local colonial history with current immigration issues and population displacement in contemporary Africa. Provocative and controversial, *Exhibit A* was designed to trigger a recognition of the observers' complicity in the history of South African oppression while also implicating museum culture in preserving artefacts while ignoring the implications of those artefacts for the people from whom they came. There is particular emphasis on the Western proclivity for putting the black body on display, such as in the well-known case of Saartjie Baartman, who left South Africa for London and was displayed in life and her body displayed in death and not returned to South Africa until 2002. The final room at Grahamstown also 'made explicit the continual displacement and abuse of black bodies transnationally'.[30] Since his return to South Africa in the mid-1990s, when Brett Bailey chose to self-identify as an African, his exploration has been of not just South Africa, but also the larger pan-African identity.

Exhibit B, the next in the series, was presented between 2010 and 2014 in twelve different cities to mixed reactions and controversy especially in Berlin, culminating in performances at the Playfair Library in Edinburgh as part of the 2014 Edinburgh Festival. The piece followed the same model as *Exhibit A*, focusing on the British and Dutch colonies. Bailey employed the juxtaposition of the material culture of British 'civilization' placed in tableaux alongside narratives and images of torture, enslavement and murder, once again employing silent, live performers as part of each exhibit. For example, in a display of a bone china tea set arranged for afternoon tea, the story of a Kenyan man castrated during the Mau Mau uprising is presented as a black male figure looks on. In another 'exhibit', a woman was chained to a bed, facing away from the audience but her stare visible from a mirror placed behind the bed, serving to indict the sexual violence of British colonial history.

Although acclaimed in Edinburgh, when the piece moved to London for a planned performance at the Barbican, controversy shut the show down on opening night and the rest of the planned presentations were cancelled. The Barbican announced that the decision to close was due to protests that the piece was racist and objectified and fetishized the black body. Groups of protestors at the opening night and other public figures objected to Bailey's own ethnicity, calling the exhibit 'an exhibition of white privilege'. Claiming it could not guarantee the safety of performers, audience or staff, the Barbican shut down the production.[31]

In response, Bailey issued his own statement, arguing:

Those who have caused Exhibit B to be shut down brand the work as racist. They accuse me of exploiting my performers. They insist my critique of human zoos and the objectifying, dehumanising colonial/racist gaze is nothing more than a recreation of those spectacles of humiliation and control ... I shudder to think that an artwork made in love against the hate of racism could spark a violent riot. Do any of us want to live in a society in which expression is suppressed, banned, silenced, denied a platform? My work has been shut down today, whose will be closed down tomorrow?[32]

He concluded the statement by asserting that *Exhibit C* 'will build on *Exhibit B* to include the British, Portuguese and Italian colonial excursions in Africa' and be performed in unspecified locations in 2015.

Summary

Brett Bailey is both iconoclast and indicative of a wider trend in South African theatre. A critical darling, Bailey's work and Bailey the artist are heralded with equal fervour. Johann van Heerden calls his projects 'original, innovative, brave and intriguing'.[33] In 1999, theatre critic Robert Greig referred to Bailey himself as 'the best thing in South African theatre today'.[34] Anton Krueger sees him as 'one of the most important writer/directors in post-apartheid South Africa', dedicating an entire chapter to Bailey in his survey of new South African drama.[35] Clearly, the critical reception of Bailey has been one of overwhelming admiration and recognition of his unique theatrical vision, approach and works.

Which is not to suggest that Bailey is without critics. David B. Coplan calls him 'brave, but offensive'.[36] Miki Flockemann reports that some critics accuse Bailey of 'exoticization' and despite his self-aware productions that indict the audience, at heart his work still represents white spectators being entertained by exotic black 'savages'.[37] Keith Bain argues that the interactive and immersive experience of TWB productions seems to be a 'theme-parking' of South African history and Xhosa culture, packaging the plays to travel to Europe and Australia for the entertainment of whites without actually having to experience the real 'Africa'.[38] Still others, most notably Duma KaNdlovu and John Matshikiza, critique Bailey for his ethnicity, or, more accurately, for being a white South African who uses (they say exploits) black South African culture.[39] Based on the themes and content of his productions, Ashraf Jamal sees Bailey as the reverse of Athol Fugard. Whereas Fugard's plays present 'a moral or redemptive vision', Bailey and TWB present 'a descent into indistinction'.[40] His works 'refuse consolation, exoneration, reprieve', according to Krueger, which is much more in keeping with the national identity after the fall of apartheid.[41]

Many critics find Bailey's work to be truly emblematic of and responsive to a syncretic, hybrid nation with multiplicities of identities. Ashraf Jamal believes Bailey's theatre 'emerges as an innovative response to the contradictors that, necessarily, define the making of Africa', while also offering 'a brilliant critique of prejudices about Africa' held by South Africans and non-South Africans alike.[42] Likewise, his commitment to accurate and honest use of *sangomas*, demonstrated by his own lengthy time studying with them and incorporation of them in his productions as well as his commitment to training actors from impoverished backgrounds, has been recognized by many.

Critics recognize the complex, contradictory and sometimes disturbing nature of Bailey's work. As David Graver writes of *ipi Zombi?*, Bailey 'neither dismisses nor idealizes the past, but, rather, shows how it both haunts the present with atavistic prejudices and offers psychological solace and communal ties to a fragmented, stress-laden society'.[43] Daniel Larlham, in summarizing both the positive and negative criticisms of Bailey, perhaps encapsulates his position in South African theatre best: 'variously charged with trespassing onto sacred cultural terrain and hailed as a trailblazing visionary forging the way to a new South African theatre', Bailey might just be 'the nation's most consistently innovative and controversial theatre maker ... a globe-hopping, extreme theatre provocateur ... [and] an outsider artist with insider knowledge of Africa's performance traditions'.[44] Bailey is himself a paradox, but one that results in exciting, dynamic, provocative theatre that always brings about an audience reaction.

If Bailey is indeed the *enfant terrible* of South African theatre in the first decade of the twenty-first century, then his maturing as an artist has shown him to be evolving into one of the most inventive, dynamic, prolific and provocative artists working today. As for the future, perhaps the last word should be Bailey's: 'I continue to look for stories that encapsulate the spirit of these luminous and uncertain times we are living through in South Africa' and he does so 'to aid [Third World Bunfight] in becoming the kaleidoscope African troupe we strive to be'.[45]

Notes

1. Quoted in Daniel Larlham, 'Brett Bailey and Third World Bunfight: Journeys into the South African Psyche', *Theater* 39:1 (2009): 10.

2. Anton Krueger, *Experiments in Freedom: Explorations of Identity in New South African Drama* (Newcastle-upon-Tyne: Cambridge Scholars, 2010), 154.

3. David B. Coplan, *In Township Tonight! South Africa's Black City Music and Theatre*, 2nd edition (Chicago: University of Chicago Press, 2008), 378.

4. Ashraf Jamal, '... nothing is / But what it is not: Macbeth in Africa', *South African Theatre Journal* 18:1 (2004): 35.

5. More information can be found on the company's website: www. thirdworldbunfight.co.za (accessed 15 April 2015).

6. Brett Bailey, *Plays of Miracle and Wonder* (Cape Town: Double Storey Books, 2003), 10.

7. Johann van Heerden, 'Beyond the Miracle: Trends in South African Theatre and Performance after 1994', in Kene Igweonu (ed.), *Trends in Twenty-First Century African Theatre and Performance* (Amsterdam: Rodopi, 2011), 104.

8. Keith Bain, 'Hyper-Theatrical Performance on the Post-Apartheid Stage', in Herman Wasserman and Sean Jacobs (eds), *Shifting Selves: Essays on New Media, Culture and Identity* (Cape Town: Kwela Books, 2003), 146.

9. Krueger, *Experiments in Freedom*, 153.

10. Bain, 'Hyper-Theatrical Performance', 158.

11. Bailey, *Plays of Miracle and Wonder*, 95.

12. Ibid., 145.

13. Pamela McCallum, 'Postcolonial Performances', *Ariel* 34:1 (2003): 128.

14. Judith Rudakoff, 'Why Did the Chicken Cross the Cultural Divide?: Brett Bailey and Third World Bunfight's *iMumbo Jumbo*', *TDR* 48:2 (2004): 81.

15. Quoted in ibid., 89.

16. See ibid., 85–90.

17. Background events are taken from both the 1998 National Arts Festival programme and Bailey, *The Plays of Miracle and Wonder*, 30–1.

18. Loren Kruger, *The Drama of South Africa: Plays, Pageants and Publics since 1910* (London: Routledge, 1999), 137.

19. Ibid, 202.

20. Bailey, *Plays of Miracle and Wonder*, 53.

21. Kevin J. Wetmore, Jr, 'Third World Bunfight's *Ipi Zombi?*', in John Freeman (ed.), *The Greatest Shows on Earth* (London: Libri, 2011), 95.

22. Brett Bailey, 'Performing so the spirit may speak', *South African Theatre Journal* 12:1–2 (1998): 191, 193.

23. Ibid., 197.

24. Quoted in Anton Krueger, 'On the wild, essential energies of the forest: An interview with Brett Bailey', *South African Theatre Journal* 20:1 (2006): 324.

25. Ibid.

26. Bailey, *Plays of Miracle and Wonder*, 199.

27. Quoted in Krueger, 'On the wild, essential energies of the forest', 325.

28. Ibid, 327.

29. Larlham, 'Brett Bailey', 22.

30. April Sizemore-Barber, 'Review: South African National Arts Festival', *Theater Journal* 65:2 (2013): 262.

31. http://www.barbican.org.uk/news/artformnews/theatredance/barbican-statement-cancellation (accessed 15 April 2015).

32. Brett Bailey, 'Statement by Brett Bailey on the Closure of *Exhibit B* in London', Third World Bunfight.com, 26 September 2014, http://www.thirdworldbunfight.co.za/productions/exhibit-a-b-and-c.html (accessed 15 April 2014).

33. Van Heerden, 'Beyond the Miracle', 104.

34. Robert Greig, 'Genre-bending operas breach fresh frontier', *Sunday Independent*, 4 July 1999, 12.

35. Krueger, *Experiments in Freedom*, 153.

36. Coplan, *In Township Tonight!*, 377.

37. Miki Flockemann, 'South African Perspectives on Post-Coloniality in and through Performance Practice', in Lizbeth Goodman and Jane de Gay (eds), *The Routledge Reader in Politics and Performance* (London: Routledge, 2000), 237–8.

38. Bain, 'Hyper-Theatrical Performance', 158.

39. Although John Matshikiza subsequently wrote the foreword to *The Plays of Miracles and Wonder*, calling his work 'bold, inquiring theatre', while still acknowledging the 'taboo' of being a white man 'dabbling in black territory' (7, 6).

40. Jamal, '… nothing is / But what it is not', 33.

41. Krueger, *Experiments in Freedom*, 169.

42. Ashraf Jamal, *Predicaments of Culture in South Africa* (Pretoria: University of South Africa Press, 2005), 143.

43. David Graver, 'Introduction', *Drama for a New South Africa* (Bloomington: Indiana University Press, 1999), 7.

44. Larlham, 'Brett Bailey', 7.

45. Bailey, *Plays of Miracle and Wonder*, 199.

Bibliography

Primary sources

Works by Brett Bailey

'Performing so the spirit may speak', *South African Theatre Journal* 12:1–2 (1998): 191–202.

'ipi zombie?', in David Graver (ed.), *Drama for a New South Africa* (Bloomington: Indiana University Press, 1999), 200–20.

The Plays of Miracle and Wonder (Cape Town: Double Storey Books, 2003).

'Statement by Brett Bailey on the Closure of *Exhibit B* in London', Third World Bunfight.com, 26 September 2014, http://www.thirdworldbunfight.co.za/ productions/exhibit-a-b-and-c.html (accessed 2 November 2014).

Secondary sources

Bain, Keith, 'Hyper-Theatrical Performance on the Post-Apartheid Stage', in Herman Wasserman and Sean Jacobs (eds), *Shifting Selves: Essays on New Media, Culture and Identity* (Cape Town: Kwela Books, 2003), 145–65.

Coplan, David B., *In Township Tonight! South Africa's Black City Music and Theatre*, 2nd edition (Chicago: University of Chicago Press, 2008).

Flockemann, Miki, 'South African Perspectives on Post-Coloniality in and through Performance Practice', in Lizbeth Goodman and Jane de Gay (eds), *The Routledge Reader in Politics and Performance* (London: Routledge, 2000), 235–40.

Flockemann, Miki, 'Spectacles of Excess or Thresholds of "Newness"?: Brett Bailey and Third World Bunfight Performers', *Kunapipi* 24:1–2 (2002): 275–90.

Graver, David, 'Introduction', *Drama for a New South Africa* (Bloomington: Indiana University Press, 1999), 7.

Greig, Robert, 'Genre-bending operas breach fresh frontier', *Sunday Independent*, 4 July 1999, 12.

Jamal, Ashraf, '… nothing is / But what it is not: Macbeth in Africa', *South African Theatre Journal* 18:1 (2004): 31–8.

Jamal, Ashraf, *Predicaments of Culture in South Africa* (Pretoria: University of South Africa Press, 2005).

Krueger, Anton, 'On the wild, essential energies of the forest: An interview with Brett Bailey', *South African Theatre Journal* 20:1 (2006): 323–32.

Krueger, Anton, *Experiments in Freedom: Explorations of Identity in New South African Drama* (Newcastle-upon-Tyne: Cambridge Scholars, 2010).

Kruger, Loren, *The Drama of South Africa: Plays, Pageants and Publics since 1910* (London: Routledge, 1999).

Larlham, Daniel, 'Brett Bailey and Third World Bunfight: Journeys into the South African Psyche', *Theater* 39:1 (2009): 6–27.

McCallum, Pamela, 'Postcolonial Performances', *Ariel* 34:1 (2003): 127–31.

Rudakoff, Judith, 'Why Did the Chicken Cross the Cultural Divide?: Brett Bailey and Third World Bunfight's *iMumbo Jumbo*', *TDR* 48:2 (2004): 80–90.

Sizemore-Barber, April, 'Review: South African National Arts Festival', *Theater Journal* 65: 2 (2013): 261–4.

Van Heerden, Johann, 'Beyond the Miracle: Trends in South African Theatre and Performance after 1994', in Kene Igweonu (ed.), *Trends in Twenty-First Century African Theatre and Performance* (Amsterdam: Rodopi, 2011), 85–113.

Wetmore, Jr, Kevin J., 'Third World Bunfight's *Ipi Zombi?*', in John Freeman (ed.), *The Greatest Shows on Earth* (London: Libri, 2011), 87–104.

CHAPTER 16
PIETER-DIRK UYS
Mervyn McMurtry

God's Forgotten; Revues; *Auditioning Angels*

Introduction

> Satire? ...
> The only thing I can do
> besides going out and shooting people,
> is to write about them,
> and make people laugh at them ...[1]

Pieter-Dirk Uys is one of South Africa's most prolific and high-profile playwright-performers: in a career spanning forty-four years, he has written, directed, produced and, most often, performed in seventy-three plays, monodramas, cabarets and revues, and twenty-six films, videos and TV series (many viewed in prison or exile by members of the present government). In addition, he has published thirteen novels, memoirs, anthologies and e-books. He has performed to royalty and schoolchildren, in parliament and community halls, in South Africa, the United Kingdom, the United States of America, Canada, Australia, the Netherlands (in Dutch), Germany and Austria (in German), Switzerland, Denmark, Israel and Slovenia.[2]

Uys was, as he puts it, 'invented'[3] in Cape Town on 28 September 1945, and christened Pieter-Dirk after two Afrikaner folk heroes. The son of an Afrikaner Calvinist father with prominent political associations and a Jewish mother forced to flee Germany in 1938, he quips that he 'belongs to both chosen peoples'. If, in his early plays, the characters are affected by the loss of a mother, and the paterfamilias is an omniscient presence, nevertheless his heritage has informed all his work, particularly 'the problems that [his] father's people created' for him and for his fictional characters.

After graduating from the University of Cape Town, Uys studied at the London Film School, where he produced his first play, *Faces in the Wall*

(1969). He returned to South Africa and joined the Space Theatre in 1973, where he wrote, directed and performed in more than fifty productions in two years; since then, he says, he has been 'officially unemployed'. His unofficial employment has been 'fighting fear and political madness with humour'.[4]

Employing 'laughter as a weapon', Uys's work arises from or targets the personal, the topical and the recognizable, to examine 'the human condition against the chaos of political upheaval'. His revues are updated daily; likewise he has revised his plays. *Paradise is Closing Down* (1977) was first set during the 1976 uprisings, then rewritten in 1988 and 1992 to incorporate contemporary 'political upheaval'. Even his fictional creations have recognizable referents within a specific context: all his plays are about South Africa (even if set elsewhere, such as *Just Like Home* (1989), which satirizes the attitudes and values of exiles in London). Because he believes that prejudice and fear are international scourges, Uys adapts the content of his revues to the time and place of performance: 'Apartheid was so successful we couldn't kill it: we sold it to [among others] Yugoslavia'; for *Foreign Aids* (2001) in New York, he added material to reflect the dual fears of viral and virtual terrorism.

By the end of the 1970s, Uys was considered the *enfant terrible* of South African theatre, having had more of his plays banned or censored than any other playwright: in the month of July 1975 alone, on the grounds of indecency, obscenity, blasphemy and ridicule of a section (Afrikaner) of the population, the script of *Selle ou Storie* ('Same old story') (1974) was banned, but not the production, whereas the production of *Karnaval* ('Carnival') (1975) was banned, but not the script. In response, Uys began working in a fugitive, non-literary performance form: the political revue. With Uys as raconteur, *conferencier*, ventriloquist and mimic, narrating, introducing, manipulating and impersonating an array of characters, he gained international recognition for his 'one-man, three-woman, twenty-politician' revues (as *Adapt or Dye* (1981) was billed in London) and, more recently, for his theatrical and media campaigns to banish fear and ignorance about HIV/AIDS.

As a playwright-performer and human rights activist, Uys has received four Honorary Doctorates from South African universities (1997–2004), the Truth and Reconciliation Award in 2001, the Obie Award in New York for *Foreign Aids* in 2004 and a lifetime achievement Special Teddy Award, with his alter-ego Evita Bezuidenhout, at the Berlin International Film Festival in 2011. Evita herself received the International Living Legacy Award in San Diego in 2000, for her 'contribution to the place of women in the last century'.

Uys resides in Darling in the Cape, where he converted the railway station into a theatre-conference-restaurant venue named Evita se Perron (Evita's 'station platform', and a pun on Perón), and a garden, Boerassic Park, arguably the only satirical museum of apartheid artefacts. Besides productions of revues, cabarets and plays, Uys serves on the board of directors for the Desmond Tutu HIV Foundation. He is also the subject of a 2007 documentary, *Darling! The Pieter-Dirk Uys Story*,[5] directed by Julian Shaw, which won awards at film festivals in, among other places, Berlin, London, Hamburg and Lisbon.

The productions

God's Forgotten *(1975)*

God's Forgotten opened at the Outer Space Theatre on 22 May 1975, in a season of South African plays, with *Selle Ou Storie* and *Karnaval.* While the form of the trilogy is conventional, employing 'the structure of the quote well-made play unquote', the plays 'smashed their way into the consciousness'[6] of theatregoers through their choice of characters and subject matter, their skilful bilingualism and use of vernacular, and their iconoclastic humour.

Primarily, during the 1970s and 1980s, Uys wrote 'for the whites, for the lawmakers';[7] in *God's Forgotten*, he examines those who reinforce the ideology and theology of apartheid. The action takes place in Excelsior, the home of the Honourable J. J. Brand; the four onstage characters are his daughters, Tosca, Sarah and Aliza, and his new wife, Gudrun (Imogen in the 1989 Anglicized version); the time frame 'is the future in white South Africa'.

The programme cover for the first performance featured a Cape-Dutch façade below the sentence '*God's Forgotten* is a black comedy or a white tragedy – depending on whose side you're on.' Whether the title refers to those forgotten by God, God has forgotten or God is forgotten,[8] Uys examines the Afrikaner Calvinist belief in 'an active sovereign God, who calls the elect, who promises and punishes'.[9] If the apostrophe in 'God's' indicates the possessive case, it plays on the opposition between God's forgotten and God's chosen. The latter interpretation recalls the covenant made on 16 December 1838 before the Battle of Blood River, in which the Boers defeated the Zulus (to avenge the killing of their leader, Piet Retief, by Dingane), and the belief that the *volk* had therefore a God-given destiny, a belief reinforced by presidents and theologians who associated God's biblical chosen, the Israelites, and the Afrikaners.[10]

Gudrun inadvertently switches on a recording of a speech by her husband which affirms that destiny:

> We are white. We are right … Kneel and pray with me: the sacrifices made by our fathers, inspired by our faith in God and passed down to us, are our heritage. We will defend, we will sacrifice our lives for the truth of our beliefs … For God in His Wisdom is with us and all will be well with our land. (177)

His speech is, however, parodied by its context: after a replay of a 1967 Springboks versus British Lions test match, and a propaganda film in which a woman believes God has remembered her pledging her sons' lives for the land (176–7). But South Africa is not remembered, even in international sport. The elect are being punished, God has forgotten 'the lawmakers', in favour of (depending 'on whose side you're on') the majority oppressed by the minority in power. In enforcing and justifying political hegemony on theological grounds, God is forgotten (in the present). The most pessimistic of the three interpretations is the perfect-tense-title: God has forgotten all South Africans, white and black.

Each daughter is an exponent of the interpretations: Tosca, the Secretary for Information, regards herself, in her father's absence, as divinely appointed to lead the chosen out of the 'political wilderness' (145); Sarah ironically claims that her father has joined 'the Great White God on his segregated Cloud to celebrate the triumph of the Great South Africa Dream' (143); to Aliza, 'South Africa has ceased to exist' (153).

Excelsior symbolizes white South Africa, an isolated state facing a bloodbath, but believing it can maintain power. Tosca will not acknowledge alternatives: Excelsior is 'old, it's musty, it's boring, it's impractical, but it's all we've got' (159). However, as Sarah says, Excelsior has a 'cancer inside' (174). The present generation will die out (they have no children), as will their heritage; to connect the past and the present, throughout the action the antique Cape-Dutch furniture is being eroded by borer, until the foundations of the ideology are demolished.

Before then, however, the family itself is 'ideologically contaminated' (184) and forgotten by the very mechanisms it has created to maintain its hegemony. The security walls surrounding the home and the ideology are illusory safeguards. Excelsior becomes 'a political prison' (179), the next Robben Island which had been 'deleted from the official records' (179).

The three daughters in *God's Forgotten* are exiles in time as well as place, nostalgically recalling the past, while dreams of the future are gradually fractured. The intertextual link, noted when the play was produced at La Mama in New York in 1979[11] with Chekhov, is deliberate. They are, in effect, Chekhov's 'three sisters' (their names are syllabically similar), remembering their father, maintaining the pretence of normality (a recurring theme of Uys's plays; here Tosca demands they 'Pretend everything's normal' (57)), even as they witness the destruction of 'the cherry orchard', the family estate. When Imogen (the Natasha-figure) points out the 'amazing similarity between [Chekhov's] white Russians and you people', Sarah answers: 'Not really. They lost their revolution' (40).

In Uys's plays the characters appear unwilling to affect qualitative change, but enforced change is already taking place: in the streets in *Paradise is Closing Down*, beyond the walls in *God's Forgotten*, on the mainland in *Panorama* (1987) (set on Robben Island, and exposing the self-imposed captivity of the country's nominally free whites), back home in *Just Like Home* – paradise, in the manner in which whites experience it, is closing down, yet reality seldom intrudes on their insular concerns.

Uys often quotes the Soviet quip, 'The future is certain; it is the past that is unpredictable.' *God's Forgotten* was a prediction of the future that reflected South Africa in the then present, a present founded on the ideologies of the past. But, when *God's Forgotten* was revived in 1995, after the 'revolution', it became a bleak reminder of what South Africans had forgotten, or chosen to forget, and 'an eloquent argument for the necessity of a Truth Commission.'[12]

The revues

The titles of Uys's first solo revues were signifiers of their content and targets: *Adapt or Dye* (1981), *Total Onslaught* (1984) and *Beyond the Rubicon* (1985) were from policy-making speeches delivered by Prime Minister Pieter Willem (P. W.) Botha, whom Uys frequently thanked for providing his 'bread and botha'. Uys regards the revue format, with its stylistic flexibility, as the ideal vehicle for topical satire, 'here-today and gone-tomorrow', dramatizing 'headline issues' for the public (whether denied access to information during successive States of Emergency in the 1980s or unaware of AIDS policies in the late 1990s). To ridicule and subversively circumvent censorship, Uys acknowledged the government as his scriptwriters, stating that he did not pay taxes, but royalties. By presenting facts as stage material (racial classification changes from the *Government Gazette*, for instance), and by superb mimicry of the words, paralanguage and kinesics of real individuals, Uys made (and continues to make) ideologies and politicians satirize themselves: 'I hold up a true mirror and leave the comedy to the eye of the beholder.'

Uys's revues focus on the craft of performance, with minimal technical assistance and properties, to reflect the situation through a spectrum of characters (black and white, male and female, young and old, racist and liberal, oppressor and oppressed) from four perspectives: fictional monologues by sympathetically drawn victims of the system in power; fictional monologues by the exploiters and perpetuators of the system; non-fictional lampoons of national and international political figures; and, as an authorial mask for himself, a stand-up discourse with the audience that engenders rapport and a sense of conspiratorial collaboration. Of these, his most enduring and internationally-known fictional persona is Evita Bezuidenhout.

Like her namesake, Evita Perón, Evita Bezuidenhout is glamorous, infinitely adaptable, with a desire for self-aggrandizement and celebrity status. Uys created her to be his own devil's advocate and express 'things that [he] would not say because [his] politics are different from hers ... and things that have to be said', and, as a further distancing device, they were (and are) said by a woman, 'swaddled in chiffon and blazing with costume jewellery'.[13]

As a stage persona Evita evolved from a weekly column Uys wrote in the late 1970s, to reveal, as the wife of a National Party (NP) Member of Parliament, details of the activities of the Department of Information. Protected by the guise of gossip overheard at social functions, Uys exposed facts which were sub judice, restricted by media regulations or even libellous. This became a notable feature of the character: audiences wondered how far Uys, through her, could draw them into a collusion in which laughter could be release and an indictment.

Evita gave Afrikaans women power they had not previously 'been allowed – a political voice', says Uys[14] (between 1917 and 1974, only three Afrikaner women were elected to parliament).[15] The Security Man was 'ordered to close' *Beyond the Rubicon* because it was 'subversive ... obscene ... blasphemous [and] just an excuse to wear woman's clothes. And that's illegal and also against the law in South Africa.'[16] By reversing accepted sexual and public roles and depicting a woman who supposedly succeeded and exerted political influence in a society of hidebound prejudices and patriarchal values, Uys guyed those prejudices and values: 'This is a republic', Evita stated, '[t]here are no queens in South Africa.'[17]

For Evita to succeed as Uys's satirical mask, she not only had to be too much part of the *status quo*, but too lifelike to be suppressed: 'She's not a "drag queen". She is as *real* as I can make her because the audiences' recognition of her reality makes her work for them.' That fictional actuality is a result of the meticulous detail Uys has invested in her visual appearance and mannerisms, and from her conviction in what she says. Throughout her career she has been completely in control and completely in character, no matter what the circumstances. To reinforce her independent existence in the eyes of the public, her family (all played by Uys) appeared on stage in *Farce About Uys* (1983) and on screen in *Skating on Thin Uys* (1985) (with NP politicians), and her pseudo-biography, *A Part Hate A Part Love*, which merges fiction and history, was published in 1990. Through such ploys, Evita became a national celebrity, 'the most famous white woman in South Africa', hosting her own television talk shows with well-known figures, corresponding with world leaders (including Margaret Thatcher), calling conferences attended by local and international media correspondents, all without any acknowledgement of her being a fictional character, but 'just because she doesn't exist, doesn't mean to say she's not real'.

Individualized by her personality, her manners and her appearance, Evita is also the representative politician, ambitious and self-interested, critical but hypersensitive to criticism (to her, Uys is a 'third-rate comic who keeps making fun of me'),[18] unable to adapt the system but infinitely adaptable to changes in the system. Her duplicity reflects that of politicians in general yet, as she often reminds audiences, 'Hypocrisy is the Vaseline of political intercourse.' To Uys, Evita 'cannot have wit, she cannot have a sense of irony, she must always be deadly serious, and that's how she works as a character'.

As an apologist for the system, Evita initially affirmed her support for the 'God-given policy of apartheid, without which we wouldn't be here tonight, but working in someone's kitchen',[19] adding stereotypical racial slurs, delivered, usually, in Afrikaans: 'They say Black Power will break White South Africa? What do they expect – the blacks break everything!'[20] When her husband was disgraced by his involvement in the Information Scandal, Evita was elevated to the status of South African Ambassador to the Independent Homeland Republic of Bapetikosweti. If Bapetikosweti

was Uys's means to satirize bantustan policies, the Bezuidenhouts epitomized corruption within the NP. After a failed coup d'etat in Bapetikosweti,
she claimed that P. W. Botha had persuaded her to resume her position as
ambassador in order 'to keep things quiet'.

When a change in government became inevitable, she resigned from
the NP and adapted her public and political profile for the new dispensation, using her Afrikaner traditional recipes for *bobotie* and *koeksusters* as
weapons of reconciliation. She appeared on podiums with Nelson Mandela
in African National Congress (ANC) rallies in 1994, to encourage fair and
free elections. Uys created a twelve-part television series, *Funigalore* (a pun
on 'fun' and 'fanagalo', pidgin language, roughly 'like this') (1994), in which
she interviewed members of the new democracy. In the Mandela episode,
the new president called Evita 'his hero', and '[t]he contrast between Evita,
a symbol of Afrikaner racism, and Mandela, a symbol of freedom from
oppression, sharing the screen gave hope that South Africa had begun
to heal its wounds'.[21] By 2000, Evita had elevated herself to Ambassador
without Portfolio, and chief liaison person with Mandela's office with regard
to Afrikaans cultural affairs.

Evita had to adapt again: formerly, she maintained that 'democracy is
too good to share with just anybody', but she became a passionate supporter
of a corruption-free, non-racial future for her mixed-race grandchildren,
Winnie-Jeanne, Nelson-Ignatius and La Toya-Ossewania. In September
2008, she launched a new party, Evita's People's Party,[22] as part of a mock-
serious campaign for president in the 2009 general election, and to make
South Africans aware of their democratic rights. In the revue *Elections &*
Erections (2008), she interviewed politicians of all parties on stage, criticizing any who did not keep to their promises to the electorate. On 1 April
2012, she joined the ANC.

Before then, however, because 'the minefield has moved: from politics to
sex',[23] Uys and Evita took on new roles for the future of South Africa.

HIV/AIDS 'actor-vism': Auditioning Angels

Uys decided to retire from theatre in 1999; however, angered by the 'AIDS is
from Venus and HIV is from Mars' attitude of President Thabo Mbeki and
the Ministry of Health, and 'realising how little hope there is for the youth
amidst the present government paralysis with regard to information about
HIV/AIDS',[24] he (and Evita) embarked on self-funded educational tours
which, by 2011, had been performed to more than one and a half million

pupils. Evita performed the AIDS awareness show, with a dildo and condom as aids, in the House of Assembly in Cape Town in 2001, and received a standing ovation.

Uys's experiences on the tours were incorporated in a series of revues: *For Facts Sake* ('99% of the world knows that HIV leads to AIDS. We're governed by the 1% who doesn't'), *Foreign Aids* (which ended with an appeal, in South Africa, Europe, Australia and the United States, for donations to a refuge for HIV-positive teenage mothers of which Uys is the patron) and *The end is naai* (a pun on 'nigh' and an Afrikaans slang term for 'fuck') (2004).

For not providing antiretroviral treatment to HIV-positive South Africans, Uys accused the Mbeki government of genocide: 'We had an apartheid regime in South Africa that killed people. Now we have a democratic government that just lets them die.'[25] To encourage open debate around the causes and treatment of the virus, Uys revealed how his early life was informed by fear, fear of apartheid, fear of sex and the added later fear of HIV/AIDS, and how he overcame those fears.[26] In his second memoir, *Between the Devil and the Deep: A Memoir of Acting and Reacting* (2005), Uys surveys his theatrical career and, as the title suggests, how his work was a reaction to apartheid. One event in the memoir, which he incorporated in the *Elections & Erections* revue, was the crucial moment when he 'discovered politics' and began to question his 'white, racist background'. Uys had never before discussed his sexuality on stage, but, he said, 'I've got to be honest; if I can't speak about myself, why should others listen to me when I speak about them.'[27] When he was twenty-two, he had a sexual relationship with an unnamed man, a man who was Coloured, a doubly illegal act. Uys felt compelled to publicly reveal and re-act the experience for himself and his partner, to raise awareness of the circumstances afflicting the country, in the past and in the present.

As an 'actor-vist', Uys presented facts about HIV/AIDS in the educational shows and in corporate information videos, while in the revues he satirized the policies of the government. In his first play since 1991, *Auditioning Angels* (which premiered at the National Arts Festival in Grahamstown on 27 June 2003), he showed the results of those policies, in a 'searing, withering invective against the complacency, undisguised self-interest, apathy and stupidity that has characterised the debate around HIV/AIDS'.[28] The action takes place in a single room (Uys's plays are virtually all set in single interior locales) in 'the largest working hospital in the Southern Hemisphere' (21), with 'no service, no water, no food, no medical staff. Only patients being patient' (39). Uys aimed to shock, to make audiences aware that in such hospitals there is 'one respirator for every twenty babies' with AIDS; that for those under a kilogram in weight the respirator is switched off (53); that ignorance about the pandemic's prevention and transmission resulted in the belief that a man can cure himself of the so-called 'thinning sickness' by sex with a virgin, so that raping a child is 'the new national sport' (21); that members of the government are not treated at state hospitals: 'they go to private places ... or overseas when they get sick ... and then die of natural causes' (18).

Besides containing the letters that spell A-I-D-S, and playing on the various meanings of the word angel, Uys leaves open who is being auditioned and by whom, and who the angels are or will be: initially, one imagines them to be the abandoned and dying babies kept in cardboard boxes because the hospital cannot afford cots ('thirteen yesterday, sixteen today, maybe twenty tomorrow' (17)), or in the 'hell' (82) that is this hospital. Is their ministering angel Nurse Tessie Bredenkamp, who has made, if not heaven, at least a haven for the babies, and who 'steals [drugs] from the living to give to the dying' (48)?

To examine its theme of betrayal and abandonment, *Auditioning Angels* has a dual focus: the health care system and rhetoric concerning the pandemic, and the members of the Nathan family who confront what divided them in the past in an attempt to understand the present. What connects the two is the alleged rape of an eight-year-old; faced with the reality of the New South Africa, Gerald Nathan, a former ANC activist and the child's grandfather, asks, 'Is this what we fought for?' (34). Uys satirizes the reality of the regeneration espoused by Mbeki's call for an 'African renaissance' by juxtaposing the factual ('We have everything here now. Three minutes from the hospital ... pornography, democracy, crime, crack, AIDS, corruption' (55)) with the unreal fragments of a hospital soap opera heard on a malfunctioning television monitor. The toys scattered about the stage are visual reminders of those who will become statistics[29] without the 'drugs [that] are embargoed, because politicians must still work out with pharmaceutical companies who gets the highest cut' (57), while the only numbers of concern are the winning combinations of the state lotto announced over the intercom.

Yet there is hope in this seemingly hopeless situation. After the Nathan family has confronted the lies and deceit of the past, their future is connected with the betrayals and deceptions in the present, as they 'audition' for the roles of guardian angels to the babies. Uys, who describes himself as a 'terminal optimist', responded to an interviewer who found the resolution 'unrealistic': 'That's the joy of theatre. Everyone has the right to make up their own minds. The end is prophetic; we will soon have to adopt babies … Unrealistic? Is anything unrealistic, from 9/11 to the rape of a baby?'[30]

Summary

My work is the comedy of prejudice, not just in South Africa. In every country I've been to, I've reflected the prejudice of the people there. Prejudice is absurd. When you see it in a theatrical context, you laugh at it because it's ridiculous.[31]

If the satiric spectrum is customarily ranged between the scathing contempt of Juvenal's tragic satire and the sharp raillery of Horace's comic satire, Uys has strived to maintain 'a balance of forty-nine per cent anger and fifty-one per cent comedy' (a definition gleaned from the comedienne Joan Rivers). Humour and criticism are his means to ridicule all forms of prejudice, and promote a release of fear through the beneficial power of laughter. As a scourge and benefactor he personifies the meaning he bestows on his Christian names: 'Pieter and Dirk … Half fascist, half freedom fighter … The hyphen keeps them apart.'[32]

His work has always been popular: in the ten weeks after its opening on 1 April 1981, *Adapt or Dye* had been seen by 25,000 people at fifty-six performances. His popularity has been double-edged, however: while 'holding up the cracked mirror for South Africa to view itself' during apartheid, Uys was 'at another level cast as a safety valve for … white South African liberals'.[33] If a satirist has to convince the audience of the necessity for criticism, there has to be a shared recognition of attitudes or beliefs against which the targets can be seen to deviate. For the revues, he structured 'a character called Pieter-Dirk Uys'[34] so as to make personal commentary in his 'own' voice, distinct from the markedly theatrical personae, and be a norm against which the targets could be measured. By explicitly informing audiences of what they should be against, Uys implicitly advocates what they should be for. When he was accused of 'preaching to the converted', he responded that the 'converted are all in Perth'.[35]

Being a white Afrikaner initially entailed working from within the laager, with Uys reminding his audiences that they could not ignore the inequalities and injustices of a system perpetuated by whites; when he revealed the oppressions endured by blacks, it served as a reminder of white culpability and ignorance. While conceding that Uys demanded change, a black reviewer criticized him for not stating 'how that change should come about'.[36] Uys, who modelled his approach on Lenny Bruce's '[p]eople should be taught what is ... not what should be', has said that, instead of presenting 'protest' theatre which provides 'answers', a satirist's function is to 'ask questions'.

By the late 1980s, Uys could no longer be regarded as a court jester living off the system: his 'anger had become contempt'. In *Rearranging the Deckchairs on the SA Bothatanic* (1986), Uys literally and figuratively exposed the pornography of the South African state. As an erstwhile critic of Uys's 'harmless mixture of affectionate parody and gentle caricature'[37] noted, 'Now his portrait of Captain P. W. Botha as a mad dictator is chilling and prescient', and the revue's conclusion was Uys's cry of 'despair against blind, totalitarian rule'.[38]

If Uys likened performing satire before largely white audiences, such as those at the State Opera House in Pretoria, to 'doing the tango in front of the firing squad'[39] with the government writing his best material, after 1994 'the new government caught up fast' and he could satirize the new 'designer democracy' by being 'careful to offend everybody equally'[40] (he found it difficult, however, to lampoon Mandela). Satire was still essential when South Africa had accrued all the features of 'a truly successful African democracy ... corruption, inflation, a gravy train, strikes ["affirmative inaction"], squatting ["affirmative camping"], crime ["affirmative shopping"]'.

He (and Evita, for different reasons) addressed audiences from a politically central position, promoting a better present in relation to an imperfect past. The ideal – never present, but always implicit in satire – did not exist; we had not, to paraphrase the title of his 1995 revue, seen it yet (*You ANC nothing yet*). As Uys was told in a self-funded Voter Education Tour before the 1999 elections, 'We voted for freedom in this country and all we got was democracy'.

Before freedom of expression was enshrined in the constitution, Uys ascribed the frustrations experienced by South Africans to being prevented from expressing social and political comment. In 2012, after a tour of *Adapt or Fly* (the title, echoing that of his first revue, was a warning to whites afraid of land takeovers by a spokesperson for the ANC Youth League), Uys began rehearsing *The Merry Wives of Zuma* (a follow-up to his 2009 parody, *Macbeki: A Farce to be Reckoned With*), which was to open with the ANC Conference in October. Loosely based on Shakespeare's comedy, *The Merry*

Wives of Zuma is set in the fictional town of Zuma, where the mayor, Mr Gedley (President Jacob Zuma's middle name is Gedleyihlekisa), aims to be re-elected for a further term of office. While satirizing the polygamous and corrupt lifestyle of its central character and his associates, Uys's 'political pantomime' is an overt metaphor for the state of the nation, and the indifference of 'the affluent political elite' to the living conditions of the majority 'whose interests they claim so grandly to represent'.[41] The personae include characters based on Julius Malema, president of the ANC Youth League, and Zapiro (Jonathan Shapiro), the cartoonist.

In the same month, Zuma's R15-million defamation lawsuit against Zapiro for three cartoons (one depicted Zuma about to rape a female 'Justice System', held down by four of his then closest allies, including Malema) was scheduled to be heard in the High Court. The artist Brett Murray likewise faced a lawsuit for 'The Spear', a painting of a Lenin-like Zuma with his genitals exposed, which subsequently had an age restriction imposed by the Film and Publication Board. Uys's response to the Murray furore was that '[t]he cracked mirror of satire reflects a cracked society'.[42] And, at the time, the Protection of State Information Bill, despite widespread criticism from media and civil society organizations, was being amended before being signed into law by Zuma.

After a staged reading of *The Merry Wives of Zuma*, Uys stated that that was its world premiere and possibly its last production, as potential sponsors had 'suddenly developed cold feet – allegedly fearing political pressure and intimidation', and he made a direct connection between his farce and the reactions to Murray's painting.[43] In part response, Uys made many of his plays freely available on his website. Despite the presidency withdrawing its R63-million claims against the media, in the interests 'of reconciliation and nation building [and Zuma's commitment] to redressing prejudice and inequality',[44] South Africa's 'freedom of expression is again under threat, this time by more covert yet no less insidious means than during apartheid'.[45]

Plus ça change …

Notes

1. Uys quoted in Avril Herber, *Conversations* (Johannesburg: Bateleur Press, 1979), 90.
2. These details are to be found on Pieter-Dirk Uys's website (www.pdu.co.za), shared with Evita (www.evita.co.za), which gives a comprehensive account

of their achievements and activities, with archived interviews, articles and reviews (accessed 15 April 2015).

3. Unless noted otherwise, quotations by Uys are from personal interviews and correspondence; similarly, unless cited, extracts from his revues are from unpublished manuscripts or video recordings.

4. Uys, *Elections & Erections: A Memoir of Fear and Fun* (Cape Town: Zebra Press, 2002), 6.

5. www.darlingmovie.com.au (accessed 17 March 2015).

6. Brian Astbury, *The Space/Die Ruimte/Indawo* (Cape Town: M and A Fine, 1980), 53.

7. Quoted in Alan Cowell, *The New York Times*, 5 July 1984.

8. See Jacoba Bedford, 'The Presence of the Past in Selected Works by Pieter-Dirk Uys', MA dissertation (University of Potchefstroom, 1988), 64–7.

9. Thomas Moodie, *The Rise of Afrikanerdom: Power, Apartheid, and the Afrikaner Civil Religion* (Berkeley: University of California Press, 1975), ix.

10. Ibid., 26–8.

11. Eileen Blumenthal, *Voice*, 4 June 1979.

12. Peter Frost, *Cape Times*, 8 August 1995.

13. Uys, *No One's Died Laughing* (Harmondsworth: Penguin, 1986), 64.

14. Quoted in Daniel Lieberfeld, 'Pieter-Dirk Uys: Crossing Apartheid Lines', *TDR* (Spring 1997): 61.

15. Hermann Giliomee, *The Afrikaners: Biography of a People* (Charlottesville: University of Virginia Press, 2003), 376.

16. Uys, *No One's Died Laughing*, 159.

17. Quoted in Alan Cowell, *The New York Times*, 5 July 1984.

18. Uys, *A Part Hate A Part Love* (Sandton: Radix, 1990), 14.

19. Uys, *No One's Died Laughing*, 61.

20. Ibid., 62.

21. Sam Stiegler, '"There are no [drag] queens in South Africa": Pieter-Dirk Uys's Satire and Evita Bezuidenhout's Rise to Power', paper (Tufts University, Massachusetts, 2005), 26.

22. www.epp.org.za (accessed 15 April 2015).

23. Uys, *Elections & Erections*, 3.

24. Quoted in Christine Whitehouse, *Time*, 23 July 2001.

25. Uys, *Elections & Erections*, 1.

26. See Sheldon Campbell, 'Stages on Pages: A Comparative Study of Pieter-Dirk Uys' One Man Shows as an Autobiographical Alternative to Memoir', MA dissertation (University of KwaZulu-Natal, 2012), 102–7.

27. Quoted in Chris Thurman, *Business Day*, 14 March 2009.

28. Wilhelm Snyman, *Cape Times*, 19 August 2003.

29. Daniel Dercksen, *News24*, 15 August 2003.

30. Quoted in 'Interview with an Angel', 4 July 2003, www.capetowntoday.co.za/Interviews/Actors/Uys.htm (accessed 15 April 2015).

31. Quoted in Penny Smythe, *Fair Lady*, 14 February 1990, 58.

32. Quoted in Herber, *Conversations*, 95.

33. Peter Nichols, *Time Out*, 9–15 April 1986.

34. Uys, *No One's Died Laughing*, 40.

35. Quoted in Darryl Accone, *Cue*, 4 July 1990.

36. 'The artist will not stay unscathed', *New Nation*, 4–10 June 1987.

37. John Campbell, *Weekly Mail*, 12–18 July 1985.

38. Ibid., *Weekly Mail*, 22–28 May 1987.

39. Quoted in John Connor, *City Limits*, 10–17 April 1986.

40. Quoted in Christine Whitehouse, *Time*, 23 July 2001.

41. Christina Kennedy, *Business Day*, 9 October 2012.

42. Quoted in Charl Blignaut, *City Press*, 26 May 2012.

43. Quoted in Lindile Sifile, *Sowetan*, 10 October 2012.

44. Janet Smith and Kashiefa Ajam, *The Independent*, 1 June 2013.

45. Kennedy, *Business Day*.

Bibliography

Primary sources

Works by Pieter-Dirk Uys

'God's Forgotten', in Stephen Gray (ed.), *Theatre Two: New South African Drama* (Johannesburg: AD Donker, 1981).

No One's Died Laughing (Harmondsworth: Penguin, 1986).

Paradise is Closing Down and Other Plays (Harmondsworth: Penguin, 1989).

A Part Hate A Part Love (Sandton: Radix, 1990).

Evita's Funigalore (TV Series, M-Net, 1994).

Foreign Aids (DVD, PDU Productions, 2001).

Elections & Erections: A Memoir of Fear and Fun (Cape Town: Zebra Press, 2002).

Auditioning Angels (Cape Town: PDU, 2003).

Between the Devil and the Deep: A Memoir of Acting and Reacting (Cape Town: Zebra Press, 2005).

Blast from the Past: Adapt or Dye & Beyond the Rubicon (DVD, NuMetro, 2007).

Elections and Erections (DVD, PDU Productions, 2009).

Secondary sources

Astbury, Brian, *The Space/Die Ruimte/Indawo* (Cape Town: M and A Fine, 1980).

Bedford, Jacoba, 'The Presence of the Past in Selected Works by Pieter-Dirk Uys', MA dissertation (University of Potchefstroom, 1988).

Campbell, Sheldon, 'Stages on Pages: A Comparative Study of Pieter-Dirk Uys' One Man Shows as an Autobiographical Alternative to Memoir', MA dissertation (University of KwaZulu-Natal, 2012).

Giliomee, Hermann, *The Afrikaners: Biography of a People* (Charlottesville: University of Virginia Press, 2003).

Herber, Avril, *Conversations* (Johannesburg: Bateleur Press, 1979).

Lieberfeld, Daniel, 'Pieter-Dirk Uys: Crossing Apartheid Lines', *TDR* (Spring 1997): 61.

McMurtry, Mervyn, 'Performing Satire in the New South Africa', *Current Writing* 8:1 (1996): 121–5.

McMurtry, Mervyn, 'Reflections in a Cracked Mirror: Pieter-Dirk Uys interviewed by Mervyn McMurtry', in Judith Lütge Coullie, Stephan Meyer, Thengani H. Ngwenya and Thomas Olver (eds), *Selves in Question: Interviews on Southern African Auto/Biography* (Honolulu: University of Hawai'i Press, 2006), 345–56.

Moodie, Thomas, *The Rise of Afrikanerdom: Power, Apartheid, and the Afrikaner Civil Religion* (Berkeley: University of California Press, 1975).

Stiegler, Sam, '"There are no [drag] queens in South Africa": Pieter-Dirk Uys's Satire and Evita Bezuidenhout's Rise to Power', paper (Tufts University, Massachusetts, 2005).

CHAPTER 17
FATIMA DIKE
Miki Flockemann and Rolf Solberg

The Sacrifice of Kreli; The First South African; Glass House; Street Walking and Company; So What's New; The Return

Introduction

The most commonly cited observation about Fatima Dike is that she is South Africa's first published black woman playwright. However, the deeper significance of her work is exemplified by the trajectory of her career, which runs from the height of apartheid in the 1970s and 1980s to the (unfinished) period of social and political transition which extends into the present. As a playwright, Dike aims to put a finger on the pulse of events that speak to the historical moments of her time, yet she also taps out her own beat. In an interview with Marcia Blumberg she acknowledges that she writes from her own life experiences, with a special focus on what she regards as 'conscience-killing' situations.[1] Claiming that 'my work is based on truth', she understands the need to fictionalize these 'truths'.[2] As a result, the often unresolved internal contradictions that surface in some of her works are indicative of Dike's unabashed embrace of the complexity of her own responses to her fast-changing world. While Dike's body of work thus provides a window on shifts in cultural politics over the past forty years, there is nevertheless something fresh in her approach which goes beyond, or problematizes, prevailing theatre trends of the time. The critical reception to her work over time reflects these shifts; however, it can also be argued that a number of her early productions anticipate later trends.

Royline Fatima Dike was born in 1948, the year that the Nationalist Party came to power and apartheid became entrenched. Her isiXhosa-speaking parents moved to Cape Town in the 1930s – however, as a result of the apartheid legislation, they were later forced to resettle in Langa, one of the earliest black townships established on the outskirts of the city. Fatima (or Fatts as she is commonly called) was the youngest of six in a close-knit family. Some of the contradictions that she grapples with in her work stem from the complex straddling of the values embedded in the traditional rural and urban environments that she was exposed to while growing up in Langa. Her family, especially her father, was deeply rooted in isiXhosa traditions, and, until his death in 1955, he served his community as one of the guardians of maintaining these values within the urban setting. This early experience of her family's clan rituals and practice became integral to her sense of cultural belonging as an African from a young age. Her mother, on the other hand, was a devout Methodist stalwart, and worked as a cook for the white superintendent of the township (or 'location' as it was called then), who also resided in Langa. Dike was thus integrated into both traditional, black urban, and 'White' cultural contexts through her mother's close involvement (much to Dike's chagrin at the time) with the superintendent's household and family. These experiences became the bedrock of much of the material she draws on in her writing.

Dike was a precocious child with a facility for languages. At her father's insistence, in addition to her mother tongue, she was taught Afrikaans and Sesotho in primary school, and later Sepedi and English at a convent high school in Rustenberg, Transvaal, where she devoured the English literary canon that she discovered in the school library. Her oldest sister notes that the family wanted Dike to become a teacher because of her 'gift of the gab', but Dike had other plans: 'she had this thing about theatre, about writing, and reading was her interest number one. Listening to stories over the radio was another favourite.'[3] It is thus not surprising that even as a child, Dike was acutely aware of the absurdity of the racially-based social inequalities that she encountered. Her sister notes that even 'in the middle of the apartheid era she wanted to know what there was in a white skin that blacks didn't have. Why would a person you didn't know say to you: "No, no, no, you can't enter here?; No, no, no, you can't eat here"?'[4] The gift of seeing the 'story' in both the ordinary and the extraordinary runs through Dike's work, and also explains why the many interviews conducted with her over the years make such entertaining and often riveting reading, as anecdotes of events that have been formative to her as an individual and as an artist are recounted again and again with different inflections that make them come alive and present again to the listener.

Her introduction to the Space Theatre, which had just opened its doors in the centre of Cape Town in 1972, initiated an extremely productive period in which Dike was exposed to play making by a group of highly talented and committed theatre practitioners who challenged apartheid legislation by running what was in effect a non-racial theatre.[5] An event that she regards as life changing at this time was watching Nomhle Nkonyeni's performance as Medea's nurse who confronts her mistress (the acclaimed actress Yvonne Bryceland) in Barney Simon's adaptation of Grillparzer's *Medea*. The dramatic resonance of such intimate, though socially unequal, encounters has remained a focus of interest throughout Dike's life and work. At the same time, Nkonyeni's performance opened a window for Dike to become more actively involved in theatre herself. Brian Asbury, who founded the theatre together with Athol Fugard and Yvonne Bryceland, immediately recognized Dike's potential, and decided to appoint her as stage manager. It was during this period of involvement with the Space Theatre which lasted until 1979 that Dike developed her first three plays.

The Sacrifice of Kreli was written and produced between 1975 and 1976, the year of the Soweto uprising. This event had a profound effect on Dike, who had by this time become strongly influenced by the ideas of the Black Consciousness Movement. The genesis of this work also signals another characteristic of Dike's dramaturgical method, namely her openness to creative collaboration: Rob Amato, another founding member of the Space Theatre, was deeply engaged in encouraging Dike in this venture. Dike's next play, *The First South African* (1977), marks a shift in terms of staging aesthetic and focus, since in this work Dike turns to the contemporary urban and domestic sphere to explore the psychic damage inflicted by apartheid racial categorization. *Glass House* (1979) comes after a dark period in Dike's life, triggered by an event she witnessed from the window of her Langa house: a schoolboy participating in a protest against the implementation of Afrikaans as language of instruction being brutally shot in the head by a policeman. This traumatic incident heralded a period of intense anger, disillusionment and confusion, and she returns to the lasting effect of this incident in several interviews. It also meant that she felt unable to write for some time (apart from a play for children based on an African folktale, *The Crafty Tortoise* (1978)). Eventually, however, she decided that she simply 'had to get it out' because 'I just did not know I could hate that much.'[6] After *Glass House*, Dike left the country and lived on and off in the United States until 1988. It was only after Mandela's release in 1990 during the transition to democracy that Dike began producing plays again. *So What's New* (1990) tracks the everyday experiences of three upwardly mobile (and refreshingly irreverent) black women who demonstrate that they are more than the aggregate of their race/class/gender positions.

In the mid-1990s Dike wrote a series of situational and satirical vignettes for a Nelson Mandela Concert at La Villette in France. This period brought another change in that she now found herself engaged not only in writing plays, but also in teaching a young generation about play making when she joined the New Africa Association. New Africa (as it was called) became a bridging school which presented a performing arts course for township youth. During this time the students performed issue-driven plays written by Dike, including *Aids the New Generation* (1998).

It was during her tenure at New Africa that she wrote *Street Walking and Company* (2000). This was a play aimed at young people that explored the drug culture that has gained such a powerful foothold, particularly in economically oppressed communities. After Dike left New Africa in 2002, she, together with Roy Sargeant and Paul Regenass of Artscape, and Dumile Magodla (also from New Africa), founded the Siyasanga Theatre Company in August 2003. At first the aim was to produce plays at the Guga S'thebe Cultural Centre in Langa, both for visiting tourists and the local community, but eventually the company moved to the Artscape Theatre complex which could offer it a stable infrastructure. Amongst the first works that were produced under the auspices of Siyasanga was *Middle Passage: A Healing Ritual*, a collaborative project with the University of Louisville, Kentucky, which explored cultural connections between South African and African American experiences. The play was performed locally at the Grahamstown Festival in 2003 and travelled to the University of Louisville in 2004. Dike was appointed dramaturge for another collaborative project, *New Day* (2004) (commissioned by Artscape), which presented a review of the first decade of democracy. The production included two of her sketches, *Sandulela* (The Dawn) and *Housing for All*.

The Return (2008), like *The First South African*, is set in a Langa home and indicates a return of sorts to some of Dike's earlier preoccupations, such as the viability of maintaining Xhosa cultural traditions in an urban setting. Dike's most recent venture is a work in progress called *Embo – A Place in Time*. She envisions this as another traditional Xhosa epic, like *The Sacrifice of Kreli*. This time the focus is on the migration of the amaMpon-domise from the north to the southern parts of South Africa. The section on individual plays which follows focuses only on her published works.

The plays

The Sacrifice of Kreli *(1976)*

The Sacrifice of Kreli was first performed in 1976 at the Space Theatre, and also at the Market Theatre in Johannesburg during the same year. The director was Makwedini Mtshaka of the Sechaba company, who also played the role of Kreli. *Kreli* was remounted in 2001 at the Baxter Theatre, directed by Roy Sargeant. Unfortunately, a plan to perform the play outdoors during dawn performances at the magnificent Kirstenbosch Gardens at the end of 2012 fell through because of lack of funding.

Seen against the backdrop of the 1976 Soweto uprising, the play speaks to an act of resistance from an earlier historical era by drawing on archival accounts of the aftermath of the ninth Frontier War between the Xhosa and the British settlers. Dike decided to focus on an event that took place seven years after the war, involving King Kreli of the Gcalekas, who had refused to surrender to the British and had gone into exile in a remote mountain gorge, a place he refers to repeatedly as a 'hole', where he and his warriors wait it out. The play draws closely on an account by a journalist in the *Daily Dispatch* of 1885 who had gone to interview Kreli accompanied by Dr Tiya Soga.[7] In order to stage this encounter, Dike uses a bare set, except for three rocks, one of which is Kreli's throne. With 16 actors, this play has the largest cast of all her plays to date.

Dike originally wrote the work in poetic isiXhosa which she then translated literally in order to keep the rhythms of the original language. For instance, when the praise singer Mpelesi presents his case to the King he says:

Mntan'omhle,
You are great
Let us not stumble over each other
For our hearts are wounded.
The corn is burnt,
The baby on your back is crying./Its cry is cutting.
Don't you feel it in your womb?
Throw your breast over your shoulder
And let it suckle.[8]

At the same time, she also deliberately evoked the 'feel' of ancient Greek theatre through the inclusion of a chorus.[9]

Another aim of the play was to depict a coherent and viable black culture. The visit by the 'strangers' exacerbates a split between those who distrust Kreli's diviner, the priest Mlangeni, who insists that they must wait for a favourable sign, and those warriors (spurred on by the praise singer) who are impatient to return and reclaim their land by force. Things come to a head when Mlangeni is accused of treachery and put to the test by being sewn into the fresh bull-hide which slowly crushes him as it dries in the sun and shrinks. Just before he dies, Mlangeni speaks and this is taken as a sign by Kreli that 'our sun is rising' (79); he commands that his son should go and 'tell our people we will defend the honour of what we are' (79).

A characteristic focus that is developed more fully in later plays is already evident: Dike notes that while writing the play she was aware of the fact that at the time there was little scope for women to tell their stories; after all, Kreli's is a man's story given to her by a man, and 'I had to get a woman's angle into it in some way'.[10] She tackled this through the character of Khulukazi,[11] who had left her clan to marry Mlangeni, which meant that for the rest of her life she has to negotiate different identities and allegiances in order for her 'to make a place for herself'.[12] However, while Khulukazi is 'bringing women together', as someone who younger women from different clans can communicate with, she is also absorbed into patriarchal practices (such as 'virgin testing' to assure the King that the young women have 'guarded their virginity' successfully). This unresolved tension between straddling a world of tradition while also 'trying to make a place for oneself' in the modern world resonates throughout other works as well.

The First South African (1977)

The First South African was written in 1977 and produced at the Space Theatre that same year. The work is inspired by a man Dike knew who lived in Langa, whose conflicted sense of identity eventually led to violence and insanity. This in itself offers a searing critique of the destructive absurdity of racial classification systems. Dike notes that the man looked white because his father was a European, though he lived as a black person with his black mother. Dike asks, 'My question is this: what is this man? He is not black – he is the shadow of a black man. He is not white – he is the shadow of a white man. And he is definitely not coloured.'[13]

In the opening scene, the man, Zwelenzima or 'Rooi' ('red' in Afrikaans), appears on a platform in semi-darkness, stripped down to a pair of shorts, quoting an incantation from Genesis: 'God created man in his image, male and female' (1). He then extrapolates from this to speak about the fear generated by the one who is 'different'. Zwelenzima describes a bloodbath that ensues as a result of this fear, until, prophetically, he claims that he will find that his colour has changed to ochre (a colour associated with a transitional phase):[14]

He'll look at himself in the mirror,
And see himself for what he is.
He'll turn around to find his brother looking at him,
And the reflection in the mirror will be the image in front of him.

This opening, which ends with the rhetorical question, 'Am I not a man then?', provides a frame for the events unfolding in the play which track Zwelenzima's unravelling sense of self after being classified 'Coloured', which means he must move out of his familiar world. At the same time, the play problematizes what is meant by 'man', since there is a constant tension between the generic concept of man as human being invoked in the opening frame scene and traditional notions of manhood. This is exacerbated by the fact that Zwelinzima has just undergone the circumcision ritual that marks him as a 'new man', deserving of respect, something that he keeps reminding others of. On the other hand, he and his friends, the dashing anti-hero shoplifter Max and his rival Solly, as well as Rooi's girlfriend Thembi, are deeply entrenched in pernicious discourses of masculinity, where maleness is juxtaposed with those who are identified, generally in the township vernacular (characterized by a mixture of Afrikaans, isi-Xhosa and English slang), as 'chicks', 'sissies', 'moffies' (gays), and so on. (On the other hand, this needs to be seen against the backdrop of the apartheid social contexts where people like Freda were 'the girl', and men like her husband Austin and son Zwelenzima were 'boys'.)

The staging juxtaposes the intimacy and constraints of the small rented family house in Langa (with the ubiquitous wall bed that folds away during the day) and an empty space where the rest of the action takes place, either in the street, in the police cell, and so on. This spatial juxtaposition gives visual content to the significance of home – the very home that Zwelenzima now finds himself exiled from: after all, as his stepfather Austin remarks, 'home is home, even if it is as small as a toilet' (14). Moreover, as Freda, his long-suffering but feisty mother, claims, 'If we can't have our self-respect within these four walls where else can we have it' (14). These claims are contrasted by scenes where Freda's and Zwelinzima's interactions with state functionaries are depicted by a spotlight to indicate the facelessness of the state machinery. This becomes palpable in the obsequious language littered with 'sir' and 'baas' (master) used by Freda and Zwelenzima in attempting to placate mindless authority. Unlike the poetic language which is maintained throughout *Kreli* in order to establish the cohesiveness of that world, in this play Dike's ear for colloquial vernaculars communicates the complex social layering of the contemporary black urban experience. At the same time, the play also becomes a way for Dike to work through the complexities of the relationship between her own mother and the white township super-intendent (who had in effect offered to adopt the 'white-looking' boy on whom the play is based).

Glass House *(1979)*

Glass House was the last play hosted by the Space Theatre before it closed its doors. The play was remounted at La Mama's off Broadway in 1980, and also at the White Barn Theatre in Connecticut. Fifteen years later, *Glass House* was revived, during Dike's tenure as Writer in Residence at the Open University at Milton Keynes, at the King's Head, London, in 1996.

The play is a two-hander and focuses on the relationship between two women from different sides of the apartheid divide. Phumla and Linda grew up together because Phumla's parents worked for Linda's white liberal father. The play shifts between present and past to explore their relationship which veers between intimate friendship and racially-based resentment and anger, during the lead-up to, and aftermath of, the traumatic political events of 1976. This includes Phumla's witnessing the killing of a protesting schoolboy (based on the incident Dike witnessed herself), and her later detention and persecution by police and comrades alike. On the other hand, Linda experiences an apparently illogical resentment of Phumla when her father is killed in an accident caused by protestors after he insists on collecting Phumla from her township home. Linda later confides to Phumla, 'The day I saw my father's face smashed in by stones, I hated you … I could see your head on that white pillow, it was a black woman's head. It was whole' (2002: 153). In facing up to their conflicting feelings about each other, and the ethical dilemmas which stem from deep-seated race-based injustice, Phumla claims, 'This is a war. You kill one of us. We kill one of you in return' (143).

Dike claims that she wrote the character of Phumla in hate, and for that reason the 1979 play was 'a foetus, not a baby'.[15] In the revised 1996 version, she changed the ending to be in keeping with the new era ushered in with the election in 1994, and to suggest the possibility of reconciliation. However, the revised ending in which both women pledge love and care for one another, as they settle in to watch Mandela's release, feels somewhat strained as the dramatic tension is not as sustained as in the previous two productions.

So What's New *(1990, 1991)*

So What's New was first produced at the Market Theatre in Johannesburg. A revised version was performed at the Artscape Theatre in Cape Town in 1994. The most recent production took place in 2011, again at the Market Theatre. Unlike her previous plays, this work underwent a workshopping process, first with Barney Simon, during the initial Johannesburg run, and then with Mavis Taylor in Cape Town.

So What's New is a comedy that reflects the slackening of the stranglehold of apartheid during the 1990s. Instead of the rather minimalist staging used in the previous plays, this production opts for a naturalistic stage aesthetic. The events unfold in a kitchen and a comfortable lounge, 'decorated in bold, nouveau riche-style' (26), with a large TV set dominating the downstage area, in keeping with the upwardly mobile aspirations of the characters. At the same time, limiting the action to this interior domestic haven (perhaps paradoxically) offers a safe space for the women to negotiate identities and relationships away from the public 'male' domain. The owner of the house, Big Dee, runs a shebeen (or tavern) from her home. There is much stage business of coming and going by close female friends, namely Pat (an aspirant estate agent) and Pat's sister Thandi (a drug-dealer).

While men are physically absent from the play, the women talk about them in racy and sexually graphic ways (similar to the way men talk about women). Dee fantasizes a scenario with her philandering boyfriend (aptly named Willie) in which she comes home to find Willie apologizing for not having her tea ready, saying, 'Mama I am so sorry, but I went to the clinic today and the doctor told me I was pregnant again', in response to which Dee throws Willie out, saying she does not need a bad housekeeper and now a 'breeding machine' to boot (27). This gender-role subversion is integral to the comedic framework, while also challenging traditional cultural taboos which prohibit women from speaking about their sexuality as desiring subjects.

The fast-paced dialogue switches between colloquial English and isiXhosa to highlight the deep personal histories that the three friends share, despite their constant bickering. The women (formerly members of the Chattanooga Singers) see themselves as agents in attempting to determine their own lives (albeit with mixed and limited success). The methods they use to achieve this are either risky, illegal or unethical. This is typical of the internal contradictions associated with Dike's work, while at the same time the play also draws on the figure of the 'shoplifter' as somehow a potentially heroic figure for flouting the law in an unjust system (not unlike Max in *The First South African*). As Chris Thurman points out, the production exposes the 'tragic false consciousness'[16] that underlies the characters' actions. One of the most significant features of the play is the way the women refuse to respond to (or, in Fanonian terms, refuse to be 'hailed' by) the discourses of patriarchy, as well as the apparently random and state-sanctioned violence raging outside the domestic haven. Moreover, the pervasive references to the events unfolding in the popular American soapie that they watch intermittently throughout the play indicates how they engage with the highly stylized fictional world constructed in *The Bold and the Beautiful* not as an unrealistic longed-for ideal or as an escape, but as a frame for negotiating their own relationships with men.

Dike includes the serious-minded young Mercedes, Big Dee's daughter, as counterpoint to the materialistic values of her elders. Mercedes reminds them of the ongoing struggle for political equality that still needs to be addressed. This is not to negate their self-fashioning efforts, but to provide a cautionary balance, since the schoolgirl seems to embody both the past ideals of the Soweto uprising as well as the need for future political involvement to achieve equality. The ending of the play points to the fact that though the women are claiming certain personal freedoms, political freedom has not yet been achieved.[17]

Street Walking and Company *(2000)*

Street Walking and Company was performed at the Baxter Theatre by the New Africa interns in 2000. This play explores the relationships between four young township women from different backgrounds who are caught in a self-perpetuating trap in which drugs are used to feed both addiction and financial greed.[18] While the play was written in the context of the issue-driven plays produced during Dike's time at New Africa, in a number of ways, *Street Walking* continues some of the trends explored in *So What's New*. For instance, there is a similar focus on popular culture and consumer values, as well as the self-fashioned identities adopted by a group of upwardly mobile women (in this case in their twenties). Similarly, the dialogue is characterized by racy and irreverent code-switching between linguistic registers. However, the play struggles with what seem to be somewhat ambiguous responses to the ubiquitous drug culture, which at one level appears vibrant and even glamorous. This sits uneasily with the sudden turn-about at the end when a moral message is delivered by one of the four women, who reveals that she is in effect a member of the 'Guardian Angels', a group of young people who are dedicated to fight crimes against young people. This strained ending stems from a tension between Dike's fine ear for observation, as well as her appreciation for the everyday drama of life in the 'new' South Africa, and the impulse here to use theatre to offer a response to a destructive social problem.

The Return *(2008)*

The Return was first performed as part of the Artscape New Writing Programme in 2008, directed by Roy Sargeant. In 2009, the production featured on the Main Programme of the National Arts Festival in Grahamstown, and later that year it travelled to Winston-Salem, North Carolina, as part of the National Black Theatre Festival.

As with *So What's New*, the play employs a naturalistic stage aesthetic, and most of the action takes place in the comfortable Sondaka home in Langa. The play explores generational and cultural tensions that emerge when an elderly couple's son (Buntu) returns home after 18 years in the United States, where he now lives with his African American wife, Isis. Buntu had gone into political exile secretly, much to the distress of his parents at the time, while his brother Sipho had stayed in South Africa. Tensions come to a head when family secrets emerge during the course of the visit, which further exacerbate the disjuncture between the values of the modern professional couple and the deeply entrenched traditional cultural expectations of the parents. A further complication is that the notion of 'family' is challenged by the arrival of Isis, who both is and isn't part of the family in terms of cultural affiliation. When Isis expresses discomfort at the notion of a ritual animal sacrifice, Mama tells her, 'Be silent and learn, my daughter. You are in Africa now and must do as we do' (60).

The Return revisits some of Dike's earlier concerns, explored in *Kreli*. In her author's introduction, she claims that '[w]e need to go back to our roots and find out about these issues of respect and freedom of worship' (12). However, this mutual 'respect' is hard-won and not before bitter words are spoken by both older and younger generations. For instance, when Isis realizes that Mama had referred to her as 'idikazi' (a bitch), Isis reprimands her mother-in-law (unheard of in traditional custom) by sarcastically requesting, 'if you want to insult me, will you do it in English so that I can understand?' (86).

At another level the play speaks strongly to Dike's preoccupation with notions of restorative justice and reconciliation. The question that hangs over the death of the son and brother who died during the struggle – was he a freedom fighter or a betrayer of his people? – points to the way the past needs to be addressed: as Dike mentions elsewhere, 'Truth is like a body that will inevitably rise to the surface.'[19]

Summary

The shifts in Dike's works that have been highlighted above also resonate with shifts in the critical approaches to her oeuvre. For instance, Stephen Gray claims that Dike's early plays 'were watershed points in the development of South African fringe drama'.[20] He links this to the way she connected to the cause of black rights through a dramaturgy that was ceremonial and sensuous (and here he speaks of *Kreli* in particular). At that time, says Gray, 'she was an original'.[21] These works were primarily viewed in terms of speaking to Black Consciousness ideals or to a rediscovery of 'Africanness' as a form of resistance to colonial and apartheid discourses. However, by focusing on the way apartheid racial classification resulted in a form of 'cultural schizophrenia from which we all suffer in one way or another',[22] *The First South African* also reveals how Dike's work runs against the grain of the prevailing protest theatre discourse of the time.

During the late 1980s and 1990s, critics tended to approach her works through feminist and gendered perspectives, especially those works produced in the transitional period of the 1990s. At the time, Dike was often paired with Gcina Mhlophe, as both were black women playwrights who explored gendered experiences in a field dominated by men.[23] Blumberg notes that while Dike and Mhlophe resist the description of their work as feminist theatre, Dike nevertheless 'writes from a particular understanding of the range of positions of black women'.[24] *Glass House*, for instance, although lacking the vigour and textured engagement of the earlier plays,[25] undoubtedly has an important place in the South African theatre history in offering a gendered and cross-cultural perspective at a period when this was rare.

Another angle has been to situate her work within comparative discussions of black aesthetic movements in Africa and the diaspora; it has been argued that Dike was developing a similar 'aesthetics of self-affirmation'.[26] Most recently, her work has been viewed in terms of discussions on social and restorative justice, reconciliation and restitution. For instance, Naila Keleta-Mae comments on the significant role of play makers like Dike who work with 'symbolic reversals' that challenge and 'disentangle the assumptions projected by dominant culture'.[27] *The Return*, by uncovering and dealing with a dark family secret which is imbricated in larger political processes of the time, can be seen as forming part of a sub-genre that Blumberg has termed 'restorative theatre'.[28]

As noted earlier, one of the notable features of Dike's work is that she is not afraid of 'performing' contradictions. The disjuncture between women's social roles and their agency in managing their lives has been evident as early as *Kreli* where the priest Mlangeni's oldest wife unsettles the warriors by confronting them with her apparently alternative frame of gendered experience. It might thus seem surprising that the feisty and independently-minded women one has come to associate with Dike's work (especially in *So What's New*) sometimes appear (as in *The Return*) to acquiesce to traditional expectations embedded in patriarchy. This suggests that maintaining cultural tradition as part of a restorative process of healing and renewal eclipses her earlier focus on gender inequalities. However, her comment in an early interview with Stephen Gray about the making of *Kreli* throws some light on this apparent 'about turn' in *The Return*: '[W]hen I talk about my blackness, I am honest. I am not ashamed of my customs. They are my customs, but what I would like to do is put them across in such a way that they cannot be misinterpreted.'[29] Dike in fact claims that she enjoys foregrounding the contradictions encountered in negotiating traditional values in modern urban contexts.

One of the most fascinating aspects of Dike's work is the way her plays anticipated theatre trends that have resurfaced or become more clearly articulated subsequently. For instance, some of her comments on her use of language in *Kreli* find strong reciprocities with the work of Mandla Mbothwe, a director who introduces an archaic style of isiXhosa as a form of restoration. Significantly, a line from *Kreli*, where the King speaks of the loss of land as an 'oozing wound',[30] is echoed in Mbothwe's *Inxeba Lomphilisi* (The Wound of the Healer), where the action is punctuated by the injunction to 'peel the scab off the wound' (in this case the leaking wound of dislocation from home is caused by the apartheid migrant labour system). Similarly, *The First South*

African points ahead to the focus on marginal identities in the post-election context and even to the fear of 'the stranger in our midst', associated with plays dealing with xenophobia such as Gina Schmukler's *The Line* (2012), or marginalized sexualities as in *I Stand Corrected* by Mamela Nyamza and Mojisola Adebayo (2012). At the same time, the title resonates with Toni Morrison's claim that instead of seeing African Americans as a 'marginal' group in their country of birth, they should be seen as 'a brand new human being in this country'.[31] This provocative claim (like the title of Dike's play) defies the notions of racialized and exclusive identity dominant even in the protest theatre of the time. On the other hand, *So What's New* points ahead to a plethora of works (most notably by young theatre practitioners) which explore a new urban and potentially liberatory, future-directed sensibility. From this, one can conclude that while demonstrating an engagement with the shifting cultural politics of the time, works like *The Sacrifice of Kreli*, *The First South African*, *So What's New* and *The Return* are not just works of their time; instead, they speak back to the past, and forward to the future.

Notes

1. Marcia Blumberg, 'Fatima Dike and the Struggle: An Interview by Marcia Blumberg, London, May 1996', in *South African Theatre as/and Intervention* (Amsterdam: Rodopi, 1999), 232.

2. Ibid.

3. Rolf Solberg, *The Life and Times of Fatima Dike* (Durban: University of KwaZulu-Natal Press, forthcoming), 13.

4. Ibid.

5. They got around these strictures by claiming that they were running a theatre club, and patrons were thus 'members' of the club.

6. Solberg, *The Life and Times of Fatima Dike*, 46.

7. The elderly Kreli (described in the report as bearing a remarkable likeness to the dignified King Ramses II) claims that he did not care to see strangers, for he was 'living like a baboon in a hole': 'Where is my country? Where are my children? My country was there – sweeping the horizon. Now I've no country' (*Dispatch*, 18 July 1885).

8. Solberg, *The Life and Times of Fatima Dike*, 31.

9. However, as Stephen Gray points out, Kreli cannot be reduced to a version of 'African Greek', and remains 'utterly original' ('The Theatre of Fatima Dike', *The English Academy Review* 2 (1984): 57).

10. Solberg, *The Life and Times of Fatima Dike*, 36.

11. She notes that to her Khulukazi was like Gagool in King Solomon's mines (in Solberg, *The Life and Times of Fatima Dike*, 28).

12. Solberg, *The Life and Times of Fatima Dike*, 36.

13. Ibid., 41.

14. Dike notes that the colour ochre works metaphorically to signify a rite of passage phase: for instance, when Rooi returns from the circumcision ritual he is covered in ochre (in conversation with Miki Flockemann, 'On Not Giving Up: An Interview with Fatima Dike', *Contemporary Theatre Review, Special Issue: Women, Politics and Performance in South Africa Today* 9:1 (1999): 17–33).

15. Quoted in Blumberg, 'Fatima Dike and the Struggle', 231.

16. Chris Thurman, '*So What's New*: A Review', *Arts and Culture*, 14 July 2011, http://christhurman.net/art-and-culture/item/review-so-what-s-new.html (accessed 24 August 2013).

17. Chris Thurman notes that as the 2011 production is set in the present, there was a poignant irony to the title, since nothing much has changed since the dying days of apartheid which is when the original version is set.

18. Dike initially envisioned an ambitious multi-media stage production, dominated by a 'beautiful open coupe' used to transport the merchandise, and as meeting point. However, this was considered too ambitious for the Baxter production.

19. Blumberg, 'Fatima Dike and the Struggle', 236.

20. Gray, 'The Theatre of Fatima Dike', 60.

21. Ibid.

22. Dene Smuts, 'Meet fats – Fatima Dike', *The Fairlady Collection: 40 years of fine writing*, 1978, pp. 18–23, http://www.worldcat.org/title/meets-fats-fatima-dike/oclc/775978507 (accessed 26 August 2013).

23. See Blumberg, 'Fatima Dike and the Struggle'; Miki Flockemann, 'Women, Feminism and South African Theatre', in *The Routledge Reader in Gender and Performance* (London: Routledge, 1998), 'Watching Soap Opera', in *Senses of Culture: South African Cultural Studies* (Cape Town: Oxford University Press, 2000), 141–54; Olga Barrios, *The Black Theatre Movement in the United States and in South Africa* (Valencia: Publicacions Universitat de Valencia, 2009), 'Male Violence Against Women and Hybrid Identities in Post-Apartheid South African Black Theatre', *International Journal of Arts* 2:5 (2012): 39–48; Michael Picardie, 'The Drama of Two South African Plays Under Apartheid', unpublished M.Phil. diss. (Aberystwyth University, Wales, 2009).

24. Blumberg, 'Fatima Dike and the Struggle'.

25. Tamsin Wolff, '*Glasshouse*', review, *Theatre Journal* 49:1 (1997): 31, http://muse.jhu.edu/journals/theatre_journal/summary/v049/49.1pr_dike.html (accessed 10 June 2013).

26. Barrios, *The Black Theatre Movement*, 193.

27. Naila Keleta-Mae, 'Contemporary Social Justice Theatre: Finding, Sharing, Healing', *Canadian Theatre Review* 132 (2007): 31.

28. Marcia Blumberg, 'Reconciling Acts: Theatre Beyond the Truth and Reconciliation Commission', in *SA Lit Beyond 2000* (Scottsville: University of KwaZulu-Natal Press, 2011), 148.

29. Stephen Gray, 'An Interview with Fatima Dike', *Callalloo* 8:10 (1980): 159–60.

30. Dike, 'The Sacrifice of Kreli', in Stephen Gray (ed.), *The Theatre One: New South African Drama* (Johannesburg: AD Donker, 1978), 66.

31. Christina Davis, 'An Interview with Toni Morrison', *Présence Africaine* 145 (1988): 143.

Bibliography

Primary sources

Works by Fatima Dike

'The Sacrifice of Kreli', in Stephen Gray (ed.), *The Theatre One: New South African Drama* (Johannesburg: AD Donker, 1978).
The First South African (Johannnesburg: Ravan Playscripts, 1979).
'So What's New', in Kathy Perkins (ed.), *Black South African Women: An Anthology of Plays* (New York: Routledge, 1998).
'Glass House', in Jane Plastow (ed.), *African Theatre: Women* (London: James Currey, 2002).
'Housing for All', in Michael Williams (comp.), *District Six and Other Plays* (Cape Town: Oxford University Press, 2005).
The Return (Cape Town: Junkets Publishers, 2009).

Secondary sources

Barnard, Rita, *Apartheid and Beyond: South African Writers and the Politics of Place* (Oxford: Oxford University Press, 2007).
Barrios, Olga, *The Black Theatre Movement in the United States and in South Africa* (Valencia: Publicacions Universitat de Valencia, 2009).
Barrios, Olga, 'Male Violence against Women and Hybrid Idenities in Post-Apartheid South African Black Theatre', *International Journal of Arts* 2:5 (2012): 39–48.
Blumberg, Marcia, 'Fatima Dike and the Struggle: An Interview by Marcia Blumberg, London, May 1996', in *South African Theatre as/and Intervention* (Amsterdam: Rodopi, 1999), 231–40.
Blumberg, Marcia, 'Reconciling Acts: Theatre beyond the Truth and Reconciliation Commission', in *SA Lit Beyond 2000* (Scottsville: University of KwaZulu-Natal Press, 2011).

Davis, Christina, 'An Interview with Toni Morrison', *Présence Africaine* 145 (1988): 141–50.

De Beer, Diane, 'Sisterhood Show Gives a New Slant on "Same Old"', *Tonight*, 2011, http://www.iol.co.za/tonight/what-s-on/gauteng/sisterhood-show-gives-a-new-slant-on-same-old-1.1094102 (accessed 7 July 2013).

Dike, Fatima, 'So What's New? The Story Behind the Play', in *Theatre and Change in South Africa* (London: Routledge, 1997), 242–5.

Flockemann, Miki, 'Women, Feminism and South African Theatre', in *The Routledge Reader in Gender and Performance* (London: Routledge, 1998).

Flockemann, Miki, 'On Not Giving Up: An Interview with Fatima Dike', *Contemporary Theatre Review, Special Issue: Women, Politics and Performance in South Africa Today* 9:1 (1999): 17–33.

Flockemann, Miki, 'Watching Soap Opera', in *Senses of Culture: South African Cultural Studies* (Cape Town: Oxford University Press, 2000), 141–54.

Gray, Stephen, 'An Interview with Fatima Dike', *Callalloo* 8:10 (1980): 157–64.

Gray, Stephen, 'The Theatre of Fatima Dike', *The English Academy Review* 2 (1984): 55–60.

Greene, Alexis (ed.), *Women Writing Plays: Three Decades of the Susan Smith Blackburn Prize* (Austin: University of Texas Press, 2006).

Keleta-Mae, Naila, 'Contemporary Social Justice Theatre: Finding, Sharing, Healing', *Canadian Theatre Review* 132 (2007): 30–3.

'Kreli at Home', Cape Town Correspondent, *Dispatch*, 18 July 1885, http://lit.alexand erstreet.com/v4/services/get.pdf.aspx?id=1000001821 (accessed 10 June 2013).

Kruger, Loren, *The Drama of South Africa: Plays, Pageants and Publics since 1910* (New York: Routledge, 2007).

Picardie, Michael, 'The Drama of Two South African Plays Under Apartheid', unpublished M.Phil. diss. (Aberystwyth University, Wales, 2009).

Plastow, Jane (ed.), *African Theatre: Women* (London: James Currey, 2002).

Rahmer, Christine, 'Community Theatre and Indigenous Performance Traditions: An Introduction to Chicana Theatre, With Reference to Parallel Developments in South Africa', *Literator* 17:3 (1996): 61–76.

Smuts, Dene, 'Meets fats – Fatima Dike', *The Fairlady Collection: 40 years of fine writing*, 1978, pp. 18–23, http://www.worldcat.org/title/meets-fats-fatima-dike/oclc/775978507 (accessed 26 August 2013).

Solberg, Rolf, *Alternative Theatre in South Africa: Talks with Prime Movers since the 1970s* (Durban: University of KwaZulu-Natal Press, 1999).

Solberg, Rolf, *South African Theatre in the Melting Pot: Trends and Developments at the Turn of the Millennium* (Grahamstown: ISEA, 2003).

Solberg, Rolf, *The Life and Times of Fatima Dike* (Durban: University of KwaZulu-Natal Press, forthcoming).

Thurman, Chris, '*So What's New*: A Review', *Arts and Culture*, 14 July 2011, http://christhurman.net/art-and-culture/item/review-so-what-s-new.html (accessed 24 August 2013).

Wolff, Tamsin, '*Glasshouse*', review, *Theatre Journal* 49:1 (1997): 60–1, http://muse.jhu.edu/journals/theatre_journal/summary/v049/49.1pr_dike.html (accessed 10 June 2013).

Zvomuya, Percy, 'Women's Theatre Comes Home', *Mail and Guardian*, 12 August 2012, http://mg.co.za/article/2011-08-12-womens-theatre-comes-home (accessed 10 June 2013).

CHAPTER 18
YAËL FARBER
Marcia Blumberg

He Left Quietly; Molora; Mies Julie: Restitutions of Body and Soil Since the Bantu Land Act No 27 of 1913 & The Immorality Act No 5 of 1927; Nirbhaya

Introduction

Yaël Farber was born in Johannesburg, South Africa, on 22 January 1971 and now lives in Montreal, Canada, but calls South Africa 'home'. She received a BA (Honours) in Dramatic Arts from the University of Witwatersrand. In her early career she directed plays at the Market Theatre (Johannesburg) including Mark Ravenhill's controversial 'in-yer-face' play *Shopping and Fucking*, which received seven national awards. She is an internationally acclaimed playwright, director and co-creator of testimonial theatre with an impressive oeuvre of eight plays, which have won multiple awards including the Best of Edinburgh Award in 2012. *Nirbhaya* (2013), her most recent creation, which won a Herald Angel Award and an Edinburgh Fringe First Award on 9 August 2013, is translated from Hindi as 'the fearless one' and refers to the female medical student who was gang raped and brutally injured on a bus in Delhi and soon afterwards died. The descriptor, the fearless one, is also apt for Farber, who deals with provocative theatre, urgent and unpopular issues, and exhibits a refusal to live in denial or sanitize complex predicaments. In a recent interview Farber spoke about her desire to 'create theatre that wakes people up, not anesthetizes them' (December 2011 – Alt theatre). Her work certainly fulfils this aim.

Her productions, under her company Farber Foundry, established in 2004, have toured the world including Africa, Australia, Canada, Europe, Japan, the United Kingdom and the United States of America. She has also been invited to participate in labs in New York with Anna Deveare Smith and in Berlin. She has been artist in residence at the Nightwood Theatre in Toronto and in New York at the Mabou Mines Theatre and Joseph Papp Public Theatre.

Farber specializes in two totally different forms of theatre: testimonial theatre and reworkings of the classics, resituating them in South Africa. In an interview from 2008, she encapsulates her oeuvre thus: '[A]ll my work tends to be about pursuing a certain truth and getting to the marrow of South Africa's past and present.'[1] In her testimonial plays her role is that of creator of collaborative theatre. Farber conducts many interviews, analyses dreams, mines memories and encourages an openness that comes with trust gained during the creative process with people whose lives have been tough and who have experienced oppression, poverty and devastating violence. These interviews have not been used verbatim; rather, they have been shaped and constructed collaboratively deploying dialogue, poetry, gesture and song in different languages appropriate to the casts in order to position audience members to bear witness to their actual experiences. Farber emphasizes that 'the plays are created with and based on the lives of the casts'. In the Foreword to *Theatre as Witness: Three Testimonial Plays from South Africa*, Desmond Tutu foregrounds the value of her theatre: 'Acknowledging the past through sharing one's personal story is the single most powerful action in the battle against the silence of indifference or fear. To testify not only uncovers what lay hidden in a regime's enforced silence – but heals the speaker and the listener alike' (7). While some would challenge his certainty about healing, Farber's testimonial plays are powerful vehicles through which the disempowered and oppressed can call attention to the plight of people positioned in previously unspeakable scenarios that have been theatricalized to transform silence into powerful verbal and corporeal communication. She draws in the audience and expects them to play a vital and active role as witnesses. Catherine Cole reminds us with reference to the Truth and Reconciliation Commission that with a reciprocal process of telling and listening there is a 'fundamental anxiety that springs from the process of witnessing: to witness is to see, to witness is to tell, to witness is to *be implicated*. And that is never comfortable' (120, my emphasis). The same dynamic operates in Farber's plays.

Secondly, as playwright, she has reworked Western classics that range from Greek tragedy and Shakespeare to modern drama and from the East, *Ram: the Abduction of Sita into Darkness*, the ancient Hindi tale of *The Ramanyana* from about the fifth century BC. These plays are re-visionings, which Adrienne Rich defines thus: 'The act of looking back, seeing with fresh eyes, of entering a text from a new critical direction – is for women more than a chapter in cultural history: it is an act of survival.'[2] I extend that definition to include men and women since unless they both raise their awareness and change, society will not transform; the latter is a goal of all Farber's work. In focusing upon the overarching themes of the classical plays and at the same time attending to the specificities, Farber utilizes these intertexts and resituates them in contemporary South Africa (except for *Ram*); she transforms the theatrical texts by altering categories of race and class, socio-political issues and modes of staging. In each case, mythological or timeless stories are regenerated to represent complex and volatile scenarios that speak to what has often been unspeakable in South Africa; she also places spectators in confrontation with traumatic historical material and its urgent ramifications that still apply in the present.

The staging for both forms of theatre requires that the actors stand level on the floor with the spectators who occupy raked seating and look directly at the performers. This dynamic allows for a close engagement with the stage and at times an interactive possibility: for example, when the audience is asked to come to the stage and pair up missing shoes of the prisoners who have been executed (*He Left Quietly*). Most importantly, the stage design situates the audience as witnesses, who will engage actively and empathetically. She thus challenges audiences to wake up and take responsibility for problems in the world around them.

The plays

He Left Quietly *(2002)*

Duma Kumalo performed himself in this production and passed away in 2006. The production has never been remounted. Yaël would have been prepared to consider a new run as long as the audience was made aware that Duma initiated the role and that it would then be an actor taking it on.

This is the third play in the collection of Farber's testimonial plays. After co-creating *A Woman in Waiting* with Thembi Mtshali, and *Amajuba: Like Doves We Rise* with five young South African actors, Farber turned her attention to the story of Duma Joshua Kumalo, one of the Sharpeville Six who were arrested for killing a town councillor, Jacob Dhlamini, on the grounds of Common Purpose, which allows anyone near a crime scene to be convicted; but they didn't commit this crime. As prisoner V3458, Duma spent three years on death row. Immense international pressure was exerted and fifteen hours before he was scheduled to be hanged there was a stay of execution. Duma served a further four years in prison and was released in

1991 when negotiations about prisoners took place, but his name was never cleared.

Farber worked in a different fashion on this text. She knew that she couldn't do another solo show as Duma was not as robust as Thembi Mtshali, so she devised two Dumas – the older Duma who would narrate and play himself in some scenes and a young actor to take the role of Duma as a younger man. Eventually she added a white woman who takes multiple roles – that of the co-creator Yaël as well as the voice of white authority, sometimes an Afrikaner and Duma's black girlfriend who would later become his wife. The Woman sits inconspicuously in the audience and lights a cigarette while speaking quietly. Duma challenges her statement 'I am here to observe' with 'You are in or you are out' (191). The stage direction instructs that she move into the performance space. Since she has initially been placed in the audience with other spectators and performs many roles, she subtly reminds us that the entire audience is complicit with the oppressive structures of apartheid South Africa and even with the many disturbing aspects of the new democratic South Africa. She acknowledges that 'You don't grow up in South Africa not knowing. You know. Where were we when the truth was finally being told? How could there be empty chairs in the halls?' (198). This dialogue hinders potential audience distancing or disengagement. The Woman's final words are addressed to the audience: 'And I know that I am home. For better or worse – we call this place "home"'. (*She moves away and out of the performance space back into the auditorium*) (237). This stage direction challenges the apathy and indifference of many white South Africans and reinforces Farber's emphasis on participation and engagement to facilitate transformation in her home and nation. Amanda Stuart Fisher argues that:

> Farber directs our attention away from the politics of the situation and instead explores the existential trauma of Kumalo himself … By drawing attention to those who did not survive, whose stories will never be told, Kumalo bears witness on behalf of the other … [He] personifies the double imperative of bearing witness: the desire to tell one's own story and the need to speak for others.[3]

The two versions of Duma (old and young) work powerfully so that Duma Khumalo narrates and evaluates his younger self and past events while the actor performs them. Young Duma initially appears from under the pile of green uniforms worn by prisoners who were executed and circles the older

Duma, who introduces himself and includes his Zulu praise names: Zulu is often spoken, for example, when Duma offers an incantation from Jonah's psalm of thanksgiving for survival and later young Duma repeats this prayer as he walks to death row. Farber's use of the vernacular accords respect and authenticity to their storytelling, which ranges from philosophizing about life and death and analysing the unjust and cruel justice system to providing minute details about the experience of death row. Spectators are emotionally connected to Duma through his trauma and painful experience and remember that in his mind he always returns to death row. The epilogue offers some hope. Duma, seated alone on a chair, as in the opening of the play, now speaks about the birth of his son on the anniversary of his scheduled hanging: 'Telling my story to those willing to listen. I speak for the dead. For we who have survived must tell the world.' (*He walks out of the door, leaving it open and the audience with themselves*) (238). His exit marks a physical leave-taking from the audience, but they will not easily be separated from or forget his compelling story and his humanity.

Mies Julie: Restitutions of Body and Soil Since the Bantu Land Act No 27 of 1913 & The Immorality Act No 5 of 1927 *(2012)*

This play is a re-visioning of August Strindberg's *Miss Julie* (1899) and shifts time and place to Freedom Day (27 April) 2012 on *Weenenplaas* (weeping farm) in the Karoo. Farber adds a character, Ukhokho, who represents the ancestors, an otherworldly but significant component of Xhosa culture replete with ancient musical instruments and throat singing, and recasts Christine as John's mother rather than as his fiancé. Here the servants are black and the troubled relationship between John and Julie evokes tensions among putative 'siblings' vying for the attention of their 'mother'. This complex relationship foregrounds the dichotomy between a black mother who, as the domestic worker, also serves as a second mother to the children of the house, here Mies Julie, especially since Julie's mother committed suicide when she was thirteen. John repeatedly mentions that his mother had no time for him but plenty of time for Mies Julie. In Farber's play, John and Julie also exhibit extremes of emotions between love and hate, desire and repulsion, and vengeance and forgiveness. Miki Flockemann comments on the post-coital scene (in contrast with Strindberg's offstage sexual relationship): '[It is] only when asleep that they can be unequivocally tender with one another, because once awake they are sucked back into the maelstrom of the past and its apparent stranglehold over their futures.'[4]

Crucial to this re-visioning is the subtext of the play that focuses on land ownership, sexual relationships across race and issues of power. Land dispossession is a complex process that has been operative for a century. Land, according to Jary and Jary, has two broad meanings: 'the landscape valued for its natural resources and the territory with which a particular people identify'.[5] Vital issues include who holds rights, how it was acquired and how it is currently used. Land has political and economic as well as identity ramifications. Many black people retain strong links to their birth-place, where their ancestors lived. Xhosa people speak of their home as their *umnombo*, meaning their roots. Farber materializes this concept in her placement of a tree from the ancestral burial ground beneath the kitchen, a tree that is breaking through the floor to connote the impossibility of being buried and being at rest.

In an interview with Jeremy Daniel,[6] Farber commented on her new play:

Sexual relations across the colour line – while still interesting and/ or shocking for some – is hardly the shocker (not to mention the law breaker) – in SA that it once was … The compelling point of *Miss Julie* in contemporary SA concerns land issues, ownership, power, sexuality, mothers, memories. These are what remain as shrapnel from our history. The battle of these primal issues in a kitchen over a single night between a farm labourer and his Baas's daughter is what *Mies Julie* has its hand in. Kitchens are places of steam and heat and making and devouring and talking. We aim for this *Mies Julie* to bring heat to the fore in all senses.

John's and Julie's worlds are irrevocably changed. In the final moments, Julie, convinced that she may be pregnant with John's child, remonstrates with him: 'You think my body your restitution? My womb your landgrab' (56). She takes the sickle and horrifically thrusts the blades up into her womb. After a gush of blood, John carries her lifeless body to the kitchen table. There is no simple way out of this race/class/gender/power battle, but we, the audience, have been 'woken up' and stimulated to ask new questions; we are amazed at the power of Farber's theatre and the role it plays.

Nirbhaya *(2012)*

Farber's most recent co-creation of testimonial theatre was inspired by the gang rape of Jyoti Singh Pandey in Delhi on 16 December 2012. Reports of this violent assault and her subsequent death went viral, garnering world outrage, and prompted Pooma Jagannathan to invite Farber to do a workshop in India with local actors to foreground this brutal event and men's treatment of women in India. Five of the seven performers share unspeakable stories drawn from life experience. Farber returned in May 2013 to create the piece with the Indian actors. Well aware of her outsider status, she was cautious and at the same time decisive about the importance of the event as a focal point, a watershed moment, in which these assaultive gender dynamics could not continue. Cognizant that conditions in India could be compared with the unbelievably high statistics of rape and sexual violence in South Africa and other countries throughout the world, Farber never wavered.

She argues that putting real survivors on stage in front of a paying audience could be seen as, in her own words, 'grief porn'. The challenge, she says, is to make the audience witnesses not voyeurs.[7] John Nathan records Farber's lack of fear of opposition: 'The beauty of freedom of speech is that people will have something to say. But certainly it is a volatile issue. And if we don't encounter opposition we haven't done our job.'[8] The play is performed in English interspersed with Hindi lines. The prologue ends with Priyanka's question, 'Who knows why one's fate touched so many of our lives? But people began to break the silence and speak. This then is our story.' The breaking of silence and the exposure of a code of male behaviour that reeks of entitlement, disregards women and considers their bodies no matter how old or young as property to be abused in a myriad of ways sends shock waves through the audience when the women unburden themselves through storytelling. The women speak of the ordeal of bus travel, when they are groped and grabbed; Rukhsar comments: 'Even in a Burka holding a child. No one is off limits.' Jyoti's world is contextualized by the women, and pre-death reactions to the horrific rape and assault provide details of her massive injuries: they pushed a rusted crowbar into her and tore out her intestines. The women pray for her recovery and beg her to keep fighting; she battled for her life for thirteen days and eventually died. Then five women in the cast speak the unspeakable and tell their stories in public to break their silence, reveal their deepest secrets and release their shame. Poona speaks of abuse by an 'uncle' from the age of nine:

> Over those years I tell no one ... To tell our parents, the court rooms, the police – is the risk of not being believed. Or worse – having broken some rule and brought shame upon ourselves ... And so our

bodies carry it all … Nirbhaya. I repeat the word 'fearless' like a prayer into the night. I tear away the silence. And begin the journey home …

Other women refer to angry and assaultive fathers, the hell of marriage and the imprisonment by husbands, physical disfigurement as a consequence of what is perceived as being shamed, attempted suicide as a means of escape. Sneha, a dowry bride, is set on fire and loses her son who is abducted by her husband. Sapna from Bombay has relocated to Chicago. She also endures sexual violence: '[t]o be gang raped in America'. Farber's deliberate inclusion of Sapna's story precludes the possibility of attributing these horrific stories and the culture that supports these dynamics to India. This happens in America, in South Africa and in many countries across the world. These stories are theatricalized so that not only are the words powerful but the staging makes its mark and leaves an indelible impression.

Some reviews from the Edinburgh Festival have raised the problem of criticizing such a powerful but harrowing experience that positions women on stage who share their real life traumatic experiences. Lynn Gardiner argues that 'we are not just watching[,] we are bearing witness'. She also notes that 'it gives us the tools to empathise, but not the tools to take action. In an intimate Nirbhaya venue with opportunity for discussion afterwards, *Nirbhaya* could start to change the world.'[9] Another reviewer, Eleanor Turney, refuses to give a star rating and admits that she isn't writing a real review:

> Go and see it … the show is about the power of words, the power of broken silences and being prepared to speak out. It's about reclaiming the night, speaking up for those who are silent and powerless. It's a show about unspeakable things, spoken of. It will leave you speechless.[10]

The *doyenne* of Edinburgh critics, Joyce McMillan, acclaimed *Nirbhaya*:

> Farber uses all her skill as a theatre-maker to create a show that is as beautiful as it is hard-hitting, evoking all the beauty and potential that is destroyed by Jyoti's death, and all the powerful and exquisite female imagery that pervades Indian culture, even as ordinary women are violated and disfigured'.[11]

Nirbhaya was awarded a Fringe First and a Herald Angel Award.

Notes

1. Belinda Otas, 'On Molora and Moving Forward in South Africa', *The New Black Magazine*, 29 April 2008.

2. Adrienne Rich, 'When We Dead Awaken: Writing as Re-Vision', in *On Lies, Secrets, and Silence: Selected Prose 1966–1978* (New York: Norton, 1979), 33–49.

3. Amanda Stuart Fisher, 'Introduction', in *Theatre as Witness: Three Testimonial Plays from South Africa* (London: Oberon Books, 2008), 15–16.

4. Miki Flockemann, 'Repeating and Disrupting Embodied Histories Through Performance: *Exhibit A, Mies Julie* and *Itsoseng*', *Critical Arts* 27:4 (2013): 403–17.

5. D. and J. Jary, *Collins Dictionary of Sociology* (Glasgow: Harper Collins, 1995).

6. Jeremy Daniel, 'Mies Julie: "Exploring the national within the realm of the personal"', *The Baxter Blog*, 20 June 2012, http://thebaxterblog.wordpress.com/2012/06/20/mies-julie-exploring-the-national-within-the-realm-of-the-personal/ (accessed 16 August 2012).

7. Mark Fisher, 'Interview: Yaël Farber on Her New Play Nirbhaya', *Scotland on Sunday* (2013), http://www.edinburgh-festivals.com/blog/2013/07/30/interview-yael-farber-on-her-new-play-nirbhaya/ (accessed 30 July 2013).

8. John Nathan, 'Nirbhaya: Play About the Delhi Rape that Shocked the World Set for Edinburgh', *The Independent*, 14 May 2013.

9. Lynn Gardner, 'Interview: Yaël Farber on Her New Play Nirbhaya', *The Guardian*, 5 August 2013.

10. Eleanor Turney, 'Nirbhaya', review, 7 August 2013, http://www.ayoungertheatre.com/edinburgh-fringe-review-nirbhaya-assembly-hall/ (accessed 17 March 2015).

11. Joyce McMillan, 'Theatre reviews: The Events; Nirbhaya; Quietly', *The Scotsman* (2013), http://www.edinburgh-festivals.com/blog/2013/08/05/theatre-review-the-events-nirbhaya-quietly/ (accessed 5 August 2013).

Bibliography

Primary sources

Works by Yael Farber

He Left Quietly, in *Theatre as Witness: Three Testimonial Plays from South Africa* (London: Oberon Books, 2008).

Mies Julie: Restitutions of Body and Soil Since the Bantu Land Act No 27 of 1913 & The Immorality Act No 5 of 1927 (London: Oberon Books, 2012).

Nirbhaya, unpublished draft of the text kindly made available by Yaël Farber.

Secondary sources

Cole, Catherine M., *Performing South Africa's Truth Commission: Stages of Transition* (Bloomington: Indiana University Press, 2010).

Daniel, Jeremy, 'Mies Julie: "Exploring the national within the realm of the personal"', *The Baxter Blog*, 20 June 2012, http://thebaxterblog.wordpress.com/2012/06/20/mies-julie-exploring-the-national-within-the-realm-of-the-personal/ (accessed 16 August 2012).

Fisher, Amanda Stuart, 'Introduction', in *Theatre as Witness: Three Testimonial Plays from South Africa* (London: Oberon Books, 2008), 9–17.

Fisher, Mark, 'Interview: Yaël Farber on Her New Play Nirbhaya', *Scotland on Sunday* (2013), http://www.edinburgh-festivals.com/blog/2013/07/30/interview-yael-farber-on-her-new-play-nirbhaya/ (accessed 30 July 2013).

Flockemann, Miki, 'Repeating and Disrupting Embodied Histories Through Performance: *Exhibit A, Mies Julie* and *Itsoseng*', *Critical Arts* 27:4 (2013): 403–17.

Gardner, Lynn, 'Interview: Yaël Farber on Her New Play Nirbhaya', *The Guardian*, 5 August 2013.

Jary, D. and J. Jary, *Collins Dictionary of Sociology* (Glasgow: Harper Collins, 1995).

McMillan, Joyce, 'Theatre reviews: The Events; Nirbhaya; Quietly', *The Scotsman* (2013), http://www.edinburgh-festivals.com/blog/2013/08/05/theatre-review-the-events-nirbhaya-quietly/ (accessed 5 August 2013).

Nathan, John, 'Nirbhaya: Play About the Delhi Rape that Shocked the World Set for Edinburgh', *The Independent*, 14 May 2013.

Otas, Belinda, 'On Molora and Moving Forward in South Africa', *The New Black Magazine*, 29 April 2008.

Rich, Adrienne, 'When We Dead Awaken: Writing as Re-Vision', in *On Lies, Secrets, and Silence: Selected Prose 1966–1978* (New York: Norton, 1979), 33–49.

Turney, Eleanor, 'Nirbhaya', review, 7 August 2013, http://www.ayoungertheatre.com/edinburgh-fringe-review-nirbhaya-assembly-hall/ (accessed 15 April 2015).

Tutu, Archbishop Desmond, 'Foreword', in *Theatre as Witness: Three Testimonial Plays from South Africa* (London: Oberon Books, 2008), 7–8.

CHAPTER 19
EMERGING PLAYWRIGHTS AND SIGNIFICANT PLAYS
Greg Homann

Nothing But the Truth (Kani); ***The Boy Who Fell from the Roof*** (Jenkin); ***Abnormal Loads*** (Coppen)

Introduction

In the first decade of democracy in South Africa very few plays by new playwrights made a lasting impact. In addition, it took almost a decade before some truly post-apartheid themes came to the fore.

In this chapter we focus on two areas of interest. Firstly we deal with dramas that have had a substantial influence on the theatrical landscape of the country but that have not been covered elsewhere in the book. These are works that have, for different reasons, contributed to a shift in paradigm or that are good examples of plays that represent a recurring theme or practice in contemporary South Africa. Secondly we consider playwrights that are, at the time of writing, emerging as prominent new voices.

Significant plays

It is unlikely that South Africa will ever produce a 'state of the nation' play. For one, the attainment of a unified sense of national identity is almost inconceivable considering the sheer economic contrast and vast cultural diversity of the country. There is, however, a strong desire amongst producers and theatres to find quality plays that speak specifically and truthfully to the post-apartheid condition.

In the search for stories, one approach has been to look to existing literary texts that could work in a theatrical form. Two dramatic plays adapted from literary works stand out: James Ngcobo's delicate stage adaptation of a short story written in 1954 by Es'kia Mphahlehle, entitled *The Suitcase*; and Janice

Honeyman's moving staging of Chris van Wyk's memoir, *Shirley Goodness and Mercy*.

The Suitcase (2006) is a beautifully crafted and touching play centring on a young rural couple, Timi and Namhla, who betray their respective families' wishes by marrying. They run away to the city of Durban. Their lives are thrown into chaos when a suitcase is discovered, at first offering hope but later revealing an inconceivable content.

This simple play shaped by Ngcobo poignantly captures the hope of the 'new South Africa' in contrast to the disappointment many have felt a decade into democracy. More significantly though it is a love story between two black characters, a type of story scarcely seen in mainstream South African theatres.

Shirley Goodness and Mercy (2007) is set in apartheid and is a playful account of a boy coming of age in the Coloured township of Riverlea in Johannesburg.[1] What makes the play unique is that it manages to avoid a heavy-handed account of racial tension; rather it explores the family relationships and friendships that the lead character has within his community.

Then there is the proliferation of 'identity plays' that address the disjuncture between old and new cultural practices, generation gaps, and the struggles to define identity under the new political system – a theme that has become an important trope in the second decade of democracy.

Many of these identity plays emerged in one-person format (see Baxter) where issues of being South African are explored from a singular cultural standpoint. The dramatic tension arises from an internal struggle between family pressures, usually cultural, and a desire to break free from those constraints. This is evident in the early part of the new century in plays like Nadia Davids' *At Her Feet* (2002), Geraldine Naidoo's *Chilli Boy* (2002) and *Hoot* (2005), and Motshabi Tyelele's *Shwele Bawo* (2004).

If there are any plays that come close to being 'state of the nation plays' then John Kani's *Nothing But the Truth* and Gregg Latter's *Death of a Colonialist* are arguably the best contenders for the title.

Death of a Colonialist premiered at the Market Theatre in 2010. It has been presented at the National Arts Festival and had a highly celebrated season in 2014 at the Baxter Theatre in Cape Town. The play is significant in that it is among the best of contemporary South African drama that deals with the relationship between identity and history, a recurring theme in the majority of post-apartheid plays.

More specifically, the play is a look at the politics of whiteness through patriotic eyes. Harold Smith is an ageing high school history teacher living in Grahamstown. He is passionate about indigenous South African history but his eccentric teaching style gets him in hot water when a student accuses him of being racist.

One play that the academy and audiences seem to agree about is John Kani's debut play, *Nothing But the Truth,* which stands in many eyes as the first truly post-apartheid drama of the new democracy.

John Kani

John Kani's presence as an actor, playwright and director looms large across the South African theatre landscape. He has received honorary doctorates from four South African universities,[2] the Order of Ikhamanga in Silver[3] for his unprecedented contribution to South African and international theatre, two OBIE awards, a Tony Award, the Hiroshima Award for Peace, as well as countless other accolades: a career which spans more than 40 years. On 10 June 2014 the Market Theatre renamed its main stage the John Kani Theatre in honour of a man who stands iconically as a representation of the South African stage.

Kani was born on 30 August 1943 in the township of New Brighton in Port Elizabeth. He first came to prominence through his association with the Serpent Players, a drama group founded in 1963 by industrial workers led by Norman Ntshinga. This group worked alongside other drama groups like the East London-based Imitha Players and the Ikhwezi Players in Grahamstown. The Serpent Players forged an invaluable partnership with a young Athol Fugard (see Walder) who directed some of their first productions of European classics. They later explored improvised and workshop-based collaborations.

With the Serpent Players, Kani emerged as a co-writer/collaborator and actor in some of the most important plays created during apartheid. His partnership with Winston Ntshona (a key member of the Serpent Players) and Athol Fugard brought them to international prominence, jointly winning Ntshona and Kani the Tony Award for Best Actor in 1975 for their performances in *Sizwe Bansi is Dead* and *The Island.*

Kani became a household name as an actor, working in TV, film and theatre, but he was not known before *Nothing But the Truth* as a solo playwright. This changed after the play's world premiere at the National Arts Festival in Grahamstown under Janice Honeyman's direction. In the Festival's daily newspaper the next day, arts commentator Darryl Accone and theatre director Alan Swerdlow debated the overnight success of the work. Accone stated it was the play the new South Africa had been waiting for. Swerdlow celebrated Kani's astounding debut saying that this 'work instantly places him (Kani) at the top of the ladder'.

Kani took more than ten years to complete his second offering as a sole playwright, entitled *Missing...*, which is a story of exile and return, a common theme in dramas in the first half of the mid-90s. Although *Missing...* has enjoyed seasons at the Baxter Theatre, the Market Theatre and a few outings at international venues, the play simply does not match the craftsmanship, weight or contemporary relevance that *Nothing But the Truth* does.

Nothing But the Truth *(2002)*

Nothing But the Truth premiered on 4 July 2002 at the National Arts Festival. It went on to enjoy over a decade of intermittent seasons, return seasons and tours across South Africa, America, Australia, the UK and Windhoek in Namibia, with Kani in the lead role. It has become a high school set work and a feature film.

Set in 2000, *Nothing But the Truth* is the story of Sipho Makhaya, the assistant chief librarian of a small public library in Port Elizabeth. Sipho lives in a 'simple four-roomed house in New Brighton' with his only daughter, Thando, who is a teacher and an interpreter at the amnesty hearings of the Truth and Reconciliation Commission (TRC) (2).

The play begins with Sipho and Thando nervously awaiting the arrival of Mandisa Mackay, Sipho's English-born niece who is visiting them to help facilitate the burial of her father (Sipho's brother), Themba Makhaya. She has never met her estranged family. The situation is set for the sharing of family history and contested truths.

Cleverly foregrounding the TRC, the play revolves around the reveal of hidden stories of a family affected by the political struggle responsible for Themba's exile. Mandisa's arrival as an outsider acts as a catalyst for father and daughter, uncle and niece, cousin and cousin, to share their stories of deceit, animosity and betrayal. The audience witnesses the family coming clean on what had been secreted between them and, in turn, the play manages to mirror broader public debates that were common at the turn of the century.

Annie Coombes points out that the TRC only ever 'staged' individuals in one of three ways: as victim, perpetrator or hero.[4] The post-apartheid narrative continues this legacy.

Kani's *Nothing But the Truth* makes a strong argument that the real champions of the struggle were not the celebrated freedom fighters who dominate South Africa's seats in parliament but rather those 'faceless South Africans' who took part in the struggle.[5]

> **Sipho** … I was part of the Struggle. I too suffered as a black
> person. I went to the marches like everyone else. I might not have
> been detained. I might not have been to Robben Island. I did not
> leave this country, but I suffered too. The thousands that were tear
> gassed, sjamboked[6] by the police, mauled by Alsatian dogs, that was
> me. When Bishop Tutu led thousands through the streets of white
> Port Elizabeth, that was me. I WAS THOSE THOUSANDS! (51–2)

Documenting social and political history through theatre was a dominant project of the protest genre during apartheid. The inclusion of factual information – the names of real people, the mention of real events, places, historical moments, etc. – was a common practice. In *Nothing But the Truth*, Kani weaves a layer of historic events into the action. This makes the play specific to a locale, a time and a place.

Sarah Roberts, the designer of the original production, shares:

> I think it is directly lived in experience because it is John's memories
> of a very particular community and a very particular way of living.
> It is that Fugard sense of being a very intensely regional writer who
> knows the world being written about; in the best tradition of an Ibsen
> or a Chekov. It is so closely observed and understood that the texture
> of that life is intensely credible.[7]

Thando supports the process being followed by the TRC, recognizing the personal truths being given in testimony as due process to the granting of full amnesty. She supports this process for the sake of peace, stability and reconciliation. Mandisa counters Thando's position, reinforcing a 'guilty, must be punished' standpoint: a judicial process like the Nuremberg trials. Earlier in the play Sipho has shared his position on the TRC.

> **Sipho**   How was your day?

> **Thando**   Oh! The same grind. Former soldiers, policeman and
> security people applying for amnesty. Saying they are sorry.

Sometimes I sit there translating, interpreting, and not even feeling. It's easy to get numb you know.

Sipho That's why I do not go anymore. It's pointless.

Thando The truth does come out, and at least the families get to know what happened.

Sipho Their version of what happened.

Thando Don't start! Don't start! I know how you feel about that. (6)

Kani gives the audience three quite different perspectives on the TRC and its process. What Kani managed to skilfully do with *Nothing But the Truth* is guide the audience to understanding how personal aspirations inform political practice – aspirations new to a country experiencing democracy for the first time. The play raised the same questions that Rustom Bharucha identifies, 'How does one justify the valorization of one truth at the expense of ignoring another? And conversely, how can one not critique a particular truth if it offends one's moral sense?'[8]

Mandisa is British. Her position comes from an understanding of living in a stable society, a democracy that has been in place for over 800 years. Thando yearns for this type of social structure but concedes that revengeful justice would not be constructive in building a young democracy.

Kani effectively charts three dialogical points-of-view informed by South Africa's political history and his own lived experience. Through the carefully selected inclusion of well-known political events, he further guides the reader to an enlightenment on the importance of the TRC, not only for a country that was on the brighter side of change, but also for every home that is grappling with questions of forgiveness.

Emerging playwrights

During the period of transition from an apartheid State to a democratic one, an eight-year period from around 1990 to 1998, there was an absence of what could be considered, in a Western sense, skilled new playwrights.[9] There was, however, a desperate need to stage work that would speak to the 'new South Africa' in a way that could help articulate the contemporary situation. But where would these plays come from?

There had not historically been a need to train or nurture new playwrights in the country, partly because under apartheid the dominant mode of play making had been workshopping and devising, but also because there has been, and still is, a political tension between playwrighting and collective modes of authorship. Where many, including myself, argue that playwrighting is a growing and necessary practice, other academics and practitioners like Mark Fleishman resist this, arguing that what is needed is accomplished theatre-makers who serve as dramaturges in the broadest sense and who, like Barney Simon, facilitate the creation of collective playmaking.[10]

This is perhaps not the place for this debate. It is also unfair to reduce Fleishman's position to a single reductive statement, but it is nonetheless important to acknowledge that the training of playwrights is contested as the best way to address the complexity of a country with eleven official languages and a history of oppression. Words possess a powerful ability to alienate, segregate and destabilize, and I am not talking here of words as a desirable dramatic device or in a Brechtian alienation sense. The politics of language in South Africa makes the process from page to stage an intricate and frequently limiting one, especially if you are working across mother tongues.

In short, post-apartheid plays of quality by new voices were few and far between for at least a decade into the democracy. It was a time where theatres were eager to get new work on stage but where there was limited to no formal structure that allowed for the nurturing of new work. A lot of good ideas ended up becoming fully produced plays long before the work was ready. So the roughness of the drama, often half-baked, meant that audiences left unsatisfied. Plays by new playwrights and theatre-makers that were lucky enough to receive first seasons in mainstream venues rarely led to subsequent performances, and almost never travelled. The ideas were good, but the plays were not. The audiences interested in watching new plays dwindled. Theatres interested in staging indigenous new work were in crisis.

***

From around 2001 the six State-subsidized theatres[11] and the Baxter Theatre in Cape Town responded to the absence of new voices by adding playwriting programmes or new work programmes to their offering. In varying levels of success these have helped produce a quickly growing group of emerging playwrights.

In addition, international arts-related foundations, councils and organizations have supported play development programmes. The NLDTF/PANSA Festival of Contemporary Theatre Readings was a national playwriting competition that gave new work and new writers a platform. Mike van Graan's *Green Man Flashing* (see Meersman) and Nicholas Spagnoletti's multi-award-winning *London Road* are two examples of plays that emerged through this competition.

At the Market Theatre the Dutch-based DOEN Foundation supported the DOEN Emerging Writers project, a script development programme that focused on six scripts per year, coupling respected theatre directors with young playwrights. The British Council has partnered on two similar projects, one with the Wits Theatre and the Department of Arts and Culture (DAC), and the other with the Royal Court in London.

The Royal Court in London spent a year (2013 to 2014) guiding twelve young playwrights in the development of their playwriting projects. Six of the writers – Napo Masheane, Neil Coppen (see below), Omphile Molusi (see Baxter), Mongiwekaya Mthombeni, Amy Jephta and Simo Majola – received staged readings in London under the banner of New Plays from South Africa: after twenty years of democracy, directors including Phyllida Lloyd, Vicky Featherstone and Ola Animashawun directed casts with some very established British actors. Subsequently the same plays have been showcased in abridged readings in Johannesburg. Similarly the Chicago Shakespeare Theatre, under the direction of Richard Gordon, identified Omphile Molusi as a talent worth investing in. This led to his highly successful play *Itsoseng* (see Baxter) which won the Scotsman Fringe First Award in Edinburgh in 2008.

In addition, where playwriting courses hadn't previously been part of university degree programmes, there are now playwriting modules and degrees offered at Rhodes University, Wits University, University of KwaZulu-Natal and at an MA level at the University of Cape Town. These major universities have graduated playwrights and theatre-makers like Juliet Jenkin (see below), Tara Notcutt, Khayelihle Dom Gumede, Pusetso Thibedi and Genna Gardini, all of whom have made a mark with their dynamic plays that reflect South Africa today.

The terrain for training, nurturing and supporting new work has undoubtedly increased but spaces to test, grow or nurture new indigenous plays at low risk and low cost are limited. Independent fringe spaces, like

POPArt in Johannesburg and Alexander Bar in Cape Town, fulfil a vital role in showcasing new work of diverse appeal, but the platform that undoubtedly offers emerging playwrights and theatre-makers the best opportunity to showcase their new plays are the multiple arts festivals that take place annually in the country.

Tara Notcutt, Albert Pretorius and Gideon Lombard graduated together from the University of Cape Town. Their workshopped play ...*Miskien* has had an extraordinary life at festivals locally and internationally, culminating in a season at the Baxter Theatre. Over a five-year period the play has toured to New York, Perth and Amsterdam fringe festivals and almost every arts festival in South Africa, raking up awards.

At festivals, passionate young artists defeat the financial limitations of producing mainstream theatre and surpass the gatekeeping that has become common in mainstream venues. Helen Iskander, Rob van Vuuren, Daniel Buckland, Tara Notcutt, James Cairns have all used these festivals as opportunities to launch their new work, with the more appealing of their plays having gone on to play in mainstream venues.

Juliet Jenkin

Juliet Jenkin was born in Johannesburg. She grew up in the Midlands in KwaZulu-Natal and studied at the University of Cape Town where she graduated with a BA in Theatre and Performance. Her debut play, *The Boy Who Fell from the Roof*, was one of four plays staged in 2005 as part of the first Artscape Spring Drama Season, a new plays programme aligned to Artscape in Cape Town.

The Boy Who Fell from the Roof has toured to the National Arts Festival, the Witness Hilton Arts Festival, the Klein Karoo Nasionale Kunstefess, and the International Dublin Gay Theatre Festival in Ireland. Jenkin's other plays include *Library*, *The Night Doctor* and *Mary and the Conqueror*, all of which premiered as part of the Artscape New Writing Programme where she worked as an editor and administrator, and a trilogy that includes *More South African Deep Freezing* (co-written with Frances Marek), *Poisson* and *Big Girl*.

The Boy Who Fell from the Roof *(2005)*

In Anton Krueger's doctoral study he investigates the representation of identity as evidenced in contemporary South African drama. He writes of how post-apartheid drama seeks to redefine the staunch categories of race and gender that apartheid rigidly enforced. He inspects a theatre that relinquishes identities instead of consolidating them.[12] He frames his study by saying:

> I would like to keep under consideration the question of what it means to have a fixed, and firmly grounded sense of identity (which might provide one with a sense of rootedness and belonging) and to contrast this with a more flexible identity (which might allow one to be more open to change, but which runs the risk of becoming inchoate).[13]

It is this idea of identity as malleable, rhizomatic and in flux that underpins the thematic concern of *The Boy Who Fell from the Roof*, a play that stands as one example of many post-apartheid plays by young writers where characters consistently question and challenge firm or boxed ideas of personal identity.

In *The Boy Who Fell from the Roof*, Simon Thomas Lyndsay, an 18-year-old boy, falls from the roof of his house while trying to fetch a tennis ball. His best friend, Georgina Marais, an 18-year-old girl, witnesses the event. Over the course of 20 short scenes, Jenkin constructs a character study of Simon leading up to and immediately preceding his fatal fall. The play investigates the relationship Simon has with three key figures in his life – his mother, best friend and a 25-year-old gay man and love interest called Leonard.

Jenkin quickly sets up a relationship between naming and identity. In scene two, Simon challenges his mother over what he says is a combination of names given to him (Simon Thomas Lyndsay) that he believes sound 'slimy'. While the scene progresses, the Chorus, which can be played by a single male or female, drops in interjections. The Chorus both comments on the action and questions the path that the story takes. There are moments of metatextual writing that keep the playwright's voice present. This combination of what Jenkin calls 'choral, dialogue and monologue performance' (5) creates a mischievous storytelling tone that is charming and humorous.

Simon is called 'Sime', 'Son', 'Friend' and 'Lover'. Similarly his mother is called 'Patricia', 'Mother', 'Patricia Mary Lyndsay', 'Patricia Mary Barton', 'Pat', 'Pattie' and 'Mrs Lyndsay'. In scene 15 George and the Chorus explain how Simon's mum calls George a long string of pet names. Naming becomes a game for Jenkin, underpinning the action as a motif, reinforcing the core theme and challenging notions of how we label each other or box our identity as one thing. This systematically builds an argument against the labelling of someone as, for example, 'gay'.

In Simon's monologues he further challenges common labels. He questions the experiences that a teenager who is trying to come to terms with his sexuality might have. Simon and George debate gender politics and stereotypes. George asks Simon in scene 18, 'What is it about boys that makes them boys?' (62).

In scene nine, George is offended that Simon speaks to Leonard, a man he meets in a convenience store, about being gay, something he has never spoken about with her. George says, 'So you refuse to speak to kids at school unless they've read *War and Peace*, but some dude moseys into the Seven Eleven and you're best friends. Cool' (25). In selecting Leonard to talk to about his sexuality rather than George or Georgina or 'Gina or Georgie', as Simon prefers to call her in this scene, she makes the point that Simon has used the same gender-based stereotyping that he judges others for using. Ironically, when Leonard meets George a little later in the play he reveals that he thought George was a boy from the way that Simon talks about her.

The apartheid conditioning that South Africans carry is apparent even in a young generation, despite them having never lived under apartheid laws.

Simon holds his ground with both George and Leonard about not admitting to being gay, or rather, not being willing to be boxed. He also holds a firm position on the diatribe of apartheid categorizing that has conditioned the world he finds himself in.

> **Simon** I can't listen to these fucking diatribes on cultural identity and race and creed and whatever.

> **George** Creed isn't even a word. Why do you say creed as if you know what it means?

> **Simon** I do. It's like in that Wordsworth poem 'by God I'd rather be something something in a worn out creed' so these national identity things everyone's always going on about, I mean, you can't go to a film or a play without –

> **George** You don't watch plays.

> **Simon** If I did I know what I'd say, I mean that's why I don't watch them, 'cause I already know what they're going to say. Y'know race

and acceptance, and the black people oppressed, the black people
struggling with their place in the country, but mostly these plays
are, I mean they're about white people struggling with black people
struggling with black identity, and the white people sit there in the
audience –

George   At plays you've never seen.

Simon   I have seen some plays, Jesus man, I saw *Hamlet* once and
the king, the dead king was black, shut up. So it's all these white
people just getting weepy about how bad they are or were or how
complacent or whatever – and sure it's relevant but relevant things
get boring hey? Fucking sins of the fathers … I mean I'm bored.
(13–14)

Here we hear a common resistance by young South Africans to reject a
history that they are tired of hearing about, a history that informs who
they are as a generation but which they are collectively trying to move
beyond.

Racial politics is brought more prominently into focus by Jenkin when
Leonard enters the story. Soon after we meet him, the Chorus offers this set
of questions:

Chorus   What does our Leonard do? He is at university. He is
involved in some sort of manual labour. He is a mechanic? No.
He studies mechanics? What are the repercussions of him being
working class, and the rest being middle class, and those middle-
class people being white? They are all middle class. Still, the
man is coloured. Does he have to be? I am unsure. Is it relevant?
Contextually, yes; thematically, I am unsure. Token. Token. Token.
Okay, one day these two meet. And this is how it happened. (22)

Leonard we learn is in fact tutoring at the university and is busy completing
a Masters degree in mathematics. He is far from the stereotypical Coloured
identity associated with the Cape Flats.[14]

Leonard   Christ Simon, what? You think all coloured people are
drinking meths on street corners or shooting each other on the flats,
shrieking Jou Ma se Poes[15] whenever they can? (48)

At one point he comments that '[n]umbers are apolitical' (48), a tongue in cheek aside to announce the racialized questions raised by the Chorus.

The success of this play is in the way it deals with some rather weighty issues but with a lightness of touch. Jenkin both embraces the theme of identity, but in doing so she resists a world that is obsessed with the theme. Simon says, 'I wish people would shut up about fucking identities and go and identify polar bears in Cambodia' (15).

There is a playfulness in Jenkin's writing. She casually drops in some very erudite references – Byron, Wordsworth, *Winnie the Pooh*, *War and Peace*, *Peter Pan*, Dylan Thomas, *Hamlet*, *Romeo and Juliet*, *Titus Andronicus*, Dorothy Parker and Oscar Wilde all get cited but without the text becoming imposing. In addition, projections of iconic Western artworks act as ironic and counter juxtapositions at the top of each scene.

The world of the play is youthful with a 'throw-away' quality that superbly offsets the tragic event that frames the action.

After Simon's death, Patricia debates whether to share with people that she knew her son was gay, although he had never openly acknowledged that to her. She questions the relevance of this bit of information, unsure whether it is in fact relevant at all.

Neil Coppen

Neil Coppen won the Standard Bank Young Artist Award for Theatre in 2011. With the commission that comes with that award he wrote, co-directed (with Janna Ramos-Violante) and designed his most acclaimed play, *Abnormal Loads*. His other plays include *Suicidal Pigeons*, *Two …*, *The Beginning of the End* (co-written and performed with Clare Mortimer), *Tin Bucket Drum*, *Tree Boy* and a South African adaptation of George Orwell's *Animal Farm*.

Coppen lives in Durban but works nationally with visual artists, sound designers and choreographers crafting work that typically fuses multi-media and powerful audio and visual overlays into the creation of almost cinematic-styled productions. A recurring thematic interest in his plays is the relationship the characters have to history and memory, a contemporary theme that is evident in many young artists' work.

Abnormal Loads (2011)

The fictional setting for Neil Coppen's play is the small coal-mining town of Bashford, a place where Anglo-Zulu, Anglo-Boer and Boer wars were once fought. This is a place reminiscent of the South African towns of Dundee and Ladysmith. Coppen has remarked, 'such politically loaded terrains, where various histories and cultures have collided over centuries, are fertile grounds for new South African stories'.[16]

The action in *Abnormal Loads* spans from 1860 to 2011 – 150 years of history. Four parallel and complementary narratives are intertwined revealing the politics of three families: the Bashford family who are of English descent, the Joubert family who are Afrikaans[17] and the Ngobese family who are of Zulu ancestry. In Bashford, one character comments, 'history is the currency of conversation' (33).

Vincent, the protagonist, is 29. We first discover him trying to learn Zulu by listening to an instruction CD. He is the son of a mixed-race couple. His parents, Sizwe Gumede (Zulu) and Linda Bashford (English ancestry), were political activists during apartheid. Vincent believes that his mother and father died in a car accident while they were on the run from the Apartheid Security Police. He was a baby at the time and was too young to remember so he has, till now, accepted his grandmother's version of the story. She is the woman that has raised him.

This narrative thread is loaded with the information that Vincent has been suffering from headaches. Prudence, the maid who works in the house, questions Vincent about them. She thinks he might be repressing an ancestral calling that is making him sick.[18] He however is convinced that they are symptoms of him being HIV positive, which he is not – he admittedly hasn't had sex in the past five years. The combination of the headaches, strange nightmares of an unrecognizable figure crying out to speak to Moira and Vincent's desire to learn Zulu set up his repressed need to discover the truth about his past.

The second narrative line focuses on his grandmother, Moira Bashford Liversage, who is planning the 120th anniversary of the town. She is heading up the Bashford Tourism Board's committee that consists of representatives of the three community groups living in the area – Zulu, English and Afrikaans. The town is planning to present reenactments of their shared history. Moira firmly recommends that they choose to honour the events that led to the naming of the town by focusing on the story of the town's founding father, William Bashford, her bloodline.

Johan, the NG Kerk *dominee,* raises the issue of disputed versions of the past.[19]

> **Johan**   What I mean to say, is that we from the Afrikaner
> Re-enactment Society are in full support of the re-enactments
> this committee organizes. It is our opinion, that for too long the
> Zulu and redcoat [English] scraps have been favoured over Boer
> [Afrikaans] ones. I applaud you for choosing this particular incident.
> I only want to make sure that if we are to make history live, Mrs
> Liversage, we are in agreement on whose version of the story we are
> telling. (25)

Moira accepts Johan's position and goes one step further. She recommends that each participant in the reenactment must be related to the person they are portraying. Not thinking that this is unreasonable, Johan proudly offers up his son to play his great-great-grandfather. Moira however has a plan, and matches Johan's proposal by stating that her grandson, Vincent, will play the English hero. Johan is shocked. How can a man of mixed-race parents stand in as the representation of an English hero? Johan claims that Vincent playing the role would be 'historically inaccurate' (26).

Coppen contrasts the three families, revealing patterns of racial tension and injustice from the past and the present. He constructs an argument within the play that history of 150 years ago does not look that different to today.

The planned reenactments by Moira and her committee are one kind of reenactment but there are others within the play. Katrien, Johan's 16-year-old rebellious daughter, for example is involved in planning how she will mirror the newspaper report of two Bonnie-and-Clyde-type killers that are on the run when she plans to run away from the town that she feels trapped in. She pulls Vincent into this as they begin a flirtatious new relationship.

Vincent and Katrien find themselves in a relationship that parallels their great-great-great-grandparents' love story – another kind of reenactment of the past. Where their love story makes up the third narrative thread, the slow reveal of the story of their ancestors makes up the fourth, all intertwining in a play that is epic in its structure.

On a micro level, Coppen also announces cycles of history that repeat themselves within the South African context. One understated but powerful example is how Prudence's situation is crafted.

When the play begins we see Prudence's mother, Gerty, the Bashford's elderly longtime maid, clasp her chest and collapse to the floor. She is dead. Prudence takes over the lifelong duties that her mother performed – a commentary by Coppen on the kind of oppressive South African legacy of maids who pass their duties on to their daughters in some unjust succession plan, a pattern that limits the possibility of breaking the history of oppression, or at least breaking it anytime soon.

Abnormal Loads is an unusually ambitious play within the context of South African theatre. The story is told through twenty-nine scenes in a filmic structure that incorporates voiceover, multiple locations and digital elements that work as visual layers and scene establishment devices. It requires a cast of 11 actors playing over twenty characters. Different modes of delivery are integrated, like when Vincent speaks in direct address to the audience, alternating between his recorded voice and monologues delivered live.

The set is somewhat abstracted to allow for the multiple locations to be conveniently established, but the scenic requirements are by no means minimal. There is a large raked wooden structure that cuts across half of the playing area, three spaces zoned as different bedroom areas, a bar area including a Victorian piano, and multiple other furniture pieces that are moved on and off the stage by what Coppen describes as 'generations of Ngobese women in maids' outfits' (12).

A back projector lends an epic scale to the piece with 'operatic cloud formations, stars, a moon, battle silhouettes, etc.' being projected onto a cyclorama cloth (12). A second projector casts a water effect under moonlight onto a 'mottled sepia floor cloth' that 'marks the playing space' (ibid.).

In South Africa it is almost unheard of for a drama to be staged at this scale. In economic terms it simply is not viable.

What Coppen manages to do in *Abnormal Loads* is capture a sense of what it is like to be a young South African challenged daily to grapple with the past – an abnormal load that they must carry but from which they feel a deep disconnect. It is through the collection and layering of past and present images and narratives that Coppen is able to illuminate his argument that the history Vincent owns is not his. If he is to take agency in his life then he must set out on his own path, both physically and metaphorically. This empowering message resonates strongly with young South Africans and as a result the play is now a set-work at a number of high schools in the country.

Summary

Although the rigid legislative categorizing experienced under apartheid has ended, identity politics remains at the heart of contemporary South African drama. Emerging playwrights are redressing the definitions of race and gender that they inherited by exploring issues of identity, history and memory. This is particularly evident in drama produced in the second decade of South Africa's democracy.

Remaining though is the struggle to move beyond a history of pain, struggle and hurt. As the memory of apartheid wanes, young South Africans reject apartheid history and the political concerns that continue to dominate post-apartheid South African drama. As more and more emerging theatre-makers and playwrights find their space and their voice, social concerns centred on interpersonal relationship are likely to become the theatre of Democratic South Africa, and it just might become conceivable to think of a play that supersedes these issues of oppression.

Notes

1. 'Coloured' is a commonly used and accepted racial classification in South Africa that does not carry negative connotations.
2. Durban Westville (1995), Rhodes University (1998), University of Cape Town (2006) and Nelson Mandela Metropolitan University (2013).
3. The Order of Ikhamanga is the highest recognition in South African arts and culture. It is awarded to citizens who have excelled in the fields of arts, culture, literature, music, journalism or sport.
4. A. Coombes, *History after Apartheid: Visual Culture and Public Memory in a Democratic South Africa* (Johannesburg: Wits University Press, 2004), 244.
5. J. Kani in *Sunday Times*, 28 September 2003.
6. A plastic pipe often used by police during apartheid to whip protestors.
7. Personal comment, 11 September, 2006.
8. E. Bharucha, 'Between Truth and Reconciliation', in Okwui Enwezor et al. (eds), *Experiments with Truth: Transitional Justice and the Process of Truth and Reconciliation* (Ostfildern, Germany: Hatje Cantz Publishers, 2002), 366.
9. This period is marked by the announcement made on 2 February that banned political parties would be unconditionally unbanned and that Nelson Mandela would be released up until the delivery of the Truth and Reconciliation Report on 29 October 1998.

10. Barney Simon died in 1995. He had played a key role from as early as 1960 as a kind of dramaturge to actors, poets and sometimes non-theatre-related individuals who he felt showed some capacity to write new work. Starting in a rehearsal room on the third floor of a ramshackle warehouse called Dorkay House, and later as the legendary artistic director of the Market Theatre, he facilitated and contributed to an immeasurable number of new South African plays. (See L. Henriques and I. Stephanou (eds), *The World in an Orange: Creating Theatre with Barney Simon* (Johannesburg: Jacana, 2005), for more on Barney Simon.)

11. The six government-subsidized theatres in the country are Artscape in Cape Town; the Market Theatre, the South African State Theatre and the Windybrow in Gauteng; the Playhouse in KwaZulu-Natal; and PACOFS in the Orange Free State. The legislative framework that governs these is largely defined by the Cultural Institutions Act of 1998 (Act No. 119 of 1998).

12. A. Krueger, *Experiments in Freedom: Explorations of Identity in New South African Drama* (Newcastle-upon-Tyne: Cambridge Scholars Publishing, 2010), 6.

13. Ibid.

14. A historically Coloured township in Cape Town.

15. Afrikaans for 'your mother's puss'.

16. Interview with the author as cited in N. Coppen, *Abnormal Loads* (Cape Town: Junkets Publisher, 2012), 101.

17. Their heritage is traced to the Dutch-speaking colonists who left the Cape Colony under British rule and between 1835 and 1846 trekked north from what is now known as Cape Town in pursuit of a homeland that was independent of British rule. This mass exodus of remarkable resilience and determination is today called the Great Trek.

18. The idea of an ancestral calling is common in indigenous South African culture, and Zulu culture in particular. It is believed that resisting the call to accept the honour of being called to become a traditional healer or *iSangoma* within your community can make you very ill.

19. A *dominee* is Afrikaans for church minister. The *Nederduitse Gereformeerde Kerk* (NG Kerk) is the Dutch Reformed Church in South Africa, a reformed Christian denomination that is historically aligned with conservative values and collectively a staunch supporter of apartheid.

Bibliography

Primary sources

Coppen, N., *Abnormal Loads* (Cape Town: Junkets Publisher, 2012).
Jenkin, J., *The Boy Who Fell from the Roof* (Cape Town: Junkets Publisher, 2004).
Kani, J., *Nothing But the Truth* (Johannesburg: Wits University Press, 2002).

Secondary sources

Accone, D., 'The Trouble with Freedom', *Cue*, 5 July 2002.

Bharucha, E., 'Between Truth and Reconciliation', in Okwui Enwezor et al. (eds), *Experiments with Truth: Transitional Justice and the Process of Truth and Reconciliation* (Ostfildern, Germany: Hatje Cantz Publishers, 2002), 3763–73.

Coombes, A., *History after Apartheid: Visual Culture and Public Memory in a Democratic South Africa* (Johannesburg: Wits University Press, 2004).

Fleishman, M., 'A Genealogy of Playwrighting in South Africa', Keynote address to the GIPCA symposium – Directors and Directing: Playwrights, August 2012, Cape Town.

Henriques, L. and I. Stephanou (eds), *The World in an Orange: Creating Theatre with Barney Simon* (Johannesburg: Jacana, 2005).

Homann, G., 'Landscape and Body', *South African Theatre Journal* 23:1 (2009): 149–76.

Krueger, A., *Experiments in Freedom: Explorations of Identity in New South African Drama* (Newcastle-upon-Tyne: Cambridge Scholars Publishing, 2010).

CHAPTER 20
AUBREY SEKHABI
An interview with Greg Homann (2 February 2015)

GH: I am interested to talk to you both as a significant playwright, as a director working in South Africa today, and in your position as the artistic director of the South African State Theatre. Let us start with the State Theatre. How long have you been in an artistic director position?

AS: I have been an artistic director for 20 years now. First for eight years as the Head of the Drama Company for the North West Arts Council and then, for the past 13 years, I have been in the position of artistic director for the State Theatre.

GH: So let's start with a big and quite broad question. What do you feel is the state of our theatre in South Africa at the moment?

AS: I think that there are two ways to look at, on the one hand, I think that we have a lot of artists that are making work and I think that theatre has in so many ways transformed and is continuing to do that. I also think we really need to go back and look into our funding models. I think that our funding models are making it hard for professional theatre to flourish. If you look for example at the State Theatre, we have five theatres there. We've got about R7 million to do our programmes. You know it takes about R500,000 to do one proper drama with four actors. We are fortunate in a sense that government still gives us money. You look at what has recently happened at the Market Theatre where there is no programming, but the artistic director tells you that there is money in the bank. But that money in the bank has to go to capital projects (capex) and refurbishment etc. So we really need to look at how we are funding theatre. But in terms of artists, I think they are out there, they are alive and vibrant.

GH: So am I right in saying that, because there are six theatres in the country that are governed by the Cultural Institutions Act[1] that they receive state funding but that state funding is only allocated to the running of the buildings, the upkeep of the buildings and to salaries? None or very little of that can be aligned directly to productions. Is that correct?

AS: You are right. You know when I was appointed as artistic director of the State Theatre, in the first board meeting, the first question that I asked – I was like thirty-three years old and coming into the State Theatre – this massive beast, right – I said, 'Why have you employed an artistic director if he has got no budgets? Because if you are just thinking of renting the space out, get a caretaker. To bring somebody like me here – you need a budget.' When I got there at that point, it was built on this whole notion of the White Paper[2] – the receiving house. People interpreted it the way they wanted to, but I say, I always say that, there is nowhere in the White Paper that says you cannot produce. Because if you are an institution and become a receiving house, you lose your identity in a sense because it is a free for all. Of course, the aim was to be a receiving house and close down repertoire companies so that there can be broader access. We get to the point where, yes, there is access but then your theatre starts to lack identity and then you don't need an artistic director as a result. So the State Theatre, by appointing an artistic director in essence is saying we want you to curate. From that moment on, I started fighting for budgets for what we now get from the Department of Arts and Culture.

GH: So, on exactly that topic then, if you had to imagine what it was like some thirty years ago, when the state-funded Performing Arts Councils were in operation and where directors, actors and other performers and theatre artists, ballet dancers, opera singers and orchestras were receiving full-time employment. How do you feel the current model works – does it work better? Obviously there were significant flaws around the Performing Arts Councils that had been skewed towards an apartheid politics and so on but in that relationship, there was a lot more money aligned to productions. Now it is aligned to keeping the buildings purely operational – as you have said there is 10 per cent or 15 per cent available of the state funding that ends up in productions. I mean, is there an argument to try and split the difference and return to something that is closer to the arts councils of thirty years ago?

AS: Not quite. I do not think that it is a matter of returning to the arts councils of thirty years ago. I mean they did have their successes. You had an employed group of actors. I worked in that system because I had a drama company with a group of actors and we were just making work all the time but you had the same guys making work all the time. However, the new system is all about access. I think what needs to change in the new system is the funding model and also when dealing with the NAC, they will tell you that they are not going to fund the State Theatre right? 'We are not going to fund the State Theatre', and I do not know where that comes from. I think that there has to be a direct link between the National Arts Council with the institutions. I think that there has to be a direct link between the lottery and the institutions. The institutions are where you have your expertise. We know where the skills are and if we have money, we can source out all the best directors and all the good artists to make sure that we give them the support to make the work that they want to do. I think, for me, it is re-evaluating the funding model and saying, 'hang on, the institutions must produce, they must curate but then there must also be access and things can work both ways'. For me, even now we'll say, if you come to the State Theatre and you have a play, even if it is somebody new, and he wants space, I will give you space – there is no way that we are going to turn you away as we have five theatres – we have space galore there. But the moment we give you space, you start to ask, can the State Theatre market it? I know now that so many artists that I have seen applying are good. We know the guys that need youth development and we will help them to develop. We will grow them to the level of the Malcolm Purkeys, of the Greg Homanns, of the Mpho Molepos, so the work is at the level of those people that are profes-sional. You must accept that these guys are professional and you have to treat them in a professional sense. Guys have studied, other guys have just been directing for all their lives and then you are going to treat them the same as the guy who is a beginner. No, I think that is not right.

GH: Let's move away from the funding question but stay on a related topic – you are talking a lot about directors and directors engaging with the spaces and how to make that possible and so on. How much do you feel that our new work in the country is being driven by directors trying to make work, because if I think about other places in the world, theatre is seen as a playwright's medium. Often when we talk about plays we talk about the playwright rather than the directors who initiate it, but in the conversation we are having now, it is the directors who sound like they are in some ways driving it?

AS: The makers? I think that South African theatre is driven by the directors. You have certain collaborations such as Craig Higginson who will write a play and Malcolm Purkey will direct. Who else? If you want your play on stage, you better write it and direct it if you are here at home.

GH: Lara Foot is a playwright and director. Yael Farber is a playwright and director. Mike van Graan – playwright.

AS: Yes. It is very few guys.

GH: There is Zakes Mda, Mike van Graan, there are a handful who are solely playwrights.

AS: Yes. In South Africa, it is unfortunate that theatre has become a director's medium. It is more about play making and I think it stems from protest theatre, from workshop theatre, because in the past it has just been about getting into the room and making the play. Today, 'I am no longer going to be a playwright', because if you are a playwright you must get a grant or something and a commission to then spend the next three months or next year waiting on this play making. Here at home, we do not have that, we are never going to get that. You must create relationships. Say, for example, I have worked with Paul Grootboom, if Paul could write a play and I could probably direct it or if I could write a play and then Paul could direct it. But then I have never actually had any writer come to me and say, 'can you direct my play?' We find ourselves in a situation whereby you have to write it, direct it, raise funds and produce it. That is why if you look at what we are doing now, we are employing dramaturges like you and I am sure you will be taking about three artists this year, because we are saying that we want playwrights and directors.

GH: So to be clear, at the moment you are working to enable new writing and new work. You are identifying a handful of projects that people have approached you with and you are trying to couple those with expertise and experience to develop …

AS: To develop and write the work and from then on when the work is there and it has been developed we are able to say, 'OK, who is the director that can direct this work?' Some people who have written the works are not directors. However, because of the nature of things here at home, they think that they will direct their own work.

GH: To an international reader and someone who is interested in theatre and knows theatre, this would not sound like any ground breaking intervention but, in actual fact, it has not been happening or very little. There has been very little institutionalized systems that allow for the real development of plays over an extended period.

AS: Yes.

GH: Why do you think that that model has not existed earlier?

AS: I think because of the whole confusion and misinterpretation of the White Paper. The moment we became a receiving house, that is when people forgot. Therefore we have been sneaking in and saying that we have to curate and you can see that the Market Theatre has its own programmes and the State Theatre is curating and I can see that the Playhouse is starting to do work and bring in work and so it has been creeping in. Now you realize that being a receiving house alone is not enough because you just wait, you have to really develop new work and you have to lead I think. You have to develop confidence and say, for example, like the State Theatre said, 'We want to be the home of South African Theatre, we want new work, we want exciting ideas. Now where are we going to get it?' If you send out a call-out, you will get hundreds of people submitting but then the works are not ready because people are doing it during their leisure time. Now we want to focus it and say, 'You are going to come in here and we are going to give you a little bit of money and you will be assigned to someone who is a professional who does this thing, and you will be referring to that person – going back and forth writing this thing and then from then on we are going to do readings.' Like how theatre is being done worldwide and like you say, it is not ground breaking internationally, but here at home we have not really ever been doing it like that. It has been cheaper to buy.

GH: And as you have said, because we come from a workshop/devising background we have taken a very long time to find a need for playwrights or for hooking teams together that will make our new work.

AS: Yes.

GH: Let's talk briefly about your perception of theatres that are not State-funded in any way, so the independent theatres and I suppose the independent theatre makers. I feel like there is a shift at the moment, certainly in Johannesburg, around certain independent spaces that are emerging, that are encouraging, particularly, new creative teams and new writers to stage their work in a way that is low risk but still gets some exposure. I think that in Cape Town this has been happening for a little longer. Any thoughts on the theatres and the spaces that are making new work beyond the state-funded ones?

AS: I am really excited by those spaces, like Plat4orm. I can tell you at Wits in my youth, I was performing almost every weekend and between 1984 and 1988 almost every Sunday. I was on stage, right, because there were community groups. When you walk down the streets in my township, Soshanguve, you will hear the bongo drums in a garage, you can go to a particular church and there is a concert, you go to the community hall and there is a concert organized by particular community groups and they invite other community groups from all over Pretoria. People who have been making theatre, and by the time things changed, suddenly we knew that there was this NAC, we all stopped ... 'hey I am not making work until I am getting money from NAC'. And I have seen us go through that. Artists then realized that, 'hang on, if I am to wait for the cycle of funding I am never going to make a play'. So now artists are going back to the drawing board. They are going back to their garages and making work.

GH: It feels like it is a young thing ...

AS: Yes, it is a young crop of people. I think that it is perfect because we can go to where they are and hunt and say, 'Wow, there is this new writer. We need to bring them on board and develop them.' Directors must direct and writers must write. You can't call yourself a writer when you write and then are not writing for the next five years. You must do it and do it again. It gets better. I see it with my work, there are times whereby I have not directed for a long time, when I do my first project after that, it is like ... but then I find if I am doing this one and that one by the time I am doing the third project, it is like ... I have figured everything out. Therefore writers need to be sitting there creating work, directors need to be directing over and over again. You need to look at some of the young people that we have, I look at people like Kea Moeketsane, Kgaogelo Tshabalala and Princess Zinzi Mhlunga. These are young people we have worked with. From their first play that they have been doing, I always said, 'guys, you must just direct, you cannot wait for the State Theatre, you cannot wait for the State Theatre to have a project, go initiate the project'. Come to the State Theatre with a project and then we will help you where we can. As they are doing more work – they were doing

Greek adaptations last year, exile and forgiveness – they are getting much better but that is because they are getting in there and getting their hands dirty. They were not just sitting there. So I think it is a good thing that we have all these independent spaces but what I also think needs to happen is that the established professionals should also utilize these spaces, you know, because then you also give them value. You need Paul Grootboom or Malcolm Purkey to do a play and try those venues. Because if we do not support those venues they will also die.

GH: What I like about your programme for this year which I have glanced at, is exactly that, there is a mix of really established names. I see that there is Lara Foot's new play that she did last year, *Fishers of Hope*. There's a brand new play from Craig Higginson called *The Imagined Land*. There's the new play that I am co-writing and directing based on Alan Paton's life called *A Voice I Cannot Silence*. But amongst these, there is also some international work like David Harrower's *Blackbird*, which had quite a life in the UK, and then there is also young artists and young makers who are mixed in with these very established international and local theatre makers, playwrights and directors.

AS: Yes, the first play that we are going to be doing is by Bongani Bennedict Masango with *Road to Damascus*. *Road to Damascus* emerged as a result of In The Spotlight. In The Spotlight is another hunting ground. At the same time there is John Kani, Lara Foot and Greg Homann, there is *Marikana – The Musical* and *Shwele Bawo!* So you have this whole diverse programme because I think that is what it has got to be. But if you look at the emphasis on South African work, most of this work, except for *Shwele Bawo!*, all of these works are relatively new. *Missing* came last year, *Fishers of Hope*, *The Imagined Land*, *A Voice I Cannot Silence*, all these plays are relatively new. However, artists have no funds even if they go to the NAC. Right now, what we are doing with this call-out, we programmed a lot of the 'big guns' this year. But there are a lot of young people who applied and we like their work but this needs dramaturgy and development. Therefore we are programming that work for next year.

GH: So one thing we have not spoken about at all is the audience in relation to this. We are talking a lot about what the artists need, what the playwrights need and directors need in a climate that clearly is underfunded and not structured in a way that is helping any of us really. Is part of your logic – coupling young new work with established work – a means to make sure that the audiences are getting a mix of guaranteed quality work, assuming that will come from established people?

AS: Yes. The thing is that in this environment, where we are struggling with audiences, we are trying by all means to engage somebody who is coming to the theatre for the first time – they must want to come. We are trying to eliminate risk as much as possible and say, 'you know what, I am better off taking a big risk with a director who has been there, who has the reputation and who also knows that it is his reputation that is at stake'. I am better off, and the theatre is better off like that, even when you account to your principles, you say, 'you know what, it was "Greg" but I do not know what happened to him, I do not know why but he was bankable'. You want to go to people that are bankable because you are thinking of that first-time audience. For me, I am always thinking of that first-time audience who is going to come to the theatre and see work and think, 'wow, this is what I have really been missing all my life'. You do not want them to come there and think, 'oh God, this is so messy and this is so bad'. So we want to programme like we have discussed. If the really young and fresh work is a miss, you still have hope because, you are thinking 'hang on, here is Zakes Mda coming in April and here is John Kani coming in June'. But audiences are difficult, and a classic example that I give, is when I directed the revival of *Sizwe Bansi is Dead* with John Kani and Winston Ntshona at the State. The first week we were very low, and we were then going to the UK and we were already selling tickets there but not at home, and we were going to the UK in two or three months' time. But the guys that were my classmates, the doctors, CEOs, from high school, they do not willingly go buy a ticket and come because they are not used to going to the theatre from back when we were in high school. Whereas when I went to the UK, with *Sizwe* there was one old lady who came to us, she had seen *Sizwe* in 1974 with her husband and now she was there with her children and grandchildren to come see it.

GH: So there is a culture internationally of going to the theatre whereas here our culture of going to the theatre is quite different. We certainly have a culture of performance but it is more informal. I would think that those buildings would have something to do with it because I mean the State Theatre is a monstrous colossal piece of apartheid architecture. I do not want to get too much into the audience development side but it is obviously an important factor of how those spaces engage with an audience and how they make an audience feel welcome and encouraged to be there?

AS: We must also realize that we do not have a theatre in Soshanguve, Mamelodi or Atteridgeville where now the majority of people come from. The majority of the audiences of the work that we are doing are coming from there. The people that we want to support *Fishes* and *Missing*, they are coming from those places where there are no theatres. In the 80s when you went to the community hall to see a Gibson Kente, we used to pack that community hall even though it had just four lights and bad, bad sightlines, but people were going there. Now, imagine if there was a theatre there, then the moment the doors opened at the State Theatre after 1994 and transformation, people would be coming but we still need to take it into the classroom. I showcased my first play for Barney Simon at the Market Theatre but I come from Soshanguve. So I drove past the State Theatre to go to the Market. I really think with the new disposition we have really done well with access, so now we have to say, 'hang on, for 21 years we have had access but how much of our audience has developed?' Now ask how much are we doing to take drama into the classroom and into the schools? People know that when they have read *Sizwe*, whether you want to be an actor or director and you are not in the business, but you know that there is this play called *Sizwe Bansi is Dead* from school or university, when you are working and you hear that it is being done by superstars, you will think, 'hang on, I know this thing', and you will want to go out and see it. There has to be that interaction with our communities.

GH: And you are right, it has to start at school level. It has to start early. I know many people talk about why they love theatre because of something they saw as an eight year old, ten year old or fifteen year old. They fell in love with the idea of watching a piece of theatre and that hooked them.

Let's talk about your work. You have done a significant body of work, some plays that you have directed from existing texts such as *Sizwe Bansi is Dead* but others that are completely new work. Talk about what interests you in terms of your creative work, reflecting and commenting on contemporary South African society.

AS: You know when I was asked one day why I did my work and where I was coming from with it I realized that in the past five years I did *Marikana – The Musical* which was a real life event, *Hungry* was based on real stories, we did interviews for that, and going back we did *Rivonia Trial, Kalushi: The Story of Solomon Mahlangu, Mantola* and *Rhetorical*. So all these six works – obviously the other ones were co-written and all that – are based on real stories. I was thinking, 'hey, why am I doing stories like this'. I realized that my first play that I did – I wrote my first play when I was fifteen, it was called *Save the People* – was borne out of the same thing. *Save the People* was inspired by a real life story. There was a cop in our township who had shot a young guy who was an athlete – a sprinter – and he had to get his foot amputated. When I wrote that play, I knew him, we went to school together. I was basically sad and angry that this boy used to run and he could have been one of the best and now he can't because of being shot. I wrote *Save the People* based on that. The second play that I wrote was *Back to School*. When we had not written our exams in 1985 we had to repeat Grade 11 – Standard 9 at the time – and then in the following year we were going back to school, I wrote the play based on the experiences of us not going to school and staying at home. Somehow the work that I have done has really been influenced by real life stories.

GH: And also responding to a social injustice or something that you are observing.

AS: Yes. Same as *On My Birthday*, I remember the images that came into my mind of domestic violence, it was violent, creepy and messy. I remember when I was writing, the images that used to come into my head all the time. There was this couple in our street, on a Sunday evening, he would chase her in her nightdress down the street and he would be swearing at her and beating her up. And a friend of mine had told me a story of his sister, I never told him, but she was married to somebody else, and he used to stay with them but they kicked him out. One day he said, 'I am going to fight with this guy, you cannot do that to my sister.' He said that this guy would fill the bathtub with water and half drown his sister there and he had had enough of it. So in the play there is this one image where he is drowning her in the sink. These things for me have been stories that I hear, that I witness, that I thought, 'hang on, this is not OK'. For me, I got bottled up, until I started writing these stories. It is where I am seeing a social injustice or social ill that I begin to say, 'hang on, let me write about it'. When I start to write, it comes. *My Home, My Prisoner*, we did at Wits, it was written by a friend of mine. It was almost workshop theatre but it was written by Victor Maloka. It was myself and Meshack Xaba, we had a company at Wits called VAM

Productions. We were very rebellious as we wanted to do our own African stuff. *My Home, My Prisoner* itself was real life situations. We went to Alexandra to teach drama there, they arrested us. We went to North West to fetch Meshack Xaba, they arrested us on our way back.

GH: Who is they and why would they arrest you?

AS: The cops. I do not know, we were just three black guys and they just arrested us on 12 January 1989. They arrested us and made me sing Michael Jackson, 'I'm bad, I'm bad, I'm bad.' They interrogated us until 13 January and the 13th was Victor's birthday. But that whole section was in *My Home, My Prisoner*. They found a script in my bag, we had bags because we left early in the year to go back to Wits, as we opened on the 20th but we left in January as we were rehearsing our next new play which I was writing. It was called *Strong Hold*. Then they stopped us, and they were paranoid, the cops, in Lichtenburg, they looked at the papers and then there was the script that I had that I was playing in with Janine Eser – she now lives in the USA and is a serious writer. And on the first page of that script, I say fuck the cops. And they said: 'Wie die fok is jy?',[3] ah, it was crazy, so *My Home, My Prisoner* was based on that. Therefore the work that I have done has really been relevant in that sense and that is really how I have approached my work.

GH: OK. So *Silent Voice*, let us talk about that work, which I think had its premiere in about 2008?

AS: *Silent Voice* was written in 1992.

GH: In 1992, OK so the first season was in 1992? And then it had another life in 2008?

AS: It had another life in 1999. We had one performance. We were supposed to bring it to the State Theatre and the State Theatre was shut down. That is when the State Theatre got mothballed and then in 2008 *Silent Voice* changed. In the original one, these guys had a lot of money. In one we were influenced by *Waiting for Godot* – you know we had just graduated, so we were bringing all these things to the table. Then the 2008 one was really influenced by real life occurrences because there was that Marble Hall heist and we knew some of the guys that got convicted for that. We went to the same schools together and acted together. Then if you look between the late

1990s and early 2000s, there were a lot of heists and robberies that came, a lot of those people – and most of them are dead – came from our township. Some of them from my school. So I knew them and so that is what drove *Silent Voice*. The stories of those people.

GH: So now in 2014 the play has again had a very significant, almost national, tour and a lot of the commentary around the piece, particularly some of the stuff I saw related to your season at the Baxter Theatre, is focused on the provocative form and the way in which the actors engage with the audience.

AS: Rory Appleton said, 'Of all the emotions that theatre can evoke, real fear is not often one of them. Until now that is. In *Silent Voice* writer and director Aubrey Sekhabi has created a production that will make your heart just about stop.'

GH: Talk about creating that fear and why you think that it makes the piece so strong?

AS: When I was reworking it, I thought, 'guys, it is OK, it is physical and interesting and all that but I don't think the audience are really feeling what we want them to feel'. I want to take this violence and bring it to their doorsteps because most of the time in *Silent Voice*, you have got those puppets that we are shooting and all that and it is OK – 'Ah it is a puppet and they are supposed to be killing people.' Also in theatre, you are not going to be shooting somebody and have them dying on stage and their head exploding, you know. We needed to really make it real. Therefore I said, 'guys, let us get into the auditorium, let us deal with these people and let us make them feel it'.

GH: By the people, do you mean the audience? Engaging in the auditorium?

AS: Yes, the audience. Let's hold them 'hostage'. The moment we started getting into that, and you must know that the cast are sweating and as they move they are intruding into the audience's space but that is what it is all about because when people rob you, they are intruding into your space. When you have Presley Chweneyagae there and Chuck – he is a big massive boy, he is huge – and you are afraid of him and he is wearing black stuff and he is wearing a balaclava, as he walks there, you can feel him. Sweat is dripping and I wanted the cast to intrude into the audience's space. One critic in Cape Town said, because there was one lady on opening night she was crying because she was so terrified and she had to walk out and all that, but she waited for us and she said at the end of the day, 'sorry guys, I loved the work but everything you did to me today in that auditorium has been done to me in real life so I knew exactly what was happening and you brought everything back'. The critic was saying that we took it a little bit too far but when I thought about it, no. This guy is exactly what I am up against, if he felt that Tshallo was overstepping the boundaries – it is interactive theatre – he should have stood up in that auditorium and said, 'Chief, you cannot do that.' But that is what we are doing in South Africa. They rob you here and I walk past and I do not say anything. So until there is a community sense of safety, we are not going to be safe. Here at home, they mug somebody here in front of you, nobody says anything and that is exactly what happened to that lady in that auditorium. Here you are, having a man who is thinking that this is unjust, but he is not doing anything about it because he is afraid that it is going to come to him. I felt that in *Silent Voice*, I needed to get people to that level.

GH: Do you think that in some way – what the tension is between audiences who felt wronged by the way in which you had created that relationship – that in some way it is talking to different perceptions of what theatre is and what it does? Has it got something to do with a passive, non-active way of watching theatre as opposed to a very active, present participatory approach? And to generalize in how to capture that, I suppose what I am talking about is a Western approach to watching theatre, which is passive, instead of an African approach, which is participatory and active?

AS: Yes, exactly, you hit it right on the head. David Fick said in his review, 'that the middle class Baxter audience was taken out of their comfort zone yesterday by the performance of *Silent Voice*'. Things are changing, today you have Facebook, you have Twitter, you have all these things that are happening. Look at PR, it is improving and changing. Look at movies, the screens in the movie theatres and all that. So theatre cannot be rigid. I think that theatre has to be engaging. I think that theatre has to be an experience. People need to come out of the theatre and stand and stop and say, 'wow, we have had an experience, we have seen a play that was a new experience'. We could have easily had the traditional South African theatre play of somebody standing there and saying, 'you know, I was born in Soshanguve, I grew up in this crime-ridden society, one day we went out for a heist … bru hai'. *Assinamali!* has done that. *Woza Albert!* has laid that foundation. Those people have laid the foundation, Workshop 71, they have given us that foundation of theatre of storytelling which is African but we can go anywhere with it now. I sort of think, 'hey man, what laws, what rules?' I am a scholar, I studied theatre, I understand the rules and I understand all these things but I must also understand my audience and say, 'I think my audience can survive with this sort of storytelling and I am going to go in that direction', and I want my audience to interact with all my work. I want my audience to interact. When we were doing *On My Birthday*, there was a guy in Grahamstown who said – when Richard is beating up the wife – he said: 'Hai Richard', in Xhosa, 'don't beat her.' And he got onto the stage and said, 'Richard', in Xhosa, 'stop!' For me that is what theatre should be, it should engage people and get them out of their comfort zones. When we played the Market Theatre, people were crying and people collapsed. When we did *Not with My Gun* at the Market Theatre, I was very clear with what I wanted to achieve. In *Not with My Gun* this white guy comes to steal the suit of this guy who is getting married tomorrow and he is at the bachelor's party. He leaves and comes back to steal the suit and they catch him. They start beating him up and some of the black audience were saying 'yeah' – you must know it was 1998, just as we moved from apartheid to democracy and all that. They started enjoying it and they were like, 'yeah it is about time we start beating up these white people' but then it gets rougher and then you start to become human. The mob thing goes away and you start to see reason and then you had people participating saying 'no' and people hiding and for me, theatre should really do that. It must make an audience work, they must not just come there as if it is a tea party, it is not a tea party, it is an experience and when you leave there you must know when they killed a black guy by mistake thinking that they killed the white guy – everybody is quiet and they realize that it is not good whether it is violence on black or white. But they had been participating throughout. Even when we did *Hungry*, the audience participation, it is a classic example. Our own security – on opening night – was kicking and threw out the lead of the play out of the theatre. Because he was begging there, there was a big scuffle and the security was saying out loud, 'Hey I am going to beat you up now, get out. Get out!' I was standing there seeing that. How are we treating other people in need? So for me, that is really how I have wanted to do theatre – that is really engaging and that an audience can participate in.

GH: I think in South Africa we have a very complex relationship towards violence and I think we have a very sophisticated understanding of violence, and I do not mean this in a positive sense. We experience violence as a part of our daily life and if we haven't directly experienced it in our daily life, I think a lot of South Africans imagine experiencing it in their daily lives. Therefore it is very present in how we interact with our world. You are dealing with very severe topics, you are dealing with the rape of a nine-month-old baby but in creating a visual aesthetic which forces the audience to imagine what that must be like, you are implicating them in how they watch it and you are making it very real and active. And I mean real, in the sense that, if I had a criticism of Paul Grootboom's work, the violence is too real but it is over there and it is distant. So if I think of *Relativity* – the violence is on the stage and the audience is in their seats. There is a safety there, so what you see is a lot of audience members laugh at the violence, whereas I am hearing you say, it is about making those moments of aggression, those moments of abuse, in some way more present.[4]

AS: Yes, for example, if you look at *Silent Voice* …

GH: And if I can just add, in order to achieve an understanding of humanity and an understanding of the wrong of it, rather than to make it purely a spectacle and …

AS: Yes, that is the thing. I remember even in *Silent Voice*, the cast wear black. Many years ago I would have made them wear a white T-shirt, many years ago they would have been filled with blood and you would have seen the blood. In *Silent Voice*, you do not see blood the whole time because they have been shooting dolls, except when they beat up Senzo and they damage his one ear. His one ear is maimed and they are busy maiming the other ear because he must not hear because they say he is a spy. No, we do not need to have the blood, to affect the audience. Whereas, *On My Birthday*, it was bloody because it was in a particular context. *On My Birthday* came at a time when people were asking, 'What is going to happen to South African theatre, protest theatre?' It was just 1995. Protest theatre, now we are free, what is going to happen? Then domestic violence became a thing. That was a huge success. I remember when I woke up one day, I think it was 16 August, and there were all these headlines on the streets. What did Quentin Tarantino do now? It was 'Township Tarantino'. There were these big things on the streets, the headlines. And it was about *On My Birthday*. It was

Adrienne Sichel. The review said 'Township Tarantino. Resonated. Artistic gut and social. Go!' But then the violence was really in your face, but then it was not done as a spectacle, it was done as reality … one of the nicest images that I have ever done in theatre was when this woman had been beaten up and she has no knives in the house and she starts to kill potatoes with her own fingers and dismembers a chicken with her own hand. That was violence without blood, that was violence without spectacle but which was more theatrical. So I think for me it is that, it is really achieving that sometimes without the horror. When you have the horror of it and the spectacle of it, for me, if that is the point that you want to drive home, then you should be able to do it like that. But you are able to show violence and blood without blood. Like in *Tshepang* – Lara does the rape with a bread and a broomstick. Other people did not like it and for others it was like 'eeeuw' because you can imagine what it was like – she did not have to bring a kid there with an older man on top of the kid …

GH: And also what I saw in *Tshepang* in that moment was that the audience closed their eyes and turned away from it but what they are turning away from is purely an image that they are creating in their own minds …

AS: Yes.

GH: Let's talk about Paul Grootboom's work, and more importantly, your relationship with Paul Grootboom's work. How many plays have you collaborated on with Paul?

AS: With Paul? *Not with My Gun*, *The Stick*, *Rivonia Trial*, *Rhetorical* and *Interracial*.

GH: And why do you think that that relationship has been so fruitful?

AS: Because I think that there is tolerance but also because you know we are both creative and sometimes we need each other in that space. But you must understand in the early days, the collaboration was more of a development for him, in the early days when we did *Not with My Gun*, I was introducing him to the theatre space and even when we were doing *The Stick*, he was still a very young director who wanted to be given an opportunity. I tried his work and I thought, 'this young guy really needs an opportunity to grow', and I started saying, 'You know, come and be my assistant director and let us co-write *Not with My Gun*, because I had just won the Standard Bank Young Artist Award and was doing *Not with My Gun* – 'come on board'. Then I did *The Stick*. The style of *The Stick* actually carries on in *Silent Voice*. *The Stick* was inspired by *Bring in 'da Noise, Bring in 'da Funk* by George C. Wolfe that I saw on Broadway. Therefore I worked with Paul, the early works was to introduce him to the industry, to guide him and to assist him, but also he fascinated me because he wanted to know, he fascinated me because he could go work on his own and he was not afraid of the labour, because you know it is labour intensive when writing. He had the stamina and he was interesting in a sense that he had his own stories. He told me a story that he once pitched to Barney Simon and Barney Simon said, 'go write about yourself, you cannot write about things that you do not know'. That is why we wrote *Madi* which was later called *Telling Stories*. When I read that work, it was really honest and genuine, and that is what attracted me to starting to work with him. And then when he did *Cards* originally I called him, he had assisted me as a director and writer on the two works – *Not with My Gun* and *The Stick* – and then I commissioned him to do one work – *Enigma* and then we had to release one director, I called him three or five days before to come and work with *Cards*. So he created *Cards* originally in the North West before the one we saw here. And he kept on working on it and he was slowly getting his own identity and doing work. So when he was doing his own original work I would really be there. He would say, 'Can you do the fight scenes for me', and all that but he would go back and write and rewrite. He wanted it more and I think that is what made me interested in him.

GH: I want to talk about *Rivonia Trial* which is another one of the works that focusses on real events. Although, in this instance, it's 1963/64, the trial of ten ANC leaders, eight of which ended up being imprisoned, one of them being Nelson Mandela. If I am correct, you worked from the transcripts from those trials. How did you shift the transcripts into drama? What was the process in creating *Rivonia Trial*?

AS: *Rivonia Trial* was mad because we got the money late. Until so very late we did not know whether we were going to do it. I had just come off *Kalushi* and done the story of Solomon Mahlangu. There we had four weeks or three weeks to do *Rivonia Trial*. And I had transcripts so the first thing was just to read the transcripts and understand the story. Then there was the individual books, obviously you refer to *Long Walk to Freedom*, there's a book by Joel Joffe that he wrote *The State vs. Nelson Mandela* – there were a few books that we read. And then from the information that we knew, we knew that the trial transcripts and the court cases were fine. When we were in the court scenes we could use these. But then we needed to tell the story and we needed to tell the story from a woman's point of view. Which meant that we had to go again and read – hey it was crazy, I never read so much. I had to go and read the books of Albertina Sisulu, the book of Hilda Bernstein was out, Mama Winnie's book. And then in the scene where there is interaction – that was just pure fiction, we were just creating it from what we had read in terms of those stories.

GH: So the real stories in that instance, became a sounding board for the scenes that you improvised or created ...

AS: Yes we created – we just wrote the scenes and rewrote them. Ah, but others came even while I was making it. We were writing in the evening and the first script, I think, was about 160 pages. Absolutely mad! But then say, for example, as I was doing – I was making it on the stage, I would change a monologue and make it into a scene and all that. Ideas were starting to be ...

GH: So it was another great example of how the writing process continues in the rehearsal room?

AS: Yes, it went on until the last day with *Rivonia Trial*. With the *Rivonia Trial*, we were making it more crisp until ... the first version you must remember was four hours and then we did it again the second year, which we then shaped it to about two hours.

GH: Is that a kind of work that, and I am being presumptuous here, that pleases the State Theatre council, the Government in relation to it being a Cultural Institution-governed building? Is that something that you feel is pressure for you? Being an artistic director in a space that is Government-funded or is this a work you would have done in any case despite the fact that it feeds into the ideas of 'nation building', 'social cohesion' and all the buzz words that are thrown around in relation to the Department of Arts and Culture?

AS: I think that it is a work that I would have done anyway because this story of the *Rivonia Trial* is a story about Nelson Mandela – everybody tells it. Anant Singh is doing it with the film *Long Walk to Freedom* and I think there is another movie coming out now told from a point of view of Andrew Mlangeni. For me it was interesting because it was a big story and working with the transcripts originally, I was excited by the material. But then it was easy to get funding for it.

GH: Because it was such a culturally entrenched and historical story?

AS: Exactly. But for me this was a trial that happened in Pretoria and the State Theatre is located in Pretoria and it was just a massive story, also because of the diversity it allows. Here is another opportunity to work with black and white actors, with white actors having roles not 'hey, let us write in this white actor'. It is Lionel Bernstein, he is there and he has a solid role in it, it is Ahmed Kathrada, he is there and has a solid role. So for me it was a good example of what South African theatre should be. Then it would start to attract both audiences but then there was just so much drama and it was unavoidable with *Rivonia Trial*. But at the time there was no pressure from council. Take *Marikana – The Musical* – I thought, 'what do they say, what do they do?'[5] That was the scariest time of my life.

GH: So the policy in the Cultural Institutions Act that states with 'arm's length' – it uses that phrase – you genuinely feel that in practice that is what is happening? There is a sense that there is arm's length distance to how you are empowered to approach the creative process and the programming at the State Theatre?

AS: Yes. I must be honest, we have never been harassed with that, we did *Ons vir Jou*, the De La Rey story and all that, but look what we did last year. Last year we did *Protest* and we did *Marikana – The Musical*. The Minister of Arts and Culture, Nathi *Mthethwa* was the Minister of Police when the Marikana thing happened.

GH: The Minister of Police is now the Minister of Arts and Culture …

AS: Yes. Not once have we been intimidated. Not once have we been called and asked questions and all that. I was myself scared, I was very afraid. For many reasons, politically – this thing looks like it is a political hot potato, and again for sure so many people have died. There is this conflict between AMCU (The Association of Mineworkers and Construction Union) and NUM (National Union of Mineworkers). The Deputy President of the country now was a board member at Lonmin. There was all these things that I was looking at and me – I was thinking, what am I doing? I remember when President Zuma announced the Minister of Arts and Culture. You know you wait until the day that they are going to announce who is going to be our next Minister because you want to prepare yourself. I was sitting there and I hear him say Arts and Culture – Nathi *Mthethwa*, at that time, I could not even raise my head. I had committed to the National Arts Festival that I was going to do *Marikana – The Musical*. It is in our programme and I am busy with the script and there is nothing that I can do. I just thought, you know what, there is just absolutely nothing I can do. I just have to do this. And the writing process was very difficult. At first, there is almost like a self-censorship but as you are going, Itumeleng Motsikoe, he is a good friend of mine and a director. Itumeleng, who I know to be very radical and all that, he would call me and say, 'are you sure about this thing?', and I said, 'Chief, what can I do? I am doing this play, I cannot … ', and at that point, you cannot turn back, you have already advertised and you cannot turn back. But at the same time, this thing is still fresh so you cannot do a proper candid piece – it cannot be that. But as it was going on, one day I thought you know what, no man, I am just going to do this thing. I set myself free because I felt that I am censoring myself, nobody is censoring me and I set myself free and I started to do it the way I did it. And I thought that if I think of new South African musicals that have happened in the past 20 years, I think it will rank way up there with the best, it became genuine, it became honest. There was no political pressure, there was no administrative pressure from the State Theatre and our council at the time were saying, 'come on, do it, there is freedom of expression'. Therefore I exercised that right as in our constitution.

GH: I want to go back to what you said a little while ago, you used the term 'both audiences' and you were obviously referring to a white audience and a black audience. Do you feel that the audiences are as separate as that or have things shifted? In your mind, is there an idea that there are two different kinds of audience groups or do you think it is more complex than that?

AS: There is a white audience and a black audience in South Africa. At the State Theatre this year, I have been seeing a nice shift and I am very excited at what is happening at the State Theatre. But there are those things, like when we had *Queen*,[6] you still have black people but it was predominantly white. But when you go to jazz concerts, you have black and white but then sometimes your white audience is your ambassadors and all those kind of things. For *Call Us Crazy* we had a black and white audience.

GH: Is it generational? Or are you seeing … I mean is it the younger audience that you are seeing the shift in or …?

AS: The younger audience – to the comedies, with our comedy nights, you get a younger audience but mixed – Indian guys, whites, blacks and all that. Drama, *Marikana – The Musical* for example, I would say that we were still sitting on 90/92 per cent black.

GH: And was that the same with the National Arts Festival for that work?

AS: No. At the National Arts Festival, we were almost on 50:50 or 60:40. It is also interesting that at the National Arts Festival now, back in the day when I was making *Not with My Gun* and all that, the National Arts Festival would be a lot of white people now I would say it is 50:50 or 60:40 (black:white) audience. But then the secret for me is that it must be South African theatre. If I want to attract mostly white and black audience at the State Theatre in particular, I must have a black and white cast, it works easier like that. The Market Theatre is kind of different of its history. There you will find a black and white audience but I have seen that you have a predominantly black audience for a play with a black cast and a predominantly white audience for a white cast. I remember around 1995, 1996, 1997 at the Market Theatre, it was for *On My Birthday*, we were in the Laager, there was David Kramer doing something else and I think there was *The Crucible* happening. And you know the foyer of the Market Theatre, there would be blacks, Coloureds and all that, the bell rings and white people go into the Barney Simon, black people to the Laager, and Coloured people to the Main Theatre so there has been that division. But I think that a work like *Rivonia Trial*, has shown me that you can have a black and white audience. *Hungry*, because we had Brendon Auret and Cameroon McEwan and all that, you can begin to have an audience that is really mixed. It is possible and the young people, I think that they do not give a damn about these old things, you know they are really seeing things completely different. So we need to go that direction.

GH: So one last question, what new work would you like to be seeing more of?

AS: I really think that we need to … hey man, look at what happened last week at the State of the Nation address. South Africa has got stories everywhere. Stories are like galore, look at where you have the Commissioner of Police suspended, you have the late Jackie Selebi arrested – stories are just like galore.

GH: And there is theatre everywhere.

AS: Yes. There is theatre everywhere. We must reflect the mood. And you know that theatre almost always cannot be in the middle, it's got to be against the status quo. You know that the status quo is propaganda. But I do not feel that it should be partisan – it should be genuine. You should get into a play and watch a play and if it criticizes the ANC (African National Congress) you should not feel that it is a DA (Democratic Alliance) play. It must not be beating the voice of the DA, the DA does not necessarily represent the people, it represents a section of the people. If you want to criticize in a theatre piece, then do it but do it as genuine. Do you know how many people now watch parliament television because there is so much drama? There are so many stories that are there and they are current, there are so many current stories. I want writers to see the reflection of the mood of the times so 20 years down the line you can be judged on what you have written today. South Africa is ripe. In the early years when you were thinking of writing a work that is against the status quo, you were thinking, 'hang on, it is still early days'.

GH: Like in that Rainbow Nation period?

AS: Yes. But we need to write now, it is ripe.

GH: You are talking about conflict and the country's challenges?

AS: Yes. I think that we should not be afraid. The President himself said that, during his ANC celebration speech, what theatre should stand for, what the Arts should stand for – it should reflect the movement of the time, the mood. The Minister himself said that, about two or three weeks ago, we should talk about the stories of today. He should not be telling us to do that, we should be doing it anyway.

GH: I think that this is a great way to end. What I am hearing is that we need to marry the social issues, the things we need to say in order to build our young democracy, with entertainment. We must entice people into the theatre so that our rich theatre tradition can continue its relationship of bringing to the fore social issues, and ultimately engage audiences to think about where we live and how we live.

AS: That's it.

Notes

1. The Cultural Institutions Acts (No. 119 of 1998) governs six theatres in South Africa who receive state funding. These theatres are the State Theatre in Pretoria, the Playhouse in Durban, Artscape in Cape Town, the Market Theatre in Johannesburg, the Performing Arts Centre of the Free State (PACOF) in Bloemfontein and the Windybrow Theatre in Johannesburg.

2. As a response to the shift from apartheid to democracy, in 1996 the then Minister of Arts, Culture, Science and Technology, Dr B. S. Ngubane, tabled the White Paper on arts, culture and heritage. This was to become the guidelines for the Cultural Institutions Act (No. 119 of 1998) which saw, amongst other changes, the dissolving of the Performing Arts Councils homed at theatres like the State Theatre, and the redirecting of a portion of those funds from those councils to the newly formed National Arts Council which was from then on the designated authority responsible for distributing state funds to artists, cultural institutions, NGOs and CBOs. This turned the six state-governed theatres into mere receiving houses.

3. Afrikaans for 'Who the fuck are you?'

4. For more, see Homann's 'Landscape and Body', *South African Theatre Journal* 23 (2009): 149–76.

5. The area of Marikana made international news on 16 August 2012 when 44 mineworkers were shot by police during wildcat strikes at Lonmin platinum mines. This event has subsequently become known as the Marikana Massacre.

6. *Queen* is a musical tribute show to Freddie Mercury and the band Queen.

INDEX

Index

Index

Index

Index

Index

Index

Index

Index